BLUEPRINT
for a
LITERATE NATION
HOW *YOU* CAN HELP

BLUEPRINT
—— *for a* ——
LITERATE NATION
HOW *YOU* CAN HELP

CINTHIA COLETTI

With chapters by
Carolyn D. Cowen, Margie Gillis, Rich Long, Elenn Steinberg,
and an introduction by Maryanne Wolf.

Library of Congress Control Number: 2013917371
ISBN: Hardcover   978-1-4931-0470-3
                 Softcover   978-1-4931-0469-7
                 Ebook   978-1-4931-0471-0

A Note of Appreciation

The publication of this book is made possible by a generous contribution from the Emily Hall Tremaine Foundation
171 Orange Street, New Haven, CT 06510
203.639.5544
www.TremaineFoundation.org

Rev. date: 10/10/2013

To order additional copies of this book, contact:
Xlibris LLC
1-888-795-4274
www.Xlibris.com
Orders@Xlibris.com
133227

CONTENTS

PART THREE
Literacy Science

APPENDICES

FOREWORD

We Are in Charge of a Million Tomorrows
~ Literacy can make them brighter or break them forever

Why Is Literacy Important?

ASKING WHY LITERACY is important may seem like a rhetorical question. After all, reading and writing are basic skills that we take for granted in modern society. However, a disturbing number of people cannot read and write well enough to keep up with escalating demands of life and employment in the twenty-first century. Illiteracy and low literacy are serious problems and usually are covered up with a sense of shame by those afflicted. Workers hide literacy problems from their employers. Parents hide these problems from their children. Students hide them from their teachers. Patients hide them from their doctors.

Perhaps the tendency to hide literacy difficulties, coupled with the fact that these often compound or masquerade as other social ills, helps explain why so many citizens, policy makers, and others are unaware that low literacy and illiteracy are grave concerns in the United States—that the issues extend across the socioeconomic spectrum and that they endanger our prosperity as a nation. Perhaps, too, it is because literacy competence is assumed in today's society. Nevertheless, despite unprecedented access to a comprehensive education system, millions of young people leave school with inadequate reading and writing skills and rarely make up for these deficits as adults.

Lack of awareness about the prevalence and consequences of these problems as well as insufficient knowledge about their solutions underscore the need to tackle pressing questions such as the following:

Why do literacy problems persist? What are the solutions? Why is literacy increasingly important in the age of information?

This book answers these questions. It takes you on a journey and provides not only the rationale and science but also the knowledge and specific tools you need to become involved and to help create a million bright tomorrows for all children, including those most at risk for reading failure.

INTRODUCTION TO THE AUTHOR

~What Cinthia Doesn't Tell the Reader

THE LAST THING Cinthia Coletti (formerly Cinthia Haan) ever wanted to do was write a book. This is her third book, however reluctantly and conscientiously written. They are all part of her seemingly indefatigable resolve to change how children in America become literate citizens who can contribute their potential to this country. At the start of the book, she tells some of the stories of how she came to be involved in what has become an increasingly powerful movement to provide resources to every parent, teacher, child, community, and even state so as to achieve what she calls literacy equity.

But what she tells in the book is only part of "her story." She left out most of the details of how a former CEO with over twenty years of success in the business community became the founder of several foundations and, most recently, Literate Nation—the movement that I predict will significantly change how we teach in many schools across the nation and how children and parents access resources for literacy. You can always read a book without knowing anything about the author. But in this case, it may buoy the reader to know about the utter implausibility of one woman's transformation and her subsequent battle for children.

Cinthia has one of those uniquely American histories. Raised in the bountiful, rural Central Valley of California in her early years and then the Silicon Valley in her formative years by Don and Connie Coletti, the best of hardworking, idealistic parents, "Cindy" was the "firstborn girl with three, close brothers." It is hard to say whether such a place in the Coletti's tightly knit family propelled Cinthia's later extraordinary climb through the largely male-dominated business world of the 1970s, '80s, and '90s, but after observing this family's penchant for values and conquering every difficult, competitive, outdoor sport invented, I choose to believe it prepared her well. She became one of the first female executives to break into senior management of a top corporation.

Early in her career, she was a founding team member in Southern Pacific Railroad's launch of SPRINT. Later she helped form and then became managing director of the cutting-edge Starnet Division of Ford Aerospace. These were the first days of deregulated communications, and she was in the middle of the excitement. Over the next years, she would become part of a series of highly successful mergers and acquisitions in the telecommunication and finance industries—a fact that is all the more striking since Sheryl Sandberg (COO of Facebook) recently lamented that fewer than two dozen women today are in top positions of the leading Fortune 500 companies.

By the age of forty, Cinthia Coletti was on her way to enjoying the fruits of two decades of very hard work—whether through an early retirement or simply having more time for herself, her family, and her irrepressible desire to perfect her scuba diving, paragliding, and other X-sports. To many an outside observer, Ms. Coletti had achieved the American dream. And then, for all intents and purposes, she abandoned it all. In the first chapter, she describes why. In confronting the difficult challenges and unnecessary obstacles faced by her own children, she came to powerful realizations about the country she loves and what it has and has not done for children for whom there is no adequate system in place.

She tells this part of her story best, and I will not do it here. But she does not sufficiently tell the reader what came next: how she moved out of retirement to use her well-honed business skills to begin and direct the Haan Foundation for Children; how she forged one collaboration after another between government and business, between researchers and teachers; how she helped conduct multimillion dollar studies of existing interventions that helped propel a next generation of research-based programs. She has been a driving force in the founding of numerous thriving nonprofit corporations. By now, she has been or is a director on multiple boards, educational institutions, including: the Strategic Educational Research Partnership (SERP), the California Business for Education Excellence (CBEE), the UCSF Neuroscience Initiative, the Department of Education Policy and Leadership at SMU, Dyslexic Advantage, and San Francisco RBI. She has received multiple prestigious awards for her tireless work on children's behalf, and she has started and directs the new grassroots cultural movement, Literate Nation, to make her considerable knowledge base and resources about these issues accessible to the widest number of people.

Finally, Cinthia Coletti has written three books about what others can do to disseminate and use this information: *The Power to Act: Transforming Literacy and Education, Literacy Policy: Ground-Breaking Blueprint for State Legislation,* and the present one. As I said at the outset, writing was once daunting to her—interoffice memorandums, yes; books, never! It isn't anymore. Her overarching desire—to see that all children in all schools around the country have the best chances possible to achieve and ultimately contribute their potential—trumps any burden every time.

With this new book, Cinthia Coletti gives us all an example of what Margaret Mead described years ago: the power of a single dedicated human to change the world around her.

Maryanne Wolf, EdD
John DiBiaggio Professor of Citizenship and Public Service
Director, Center for Reading and Language Research
Tufts University
Author of *Proust and the Squid: The Story and Science of the Reading Brain*

PART ONE

Stories and Facts About Literacy in the United States

CHAPTER ONE

GOING PUBLIC

You Are Not Alone

EVERY DAY, CHILDREN in elite, independent schools as well as in high-poverty schools are deprived of their dreams and opportunities because they are not taught to read or to read well enough. This is unacceptable. We can and must shift the societal norms for equality in literacy and education, and we must begin now.

Many of us have stories about what heightened our awareness of our nation's imperiled state of literacy and education. There are commonalities in these stories as well as aspects that are uniquely our own. Before building the case for changing how literacy is addressed in the United States and outlining a plan for action, at the urging of colleagues, I will share some of the events in my life that led me to write this book. Then I will invite you to tell your own story on our website and to join me in a movement for a literate nation.

I would prefer not to go public with my life, particularly since it involves the lives and challenges faced by my children. But countless similar stories of other children and families and of disappointed and frustrated teachers strengthened my resolve to fight for literacy equity—that is, literacy for all. If my story inspires you and others to join me in this fight, then I share these personal experiences gladly. In many ways, this story is your story, and yours is mine.

A Bit About Me

Although I consider myself to be a pretty average American, for many years, I was a highly successful businesswoman. With hard work and some luck, I built companies by innovating, creating, leading, negotiating, and uniting people at a time when few women were able to break through the glass ceiling. Holding senior management positions in large corporations and nurturing and growing start-up organizations was rare indeed. In short order, I became a seasoned executive experienced in P&L management, operations, penetrating new markets, and generating windfall revenues at a young age. Thinking back, I believe being the oldest sister with three brothers and a brood of male cousins prepared me well to become an entrepreneur, CEO, and leader.

Retirement was earned early, but it was short lived. I enjoyed five blissful years of freedom, exploration, and discovery that led me into previously unimaginable territory—mushing a dog team along the Canadian border in the dead of winter, biking through Morocco from the desert to the mountains, paragliding off mountains in the Swiss Alps, and diving the shipwrecks of the Truk Lagoon in Micronesia. All the while, not a museum was missed. I inhaled the richness of varied cultures that could not happen while I was in business; there was not enough time.

Cherished retirement, however, ended quickly when I was called into battle for literacy. Why? I could not bear seeing another child struggle and fail. Simply stated, there was a nagging and growing feeling that I should put to use what I had learned from my children's struggles now on behalf of the countless others who continued to face frustration and failure.

Today, I use the skills and strengths I developed in the corporate world to address the challenges of achieving literacy for all. My motivation to write this book comes from years of helping hundreds of children who struggle to learn in traditional classrooms, from a love for my country, and from the gut-wrenching feeling I get when I read how far our nation has slipped in literacy, educational achievement, and global standings. To me, it is obvious: If we do not take responsibility for turning the rising tide of literacy problems, we will be responsible for a bleak future for generations to come.

Setting the Stage

John Steinbeck writes about the consequences of failure beautifully in his book *East of Eden*. He describes how failure frequently turns into fear and then sadness. This sadness evolves into anger at oneself and at society. Over time, anger turns into hatred and then, often, into violence—perpetuating the destructive cycle of failure. The implications for education are obvious: The effect of academic failure in childhood and adolescence can be pervasive and lifelong.

Imagine that you are a child embarrassed or fearful about your schoolwork. No matter how hard you try, you keep failing. Think about waking up Monday morning feeling sick to your stomach, paralyzed at the thought of having to go to school for another day of humiliation. Within the academic realm, failure is all you know. "It must be my fault," you say to yourself. "The other kids do okay—maybe I'm the stupid one." You harbor sorrow and anger deep in your soul, both are directed at you. Tears well in your eyes when you think about reading aloud. You know you will embarrass yourself in front of everyone.

Now imagine your teacher calls on you to write on the whiteboard. Your face flushes as your heart races, and your hand shakes, unable to comply. You agonize over the thought of your friends finding out how stupid you are. What if they refuse to play with you or even talk to you? For sure, they will laugh at you, if not publicly then secretly behind your back. They may bully you, adding to your sorrow and anger. In time, your fear traps you in a cycle of helplessness. If you are very young, perhaps you lie to your parents some days, claiming you feel too sick to go to school. If you are a middle-schooler, you may cut class.

In this thought exercise, you are one of millions of students who lose valuable opportunities for education each day, shuffled through a system that disregards their potential and neglects to prepare them for grade-level classwork. Throughout their lives, these students carry impressions of a hostile education system. Feelings of stupidity and guilt follow them into adulthood. In time, sadness turns to anger. How can it not? Had these students been taught to read, write, spell, think critically, and engage in peer collaborations with good teachers and with good instruction, who knows how far such students could have gone in life? How high they might have soared?

My Intimate Truth

Difficulties in life can ignite a passion for overcoming these very hardships. So it is with the quest to heal the many consequences of illiteracy. It began for me with my own children.

I learned for the first time that hard work is not always the answer and that the secrets of school success are revealed by scientific research. My earliest battles, tempered initially by my trust in the system, soon escalated into a full-fledged war for my children's right to reach their potential and against classrooms inhospitable to their learning. Too often, my children's mental development was delayed by wasteful instructional practices. School became a desert where they were stranded, their thirst for learning unquenched, and their potential in danger of being curbed. None of this was done to my children maliciously, of course. Nevertheless, misguided practices—no matter how well-meaning—take a toll.

It began with my daughter in the early 1990s. Her schooling started with a slow stream of reassurance and appeasement that cascaded into a torrent of fear. My daughter is the first grandchild of her generation in a large, tightly interconnected family. Her birth was celebrated, as was her acceptance at four years old to a competitive private school for girls. Naturally, we expected that teacher knowledge and skill in this elite school would be exemplary and that the children they taught would flourish.

Tiffany is blessed with unique physical characteristics—a jewel of color like a glass mosaic. To this day, her eyes remain a vivid turquoise blue, her hair vibrant shades of strawberry blonde and auburn—the look of young Flemish women painted in the fifteenth century. At a young age, she had the confidence of a conductor about to lead a virtuoso orchestra. From her earliest moments in school, she was paid great attention for these attributes—attention that proved worthless, if not harmful.

My daughter's story illustrates how parents can be lulled into believing their child is "doing fine" in school. Teachers and school leaders too often are unaware of the early signs of reading problems, and bright kids are adept at hiding their struggles. Headmistress and teachers alike spoke often about how engaging Tiffany was and what a pleasure she was to have as a student. Occasionally, I questioned them about her struggles to read with me in the evenings, but I let my worries be soothed with a salve of words: "It's only a maturation issue. She is good in math and storytelling; her vocabulary is remarkable. Reading will come in time." These words took on a hollow ring in the fourth grade as both my daughter and I struggled with the agony of mounting nightly homework and occasional tears. Because she was labeled "gifted," I fell into a false sense of security about the academic picture. My daughter also managed to hide her struggles with "dyslexia" and "dysgraphia" quite well, terms that I eventually came to understand as a neurobiological difficulty with learning to read and write. By the fifth grade, we finally stopped believing her school and saw clearly her strain, her fight to work late each night on homework, and her despair as she slipped further behind. Try as she might, she no longer could go it alone.

The pain of this realization haunts me still. Her self-esteem suffered needlessly right before my inexperienced, trusting, ignorant eyes. Steinbeck's themes offer insights into my own progression through sadness and guilt over my obliviousness to her struggles, sadness and guilt that turned to self-directed anger, even rage. How could I have trusted them with my daughter's future? How could I have been so careless with her precious life? I went on a rampage and declared war. In time, we were victorious.

The timing of our recognition of Tiffany's difficulties is not unique. In fourth grade, as the focus on learning to read shifts to reading to learn, children with weak reading and writing skills start to lose any precarious toeholds they may have in school and begin to slip further behind. In grades 5 through 8, struggling students often begin thinking about dropping out of school. Their feigned illnesses, acted out in early grades, are not met with the same nurturing response. Truancy often manifests as these children flee the daily pain of failure. No longer able to endure the fight, these children start to grasp that no amount of effort will make school any easier or success more likely. Without a champion, they often succumb to the instinct to end the painful humiliation; the seeds of dropping out are sown. The promising young boys and girls who entered school, ready to succeed, fall short of their hopes and lose the capacity to go on. Who can blame them?

For my daughter, however, there was a different outcome, but only because I had the luxury of time and the means for seeking help outside school. I will share the next chapter of Tiffany's life to illustrate that every child can become literate and educated, but it is up to us to shift societal expectations and practices on education and literacy so each child can reach his or her potential.

With help, we found a highly skilled education therapist along with a new school to guide Tiffany to fully develop her reading and writing skills. She worked hard to catch up. She was five years behind grade level, and it took her determination, "a village," and a small fortune to catch up. But both high school and college proved fruitful. She finally soared, achieved honors, earned a baccalaureate degree, and started a career, followed in short order by multiple promotions. Today, she is managing director of Translation, an award-winning advertising agency headquartered in New York established to lead brands in a thriving contemporary culture. Last year, Advertising Age, the global organization that publishes information on the industry and recognizes outstanding talent in the field, honored her as one of twenty-four women from around the world—a Woman to Watch—for career achievement. And she had just turned thirty years old.

Yes, we can celebrate Tiffany's hard-earned success. She is, indeed, a woman to watch. However, if we had not caught and aggressively addressed her learning needs, her life would have gone in another direction, as it often does for millions of children with less opportunity. Even with her success, it is unacceptable that she had to work so hard to catch up, and it is riling that her heart had to break, like so many other children, in those early years. Mine, did, too. All this could have been prevented if her kindergarten had conducted universal screening and if her first-grade teachers had been properly trained in the complexities of reading development and used continuous data-progress assessments to guide instruction. If they had, my daughter *never* would have experienced years of academic struggle. Finally, without the targeted supports, she might have been like millions of other young people. Adrift.

In one girl's story, I soon began to see the elements of a plan for literacy action: universal screening in kindergarten, teachers better prepared with the necessary knowledge and skills to instruct all children in every neighborhood to read and write, and targeted supports in higher grades for those not reading and writing proficiently. My daughter's story inspired me to learn what I could to ensure her academic success. My son's story compelled me to stay the course to champion his needs and those of our nation's youth.

Backdrop: Another Story Among Many

My son Gianmarco's early warning signs were similar to Tiffany's, but different enough that they did not catch my attention. I missed them. I had no excuse. The lauded private school for boys he attended had no excuse. However, the teachers, all four of them, did have an excuse. These teachers could not know what they had not been taught themselves. Teachers of reading—all kindergarten through third-grade teachers—must have vital knowledge about how to screen for, assess, and instruct all at-risk readers. This lack of fundamental professional knowledge is why my son was held back in kindergarten for "extra time to mature." In his story, we see a few more elements in a plan for literacy action: standards and strategies to attract, prepare, support, reward, retain, and advance high-quality *teachers of reading*.

Gianmarco was a generous, inquisitive, good-natured child, a natural negotiator, and a problem solver, even at an early age. I will never forget the moment I realized that he was struggling. I was on my knees helping him from his bath. Drying him off, I looked into his eyes. They were tearful and filled with despair. His small, second-grade hands gripped my shoulders tightly. I asked him what was wrong. He gulped back sobs and asked, "Mommy, when will I be able to read the blackboard like all my friends?" Tears rolled down his cheeks, and then down mine.

This agonizing moment is etched deeply in my heart. Sixteen years later, I still tear up at the memory. It tore at my core then and continues to do so now. From that moment to the present, I became determined to fight to ensure that no other mother or father or child would feel the grief we felt at that moment. For despite all the material resources we had, our son's reading challenges required some things we did not yet possess: an extraordinary amount of research, time, and vigilance by our family overseeing our son's progress and self-concept, which had been whittled away; hard work and perseverance by Gianmarco; and the long-term support of highly trained teachers of reading. Indeed, had we not assiduously sought out and found highly qualified tutors, teachers, and schools, I am convinced that both my son and my daughter might have dropped out of high school, unable to read or write well enough to apply their superb thinking skills to their areas of strength or to succeed in our complex world.

Like my daughter, my son succeeded and has become known as a young man with wisdom and innate leadership skill. He recently graduated from a prestigious university with a degree in engineering, management, and information systems. It is an ambitious "3D" degree, infinitely well suited for the twenty-first century and typical of the gifted thinking abilities of individuals with dyslexia. Gianmarco soared through his summer internships—both national and international—and at times struggled through hard-won courses in the semesters in between. Immediately upon graduation, he was offered several positions and is now enjoying success as a rising engineer with a multinational firm in Silicon Valley.

We are proud of and grateful for what our children have achieved. But what would have happened had we not had the resources, the time, and the stamina to support their own hard efforts? The realization that countless parents have neither the resources nor the time to do for their children what we were able to for ours transformed my life from that moment forward. My children's "turnaround" became a symbol to me of why we must build a movement to drive a seismic shift in literacy instruction in order to ensure that all children, teachers, and all parents have access to the resources and knowledge we were able to leverage to ensure full literacy for our children—research, qualified tutors, teachers, and schools. Without these vital ingredients, my children might have dropped out of high school—unable to read their textbooks, pass exams, write coherently, seek careers—and unprepared to think critically and work collaboratively in this complex world.

*   *   *

The battle to preserve the potential of my children changed me. I now feel compelled to wage this battle on behalf of all children. Over the last decade, my focus has shifted, therefore, from solving the learning challenges of those closest to me to addressing our schools' failure to improve student-learning outcomes. To gain the knowledge, skills, and credibility I needed, I left my comfort zone and began to build collaborations at the state and national levels—working with the National Institutes of Health, with the National Academy of Sciences, and with eminent researchers in top universities to conduct multidisciplinary studies and clinical trials examining how we learn, how the brain develops, and how it evolves and changes with effective instruction.

All these experiences empowered and drove me. They led me to write this book and to invite you to join our crusade for a literate nation. Following the Japanese attack on Pearl Harbor in 1941, Admiral Yamamoto, who had been educated in the United States, commented that he feared that Japan had awakened a sleeping giant. Today, we must awaken that sleeping giant for another cause: to recognize the perilous inadequacies of our public education system and inspire a resolve to achieve world-class learning for all our students, including those at risk.

If my story resonates with your own story or that of someone you love, I hope you will share it on our website. No matter where you are in the arc of your story—whether the literacy-learning challenges continue or have been overcome—we would love to hear from you. Our individual stories weave into a powerful narrative and help build the case for change. You can visit our website, www. LiterateNation.org, and follow the prompts to tell us your story. As you read on in this book, you will discover tips, tools, and resources to help you become engaged in the fight for our children and a literate America.

Taking Responsibility for a Societal Issue

To blame our schools as the sole source of inadequate literacy of our citizens is not only unreasonable, it inhibits progress. While they are the major players in educating our children, there are many other social factors that play a role.

We all are stakeholders in the public education system's goal to educate the young so they can become contributing adults. The stepping-stones in a productive and purposeful life are literacy, education, graduation, and the first job, which leads to continued learning and a career path. Without reaching the first stepping-stone— literacy—the next stepping-stones are much harder to attain.

> *Literacy is not a luxury, it is a right and a responsibility. If our world is to meet the challenges of the twenty-first century, we must harness the energy and creativity of all our citizens!*
> *—Bill Clinton*

Reading Literacy

Throughout this book I use the term "reading literacy," a term that may seem redundant. It is borrowed from the Organisation for Economic Co-operation and Development (OECD), based in Paris. Among OECD's many activities is to rank fifteen-year-old students from around the world on skills in three categories: reading literacy, math literacy, and science literacy. Their assessments and subsequent rankings are used as economic indicators, bellwethers for gauging future productivity of a nation. Basing these projections on the smarts (quality education) of the upcoming workforce makes sense. OECD ranking is a respected marker, used by decision machines across the globe. This is why the decline in US student ranking is worrisome. The OECD tests the "reading literacy" of students throughout the world because reading aptitude is a key predictor of individual and national future economic success. It correlates with the power to "read to learn" for a lifetime of acquiring knowledge, a vital ability in a rapidly changing world of technology and innovation. Consider the many new things you have needed to learn in the past decade. Clearly, the world is changing very quickly. Our youngest citizens must develop skills for lifelong learning; otherwise, the well-being of our nation is undermined.

You may have heard about the "reading wars." I have had the opportunity to interact with representatives of numerous philosophical camps on literacy— deans in colleges of education, superintendents of school districts,

What Are The Reading Wars?

A debate about the "best way" to teach reading has been raging for decades. In what is often described as the "reading wars" by academic and policy insiders, there are opposing factions of experts and politicians who champion "phonics," on the one side, or "whole language," on the other. Each faction declares their respective approach as the key to effectively teaching all children to read.

Unfortunately, this "war" has been politicized and it does little to help teachers and students in the trenches, in America's classrooms.

−National Education Association

principals, classroom teachers, neuroscientists, reading researchers, professional education therapists, legislators, parents, advocacy groups, and professional associations. These camps have debated "reading" and "literacy" theories for decades, seldom bridging the divide. I believe that no camp is 100 percent correct, but together they offer the possibility of a symphony of triumph, if teachers have the knowledge, skill, and supports to tap into an integrated expertise that can address the needs of students.

"Reading literacy" is also a consensus-building term. Its connotations go beyond reading's required development of active and interactive skill attainment and beyond comprehension and analysis of rich text. We need consensus among stakeholders. Today's demands for reading literacy include employing strategy and skill as well as cognitive function, all of which are necessary for a lifetime of learning. Reading literacy also implies that there is a capacity for reflection on written material that evokes personal experiences and memories. Finally, reading literacy is fluid: It moves from the schoolroom to the workplace, to citizenship, to continual learning, all of which fulfill or are central to achieving one's aspirations, dreams, and goals, and all of which enrich individual lives.

The Roots of SEEDS

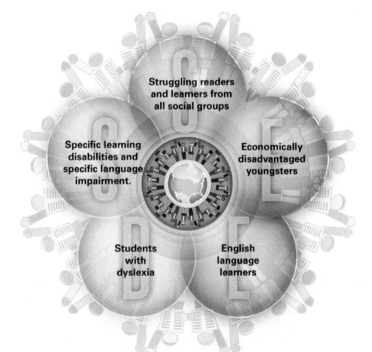

Throughout this book, I use the acronym SEEDS, with all its optimistic, metaphorical connotations—

Struggling readers and learners from all social groups,
Economically disadvantaged youngsters,
English language learners, and students with
Dyslexia,
Specific learning disabilities, and language impairment.

The term is not as overused as struggling readers, striving readers, at-risk students, English learners, or learning disabled and speaks to the potential of the students who do not learn to read easily because of inadequate instruction or lack of classroom support systems. The acronym includes all these children. Of America's eighth-graders who took the National Assessment of Educational Progress reading test in 2011, 67 percent of all students and 83 percent of students from low-income families failed to reach the "proficient" reading level. In other words, these students are reading at a level deemed basic, below-basic, or chronically-below-basic. More than 22 million students are included in the SEEDS acronym, and I have personally known hundreds of these children, including my son and daughter. Despite the various reasons for their struggles in learning to read, all are capable of full literacy.

The need for a new term hit hard as I sat in a school district meeting last year. By midmorning, many of us were infuriated as we listened to educators classify sixth- and seventh-graders as "challenged," the implication being that they lacked the cognitive ability to perform at grade level. Every "challenged" student was two or more years below grade level in reading and hence viewed as "challenged" because he or she could not perform in language tasks: reading, writing papers, or coping with written exams. It was heartbreaking to hear these educators speak about these students as if the students were at fault. I wanted to shout, "It isn't their fault! The blame belongs to our system, for failing to provide our teachers with the knowledge and skill necessary to teach all children to read before third grade!" I defy anyone to find a child who has chosen to fail to learn to read and write.

Reports and data from respected authorities on the subject demonstrate the direct correlation between low third-grade reading scores and elevated high-school dropout rates. The Annie E. Casey

Report "Early Warning! Why Reading Matters by the End of Third Grade" and the Tremaine Foundation Report "Don't 'Dys' Our Kids" agree that upon entering third grade, students must begin the journey of text comprehension so that by fourth grade and beyond, they are fluent readers, ready to become fully reading literate and literate in other subjects. Thankfully, we live in an age when superior, differentiated, data-validated, high-tech teaching models, and professional development models can guarantee success for all our students and their teachers. Sadly, we have not come close to universally employing these tools. All children suffer the consequences, particularly our SEEDS children.

For years, we have been engaged in a blame game with respect to education and our schools. We point fingers at faddish reform efforts with questionable results, at unions who protect poor teachers, at administrators and school boards caught up in politics and bureaucratic practices, at schools of education that are slow to adopt the evidence of reading research, and at policy makers and legislators who fail to establish and maintain research-based standards and licensing requirements. By now we should be ready to stop playing the blame game and redirect that energy to build bridges that bring together all the stakeholders.

We should recognize that there is enough blame to go around and that assigning blame never solves the problems our schools confront. Especially, we must reject blaming children, which I have observed in more than one gathering of parents and educators. Nevertheless, it was that one district meeting, mentioned above, that led me to reach out to colleagues in search of a term that conveyed a positive message about the potential of the "challenged" children who do not learn to read with conventional, often inadequate, instructional practices. We coined the SEEDS acronym.

Many children in the SEEDS community struggle due to unsuitable assessment and instruction in the early grades; others lag behind because of the nature of their environments. Some struggle for biological reasons (such as dyslexia); others are just learning English. According to recent research, cited in chapter 4, a growing number of SEEDS students are average middle-class students. Regardless of the reasons for their struggles, like seeds that have the potential to grow and bear fruit, these students embody human potential. SEEDS are the 67 percent of all learners in today's schools. These children have the potential to grow into valuable, capable, fully literate citizens, and they must.

Instead of replaying the blame game, let us put our time and efforts into developing programs, practices, and policies that will foster that potential of all students. That is our duty.

Going Forward

I hope that by going public with my own story, together we can begin our journey toward a literate nation. Next, you will learn about facts and research behind this evidence-based blueprint for changing today's literacy standards, a blueprint chock-full of concrete strategies that can be acted upon now. We have assembled what you need to be an informed citizen and proactive literacy champion. We hope you will help drive change in your communities. Toward that end, we have synthesized bodies of science to support your work and share inspiring anecdotes to encourage you on your journey.

Part 1—consider this a compact executive summary on the state of the nation and the United States' international standing in the world of literacy, and how they affect jobs, our economy, and the quality of life afforded to American citizens. This overview and empirical data will help you become a well-informed and influential leader of change, capable of tackling the tough problem of schooling in America.

Part 2 is filled with information about levers for change and steps necessary to ensure that every American student is literate, educated, and career-ready.

Part 3 synthesizes and curates current literacy evidence into a usable guidebook consisting of nine critical components of model policies and practices. It provides the blueprint of action for grassroots, state policy makers, districts, and colleges of education.

The appendices present in detail model policy and practice with one-page summaries, key components, detailed specifics, and language for state legislation in

> SEEDS are the students who don't arrive easily at reading acquisition in kindergarten to third grade with low-standard classroom practices.

nine critical areas. They also organize the facts, citations, science, and resources of the book.

As a whole, this work curates scientific knowledge, policy expertise, curricular guidelines, Common Core State Standards, implementation fidelity, media and messaging tactics, timelines, and responsibilities together toward one goal: a literate citizenry.

CHAPTER TWO

AMERICA'S PLIGHT

I N THIS CHAPTER, I describe the plight of the American education system, its connection to society, its worth as an economic marker, and, most importantly, how it is neglecting to meet the needs of its students and its nation. To be an effective "literacy activist," you need to understand the nature of the literacy crisis that faces us and be conversant with facts and their implications.

> The world wants to work, and emerging-market governments are racing to seize the opportunity by investing in their greatest asset—human capital.

The Times They Are a Changin'

For those over thirty-five years old, the world we knew as children no longer exists. Technology pundits speak about living in "exponential times," during which advances double every year. It was in the mid-nineties—only twenty years ago—when at the recommendation of my MIS (management information systems) department, I requested that my employees discard the use of interoffice memorandums in favor of e-mail. Today, I can't imagine life without e-mail, text messages, Facebook, Twitter, Google docs, Dropbox, and the Internet.

Exponential times? You bet. To reach a marketing audience of fifty million people, it took the radio thirty-eight years. Guess how long it took Facebook? Two years. As for Twitter messages, well, just three years ago, would you have guessed that more than one hundred million tweet messages would be sent each day? I certainly did not. Hearing that @LadyGaga was all the rage, sending 140-character messages on the Internet to almost thirty million followers, I scratched my head, never imaging that a year later, I would be tweeting every day to a thousand followers of @LiterateNation. President Obama's campaigns took advantage of technology, particularly social media, in both his runs for office. We are living in "exponential times on steroids," even before we enter the magic kingdom of mobile apps. It is a new era, but reading literacy still rules. Indeed, forty years of declining US literacy and educational standards puts our youth at a disadvantage in this new environment.

The information age began with the invention of the computer and accelerated with the launch of the Internet, both of which ushered in a series of intoxicating digital (microminiaturization) advances. Today, rapid global communication, networking, and mobile devices shape modern society. Mass accessibility, expediency, connectivity, and innovation lead almost every sector of society except one: education. All my life, I have traveled to far-off lands, enjoying foreign cultures while taking comfort in the power and progress of my homeland—the land of freedom, opportunity, education, innovation, and security. However, in the last decade of my travels, I have witnessed a change in this global dynamic.

Final Result of the International Adult Literacy Survey, 2000
Literacy in the Information Age—

Literacy skills are becoming increasingly important in the knowledge economy, both for individuals and at the macro level. Countries with higher levels of skills will adjust more effectively to challenges and opportunities opened up by globalization because their firms will be more flexible and better able to absorb and adapt new knowledge, technologies and to work with new equipment. The skill level and quality of the workforce will increasingly provide the cutting edge in competing in the global economy.

Across the nation, a consensus is growing: rapid innovation is accelerating the pace of change in daily life, creating an exponential demand for dual-literacy—the ability to read rapidly and skim for information and the ability to read deeply for knowledge and analyze information. Today, both skills are requirements for lifelong learning. If you doubt that reading has evolved, take a quick look at an instructional manual from the 1980s and then look at one from 2013. The demand to process, analyze, and apply textual content has intensified.

Business leaders point to a concern they do not have the power to address alone: our workforce does not have the skills required to perform today's jobs—jobs that support our families and our nation. Schools pass kids along with weak reading, writing, and math abilities; they still emphasize memorization of information in subject areas. But technological innovations and investments allow knowledge to be summoned instantly. Thus, students need twenty-first-century skills that are largely absent in the classroom: the ability to read deeply, to formulate important questions, to model complex problems, to solve problems collaboratively, to communicate effectively in speech and in writing, and to guides one's own learning. Unless public education is substantially revamped, our workforce will not be performing the jobs in technology, manufacturing, finance, and many others. This is why industries are joining our effort to address the critical problem of an education system that is not keeping pace.

Seven billion people and many cultures share this planet—an interconnected populace capable of working and creating communally. The statistics of multinational corporations document rapid emergence of foreign markets and of highly skilled foreign employees. These trends forecast a coming war, not over religion or territory but job creation. Six years ago, Gallup's World Poll took on the herculean task of annually polling world leaders, academics, and citizens from 150 countries to find out what they were thinking. Gallop reported that the whole world is thinking it wants a good job with a steady paycheck from an employer who can provide at least thirty hours of work a week.

Job creation is a top priority for every country. Creating jobs is one thing; filling them is another. According to the US Bureau of Labor Statistics, there are 3.1 million US jobs unfilled. Why? There are many reasons, but the most worrisome is lack of skill and education among job applicants. Yet statistics document that 12.8 million citizens are seeking employment actively, while millions more are either underemployed or have given up the job search. [1] This discrepancy raises a question: What are the skills needed to fill these jobs? The answer: The vast majority of twenty-first-century jobs

---

[1]   Bureau of Labor Statistics, accessed March 2012, http://www.bls.gov/news.release/empsit.nr0.htm.

require tertiary education, and literacy skills are crucial at institutes of higher education in science, technology, engineering, and mathematics (STEM is the acronym for these subjects) as well as in trade schools offering vocational and career training.

According to a recent study by the Association of Manufacturing Excellence, 1,100 US manufacturers report job openings for skilled workers, such as machinists and technicians, and 83 percent of companies report moderate-to-serious shortages.[2] Manufacturing in the twenty-first century is steeped in innovation technology that requires astute workers. Moreover, the US Bureau of Labor Statistics estimates that manufacturing supports almost nineteen million jobs in the United States—about one in six private-sector jobs. The bulk of the nearly twelve million Americans holding manufacturing jobs currently are baby boomers approaching retirement age. Who will fill those high-paying jobs when boomers leave the workforce? If companies cannot find qualified US workers, will they be forced to move their operations overseas to harness the labor of better-educated populations?

> Wherever I find myself—in South America, Asia, Eastern Europe, Micronesia—I see an escalating ambition for education and job creation. And, of course, in this twenty-first century, the latter cannot exist without the former.

For decades, the US education system was the envy of the world. Our education system was a key factor in expanding the post-World War II economic success of the United States. In particular, we were notable for producing a high number of college graduates who fueled gross domestic product (GDP) and innovation. In large part, this was due to the enactment of the GI Bill. In 1944, the Servicemen's Readjustment Act was signed into law to provide a college education for veterans returning from war. This was the beginning of education, innovation, and GDP supremacy for the United States.

---

[2]   Association for Manufacturing Excellence, accessed February 2012, http://www.ame.org.

Education's effect on income.

It should come as no surprise that a higher education generally means a higher income. However, education is **not a guarantee** of success. The chart below shows common jobs and salaries based on the amount of training (education) required.

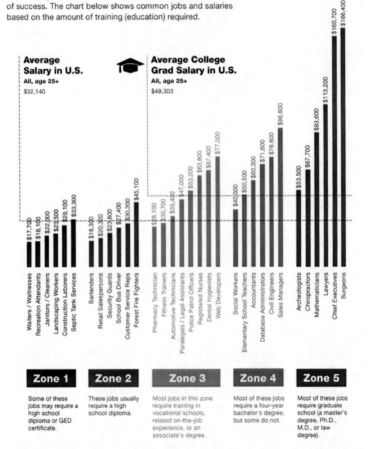

Average Salary in U.S.
All, age 25+
$32,140

Average College Grad Salary in U.S.
All, age 25+
$49,303

Zone 1 — Some of these jobs may require a high school diploma or GED certificate.

Zone 2 — These jobs usually require a high school diploma.

Zone 3 — Most jobs in this zone require training in vocational schools, related on-the-job experience, or an associate's degree.

Zone 4 — Most of these jobs require a four-year bachelor's degree, but some do not.

Zone 5 — Most of these jobs require graduate school (a master's degree, Ph.D., M.D., or law degree).

Zone 1:
- Waiters / Waitresses — $17,700
- Recreation Attendants — $18,100
- Janitors / Cleaners — $22,000
- Landscaping Workers — $23,500
- Construction Laborers — $29,100
- Septic Tank Services — $33,300

Zone 2:
- Bartenders — $18,300
- Retail Salespersons — $20,300
- Security Guards — $23,600
- School Bus Driver — $27,400
- Customer Service Reps — $30,300
- Forest Fire Fighters — $45,100

Zone 3:
- Pharmacy Technician — $28,100
- Fitness Trainers — $30,700
- Automotive Technicians — $35,400
- Paralegals / Legal Assistants — $47,000
- Police Patrol Officers — $53,200
- Registered Nurses — $63,800
- Dental Hygienists — $67,400
- Web Developers — $77,000

Zone 4:
- Social Workers — $40,000
- Elementary School Teachers — $50,500
- Accountants — $60,300
- Database Administrators — $71,600
- Civil Engineers — $76,600
- Sales Managers — $96,800

Zone 5:
- Archeologists — $53,500
- Chiropractors — $67,700
- Mathematicians — $93,600
- Lawyers — $113,200
- Chief Executives — $160,700
- Surgeons — $166,400+

Notes

A bright career outlook

All of the careers listed above are "Bright Outlook" careers. Bright Outlook careers are expected to grow rapidly in the next several years, will have large numbers of job openings, or are new and emerging jobs.

A note on salary numbers

The salaries listed above are the U.S. national average numbers from 2009, the latest data available. Numbers vary by state. To learn more about any specific jobs, you can use this helpful tool: http://online.onetcenter.org/find/zone

Source: U.S. Bureau of Labor Statistics

graphs.net

CINTHIA COLETTI

Today, among our young adult population (twenty-five to thirty-four years old), only 39 percent have attended college and received an associate's or bachelor's degree. [3] Measured by college graduation rates, the United States has made no progress in the level of citizen education over the past four decades. This has led to (1) a statistical plateau that stands in sharp contrast to the increase other advanced countries have experienced and (2) an unmet demand for a highly educated workforce. We must and can do better.

As a point of comparison, South Korea's level of educational achievement over the past two decades is astonishing. Just twenty years ago, only 13 percent of that nation's seasoned workforce had completed college; today 63 percent of Korean young adults hold a college degree. When a nation focuses on its human capital, remarkable success can occur in short order.

Exponential Threat

We are living in a 24/7 culture of Facebook, LinkedIn, Google+, Twitter, e-mails, e-marketing, mobile devices, apps, text messages, social media, forums, blogging, and other ubiquitous digital technologies that are now considered a compulsory part of life. All are rooted in reading, writing, and grammar. A semi-illiterate person has little opportunity to become a contributing member of society, start a business, be an inventor or artist, or achieve what once was considered a comfortable, blue-collar lifestyle. This lack of opportunity has negative consequences for individuals and for their communities, which do not benefit from the talent and involvement of each member.

A lackluster public education system threatens the future of our nation and will have a profound impact on all our lives. Our students are not acquiring the prerequisite skills for an increasing number of jobs that require STEM education. STEM proficiency requires a foundation in reading literacy. With the majority of our public-school youth lacking the rudimentary reading,

---

[3]   "Educational Attainment in the United States: 2011," US Census Bureau, accessed February 26, 2012.

writing, math, and science skills needed to fuel our economy,[4] there is no time to waste. We must improve our education system or be overtaken by other countries. It will not be easy, though. The failure of the "No Child Left Behind" five-billion-dollar policy and of other efforts at a fix (such as the Gates Foundation three-billion-dollar small schools initiative) underscores the fact that there is no silver-bullet solution.

A recent "warning" was published by Joel Klein, former chancellor of public schools in New York City, and Condoleezza Rice, former secretary of state, projecting that poor-quality educational outcomes are threatening not only the economy but also our national security:

> "A year ago, we brought together leaders in education, politics, business, academia, and the armed forces and diplomatic communities to assess the nation's education challenge in the context of national security. We believe education is posing direct threats to our nation: to economic growth, to intellectual property and competitiveness, to the protection of US physical safety, and to US global awareness, unity and cohesion . . . Human capital will determine power in the current century, and the failure to produce that capital will undermine America's security. Large, undereducated swaths of the population damage the ability of the United States to physically defend itself, protect its secure information, conduct diplomacy, and grow its economy."[5]

---

[4] Trends in International Mathematics and Science Study, *TIMMS 2011 International Results* (Washington DC: International Association for the Evaluation of Educational Achievement, 2011).

[5] Council on Foreign Relations–US Education Reform and National Security, http://www.cfr.org/united-states/us-education-reform-national-security/p27618?co=C007304.

Shifting Dynamic

Colin Powell, on Meet the Press, opined: "America is going to be a minority nation in one more generation,"[6] which gave me pause. These minority students are not getting educated well enough now.

51.9 million *Hispanics lived in the U.S. in 2011...*

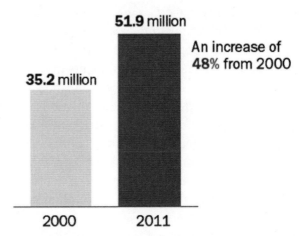

Pew Research Hispanic Center tabulations of 2000 Census (5% IPUMS) and 2011 American Community Survey (1% IPUMS)

"Fifty percent of our minority kids are not finishing high school. We've got to invest in education" was General Powell's impassioned statement. Not finishing high school should not be an option for any student in twenty-first-century America. Imagine the psychological costs of dropping out of school and of a future limited by functional illiteracy. Imagine a life without the ability to read a ballot in a voting booth, to understand directions on prescription medications, to help a child with homework, or to complete a job application. Adults often encounter text-heavy materials, such as schedules, charts, graphs, tables, maps, and forms at home, at work, or when traveling in their communities. The knowledge and skills needed to process information contained in these documents is therefore an important aspect of literacy in a modern society. Success in processing documents appears to depend at least in part on the ability to locate information in a variety of displays, and to use this information in a number of ways—like communicating, writing, and transferring information from one source to another, all impossible without full literacy.

Our forefathers wrote of the unalienable rights to life, liberty, and the pursuit of happiness; yet in some states and school districts, only four out of ten students could read these words found in the Declaration of Independence. In states like Nevada, New Mexico, Georgia, Oregon, Alaska, only six in ten students graduate from high school. Some school districts' graduation figures are far worse—even catastrophic—leading to the label "drop out factory,"[6] like Milwaukee where only 31 percent of students graduate.

Literacy and lifestyle are intrinsically linked. Literacy is the foundation for all other accomplishments in education, work or career, hobbies, knowledge attainment, self-esteem, social status—ultimately, the quality of life. Literacy is the foundation of a strong nation. The College Board, the organization that administers the SAT, began in 1900 with the goal of creating the first examination to expand student access to a college education. Then and now, the examination helps admissions departments determine whether or not a student is "college-ready." The College Board announced that the 2011 SAT student scores were the "lowest in 40 years."[7] I must admit that this caught me by surprise, so I decided to take a long hard look at the report.

In a nutshell, approximately four million kids start high school each year. Last year, 1.65 million students took the exam, and only 43 percent (710,000) met the "college and career benchmark" established by the board. Think about it another way: the other 57 percent are

---

[6] Milwaukee graduates only 31 percent, Detroit 37 percent, Baltimore 41 percent, and Los Angeles 44 percent. Statistics come from the Trial Urban District Assessment, Governing Board, National Center for Education Statistics of the US Department of Education, Council of the Great City Schools, and the urban districts sections of the National Assessment of Educational Progress. All sources can be found on associated organization websites.

[7] "43 Percent of 2011 College-Bound Seniors Met SAT College and Career Readiness Benchmark," College Board, accessed September 17, 2011, http://press.collegeboard.org/releases/2011/43-percent-2011-college-bound-s.eniors-met-sat-college-and-career-readiness-benchmark.

not—meaning 940,000 decent students declared ready for college by their high schools are not ready. These are students who passed their courses, many taking advanced placement courses, and earned a high-school diploma. Now consider that there are another 2.23 million students who did not take the exam (the 1.23 million students who dropped out of high school, and the estimated 1.0 million-plus students who received a diploma but were deemed not qualified to take the SAT[8]).

Doing the math, this means that only 710, 000 out of four million students who enter high school each year will be college-ready. Oh my! What will happen to the "American dream?" It is reported that by 2018, the nation will need twenty-two million new employees with postsecondary credentials, yet we'll fall millions short.[9]

This brings up a related topic: the unnecessary time and cost of college remedial classes. Are the high-school graduates who fail to meet the College Board benchmark doomed to remedial English classes? Over 940,000 kids take the SAT, ready to commence the journey into the world of higher education, and end up repeating work that is high-school level or below level. Whose responsibility should the financial burden for remedial classes be—students'? taxpayers'?

Observation of an Immigrant

> *Human history becomes more and more a race between education and catastrophe.*
>
> —*H. G. Wells*

---

[8]   Editorial Projects in Education, Diplomas Count 2008, "School to College: Can State P-16 Councils Ease the Transition?" special issue, *Education Week* 26 (2008): 40.

[9]   "The American Dream 2.0," HCM Strategists Report, accessed 2012, http://www.hcmstrategists.com/americandream2-0/report/HCM_Gates_Report_1_17_web.pdf.

Professor Maryanne Wolf, who conducts cognitive neuroscience research on the reading brain, gave a lecture recently in Berkeley, California. She told me something that captures one of the reasons I began this book.

In her lecture, she described her concern that children's immersion in digital media might impede formation of an "expert reading brain" and might give children less motivation to come to their own thoughts, insights, and creative ideas, a skill learned from deep reading. While speaking, she noticed a man dressed in a black suit that could have been a uniform pacing behind the audience. He seemed riveted by what she was saying. After the lecture, the man waited until everyone left before approaching her. He seized her hand and spoke animatedly about his appreciation for what she had said. And he told his story. Ali is a well-educated Iranian who was forced to flee his home country decades before. He loves America for allowing him to embark on a new life for himself and his family, but now he despairs for the United States. With an eloquence that was compelling, he said, "In my humble opinion, America is losing its ascendancy"; its children cannot read nor do math or science. He predicted that his chosen country soon would lose its place in history because we have let this happen. "Our children become 'dumber' every day," Ali said, "while other nations do everything they can to make their children succeed."

The competitive edge that the country has enjoyed from decades of investment in public education that exceeded that of other nations is now rapidly eroding. While the very best schools in the United States are as good as the best in the world, the averages are less competitive, and the bottom quartile lags well behind most other developed nations. The competitive position of the United States in the world is clearly at stake.

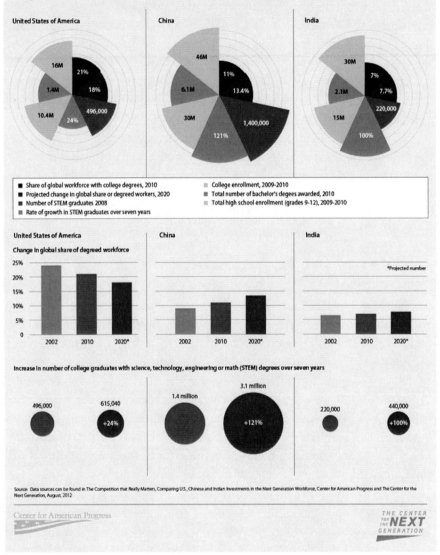

Fast facts: The competition that really matters

A snapshot of U.S., Chinese and Indian investments in the next generation workforce

United States of America | China | India

- Share of global workforce with college degrees, 2010
- Projected change in global share or degreed workers, 2020
- Number of STEM graduates 2008
- Rate of growth in STEM graduates over seven years
- College enrollment, 2009-2010
- Total number of bachelor's degees awarded, 2010
- Total high school enrollment (grades 9-12), 2009-2010

United States of America | China | India

Change in global share of degreed workforce

*Projected number

Increase in number of college graduates with science, technology, engineering or math (STEM) degrees over seven years

Source: Data sources can be found in The Competition that Really Matters, Comparing U.S., Chinese and Indian Investments in the Next Generation Workforce, Center for American Progress and The Center for the Next Generation, August, 2012

Center for American Progress

THE CENTER FOR THE NEXT GENERATION

After Dr. Wolf, author of the highly acclaimed book *Proust and the Squid: The Story and Science of the Reading Brain*, told me about Ali's indictment of American society, we were both quiet. Ali was right. For a host of reasons, a great many of our American children are becoming only a fraction of what they could become. The implications extend to the whole of society and reach into the immediate, near, and distant future. We all will be either twice blessed—with thriving citizens in a thriving society—or twice cursed. The choice is ours.

This brings me back to the SAT and high-school dropout statistics mentioned above. Ali also said to Dr. Wolf, "Dumb people are easily manipulated." History shows that when governments fail to prepare their youth for the future, the foundation of society fails. Good citizens are voters who are well informed, which requires the ability to read. This is essentially what Ali, the solid citizen and employed manager of a respected establishment, said.

We must take responsibility as citizens. We must acknowledge the needless deterioration of US literacy and education outcomes. We must unite and drive the change needed to reverse this deterioration quickly. We must move our fellow citizens intellectually and emotionally to embrace a simple truth: to sustain our freedom and quality of life, we need literate, career-ready young people.

A Look Around

Human capital is a country's greatest asset. Education, training, and health are among the most important investments a nation can make. The emerging superpower nations are acting upon the ideology today; for example, since 1998, China has invested in "a massive expansion of education, nearly tripling the share of Gross Domestic Product (GDP) devoted to it. [10] In the decade since, the number of colleges in China has doubled and the number of college graduates quintupled, going from one million in 1997 to 5.5 million in 2007."[11] What does this mean, and how do these facts apply and compare to the United States?

---

[10]   The gross domestic product (GDP) is a primary indicator used to gauge the health of a country's economy. It represents the total dollar value of all the finished goods and services produced within a country's borders in a specific time period—the output of goods and services produced by labor and property located in a country.

[11]   "The Real Challenge from China: Its People, Not Its Currency," *Time*, October 7, 2010.

China has about four hundred million students, compared to our fifty-four million. China has more students than the entire US population. But what really stands out is not the number of students, but how they are being prepared to contribute to China's society through quality education. Chinese children typically start their formal education at age two; for our children, age five is standard, though not mandatory in some states. By the first semester of first grade, Chinese children are expected to recognize four hundred characters and write one hundred of them.[12] The vast majority of our first-grade students have not learned the forty-four phonemes (distinct speech sounds) of the English language, nor are they able to match phonemes with orthography (the combination of letters to form words).

If America is to remain a world leader, innovator, and producer, then we must embrace the creed of the new global economy: invest in the education, skill, and the employability of young people. Many of us are nostalgic for the boundless potential of the US political and public education systems of the past, nostalgic for the days our beautiful coasts allowed us to be isolationists, living in towns where we knew our neighbors and considered ourselves part of a discrete community. Some of us, myself included, even long for the lazy days of low-tech simplicity, of living without digital devices glued to our body parts. Yes, I would like to be a Pollyanna, or perhaps just bury my head in the sand and do nothing to help my country; but this is very dangerous territory. Why? Because inaction cripples our ability to drive reform. And if we don't drive reform in education, we put our country and lifestyle at inordinate risk.

A report by Nobel laureate economist James Heckman argues that quality education and early intervention address both social justice and cost efficiency. In essence, he says that education and early intervention lead to a significant reduction in public expense and a brighter economic future: "Educational equity is often discussed as a moral issue. As an economist, I focus on the economic value of equalizing educational opportunities and achievement in order to identify the most effective way to increase the productivity of the American economy. We need a capable and productive workforce that will compete successfully in the global economy. Underdeveloped human

---

[12]   "China's Winning Schools?" *New York Times*, January 15, 2011.

potential burdens our economy and leaves us with a workforce that is less than it could be."[13]

Where You Stand Depends on Where You Sit

To get a clear picture of our education system, we turn to the reports by the National Assessment of Educational Progress (NAEP), nicknamed the "Nation's Report Card." These reports corroborate that we are not investing wisely in educating our future workforce—and poor returns on our investments are not limited to underprivileged students. Today, only 33 percent of our fourth- and eighth-grade students read at a proficient grade level.[14] Are you shocked? I sure as heck am. The vast majority of our students (67 percent) read at just basic, below-basic, or chronically-below-basic level, meaning nearly seven out of every ten US students are seriously underdeveloped in the number-one skill needed to succeed. Shocking statistics like these raise four key questions:

> How can a nation that spends more than $1.15 trillion per year on public-school education invest more wisely and get results?

> How can we spend more money per student on education than any other country in the world and still rank in the bottom tier of the OECD international assessment?

> How many of our students are unprepared for the jobs that lead to careers that increase the nation's GDP?

> What do these numbers tell us about our future economic health and welfare?

[13] J. Heckman, "The Economics of Inequality," *American Educator* (Spring 2011).

[14] National Assessment of Educational Progress, *The Nation's Report Card* (Washington DC: 2011).

After World War II, the United States led the world in student achievement. Since the 1970s, we have been in a downward spiral. Once, we were first in high-school graduation ranking; now we have slipped to nineteenth in the world, according to the OECD. Poland and Korea do a better job of teaching their students to read than we do. [15] Guess where we rank in reading literacy among our international competitors? The answer: a miserable twenty-fourth out of thirty-four developed countries. [16]

With its better-trained teachers, longer school days, and obligatory time for students to learn both Mandarin and English, China soon will become the number-one English-speaking country in the world. The United States still is thought to be the greatest nation on the planet; our GDP is more than double China's (which we achieve with a fraction of its population), and yet only one in three American students is proficient or higher in reading? This does not bode well for us. Are we approaching a day when China's schools are doing a better job teaching English than our own schools? We can and must do better.

Research shows that when students are taught to read with teachers skilled in using assessment data to drive instruction in an explicit, systematic, and integrated format, all but a small percentage of children will become reading literate in the English language.

This means they will be able to read for knowledge, write accurately and coherently, and think critically about subject-area printed material in order to analyze, critique, synthesize, and use information to reflect, make informed decisions, and create new ideas.

If other nations can improve their academic gains, so can we. A recent report by Harvard University's Program on Education Policy and Governance at the Kennedy School of Government found that students in Latvia, Chile, and Brazil are making academic gains three times faster than American students, while those in Portugal, Hong

---

[15] "Programme for International Student Assessment (PISA) Ranking," Organisation for Economic Co-operation and Development, accessed October 6, 2013, http://www.oecd.org/pisa/pisaproducts/48852548.pdf.

[16] Ibid.

Kong, Germany, Poland, Liechtenstein, Slovenia, Colombia, and Lithuania are improving at twice our rate:

> *Because rates of economic growth have a huge impact on the future well-being of the nation, there is a simple message: a country ignores the quality of its schools at its economic peril. Some excuse our mediocre performance, noting that we provide an education to a much more diverse population than other countries. Some argue that test scores in the United States are lower than those in many other countries because they are not providing an education to all their students. But these arguments reflect a dated view of the world.*[17]

The realities of our educational circumstances demand that we rise to the challenge together.

> We need young people to graduate from college or a skills school and get a job that becomes a career and is backed up with continuing education.
>
> —Ron Bullock, Chairman
> Bison Gear & Engineering
> Corporation

---

[17] *Endangering Prosperity: A Global View of the American School,* Harvard Program on Education Policy and Governance (PEPG), Harvard Kennedy School, accessed October 6, 2013, http://www.hks.harvard.edu/pepg/endangeringprosperity.htm.

PISA — Program for International Student Assessment: 2009 Survey Results

READING

	SHANGHAI, CHINA	556
	SOUTH KOREA	539
	FINLAND	536
	HONG KONG, CHINA	533
	SINGAPORE	526
	CANADA	524
	NEW ZEALAND	521
	JAPAN	520
	AUSTRALIA	515
	NETHERLANDS	508
	BELGIUM	506
	NORWAY	503
	ESTONIA	501
	SWITZERLAND	501
	POLAND	500
	ICELAND	500
	UNITED STATES	500
	LICHTENSTEIN	499
	SWEDEN	497
	GERMANY	497
	IRELAND	496
	FRANCE	496
	TAIWAN	495
	DENMARK	495
	UNITED KINGDOM	494
	HUNGARY	494
	PISA Average	493
	PORTUGAL	489
	MACAO, CHINA	487
	ITALY	486
	LATVIA	484

SCIENCES

	SHANGHAI, CHINA	575
	FINLAND	554
	HONG KONG, CHINA	549
	SINGAPORE	542
	JAPAN	539
	SOUTH KOREA	538
	NEW ZEALAND	532
	CANADA	529
	ESTONIA	528
	AUSTRALIA	527
	NETHERLANDS	522
	LICHTENSTEIN	520
	GERMANY	520
	TAIWAN	520
	SWITZERLAND	517
	UNITED KINGDOM	514
	SLOVENIA	512
	MACAO, CHINA	511
	POLAND	508
	IRELAND	508
	BELGIUM	507
	HUNGARY	503
	UNITED STATES	502
	PISA Average	500
	NORWAY	500
	CZECH REPUBLIC	500
	DENMARK	499
	FRANCE	498
	ICELAND	496
	SWEDEN	495
	LATVIA	494

MATH

	SHANGHAI, CHINA	600
	SINGAPORE	562
	HONG KONG, CHINA	555
	SOUTH KOREA	546
	TAIWAN	543
	FINLAND	541
	LICHTENSTEIN	536
	SWITZERLAND	534
	JAPAN	529
	CANADA	527
	NETHERLANDS	526
	MACAO, CHINA	525
	NEW ZEALAND	519
	BELGIUM	515
	AUSTRALIA	514
	GERMANY	513
	ESTONIA	512
	ICELAND	507
	DENMARK	503
	SLOVENIA	501
	NORWAY	498
	FRANCE	497
	SLOVAKIA	497
	AUSTRIA	496
	PISA Average	496
	POLAND	495
	SWEDEN	494
	CZECH REPUBLIC	493
	UNITED KINGDOM	492
	HUNGARY	490
	LUXEMBOURG	489

Challenges and Ramifications

When we took our eye off the ball of educating the next generation, we put our nation's future on the line. *That Used to Be Us: How America Fell Behind in the World It Invented and How We Can Come Back*, by Thomas L. Friedman and Michael Mandelbaum, analyzes four challenges relatively new in human history: globalization, the revolution in information technology, chronic deficits, and patterns of energy consumption. To confront and overcome these challenges requires a well-educated and productive citizenry. Friedman and Mandelbaum argue that our future depends on how we address these challenges. So far, they believe we are failing. Our schools have not adapted to changing priorities around the world and must play catch-up in teaching skills critical to the new economy's financial growth: math, physics, engineering, and technology, all demanded in a digital age and dependent on a solid foundation in reading literacy.

After surveying industry organizations and associations, I find that most agree that a lack of qualified reading literate citizens is affecting their ability to maintain production schedules. Nearly 75 percent report that the lack of skilled production employees is affecting their ability to expand operations in the United States, and 80 percent fear a shortage of qualified workers will impact their ability to continue operations here. In other words: we lose more jobs because companies are forced to move operations overseas to tap a more talented, employment pool.

> Couple poor teacher preparation with fewer hours of student education and a country has the recipe for pending catastrophe in losing the world's war for jobs. And if education budget cuts are added into the mix, then we have the perfect storm.

Decades without Our Eye on the Ball

Let us ponder why OECD measurements show our students diving in international standings compared to other countries. A few reasons stand out. The first is the inadequate knowledge, supports, and skill base of our teachers, which, of course, is not their fault. The second has to do with the number of hours our students are educated.

Compared to the highest-performing countries, American students have the shortest school days, a mere thirty-two hours a week in school. This reflects our agrarian roots, a time when children were needed at home to work in the fields, farms, and stores. Countries like Denmark and Sweden boast forty- to fifty-hour school weeks— almost 30 percent longer than ours. Among all countries, Shanghai and Hong Kong, which claim two out of the top-five rankings in the OECD International Reading Literacy standings, spend a staggering eight and a half to twelve hours a day in school,[18] spending roughly 50 percent more time being educated than America's children, and by better-trained teachers. It is not just about the amount of time spent learning. Teachers also must have deep knowledge, supports, and skills.

Teaching students in Mandarin and English simultaneously is complex; the languages have significant differences (same with Japanese, Arabic, etc.), which makes learning English a serious challenge for students who are not native speakers. The ministries of education in China and other countries deserve a round of applause for setting high standards that prepare their teachers exceedingly well and for requiring bi/trilanguage acquisition, which will help their students compete in the global economy.

The issue boils down to this: if America is to succeed, we must raise the societal value of the teaching profession through the recruitment, preparation, support, credentialing, advancement, and compensation of professional educators.

Most of China's teacher preparation originates from the work of experts in US think tanks and research institutes. Foreign ministries of education and institutions of higher education have purchased more copies of research books published by the National Academies of Sciences than have been purchased in the United States. What conclusions can we draw when such data suggests that our own research is being used more frequently abroad than here at home?

China's new teachers come from the pool of their best students, selected from the top ranks in their secondary schools, often provided scholarships, and are ushered into teaching three areas of focus: engineering, IT, and medicine. Teaching is considered of equal importance, and these teaching candidates receive advanced college

---

[18] "China's Children Too Busy for Playtime," *China Daily* (*Xinhua*), accessed September 15, 2011, http://www.chinadaily.com.cn/china/2007-05/13/content_871182.htm.

education and living stipends and are appointed mentors upon graduating. Yes, mentors—seasoned master instructors who train teachers until they are deemed "expert" in their subjects. In contrast to many other countries preparing and advancing their teachers, the United States endorses the bare minimum for candidate qualifications, course load requirement, licensure, and certification. This leads directly to our students' subpar skills in reading, writing, and learning, and to low rates of high-school and college graduation. We can do a better job!

Most of our teacher preparation programs provide little instruction in the science of teaching reading. [19] Check the index of the textbook required in courses in reading and you will seldom find more than a very few pages dealing with the structure of language or with the needs of students who learn differently. These programs maintain barely acceptable standards, leading to poor certification and licensure, and very little performance reporting—much less longitudinal data on effectiveness, which is on my top-ten wish list.

Lacking preparation in teaching reading to a diverse group of children, our dedicated new teachers are at a loss as to how to best instruct them. In 2010-2011, 3.5 million children were first-time kindergartners; 53 percent were white, 24 percent were Hispanic, 13 percent were African American, 4 percent were Asian, and 1 percent were American Indian or Alaska Native; 25 percent came from households below the federal poverty level; and 84 percent lived in homes where English was the primary language.[20]

Think about what young teachers see as they start the school year with this range of ethnicity and background—twenty-three bright, beautiful children staring up, eager to learn to read, write, and please their teacher. Sadly, most of our teachers do not have a clue what to do to give these students their best shot at achievement. If we educated

---

[19] US Department of Education, "Preparing and Credentialing the Nation's Teachers," *The Secretary's Eighth Report on Teacher Quality Based on Data Provided for 2008, 2009, 2010* (Washington DC: 2011).

[20] PEW Research Center, "English Usage among Hispanics in America," *Numbers, Facts, and Trends Shaping the World* (Washington DC: 2009).

and trained teachers more effectively, perhaps 50 percent of new teachers would not leave education within their first five years.[21]

In one of my research projects on early literacy, I worked with many recently licensed teachers. Early in the year, control classrooms were presented with picture books and bright charts, but no additional training or supports to improve teachers' deep knowledge of reading development. By the fall holiday break, the majority of these teachers were frustrated because most of their kids were no closer to grade-level reading than when they started the year. These poor teachers felt helpless, realizing they didn't have the skills to succeed in their job. When we began to provide training and increase the use of data to direct student instruction, many teachers became angry with their colleges of education for failing to teach them these skills and provide the knowledge required for differentiated instruction—especially since these young teachers still were paying off student loans.

Now, this news isn't novel. Even the deans of education at prestigious colleges of education admit that they are helpless in solving the teacher preparation problem because deans have no authority over their tenured professors. In 2010, a blue-ribbon clinical teacher preparation panel was established to seek knowledge on how to raise the bar for teacher preparation.

> Shouldn't each of us pressure the political machine to make education the nation's top priority?

The recommendation from the national commission was blunt: "Turn teacher-preparation education upside down."[22] Specifically, the panel declared that early education teaching curricula are lagging decades behind the science of teaching and learning—science that has been paid for by taxpayer dollars and ignored by the faculty in institutes of higher education across the country. The panel also

---

[21] "Teacher Attrition: A Costly Loss to the Nation and States," Alliance for Excellent Education, accessed October 6, 2013, http://all4ed.org/reports-factsheets/teacher-attrition-a-costly-loss-to-the-nation-and-to-the-states/.

[22] "Transforming Teacher Education through Clinical Practice: A National Strategy to Prepare Effective Teachers," National Council of Accreditation for Teacher Education, accessed March 8, 2012, http://ncate.org/LinkClick.aspx?fileticket=zzeiB1OoqPk%3d&tabid=669.

deemed the procedure of state teacher licensure weak when compared to international standards. The panel's findings exposed the pending disaster for future teachers, this generation of students, and this country if preparation programs are not "turned upside down."

Stakeholders Unite for a Literate Next Generation

If we can mobilize a broad-based movement for literacy and education transformation, the result will be greater employment, a growing economy, fewer citizens on social services, and more money for the folks who need these services. If we do not turn this around, we must prepare ourselves for an increasingly uneducated, unskilled, functionally illiterate population with few carrying the burden of many. In a recent article, "Are You Winning the Workforce Preparation War?" shipbuilding executive John Shifflett said, "Make no mistake. You, along with the rest of the United States, are in a war for the most competitive workforce. And, we are not winning."[23]

The quality of American life depends upon a population that can read, so they can have rewarding career opportunities, live in decent neighborhoods, raise families in homes they own, and enjoy freedom of choice. The top driver in the competitiveness of a nation and the standard of living of its people is a steady supply of highly skilled employees, scientists, researchers, and engineers. There is so much bombarding us today—national security, health costs, retirement, energy, and budgets. However, I hope I have convinced you that nothing is more important than education. How do we convince government officials and education leaders that providing a world-class education for our youth is a national imperative? We must unify. We must work together as stakeholders in our communities and states to achieve the education goals that will ensure that our children enjoy lifetimes of possibilities and opportunities.

---

[23] John Shifftlett, "Are You Winning the Workforce Preparation War?" *Target Magazine*, 2011.

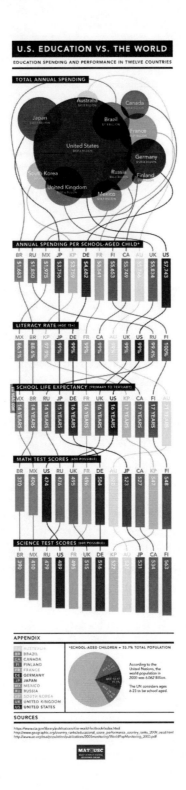

U.S. EDUCATION VS. THE WORLD

EDUCATION SPENDING AND PERFORMANCE IN TWELVE COUNTRIES

TOTAL ANNUAL SPENDING

Australia
Canada
Japan
Brazil
France
United States
Germany
South Korea
Russia
Finland
United Kingdom
Mexico

ANNUAL SPENDING PER SCHOOL-AGED CHILD*

BR	RU	MX	JP	KP	DE	FR	FI	CA	AU	UK	US
$1,683	$1,850	$1,975	$3,756	$3,759	$4,682	$5,541	$5,653	$5,749	$5,704	$5,834	$7,743

LITERACY RATE (AGE 15+)

MX	BR	KP	JP	DE	FR	CA	AU	UK	US	RU	FI
86.1%	88.6%	97.9%	99%	99%	99%	99%	99%	99%	99%	99.4%	100%

SCHOOL LIFE EXPECTANCY (PRIMARY TO TERTIARY)

MX	BR	RU	JP	DE	FR	UK	US	CA	FI	AU
14 YEARS	14 YEARS	14 YEARS	15 YEARS	16 YEARS	16 YEARS	16 YEARS	16 YEARS	17 YEARS	17 YEARS	21 YEARS

MATH TEST SCORES (600 POSSIBLE)

BR	MX	US	RU	UK	FR	DE	AU	JP	CA	KP	FI
370	406	474	476	495	496	504		523	527	542	548

SCIENCE TEST SCORES (600 POSSIBLE)

BR	MX	RU	US	FR	UK	DE	KP	AU	JP	CA	FI
390	410	479	489	495	515	516	522	527	531	534	563

APPENDIX

AU AUSTRALIA
BR BRAZIL
CA CANADA
FI FINLAND
FR FRANCE
DE GERMANY
JP JAPAN
MX MEXICO
RU RUSSIA
KP SOUTH KOREA
UK UNITED KINGDOM
US UNITED STATES

*SCHOOL-AGED CHILDREN = 33.7% TOTAL POPULATION

AGE 12-17
11.1%

According to the United Nations, the world population in 2000 was 6.062 Billion. The UN considers ages 6-23 to be school aged.

SOURCES

https://www.cia.gov/library/publications/the-world-factbook/index.html
http://www.geographic.org/country_ranks/educational_score_performance_country_ranks_2009_oecd.html
http://www.un.org/esa/population/publications/2003/monitoring/WorldPopMonitoring_2003.pdf

MAT USC

CHAPTER THREE

ROAD TO RECOVERY

THUS FAR WE have touched on undesirable contextual material—designed to help us understand where our educational malfeasance has led us, where we stand in the world as educators, what the economic impact might be, and who thinks so and why. Indeed, the negative aspects must be understood if we are to solve real education problems with real means described in the steps ahead. In this chapter, we will weave system's opportunity together with literacy's impacts. The countries cited are best viewed as examples of national determination and successful strategies, rather than foreboding comparisons.

Recognition of Opportunity

Before we get to the blueprint or action plan in part 2, it is important to think more about the current context of literacy in the United States—identify the political and social misconduct all too easily accepted in our education system and then call for a practical approach that identifies a remedy.

I am one of many who believe that voter trust in national government has eroded and that the role of state governments is perhaps strengthened and better suited for solving issues regarding each state's citizens. State governments allow citizens to establish action plans built on areas of agreement. Today, in state after state, citizens are agreeing that we can do better in public education. Education data have confirmed that the problems of student literacy and education are weighty and critical and require positive action. A high-school graduation rate that is the eighth lowest in the OECD ranking (dropout rates have tripled in the last thirty years[24]), represents a chilling certainty: "educational gaps impose on the United States the economic equivalent of a permanent national recession."[25]

These and other education indicators discussed in the last chapter paint bleak realities for our future. Yet at the same time, they give the nation and each state a great opportunity to unite and enact powerful educational change—think about a set of Common Core State Standards unifying behind the basic universal skills necessary for educational success to feed personal, economic, and political success. Americans with a history of the right to freely associate—from the Declaration of Independence to civil rights, veteran rights, women's rights, working conditions, environmental initiatives, and right to work—confirm an amazing ability to form grassroots organizations to tackle society's most difficult problems and to effect change. So if we know that America has the enormously complex problem of educating its young citizens, which, if not solved, will weaken our society, why aren't we raising our voices to demand change? Here is where I believe we can unite and advance a positive movement.

Clearly, there are many hurdles that the education system and individual students and teachers face, from hunger to absentee parents, from crumbling schools to lack of funds for technology, from learning disabilities to poor teacher preparation, and the list goes on. But they are not unique excuses for the continuing increase in the rate of failure to teach all our students to become literate, complete their education, and find careers to support themselves and contribute back to society—we can overcome these issues. We can reverse the trend of generations of functionally illiterate, unemployable citizens that will, in time, impose disturbing ramifications for every one of us. Economic Impact of the Achievement Gap in America, a recent McKinsey report, states that "the achievement gap generates the obvious: lower

---

[24]   National Center for Education Statistics, accessed September 2011, http://nces.ed.gov/pubsearch/pubsinfo.asp?pubid=2012025.

[25]   "The Economic Impact of the Achievement Gap in America's Schools," McKinsey & Company, http://www.mckinsey.com/app_media/images/page_images/offices/socialsector/pdf/achievement_gap_report.pdf, 17.

individual and community earnings, poor health, higher rates of incarceration and social dependency, and significant forfeiture of America's Gross Domestic Product."

Facts are crying out that the time has come for us to quickly and powerfully build community organizations to solve the most fundamental, singular problem that is key to our future: educating our young people. We can do this because it is being done in countries far less able than the United States of America. Research has confirmed time and again that all but a very small percentage of children can become literate; however, if children have not been taught to read by fourth grade, there is a good chance they will not be earning a high-school diploma.[26]

Now, let's be frank, every day we hear common excuses about myriad systemic problems plaguing our education system. I will rattle off the top ten: (1) an increased number of students who are learning English, (2) more children in high-poverty schools, (3) budget cutbacks, (4) old technologies in antiquated school buildings, (5) inadequate teacher preparedness programs that lag twenty years behind science, (6) no respect for the teaching profession and low pay, which leads to the inability to recruit top talent, (7) reduced school days and shorter school years, (8) meager professional development for teachers and a lack of school-based leadership talent, (9) top-heavy officialdoms, (10) tenure issues in elementary school through to universities—the list goes on. Yes, we have created a complex beast of an education system mired in government administration, union protectionism, higher-education isolationists, and so much more. Nevertheless, there are a few easily resolvable problems that we can get our arms around that will cure the functional illiteracy and educational failure that exists.

Getting Back on Track

The advent of the Common Core State Standards Initiative (Standards) in 2010, which have been adopted by forty-six states

---

[26] "Early Warning: Why Reading by the End of Third Grade Matters," Annie E. Casey Foundation, http://nces.ed.gov/nationsreportcard/naepdata/.

and the District of Columbia, presents our literacy movement with a tremendous opportunity to effect positive change. So let's quickly touch on the Standards and how they intrinsically link to our work. Advances in research and theory emphasize that education can be inclusive of all student outcomes (equity) with the goal that regardless of where students live or what school they attend, they can and will meet the same high-quality standards of education. The Standards were developed with the recognition of global competition, combined with the dizzying pace of technological innovation that creates a new urgency for fundamental, engaging, and challenging ways to educate our young people across states. Clearly, getting the common-core content right was monumental. I know, because several of my colleagues united across disciplines to accomplish the task of writing the Standards.

Local education agencies across the country are determining how schools and teachers can best advance skill and knowledge so all students can demonstrate mastery in the Standards. This is a huge and necessary task as it places great demand to change the course of instruction from one of "Lecture and Test" to "Involvement and Demonstration." It also mandates that literacy and language instruction become a larger part of all subject-area instruction, requiring teachers in grades 4 through 12 to become literacy instructors—science literacy, math literacy, digital literacy, and so on. Our literacy movement can make a big difference in how thoroughly and consistently the Standards are applied.

Many fear that the Standards may never be realized for one key reason: the void of deep teacher knowledge necessary to ensure solid student reading development in kindergarten through third grade and to ensure reading and content-area literacy proficiency in all students and in all subjects in grades 4 through 12. Why? Because this is what it takes to compete in the global society. I am heartbroken to report that already states have pushed back from achieving the

> I predict that the Standards will fail unless teachers receive intense professional development and continued support, treated as professionals whose abilities are advanced with new practice and science. Only then can we move literacy from the schoolroom to the workplace, to citizenship, and to lifelong learning—central to achieving our aspirations. Only then will America stand a chance to get back on track as a world leader in education.

Standards, filing for waivers to delay the requirements for three or more years. This is tragic, but even more tragic would be to have the movement for Standards discarded because teachers are not provided with the support they need to put it into practice.

Lessons to Ponder

The strategic road to recovery for education in the United States is a complex chess match with either an eventual loss that connotes continued decline or a triumphant win. Chess masters create strategies in which the early moves are essential to the end game. So while having this early move toward the Standards is essential, we must be strategic in ensuring it will succeed by designing scaffolding to support its construction. This is where our work comes into the game—the most important factor to reach the Standards is, first, reading literacy. If content-area teachers in late elementary, middle, and high school receive students into their classrooms who are years behind grade-level reading, they will never be able to uphold the lauded goals of the Standards.

There are many examples of effective educational strategies from around the world. In a new book by Vivian Stewart, A World-Class Education: Lessons from International Models of Excellence and Innovation, the stories of five very different educational systems unfold: those of Australia, Canada, China (Shanghai), Finland, and Singapore, which include (1) long-term vision, (2) sustained leadership, (3) ambitious standards, (4) commitment to equity, and (5) high-quality leaders and educators. In spite of differences in policy details and practices, as well as in the cultural contexts and political systems in these countries, there are clearly some common drivers of success. These drivers support the work of this book toward achieving students' literacy and the goals of the Standards. Here are the five big lessons from some of the world's top-performing systems that American education can learn from:

1. Long-term vision
The political leaders of countries with high-performing education systems share a conviction about the centrality of education to their dreams for society: to raise people from poverty, achieve greater equality, develop a well-functioning multicultural society, and,

certainly, create a thriving economy and a growing number of good jobs. Each of these countries has a long-term vision, widely shared inside and outside the education system, for achieving these goals through education. In Singapore, for example, long-term vision helped to propel the economy from third world to first; China's 2020 vision was developed with online input from millions of people and includes universal high-school graduation and world-class universities; Alberta asked all its citizens to contribute to a dialogue on what the educated Albertan of 2030 should look like; Finland's vision was to become a modern society and economy, free from domination by larger powers. Literacy and the Standards can be promising components of America's long-term vision of high education performance, if we seize the day.

2. Sustained leadership

Major reforms are often triggered by an economic, social, or political crisis and may be led by a single strong leader. Such reform efforts can bring about significant improvement within a three- to five-year period, but to make substantial changes in performance or to close achievement gaps on a large scale requires a longer time frame than most political cycles. Therefore, high leadership turnover is a fundamental barrier to sustaining change. Understanding this, the premier of Ontario regularly brought together all the key stakeholders—teachers, parents, businesses, students—to create buy-in, to iron out problems as they arose, and to maintain sustained support for Ontario's reforms over a period of many years. Our states and districts could likewise bring together a group of key stakeholders to define a vision for what the educated American should look like in 2030 and to build momentum toward this vision through political cycles and leadership turnovers.

3. Ambitious standards

Countries that excel do so by setting ambitious, universal, and clear standards for all their students, typically at the national or state/provincial level. The fundamental problem with locally set standards is that they lead to wildly varying expectations of performance and lower achievement overall. More countries are now creating common standards across all jurisdictions. We should be thrilled that the Standards are following international best practice in establishing fewer, clearer, and higher standards in some academic areas, but high-performing systems have standards in all subjects to avoid narrowing the curriculum.

4. Commitment to equity

Leaders in every country proclaim their commitment to equity, but successful education systems focus on achieving equity in a strong and deliberate way. Our mediocre performance on international assessments is due in part to the large percentage of students who score at or below basic levels. High-performing systems use a variety of approaches to minimize the impact of social background on student achievement. These include system-wide policies, like equitable funding, common high expectations for all students, and high teacher quality in every school. They also include classroom-level interventions, such as focused early literacy and math support and a variety of family and community supports outside of school. These policies don't eliminate the gap between children of parents with disparate education backgrounds, but they do significantly level the playing field to create a society that is open to talent from wherever it may come.

5. High-quality teachers and school leaders

Vision, leadership, high standards, and commitment to equity are crucial starting points, but unless they affect teaching and learning in the classroom, they won't bring about significant change. There is broad agreement between high-performing and rapidly improving countries that no matter what reform strategy they are pursuing, the quality of an education system rests on the quality of its teachers. These systems adopt policies to attract, prepare, support, reward, retain, and advance high-quality teachers. In general, high-performing systems put the energy up front in recruiting and supporting high-quality teachers and leaders, rather than on the back end of reducing attrition and firing the weak ones.

It is important to recognize that all countries face challenges in adapting their education systems to the vast transformations taking place around the world. And no nation has a monopoly on excellence. None of these five lessons, however, is rocket science, and many of the elements above can indeed be found in districts and states around the United States. The problem is, they are rarely found all together. Isn't it ironic that our education research informs other nations? As I mentioned in the last chapter, high-performing countries have, in fact, studied the peaks of American research and innovation and then adapted them, often more systematically, to their own systems. So along with analyzing other countries, you may be wondering if our education sector can take away lessons from other more-effective sectors. Yes, we can.

Education is filled with many good intentions. It is also filled with fads and practices, such as ability grouping, whole language instruction, guided reading, new math, and the self-esteem movement. Such practices drift in and out of fashion over time, with little regard for data-validated evidence. As a result, we have forty years of no progress in raising K-12 educational achievement despite a 90 percent increase in real public spending per student. Yes, you read this correctly: 90 percent! Even though we have had both time and financial resources, we could have accomplished so much more by applying our own research findings. Now, our nation's extraordinary inability to raise educational achievement stands in stark contrast to our remarkable progress in improving human health over the same time period—progress, which is largely the result of medical practice guided by scientific evidence. So let's take a look at the revolution in better medical treatments as a result of research.

> The United States is a very resourceful country. If it combines its own assets with the world's best practices—those of the countries that clearly outpace it—it could indeed develop a world-class education system for American children and grandchildren.

In the past half century, American biomedical research has produced enormous improvements in health. One of the main reasons for this progress is that in the 1920s, a gentleman by the name of Abraham Flexner was commissioned to research the practices and methods medical schools used when preparing students to become physicians. His report, the Flexner Report, still cited and highly respected ninety years later, shocked the profession and highlighted the lack of standards in physician training and the prevalence of "anecdotal practices" that were universally used and often responsible for patient deaths. Sound familiar? The report opened the eyes of institutes of higher education that were training young doctors, and in short order, the field of medical education established standards of practice and protocol, unifying curricula of instruction based on scientific evidence, national physician assessments, and ongoing professional development followed by all of medicine, including medical schools that train and accredit doctor candidates.

Following this impressive movement, in the 1950s and early 60s, the National Institutes of Health (NIH) and the Food and Drug Administration (FDA) made another fundamental departure from the way things were being done in medicine: namely, they adopted randomized controlled clinical trials as a way of conclusively establishing what medical treatments worked, for whom, and under what conditions, along with identifying which treatments did not work. [27] Randomized controlled trials are a more logical way to eliminate anecdotal teaching practices and fads that live in schools today. Science has provided the conclusive evidence of effective medical treatments that are responsible for most of the major medical advances since 1950, including vaccines for contagious diseases such as polio, measles, and hepatitis B; interventions for heart disease, such as high cholesterol and hypertension; and cancer treatments that have greatly improved survival rates for many malignancies.

In contrast to the rapid advancement in medicine, education has experienced limited progress over roughly the same time period, if not a steep decline. So it seems logical that with the world advancing as fast as it has, education could and should take a lesson from the medicine? Isn't it reasonable that this model could become the beacon that drives a new education movement with the strong societal correlation for schools of education to follow schools of medicine? I often wonder why our schools of education have missed this connection. This is not nanotechnology science, but rather a process of creating standards, curricula, and assessments as stringent as those that help certify

> As in medicine, every school and teacher that has not been provided scientific knowledge is harming the majority of their students, and most often without even being aware of the lifelong impairment outcome.

---

[27] Randomized controlled trials are quantitative, comparative, controlled experiments in which investigators study two or more interventions in a series of individuals who receive them in random order. This is one of the simplest and most powerful tools in clinical research.

attorneys and financial advisors. But how do we get there? With effective literacy standards, excellent professional development, and collection of progress data, we

- drive and sustain science-based preparation at the teaching colleges and require new certifications for licensure;
- foster support for change that requires all existing teachers and school-based leaders to be provided state of the art knowledge, support, and skill through professional development and new certifications; and
- initiate change for stringent school implementation of policy requirements using data to access impact and drive decisions.

If heeded through new state literacy policy, American education will produce a steady leap to the top tier of international standing, as did medicine—thanks to Abraham Flexner's work.

Education cannot be the guessing game that it is today if we intend to close the literacy and education gap. Personal philosophies, open curricula, hunches, sizzling marketing presentations, and student partiality are not the answers for America's education system. The most important goal is a fundamental improvement in life outcomes. Currently we spend close to a trillion dollars a year in social services devoted to underserved unprepared citizens, many of whom our public education system has failed to educate or train to survive in this knowledge economy of the twenty-first century. Unfortunately, there are few places left for uneducated populations other than crimes, welfare lines, prison, or the ranks of the homeless. Following Flexner's wise study, the medical model could lead education to propel America's future and quickly reduce our enormous societal burden and the personal burden of the young people we neglect to prepare.

US News and World Report on 2013 NCTQ rating on teach preparation programs— Teacher prep is the Wild West of higher education. Consider: In four out of five universities in our Review, the undergraduate and graduate programs can't even agree upon the core skills and knowledge an elementary teacher should have. Or this fact: There are currently no fewer than 866 different textbooks being used to teach elementary teacher candidates how to teach reading.

Kate Walsh
President, National Center for Teacher Quality

Accepting Responsibility

In the past decade, my swath in education and scientifically validated data has developed broadly. With confidence, I stand with many who are able to declare that the time is now to reform the literacy landscape. It isn't complex. It is simple, actually. Like other sectors, we look to the science. Having had the honor of working with outstanding schoolteachers and leaders in districts and school buildings, with distinguished researchers at top think tanks and institutions, with all types of celebrated educational trailblazers, and myriad alliances with other organizations, foundations, and businesses, to all of whom I am eternally grateful, our movement of collaborative efforts can now come together on the literacy solution. The solution culminates through a cohesive synthesis of knowledge, born of and committed to validated findings. Clearly, fixing our student achievement problem requires fixing our literacy problem—requires accepting responsibility. Therefore, what we have collectively learned about this very complex education system boils down to the answers to these questions:

- What works in teaching reading literacy to students?
- For whom does it work? and
- Under what conditions does it work?

Despite the many factors that contribute to a poor educational system and low international ranking previously listed, we can identify a few salient issues that seem to be the most harmful to true transformation:

- The continuing glorification of educational fads and silver bullets that in fact do not work to improve student achievement over time: open classrooms, learning styles, brain-based learning, new math, sensory integration training, invented spelling, whole language, developmentally appropriate practices, and additive free diets are just a few of the fads that promised but did not deliver;
- Uninformed teacher preparation and professional development practices that have failed to advance the profession of teaching and learning;

- Significant limitations in the preparation of school-based leaders along with a lack of knowledge of what defines good school leaders; and
- A lack of implementation criteria that can sustain systemic success.

However, what is promising about these issues is that all can be fixed by turning to science and research and to successful school models based on the same.

During my first neuroscience studies, alongside researchers from top universities, we actually witnessed the impact good teaching, leadership, and instruction has on the brain as students were engaged in extended, science-based reading interventions. That's right—using functional magnetic resonance imaging (fMRI), we watched over and over again children's basic reading, writing, language, and speaking abilities significantly improve (a standard deviation or more) and their brain patterns change under the tutelage of a skilled teacher. This was the solid proof I needed—it was tangible. Over a hundred times, I watched fMRI detect changes in areas of activity and blood flow in the brain, as the experimental group performed reading and comprehension tasks both before and after reading interventions.

However, we also saw the opposite—nothing happening with poor instruction in the control groups. What was originally difficult for me to grasp is that learning to read is a complex process,[28] and for the most part, we have poorly prepared teachers without the knowledge and skill needed to succeed. It is analogous to asking an accountant to perform the work of an actuary, who has been highly trained to apply the knowledge of statistics to assessing risks. If the knowledge and skills have never been provided, without question, both the teacher and the accountant will fail the task. For most people, until we learn something, we prove the age-old adage that "we don't know what we don't know."

---

[28] Maryanne Wolf, *Proust and the Squid: The Story and Science of the Reading Brain* (New York: HarperCollins, 2007), 130.

Tipping Point

After a decade running around in this complex world of education filling my mind with statistics, science, R&D, and implementation practices, at times I drew conclusions that were too broad for real change. So as would any good investigator, together with colleagues, I decided to take a few years to ponder all the accumulated data and to seek potent solutions that were evidenced based, achievable, expedient, measurable, and affordable. There was a story about a beekeeper who owned bees that found the best pollen because they traveled to the flowers found in the fields of his neighbors. In the same way, we all use the accumulated knowledge of others. So in a nutshell, here's what has been validated as essential pillars to get us started down our road to a literate nation. We cannot overemphasize the importance of these factors:

1. Data—the contributions that usable student, teacher, and school data, systematic assessments, tiered evidence-based instruction, and data-driven intervention will make to global student literacy and achievement;
2. Great teachers—the importance of high standards in the process of recruiting, preparing, evaluating, credentialing, retaining, advancing, and compensating skilled knowledgeable teachers, or the contributions these people, will make to global student achievement;
3. Top-notch leadership—the contributions that first-rate principals and school-based leadership will make to global student achievement. The latter point is as critical as the former two—an absence of leadership in an organization will doom any initiative, in any field, to failure; and
4. Good science in education—the impact of science-based practices and implementation will lead change and sustain transformation.

The education system is at a tipping point where we can formulate a new model for success with new policy. All the best scientific findings and past practices now offer an opportunity to effect sustainable, systemic change that will feed America's human capital for decades to come. However, this can only happen if we say "No more!" to a substandard education system—we must awaken the sleeping giant through a large and successful movement. We must recruit a huge movement that will represent social justice for our country, communities, teachers, and students. This is why I won't give up, and why I ask you not to give up either. Our work is a moral imperative. It is our duty to direct literacy policy from preschool to university and to support schools with differentiated tools and knowledge that guarantee America's young people an effective, motivating, and challenging education.

So now we've talked about literacy's commanding needs if an education is to be achieved and the economy is to thrive, the Standards, the top-performing educational systems commonalities, and the policy components that must be the central pillars for a literate nation. It is time to look more closely at how to assimilate, collaborate, and prevail in our movement.

CHAPTER FOUR

COLLABORATE AND PREVAIL

S O FAR WE have determined the critical need for literacy reform and have begun to look at important factors for achieving that. We have identified key movements that may help us compete with developed and emerging nations. We touched on the Standards and on the essential foundational research behind learning to read proficiently as central to this mission. Now let's begin to consider the method for implementing literacy change.

Quick Overview to Start Tackling the Problem

I think Robert Luce said it best in his book *Time to Start Thinking:*

> **"Sometimes it seems Americans are engaged in some kind of collusion in which voters pretend to elect their lawmakers and lawmakers pretend to govern. This, in some way, is America's core problem: the more America postpones any coherent response to the onset of relative decline, the more difficult the politics are likely to get today. Time and money are both in tight supply. The appetite to mislay both remains unchecked."**

How do we go about solving this serious problem we face? Well, the answer is simple and as old as our American history—we form support groups, grassroots teams that create the will, the impetus for state and local lawmakers to enact new policy and practices. We create the will, and it creates the capacity—this is the appetite necessary to drive the seismic societal changes in literacy. We begin with a guarantee that good reading instruction will raise the reading abilities of all children—all boats in the harbor rise. In the states of Florida and Massachusetts, when they enacted policies we will discuss later, not only did the SEEDS students become reading literate but also the percentage of the students in the top categories doubled (advanced readers)! So this isn't an us-versus-them issue—everyone wins. Thus, it is up to us, citizen voters and our elected politicians, to stop pretending this issue will go away; it simply won't. Absent citizen leadership, literacy will continue to worsen as it has for many years.

The good news is that the cultural literacy movement has already begun. Grassroots folks, many of whom we work with closely, have enacted and/or are enacting new state literacy policies in more than two dozen states. A dozen grassroots teams have done this in a few short years, and it has forever changed the lives of millions of children. It will also improve their state revenues, which sorely need a boost. New literacy laws enacted in some states met with resistance, but those states have acted forcefully to implement these laws. Massachusetts, Connecticut, and Florida are great examples.

Why are my colleagues and I, who in the past have helped push major federal legislation, now focusing our support on enacting state and local policy? In recent decades, the federal government has funded many worthy programs that rewarded states for improving reading and education standings. A few of these federal programs had significant impact and brought about relevant cultural change—for a while, that is. History notes that we seem unable to systemically sustain federally guided change. With each new administration come new ideas and consequent changes in funding that hinder deeply rooted sustainability in the state education systems. After reflecting long and hard upon this national reality, we concluded that only state and local legislative policy, created and directed through ardent community action and scrutiny, can achieve vital change—the change that is necessary to bring American educational and economic statistics back to the top—on a long-term basis.

In the next few chapters, you will see specifically outlined policies on our proposal for new literacy laws that are clear, uncomplicated, enforceable, validated, and actionable, all of which are necessary for systemic change. In a nutshell, there are five very logical components in the policy content:

First, the colleges of education will prepare teachers on evidenced-based knowledge.

Second, states will require a new certification for teachers of reading and require all schools to employ these knowledgeable, skilled teachers in every kindergarten through third-grade classroom. These teachers will be required to pass an advanced reading instruction competence assessment. Additionally, states will also require fourth-through twelfth-grade teachers of content-area subjects to pass a basic reading instruction competence assessment—for all teachers really are teachers of reading, writing, and language.

Third, data systems will be required to collect, analyze, and use data to direct student instruction toward academic achievement. All students will be screened in prekindergarten, kindergarten, and first grade for learning and language disabilities, and systematically assessed on their grade-level reading literacy acquisition through grade 12. The data collected from these screenings will identify individual student areas of weakness so that teachers can address and correct them. This will prevent a student from ever falling a year or more behind grade-level requirements. It will also identify areas of strength on which teachers can build.

Fourth, evidence-based reading development instruction (also known as explicit systematic instruction) will be taught in general-education classrooms by qualified teachers. If at any time a student in any grade falls behind as a proficient reader, that student will receive the support services necessary to regain proficiency at grade level. Students no longer will be pushed through to the next grade or given more of the same instruction that led to their falling behind.

Fifth, states, districts, schools, and school-based leaders will adhere to requirements, standards of implementation, and compliance with the law.

Sixth, requirements and implementation standards for high-quality preschool will be available to every child in America.

New literacy laws with such provisions are already succeeding in several states because of a groundswell of grassroots efforts from folks just like us. The details and model legislation language of each component are summarized in part 3 of this book.

What is both heartening and disheartening is this: we understand that there are many explanations, both reasonable and unreasonable, for why the majority of our young people are not fully literate. Granted, the problem is easy to grasp in theory and harder to address in practice. Many believe that educational failure comes down to the widely held belief that race, ethnicity, social status, and IQ are determinates. I know and I am embarrassed to say that I pondered this defense prior to immersing myself in the field. But what we need to remember is that all but a small percentage of human populations can become literate. Period. Thinking anything else is nonsense. The case in point is that if we were physicians, operating under this pretext, it would be considered malpractice, and maybe we need to concede educational malpractice.

As this book goes to press, a group of students in Michigan are suing their school for violating their "right to read." It is the first suit of its kind, and many of us agree that it is long overdue. Perhaps teachers will next unite and sue their colleges of education for failing to provide them with the knowledge and skills they need to teach all students to read. As a nation of people founded on liberty and opportunity, we cannot accept serial failure in education that compromises individual happiness and our economic fruits decade after decade.

Authenticated Model—Does It Work? Can It Work?

Several years back, I was hungry to see "model schools" that followed the five points of evidence-based practices outlined above and that were blowing the lid off of student academic standard requirements. We wanted to locate schools with difficult sociodemographics to ensure that the scientific findings we studied could transfer from research to practice in the trickiest of school populations. To do that, the Center to Close the Achievement Gap was formed in California. The state, the California Business for Education Excellence, and the Business Roundtable funded this. When the schools were identified, a team of observers was assembled to tour several school districts and schools throughout the state that fit the criteria. The team included deans of three colleges of education in the California State University system and representatives of the California Business for Education Excellence.

> Explicit Systematic Instruction . . . refers to an instructional practice that carefully constructs interactions between students and their teacher. Teachers clearly state a teaching objective and follow a defined instructional sequence. They assess how much students already know on the subject and tailor subsequent instruction, based upon that initial evaluation of student skills. Students move through the curriculum, both individually and in groups, repeatedly practicing skills at a pace determined by the teacher's understanding of student needs and progress.
>
> The Benefits of Explicit and Systematic Instruction
> Bill and Bobbie Donelson
> Council for Exceptional Children

The purpose for the tours was to observe and interview faculty, staff, and parents in high-performing schools that are closing the achievement gap. We wanted to better understand the skills, knowledge, and practices that accounted for the success of these schools. In turn, this information directs CSU's colleges of education toward the best course of study to prepare preservice teachers for the challenges of the twenty-first-century classroom. This journey was an honor—a real eye opener in my education—as we probed the most sociodemographically challenged schools in California. It led me on a pilgrimage that extended into visits to other states' schools to find the same. And time after time, what I witnessed is simply beautiful!

Successful sociodemographically challenged schools are referred to often as "90/90/90 schools."[29] These are the schools primarily made up of our SEEDS students: 90 percent or more of students are impoverished and eligible for free or reduced lunch, 90 percent or more of the students belong to ethnic minority groups, and 90 percent or more of the students are beating state standards—they meet or exceed standards in reading and English language arts, math, and more!

Students in the SEEDS schools we visited have attained staggeringly high achievement levels, as well as high-school graduation

---

[29] Organisation for Economic Co-operation and Development, accessed October 2013, http://stats.oecd.org/glossary/detail.asp?ID=1163.

rates and college completion rates. All odds are against them—violent neighborhoods, absentee parents, homelessness, abuse, drugs, hunger—yet 90 percent of them succeed! They learn to read, write, spell, speak, and think critically. They engage in classroom dialogue, pose astute questions, innovate in their science labs, and challenge dogma. Their teachers are deeply knowledgeable and skilled; their school-based leaders are strong; and, yes, these engaged, thriving students are primarily our SEEDS community of students—the youngsters of poverty, the many who are learning to speak, read, and write English or who have dyslexia and learning differences.

Many of the SEEDS students in California are Hispanic/Latino. As noted earlier, such students are our largest minority and may soon become the majority.[30] By 2020, Hispanics/Latinos are projected to constitute about 20 percent of the US population ages sixteen to eighty-four. However, in 2011, only 21 percent of these students nationwide held an associate's degree or higher, compared with 44 percent of whites, 57 percent of Asians, and 30 percent of blacks. Thus, we can argue that we must increase college graduation rates in all social groups and for all students if we want to regain the world's top ranking in college degree attainment.

And after observing the students of "90/90/90 schools" working with their teachers and principals, my colleagues and I are convinced that all American students have the aptitude to achieve literacy, irrespective of the issues related to low socioeconomic conditions. What haunts us is the indifference prevalent regarding the potential of these youth. To cut to the chase, the community of SEEDS students, often typecast as too difficult to educate, have the potential to grow, bloom, and contribute to society—no excuses, no exceptions. What is also interesting is that the cost of these schools is no more and often significantly less than low-performing schools. So let's chat a minute about costs.

---

[30] Nationwide, Hispanics/Latinos make up about 16 percent of the general population and 22 percent of the K-12 population (this number is 50 percent in California, Texas, and Florida, statistics found in US Census Bureau, Decennial Census, Hispanic Population: 2010 (accessed June 2013, http://www.census.gov/prod/cen2010/briefs/c2010br-04.pdf).

Reform: A Budget Obligation

One thing we can't do is let the impending federal and state budget cuts sway our work. Education is the best investment of state income that a citizenry can make—it is a revenue producer, a mandate for a healthy society. Just like citizens who lived in the shadow of the Great Depression, we are facing the challenges of boosting student learning and graduation rates with decreasing funds and a rising national debt. States are hard pressed to meet their education obligations with recession-driven sales and income tax levels down and unemployment up. The somber truth is that states are unlikely to accomplish any economic or education goals, whether it is "back to work" or the praiseworthy "Standards," until they solve the literacy failure rates in schools.

Case in point: California. Let's take, for example, our largest state with more than thirty-seven million people. In 2011, the Pacific Research Institute (PRI) released a landmark study showing that "failure to prepare a single cohort of freshmen for college-level work" will cost the state of California, the students, and their colleges $14 billion annually. Yes, $14 billion each year! This price tag is mind-boggling, far more than ever imagined. And California is not unique; every state has representative numbers that are as staggering.

The PRI study disclosed that the majority of students going to two-year and four-year colleges were required to take remediation classes, and the real remediation problem started long before the students entered college—it most likely began in early elementary school. On average, only 25 percent of high-school students achieve grade-level proficiency or higher in English language arts on the California Standards Test; worse, barely one in five high-school juniors (only 20 percent) are deemed college-ready in English language arts, according to the state's early assessment program. This is terrible for California's students. How sad is it for a young person to learn that after graduating from high school, getting good grades, and possibly taking advanced placement classes, that he or she still needs a college semester or two of remedial classes? I can't even imagine the personal disappointment, much less the cost to

> Education fuels jobs; jobs fuel tax revenue; revenue fuels higher budgets; and higher budgets fuel education. This stark reality should pressure lawmakers to support your work.

CINTHIA COLETTI

the state's citizens of $14 billion a year. Another way to look at it is if we were doing better in teaching all students to read in grades K-3, the same $14 billion could be spent on quality professional development and teacher recertification, on building data systems to drive improvement, on extending the school day, and on providing quality pre- and afterschool programs to kids in need. Instead, these funds go to college remediation classes? This is tantamount to malpractice.

Education's Return on Investment

A research study by Dr. Raj Chetty at Harvard concluded that the societal impact of highly skilled kindergarten teachers is profound enough to justify an annual salary of $320,000.[31] Essentially, early reading is so important to states', and our country's, future that "certified teachers of reading" in kindergarten to third grade should be a staple of US education. These certified teachers of reading would possess deep knowledge of reading development and reading literacy, be highly skilled, respected, and remunerated professionals—as educated and valued in society as engineers, doctors, attorneys, and scientists, with equivalent levels of quality training, credentialing, professional development, and knowledge obligations. As mentioned earlier, other countries are doing this—creating an incentive for the "professional teacher."

During the past forty years, accounting for inflation, we have nearly tripled the amount of money we spend per student in public K-12 education: in 1971, it was roughly $4,000; and last year, it amounted to $11,000 per student. Over that same period our students' reading and math scores have fallen. Now, I am not an investment banker but can confidently say that this is a lousy return on investments of hard-earned tax dollars. The trick is that quality investment in our teachers will provide each citizen and the economy a great return.

So is it cost barriers that keep us from enacting state literacy laws? I think not. The barrier is not cost; it is inertia. Serious change is needed immediately. State budgets benefit when we establish

---

[31]   R. Chetty, J. Freidman, H. Hilger, E. Saez, *How Does Your Kindergarten Class Affect Your Earnings?* (Massachusetts: 2011).

literacy policy—an investment that will quickly be recaptured in state revenues when 98 percent of students are reading with understanding, writing their thoughts coherently, expressing themselves by using proper grammar and appropriate vocabulary, collaborating in analysis, critiquing ideas, and making informed decisions as literate, participating citizens. Isn't this essentially the purpose of public education and ultimately citizenship?

There is another way to look at literacy law as a budget obligation, and it is the lost revenue to a community when a student drops out of school. According to Editorial Projects in Education Research Center, nationally 1,230,000 students each year fail to graduate from high school.[32] One cohort of annual dropouts costs us more than $319 billion in lost wages, taxes, and productivity over the lifetimes of its members[33]—a waste of America's paramount asset—its human capital. Stated differently: one cohort, meaning one year's class, of one decade of high-school dropouts costs our nation $4.1 trillion!

---

[32] Alliance for Excellent Education, *The High Cost of High School Dropouts: What the Nation Pays for Inadequate High Schools* (Washington DC: 2008).

[33] *Demography as Destiny: How America Can Build a Better Future* (Washington DC: 2006).

CINTHIA COLETTI

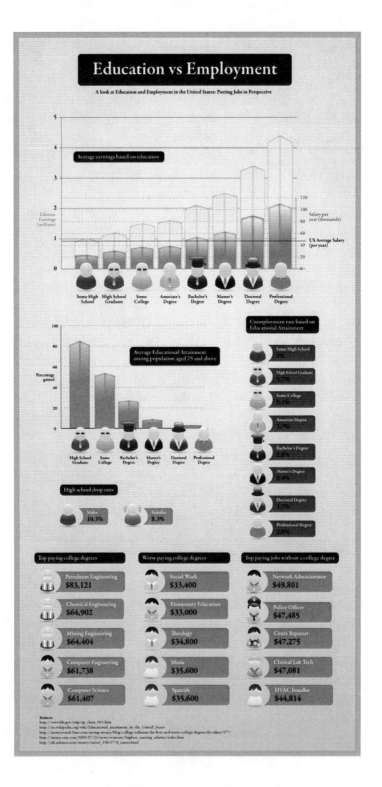

According to OECD, among the top industrialized nations, no country spends more public and private money to educate each student than US taxpayers. Americans spend more than a trillion dollars each year on an education system that statistically fails a significant percentage of its youngest citizens. So no, we are not getting value for our tax dollars spent; we are not making smart-money education decisions, and potentially we are risking our democracy. As Bill Maxwell of the St. Petersburg Times so eloquently put it,

> *Literacy is especially important in this country because we are a democracy. Here, unlike in non-democratic nations, government wants and expects citizens to make good individual decisions. To do so, we must be literate and be able to comprehend the issues that are important to the greatest number of people over time.*[34]

With a continuing shift of societal power to a functionally illiterate populace, we endanger the land of liberty and freedom; we endanger the prosperity of this great nation. Our current return on our education investment is extremely poor: our education system earns the least skilled students for the most money spent, meaning we spend more per student than any other nation and receive a poor rate of return on our investment. To this fact, we must say, "There are no *budget* barriers to literacy law." It is clear that literacy is the revenue generator for each state and for the nation. Literacy unlocks the potential of every citizen. Lack of literacy? Well, the economic costs are simply too great.

Call to Action

In chapter 7, "Actions of a Potentate," experts will teach us how to best target facts and messages that pressure politicians so they can "right the education wrong," invest in our human capital, and require that literacy be a line item in the state budget before any dollars are allocated to conventional education: It is not about how much we spend, but what we spend it on. We cannot afford to make a single

---

[34] "Literacy Is Freedom," Bill Maxwell, accessed August 17, 2011, http://rolemodels.jou.ufl.edu/rolemodels/publisher/literacy.shtm.

mistake in education funding allocations. All resource decisions need to be smart, strategic, and about all students achieving.

We have learned that for the first time in our nation's history, this generation is not as literate as the previous one. Shocking in itself and more so because of information we gathered in chapter 2, "America's Plight": (1) innovation and technological advances are rushing ahead at lightning speed, and (2) the baby boomer generation is getting ready to retire and is predicted to leave a workforce vacuum with not enough skilled, educated employees in the United States to fill their shoes. These facts could be the most important issues facing our nation in the past forty to fifty years. To maintain our freedoms and superior democracy, we cannot have inferior education. We can do better.

A literate America is the societal imperative of our time, and to achieve this, both ethical and prudent leadership is required. Together we can rally and work toward a reversal of our education's decline by investing expertise and science into retooling student outcomes and teachers' knowledge. Further, we can't think for even a minute that throwing more money at the problem will garner different results. It won't. We spend plenty of money already. Our systemic malfeasance in educational outcomes is due to many factors; spending is not one. Lack of focus, fads, compliancy, and inability to keep pace with science—the list could go on. The good news is that we have science-validated examples from all over the world on how to skyrocket student success. So we end part 1 of this book and look to part 2, our impetus for solutions that begins with each of us. It will cast light on our united voices, which will embolden our youth to boundless opportunities.

> *Those who learned to collaborate and improvise most effectively have prevailed.*
>
> *—Charles Darwin*

All players in society will benefit from our actions to prevent and end illiteracy. This is our opportunity to collaborate and prevail. The message is clear: whatever our role is in the movement, the time to act is now!

A broad range of individuals, organizations, and businesses within each state and across the nation are positioned to press initiatives and implement policies to stimulate literacy development.

PART TWO

Toolbox for Building a Cultural Movement and Literacy Overhaul in Your State

—Driving a Seismic Shift in Student Outcomes

CHAPTER FIVE

ON THE EDGE OF ACTION

We Must Be the Change We Wish to See in the World

M OST OF US go about living without thinking much about the communities around us that are organized for public service. We raise families, we work, we have hobbies, and we enjoy friends. We sometimes question the meaning of our lives, especially as we hit midlife or when the children are raised and the nest is empty. "Meaning" in our lives often comes when we put our talent, energy, and power in the service of a larger purpose. Sheldon Wolin in *The Presence of the Past* says it well:

> *Life's significance is our capacity for developing into beings who know and value what it means to participate in and be responsible for the care and improvement of our common and collective lives.*

Part 2 of this book highlights exactly that—our own capacity to participate, to take on the worthy challenges of saving students and reversing literacy failure. Everything you need to begin on this journey is here for you, researched and written, together with chapters by four of my colleagues. But this knowledge will not automatically be developed into a new skill—it will take thought and reflection. To become a change agent also takes development, and it requires practice. Bottom line is that if you have the head, the heart, and the guts to take action, I am confident you and your team will be a resounding success!

Together, we must stand poised and determined not to remain silent and inactive as this crisis looms. Our movement is passionate; it is not about people's money; it's about commitment and time for this worthwhile investment. So how does our movement, our advocacy start?

- Begin with conversations among friends, family, neighbors, community members, coworkers, church members, and associates about the statistics discussed in part 1 of this book. You will be surprised at how many people already realize the crisis experienced by students each day and are excited to help.
- Find out who would like to join a group to raise awareness and change education in your state. Determine the different expertise and talents of the group and form small working core teams of similar interests.
- Create a name for your literacy coalition. Talk about setting goals and then go ahead and establish two or three initial goals and associated tasks to reach the goals. Don't forget timelines and due dates, as all volunteer groups need structure to work cohesively and transparently.
- Lay out ideas like how best to form your message, write an elevator speech,[35] use social networking, build community awareness and critical mass, schedule trips to the capital to visit your representatives, create marketing materials, etc. (guidance on this in chapter 7).
- Ask your team to reach out and bring others to your cause. Assign responsibilities so everyone can take ownership. Communicate regularly and work together in teams toward your goals.
- Tell real-life stories of students that have been failed by the system, touch hearts, gather the flock, and unify behind your goals.

---

[35] The "elevator speech" is so named because it should last no longer than the average elevator ride. Elevator speeches are one of the most effective methods available to reach new audiences quickly with a winning message. They are an important way to spread information about what you do or what you want in a way that excites others; it should be a fundamental skill.

CINTHIA COLETTI

Soon you will see political action that often starts with a coffee at Starbucks and moves to a grand scale. Philosophers throughout time have expounded upon the nobility of gathering, giving, and improving society. What could be more meaningful?

Storytelling

Recently I was honored to be the keynote speaker at a business conference of C-Suite executives (those holding senior management positions in corporations—e.g., chief executive officer, chief financial officers). These "chiefs" wanted "frank speak"—. . . tell the facts on the demise of education and the subsequent vacuum it creates in corporate productivity and GDP." And so I began by telling a story about the largest state in the nation.

Once upon a time, in the 1960s, California schools were the model of educational excellence. The Golden State, the nation's largest public-school system, was home to education leaders and policy makers who essentially guaranteed a superior education for one out of every eight students in the United States. Now, we fast-forward forty years and find a student achievement record that is simply abysmal. And worse, it is negatively and silently affecting every one of us in this room. Rather than leading the nation in how well our children learn and achieve, California, the world's eighth-leading economy, now ranks near the very bottom of our states in student achievement! Yes, in state-by-state rankings, California students are forty-sixth in student achievement measures in reading and math, fiftieth in high-school graduations, and forty-ninth in young adults with a high-school diploma (ages eighteen to twenty-four). Furthermore, in 1960 California ranked at the top in citizens holding a bachelor's degree or higher; we now rank twenty-third.

Without question, California is rapidly losing its grip on fueling its economy, and worse, it is leaving millions of young Californians— the state's most precious resource, its future employees—behind. The numbers have trended downward each and every year since for almost all students in our schools . . .

Stories just like this can be told in state after state. The facts on your state are easy to find, in twenty minutes or less, online at the National Center for Education Statistics (***www.nces.ed.gov***). And finding the students' stories are around every corner.

First, Cross the Divide

Imagine, if you will, a United States of America that once again flourishes because it cultivates bright children, taught by knowledgeable teachers in twenty-first-century schools. Everyone benefits—you, families, neighborhoods, communities, businesses, the economy, your state, our nation, our world.

Before we can move forward and take action, we must confront the real issue at the base of poor educational statistics—reading instruction. It has devolved into a polarizing debate over whether people are "for" or "against" systematic reading instruction or rich reading instruction. Often, the voices in the middle are crowded out by extreme positions on both sides. One extreme feels that continued exposure to rich text and guided reading will provide all that is necessary to instruct a student to become reading literate; the other side claims only explicit phonics and comprehension skills will accomplish the goal. My estimation and study of forty years of education history resolves that neither side is right, but collectively, both sides make a winning team. We must stop polarizing our assets and start synthesizing our strengths!

If scientific progress had gripped education as it has other sectors such as medicine, agriculture, and genetics, we would not find ourselves suffocating in low literacy statistics. Science has confirmed time and time again that diverse children learn to read differently. Hello! It also tells us that early elementary teachers need to know what methods work for which children and under which conditions. Reading teachers need deep professional knowledge, skill, and data to deliver differentiated instruction to groups of children. In the next chapter, my colleague, a preeminent researcher, Dr. Margie Gillis, outlines this professional knowledge, along with a plan to increase teachers' knowledge of effective practices for teaching reading.

We have learned about the pernicious ramifications of literacy failure, and now our next actions are to rise, stop the noise, and solve the problem—just as they did in medicine by using science to direct practice. If we take this course, everybody triumphs and the "reading wars" end. Since 2003, Massachusetts has done this. It has required teachers to pass a test that focuses on research-based knowledge of reading instruction and literacy. Not coincidentally, the state's students boast the highest fourth- and eighth-grade NAEP scores in the nation. Following suit, the Connecticut Board of Education ruled that all pre-K-6 teachers pass that same exam. Minnesota then followed, and other citizen teams are pushing for the same in their states. The movement has begun! Our students will succeed.

While researching and studying information for this book, it occurred to me that in order to bridge the reading divide, a new definition of literacy was in order and could be of great assistance in our work. We needed a definition that took into account all the knowledge neuroscience and reading research has provided about reading acquisition skills and how best to enhance children's excitement about the written word. So we gathered the best minds, from both sides of the aisle, and together crafted a new twenty-first-century definition of "literacy." After a ton of enjoyable work and debate, there is consensus, and it is proudly on Wikipedia. See below:

Literate Nation: Official Definition of Literacy

Literacy represents the lifelong, intellectual process of gaining meaning from print. Key to all literacy is reading development, which involves a progression of skills that begins with the ability to understand spoken words and decode written words, and culminates in the deep understanding of text. Reading development involves a range of complex language underpinnings including awareness of speech sounds (phonology), spelling patterns (orthography), word meaning (semantics), grammar (syntax) and patterns of word formation (morphology), all of which provide a necessary platform for reading fluency and comprehension. Once these skills are acquired the reader can attain full English reading literacy, which includes the abilities to approach printed material with critical analysis, inference and synthesis; to write with accuracy and coherence; and to use information, background knowledge, and insights from text as the basis for informed decisions and creative thought.

Reading Literacy is Nimble

Reading literacy in a digital world will evolve over time with changes in society, the economy, and cultures. It travels with individuals through childhood, to employment, to social responsibility, to lifelong learning, which is central to being a part of today's society. Across the world, it affords interaction with peers and communities, then continues to exchanges with large bureaucracies and complex legal systems. It enriches the breadth of experiences in an individual's life, or it cripples it.

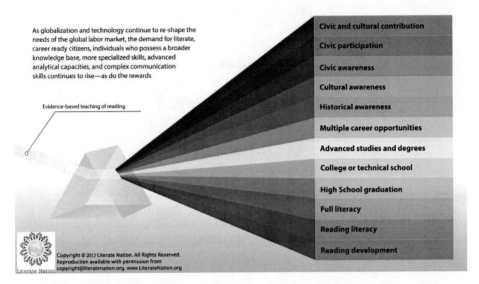

As globalization and technology continue to re-shape the needs of the global labor market, the demand for literate, career ready citizens, individuals who possess a broader knowledge base, more specialized skills, advanced analytical capacities, and complex communication skills continues to rise—as do the rewards

Evidence-based teaching of reading

Civic and cultural contribution

Civic participation

Civic awareness

Cultural awareness

Historical awareness

Multiple career opportunities

Advanced studies and degrees

College or technical school

High School graduation

Full literacy

Reading literacy

Reading development

If the new literacy definition can be applied in state literacy law, it stands a chance to unite those engaged in the reading wars, ending the dividing debates and cultivating a new understanding of how to teach diverse student populations. Neuroscience teaches us that humans are not genetically programmed to read in the way we are programmed to speak.

- Most of us have to be taught to read. Some children learn to read by exposure to almost any method, but most children need direct methods of teaching. Thus, teachers of reading need the knowledge, data, and skills to teach what works best for each child. Evidenced-based reading instruction works for all children during the development phases; some may spend more time learning different aspects of reading's complexity, but all children can soar.
- Teachers of reading cannot teach what they have not been taught, and many teachers have not been taught the deep knowledge nor provided the skills they need to be successful in teaching all students to read.

CINTHIA COLETTI

So what do we do? First, we must require instruction in differentiated teaching skills in advanced preparation programs and guarantee it be sustained in professional development. We believe that

- all teachers of reading, certainly grade K-3 teachers, should receive an advanced licensure certification as "teaching specialists." These teachers will set the foundation for all academic achievement and lifelong success. They deserve to become our most respected, best-skilled, highest-paid, and most keenly desired teachers; and
- all grade 4-12 teachers need literacy and language skills and require a basic reading competency licensure if schools are to realize the Standards requirements. The reason for content-area teachers to pass a knowledge examination may baffle you, as it did me at first. So that we can truly appreciate the complexities of a content-area teacher's job, let's take a quick peek into the work of the eighth-grade Algebra teacher.

Regardless of a student's sociodemographic standing, we can reverse the malignant cycle of literacy failure by having the courage and conviction to stand up and act. To say "enough is enough" and demand dramatic improvement in the way we prepare our teachers to teach reading.

We must unite in common voice—parents, grandparents, teachers, principals, communities, and politicians. All of us can be leaders.

Teaching algebra is complex. The algebra teacher must introduce novel vocabulary words and phrases, such as "absolute value," "additive inverse property," "exponential form," "linear equation," "planar cross section," "reflexive axiom of equality," "scientific notation," and "tessellation." Now, if you were this teacher and the majority of your students had not developed adequate skills in reading grade-level text, how could you succeed in teaching them to become algebra literate? How could they read, write, study, and debate the rules of operations and relations, and the constructions and concepts arising from them? Sadly, they are unlikely to be successful algebra students.

All subject-area literacy first necessitates reading literacy skill—language and background knowledge that provide a foundation for understanding unstated elements of a text passage. Recent research concludes that the ability to read and write language is highly correlated with students' oral language proficiency, and the ability to understand a text read aloud is a prerequisite for making sense of the same text in printed form—such as in answering an algebra question on a test. Furthermore, children must build listening and speaking competency in the earlier grades while also developing reading and writing skills so they can engage in collaborative class efforts and classroom debates. So yes, all this is required to become algebra-literate. Most math teachers are not remotely prepared for this task—a serious oversight by the colleges of education and professional development programs. Thus, new knowledge in literacy is required of all teachers so all students become lifelong readers.

Can All Kids Learn to Read?

I had the honor, through the Haan Foundation for Children, of coleading a groundbreaking clinical research project that incorporated neuroscience with reading research. It was a longitudinal randomized clinical trial that was conducted with students in twenty-seven public schools. What a privilege and learning experience to work with distinguished scientists, Drs. David Myers, Joseph Torgeson, and Marcel Just. In the study, we applied intense teacher knowledge and skill development with evidenced-based student reading programs and assessments. We used functional magnetic resonance imaging (fMRI) to observe students' brains actually change while reading. This evolution (change in patterns) led to the acquisition of students' improved fluid reading and language ability. There were hundreds of third- and fifth-graders in this study who had struggled to learn to read. After just one hundred hours of small group instruction, these children, who were previously reading at the bottom of their class, progressed to either reach or move closer to reading at grade level. As importantly, they most likely dodged the bullet of becoming high-school dropouts and prison statistics.

The results of these studies were impressive. Students gained an average of two years improvement in their skills in just one hundred hours of instruction. Additionally, the work of neuroscientist Just was groundbreaking. Never before had a community of willing and excited public-school children (and their families) had the opportunity to participate in a neurostudy. Dr. Just's neuroimaging proved that professional instruction did in fact rewire the reading brains of both younger and older students. This accomplishment is based on a term that is referred to as "brain plasticity"—the ability of the brain to respond to circumstances to create new circuitry. Brain plasticity is best understood by the pioneer, Michael Merzenich, whom I worked with in the mid-2000s on my first research project. Dr. Merzenich says:

> *Brain plasticity is a physical process. Gray matter can actually shrink or thicken; neural connections can be forged and refined or (conversely) weakened and severed. Changes in the physical brain manifest as changes in our abilities.*

The same opportunity to improve "abilities" through a change in brain plasticity holds true when our SEEDS community of students are provided with data-validated instruction that targets areas of weakness. The brain's plasticity responds, and in time and with proper instruction, it blossoms into a reading brain. Thus, with the help of technology and neuroscience, it is a fact that all but a few percent of students can become proficient readers and writers; conversely, it supports the theory that reading instruction cannot be a notion of anecdotal fads and magic bullets.

Pledge, Understand, Act

We must be the change we wish to see in the world.
—Mahatma Gandhi

When ordinary Americans unite in common voice, extraordinary things happen. Our movement must focus on the triumph of each child—a life worth saving, worth fighting for; a life to value. The inertia in our schools has resulted in creating pain and frustration for those who have experienced failure. Together, we are the force that will overcome inertia and bring about critical changes.

With knowledge and acumen, we are no longer merely spectators or critics or occasional complainers.

We can commit and pledge ourselves to building strong relationships in the public sphere, engaging in settings and venues with sustained, disciplined organizing that will spark the public and private transformation for new public policy on literacy education.

We are ordinary people who can discover worth and hidden power in a community. We can become the organizers who swell legions of citizens committed to work for each child, day by day, month by month, and year to year. We will do this until the destructive effects of bureaucratic patronage on powerless, disenfranchised children ends. We will work together to enact state literacy policy that encompasses

(1) rigorous requirements for the curricula and standards for teaching candidate preparation programs in universities and colleges of education. Requirements based on scientific findings to produce skilled, knowledgeable teachers prepared for the challenges of teaching reading, writing, and subject matter material to each and every student. Teachers prepared with the knowledge to pass stringent competence assessments, teachers who flourish under the "exponential" and technological learning demands of our times.

(2) robust requirements for school-based leadership with a firm command of data system analysis, use, and interpretation to direct instruction, to evaluate both teacher and student performance, and to create structures of support to ensure scholastic victory for both.

(3) vigorous and differentiated requirements for general-education classroom reading development and literacy instruction: instruction that is science validated and steeped in continuous assessments of student progression or delay in skill attainment.

(4) dynamic requirements that all teachers be adept at providing Multi-Tier System of Supports in general-education classrooms immediately for students who lag behind in attaining a specific area of skill development.

(5) stringent requirements and consequences for districts and schools to implement the law with fidelity and be held accountable for each child's literacy success in all subjects.

What may seem like an obvious mantra—"Every child literate, educated, and career-ready—no excuses, no exceptions"—must first be internalized if it is to become our quest. Ignore it, and nothing else matters. Our pledge, which is neither too complex nor too difficult, is as outlined above. It is dynamic, organic, and set to be enacted and implemented in part or as a whole, immediately or in time.

Tens of thousands of us in state after state are ready to pledge ourselves to the cause by forming a movement with you, a call to action for a literate nation: (1) organizing through social and personal networking, and (2) crafting clear goals, strategies, and tactical plans that outline the steps necessary to join forces, work with legislators, and enact literacy laws. In essence, let the political process begin.

The following chapters comprise your "toolbox for action!" filled with information and materials needed to draw large numbers of people from every corner of society to push literacy legislation. Chapter 8, for example, is your tool to tap into the immense power of social media and networking. Think about Lady Gaga's tweets that have rallied millions of young people to drive change on bullying, human rights politics in foreign countries, and clean energy. Think of the Twitter fight against Don't Ask, Don't Tell, and the Born This Way campaigns as perfect examples of the power of social media. How about that social media backlash that motivated a multinational corporation, Gap, not to change its corporate logo? Guess what happened?

Gap announced on its Facebook page that it was scrapping its new logo design efforts, acquiescing to a torrent of criticism coming primarily from Facebook and Twitter users.[36]

How impressive is the power of social media? Very. And this is why I asked my friend and colleague, Carolyn Cowen, who learned social media "from zero to sixty" in short order, to write a chapter for you. As Carolyn led me last year, I now kick myself for not joining Twitter sooner because it is one of the most expedient ways to quickly initiate a wave of change. If we are able to engage the young people to become part of this movement, it will become a success beyond our dreams. Think of millions of students raising their voices for "their rights" to be educated and employed in a twenty-first-century career. Imagine what potency they add to the cause, saying, "It is not our fault! Change it. Educate every one of us, for we are your future too!"

The toolbox is also loaded with powerful tactics and intricate language that communicate best the facts and emotion to ensure

---

[36]   Ben Par, "Gap Reverts to Original Logo after Social Media Backlash," http://mashable.com/2010/10/11/gap-logo/.

success in your grassroots and networking campaigns, which we will discuss in detail in chapter 7, "Actions of the Potentate." Much of this content is based on the work of focus groups assembled for this reason. Part and parcel to the messaging is a pledge to understand the tactical steps and critical elements that are involved in successful advocacy:

What is the problem? The pernicious virus affecting innocent students, our future, and our communities: schools are not teaching this generation of students how to become fully literate.

How do you fix it? By enacting stringent literacy laws that require schools and teachers to have the knowledge and skills necessary for success.

Who will fix it? Citizens will find legislative champion(s) who will take up the state literacy law issue as their own and fight for it until the law is sanctioned and school systems implement it with reliability.

When will it begin and when will it be fixed? It has begun. You have already started by reading this book, and it will be fixed relatively quickly once teachers and school-based leaders obtain the knowledge to teach each child as science has proven.

Where will it start? Right in your own community, right on your home computer and telephone, right in your neighborhood—assembling your team of networking advocates who will gather in common voice to manage legislative efforts.

Later in the book, I will highlight grassroots success stories, provide sample communiqués and scripts for your call-to-action/movement campaign, address tips for parents advocating for their children, and share my profound reflections that drive me today. The bottom line is that each of us appreciates our civic responsibility, our moral imperative for a literate nation. For more than a decade, my colleagues and I have devoted ourselves to learning, to finding educational solutions, and to understanding that in the end, of course, it is not about who is the best or who did what, but about how to bring the best out of every child—for they are the seeds of our shared future. Thus, we commit to invest ourselves right alongside you as the leaders of education transformation so young citizens can participate in freedom and attain their dreams, whatever they may be: career, culture, innovation, arts, sports, literature, technology, adventure, hobbies, charity, and all that our world offers.

Without question, you can invest yourself in this action—I know you can, because I did. And the good news is that you are going to get the crib notes! Think of these next chapters as your class or lesson filled with important information that has been written for you.

The next chapter is written by Dr. Margie Gillis, president, Literacy How, and project director, Haskins Literacy Initiative, Haskins Laboratories at Yale University. Margie has been instrumental in conducting research, along with preparing teachers and teaching students of all ages to read for over thirty years. She is renowned as an expert in promoting the science of teaching reading through professional development and classroom support for teachers.

Before we move into this vital chapter, I want to share that working with Dr. Margie Gillis is one of those unique opportunities that life seldom presents. Her intellectual expertise on this subject is in the top tier, distinguishing her as a gold-standard scientist who is capable of seeing beyond the depth of her research expertise to view problems on a long-term and far-reaching scale, with all stakeholders and interests in mind. She thinks with clarity and fairness, observing and acknowledging the hurdles educators face with an ability to grasp the most effective path offered them. She, along with a number of education and research colleagues, agrees that regardless of the student hurdles (environmental or neurobiological), all student reading failure is primarily treated with skilled teaching: impending reading failure can be recognized as early as preschool and kindergarten, if not sooner, and with appropriate, intensive, differentiated instruction, all but the most severe reading disabilities can be ameliorated in the early grades, and students can be prepared to "read to learn" by third grade. Enjoy.

CHAPTER SIX

KNOWLEDGE CALIBRATION

By Margie Gillis, PhD

"KNOWLEDGE CALIBRATION" IS the correspondence between what we think we know and what we actually know. It's often the case in life that we don't know what we don't know. It's true on many levels, and in many of those cases, that lack of knowledge or the accompanying lack of awareness of "not knowing" hurts no one. However, in education, where children's livelihoods and lives are at stake, the result of teachers not knowing what they don't know has far-reaching negative consequences for their students. And let us state right off that it is not the teachers' fault.

Knowledge calibration work conducted by Anne Cunningham and her colleagues demonstrated that elementary teachers responsible for teaching children prerequisite foundational reading skills thought they knew a lot about phonological awareness and phonics. [37] However,

---

[37] A. E. Cunningham, K. E. Perry, K. E. Stanovich, and P. J. Stanovich, "Disciplinary Knowledge of K-3 Teachers and Their Knowledge Calibration in the Domain of Early Literacy," *Annals of Dyslexia* 54 (2004): 139–167.

when they were tested on that knowledge, they failed miserably. My own research, along with that of many others, bears that out. [38, 39, 40, 41]

The good news is that there is mounting evidence for how and why to prepare teachers, as well as the importance of arming them with the knowledge needed to teach children to read. For example, we know what students need to learn to become successful readers. We even have evidence to show that teachers' pedagogical content knowledge (I'll describe that shortly) correlates with their students' reading achievement. However, there is also some bad news. Many schools of education in both public and private colleges and universities across the country are not teaching prospective teachers this information. And once teachers find a job, there are few opportunities for quality, job-embedded professional development to compensate for teachers' misguided, off-base preservice preparation.

What Students Need to Know to Learn to Read

A bleak picture has been painted in previous chapters—the country's NAEP reading scores for fourth-graders show we are seventeenth in the world. If you don't learn to read by third grade, you will most likely struggle in school and in life. Students who are at risk for experiencing difficulty in learning to read, most notably our SEEDS students, benefit from a systematic, sequential, explicit,

---

[38] S. Brady, M. Gillis, T. Smith, M. Lavalette, L. Liss-Bronstein, E. Lowe, et al., "First Grade Teachers' Knowledge of Phonological Awareness and Code Concepts: Examining Gains from an Intensive Form of Professional Development," *Reading and Writing: An Interdisciplinary Journal* 22 (2009): 425–455.

[39] L. C. Moats, "The Missing Foundation in Teacher Education: Knowledge of the Structure of Spoken and Written Language," *Annals of Dyslexia* 44 (1994): 81–102.

[40] L. Spear-Swerlin, P. Brucker, and M. Alfano, "Teachers' Literacy-Related Knowledge and Self-Perceptions in Relation to Preparation and Experience," *Annals of Dyslexia* 55 (2005): 266–293.

[41] C. Bos, N. Mather, S. Dickson, B. Podhajski, and D. Chard, "Perceptions and Knowledge of Preservice and Inservice Educators about Early Reading Instruction." *Annals of Dyslexia* 51 (2001): 97–120.

intense, and scaffolded approach to reading that includes instruction in the following five components: phonemic awareness (the insight that words can be taken apart and blended sound by sound), phonics (the mapping of those speech sounds to letters), fluency (reading words automatically in and out of connected text), vocabulary (what words mean), and comprehension (extracting and constructing meaning of various types of text).

BUILDING BLOCKS OF SUCCESSFUL READING

We haven't figured out exactly what dosages of each of those pieces each student needs. Nor do we know what level of intensity and frequency is necessary to get the job done. But we are figuring those specifics out! (Stay tuned for more on this later.) On the other hand, research has confirmed that a multicomponent approach is best and that the amount of emphasis on each of the components of reading depends on the characteristics of the individual.[42, 43]

---

[42] P. G. Aaron, R. M. Joshi, R. Gooden, and K. E. Bentum, "Diagnosis and Treatment of Reading Disabilities Based on the Component Model of Reading," *Journal of Learning Disabilities* 41 (2008): 67–84.

[43] C. M. Connor, S. B. Piasta, B. Fishman, S. Glasney, C. Schatschneider, E. Crowe, P. Underwood, and F. J. Morrison, "Individualizing Student Instruction Precisely: Effects of Child by Instruction Interactions on First Graders' Literacy Development," *Child Development* 80 (2009): 77–100.

What Teachers Need to Know to Teach Reading

First, teachers need to be masters of their language. If they're teaching English (i.e., reading, writing, and spelling), they must know how our language works. For example, all would-be readers must understand that spoken words are made up of speech sounds called phonemes. This insight, called phonemic awareness, is what prepares young children to access our English code, which is based on an alphabet of twenty-six symbols called letters. Written words translate each phoneme into a letter or letters, depending on the sound and where it comes in a word. There are forty-four sounds (phonemes) in the English language. What makes this tricky is that the English language is based on both sounds and meaning. This is both a blessing and a curse—a blessing in that English has maintained its heritage and richness over the hundreds of years since it was born—but a curse too. In order to preserve the origin of words, English spellings appear random and confusing, such as ghost, climb, and wrist. However, there is logic and an order as to how the English writing system (called orthography) works. And this is where it gets interesting.

Research studies confirm that university professors are not well versed in this knowledge of language word structure,[44, 45] so it's no surprise that our future teachers don't learn about word structure in their college courses. To add another wrinkle, our young and often newest teachers have a double whammy, since their formative years were likely spent in whole language classrooms where phonics was at best embedded in reading instruction, or at worst a dirty word and not taught at all.

And there's more than just understanding the writing system. As literacy expert Louisa Moats says, "Teaching Reading is Rocket Science."[46] Teachers not only need to know about English's rich

---

[44] J. McCombes-Tolis and R. Feinn, "Comparing Teachers' Literacy-Related Knowledge to Their State's Standards for Reading," *Reading Psychology*, 29 (2008): 236–265.

[45] R. M. Joshi, E. Binks, L. Graham, E. Ocker-Dean, D. Smith, and R. Boulware-Gooden, *Journal of Learning Disabilities* 42 (2009): 458–463.

[46] L. Moats, "Teaching Reading Is Rocket Science: What Expert Teachers of Reading Should Know and Be Able to Do" (2011).

but complex word structure but also need to know how reading develops over the course of several critical years. In fact, learning to read begins at birth when babies listen to "motherese"—the universal language that caregivers use to communicate with infants and young children. The language that children first listen to and later imitate is the foundation upon which the bricks of decoding, spelling, and writing are laid. Listening is a receptive oral language skill, just as reading is a receptive written language activity. And speaking is expressive oral language just as spelling and writing are expressive written language skills.

When children are learning to read in kindergarten and first and second grade, the skilled teacher must assess what each child knows about decoding and spelling words and then teach these skills as two sides of the same coin.[47] Moreover, teachers who understand the phases/stages of reading development know how to use this assessment information to form small instructional groups focused on the precise content needed for their students. What's more, this information has the potential to change the trajectory of students—especially those who need a targeted approach to reading and spelling words accurately and automatically. With or without fluency firmly established, children will arrive in third grade. There a seismic shift occurs. Now children are reading to learn, and so a good deal of reading instruction must focus on metacognition—that is, the ability to think critically about complex ideas and to relate them to prior knowledge and/or experiences. When children do not master the foundation reading skills by third grade, the desired reading trajectory becomes thwarted. Teachers in third grade and above do not have the luxury of going back to teach the necessary foundation or basic reading skills. And the reading gap is perpetuated year after year.

All of this information is what we in the teacher education business refer to as "pedagogical content knowledge"—that is, what teachers must know in order to teach their "subject-specific" (reading) information effectively. Teachers' knowledge of the subject they teach is the major teacher characteristic related to positive student

---

[47] L. C. Ehri, "Learning to Read and Learning to Spell: Two Sides of a Coin," *Topics in Language Disorders* 20 (2000): 19–49.

achievement.[48] High-school science teachers usually major in biology or chemistry. But a fundamental problem in the teacher preparation field is that elementary teachers don't really "major" in anything—at least, nothing that builds a deep knowledge of what should be considered their subject matter, reading. If that were to change, it would mean requiring preservice teachers to take a minimum of fifteen credits hours of research-based reading courses to master the pedagogical content knowledge and leave room for application of that knowledge in a practical setting. At present, most prospective elementary education majors take one or two reading courses that merely expose them to a myriad of methods and instructional practices rather than give them a deep understanding of that content knowledge.

What a "Reading Major" Might Include

Louisa Moats and a number of other reading experts have written a blueprint for what reading teachers should know and be able to do. The International Dyslexia Association (IDA) and the Alliance for the Accreditation and Certification of Structured Language Education (Academic Language Therapy Association [ALTA] and the International Multisensory Structured Language Education Council [IMSLEC]) have adopted the "Knowledge and Practice Standards" document. (http://www.interdys.org/Standards.htm). There are two parts to the standards:

1. Pedagogical/content knowledge (what teachers need to know—the knowledge standards):
   - the phases/stages of reading and spelling development;
   - how to evaluate and choose appropriate instructional materials for the stages and phases of reading and spelling;
   - the structure of the English language; and
   - how to engage and motivate culturally and linguistically diverse learners.

---

[48] R. Miller and R. Chait, "Teacher Turnover, Tenure Policies, and the Distribution of Teacher Quality Can High-Poverty Schools Catch a Break?", http://www.americanprogress.org/issues/2008/12/pdf/teacher_attrition.pdf.

2. How to identify risk factors for SEEDS students (Struggling readers, Economically disadvantaged youth, English language learners, and students with dyslexia, or Specific learning disabilities, and language impairment). Application of the pedagogical knowledge (what teachers need to be able to do—the practice standards):
   - how to administer and interpret various reading assessments, and
   - how to write lesson plans and deliver lessons matched to the students' documented needs.

The stated purpose of these standards is **to guide the preparation, certification, and professional development of those who teach reading and related literacy skills in classroom, remedial, and clinical settings and to specify what any individual responsible for teaching reading should know and be able to do, so that reading difficulties, including dyslexia, may be prevented, alleviated, or remediated.**

Like any professional responsible for mastering a domain of disciplinary knowledge, teachers need to know a lot to move from a "novice" reading teacher to an "expert." Catherine Snow, of Harvard, and her colleagues identified and defined five levels of increasing progressive differentiation that roughly correlate with five points in the teacher's career progression: preservice, apprentice, novice, experienced, and master teacher. [49] The five levels of knowledge are

1. declarative knowledge—learning from books or lectures about child development, stages of reading, methods of reading instruction, etc.
2. situated, can-do procedural knowledge—applied understanding in relatively simple situations under "normal circumstances."
3. stable procedural knowledge—applied understanding in more complex situations that requires more differentiation and explicit instruction.
4. expert, adaptive knowledge—a more advanced level of knowledge demonstrating the ability to deal with a full array of instructional

---

[49] C. E. Snow, P. Griffin, and M. S. Burns, *Knowledge to Support the Teaching of Reading: Preparing Teachers for a Changing World* (San Francisco: Jossey-Bass, 2005).

challenges, an interest in acquiring new knowledge and incorporating that knowledge into existing knowledge structures.

5. reflective, organized, analyzed knowledge—a knowledge that allows for a deeper analysis of what has been learned, an ability to evaluate information effectively, and to present information to others.

These five levels represent points along a trajectory "during which knowledge becomes increasingly differentiated and subject to analysis." The following graphs illustrate how the different levels of knowledge might be distributed at two points in a teacher's career as the total knowledge available grows as well.

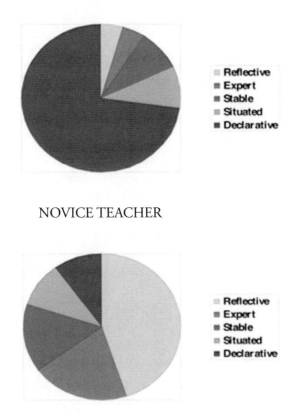

NOVICE TEACHER

EXPERT TEACHER

The accumulation of the various levels of disciplinary knowledge doesn't happen quickly or easily. It is a long and complex process that occurs as teachers learn the prerequisite declarative knowledge and continuously apply that knowledge in different situations with constantly changing variables, including children who come to school with varying amounts of skill and ability; classroom dynamics that change daily; schools with constantly changing administrators, initiatives, instructional programs, and materials; and the overarching educational landscape with its ever-changing district, state, and federal mandates.

What's important to note here is that although teachers' experiences are important in developing the "expert" status as described above, research demonstrates that experience doesn't correlate with teachers' knowledge of fundamental language structure and reading development.[50, 51, 52, 53, 54, 55, 56, 57] Studies that examined teachers'

50 S. Brady, M. Gillis, T. Smith, M. Lavalette, L. Liss-Bronstein, E. Lowe, et al., "First Grade Teachers' Knowledge of Phonological Awareness and Code Concepts: Examining Gains from an Intensive Form of Professional Development," *Reading and Writing: An Interdisciplinary Journal* 22 (2009): 425–455.

51 D. McCutchen, R. D. Abbott, L. B. Green, S. N. Beretvas, S. Cox, N. S. Potter, et al., "Beginning Literacy: Links among Teacher Knowledge, Teacher Practice, and Student Learning," *Journal of Learning Disabilities* 35 (2002): 69–86.

52 D. McCutchen, L. Green, R. D. Abbott, and E. A. Sanders, "Further Evidence for Teacher Knowledge: Supporting Struggling Readers in Grades Three through Five," *Reading and Writing: An Interdisciplinary Journal* 22 (2009): 401–423.

53 A. E. Cunningham, K. E. Perry, K. E. Stanovich, and P. J. Stanovich, "Disciplinary Knowledge of K-3 Teachers and Their Knowledge Calibration in the Domain of Early Literacy," *Annals of Dyslexia* 54 (2004): 139–167.

54 A. E. Cunningham and J. Zibuslky, eds., "Perspectives on Teachers' Disciplinary Knowledge of Reading Processes, Development, and Pedagogy, *Reading and Writing: An Interdisciplinary Journal* 22 (2009): 8.

55 L. Spear-Swerling and P. Brucker, "Preparing Novice Teachers to Develop Basic Reading and Spelling Skills in Children," *Annals of Dyslexia* 54 (2004): 332–364.

56 L. Spear-Swerling, P. Brucker, and M. Alfano, "Teachers' Literacy-Related Knowledge and Self-Perceptions in Relation to Preparation and Experience," *Annals of Dyslexia* 55 (2005): 266–293.

57 L. Spear-Swerling, "A Literacy Tutoring Experience for Prospective Special Educators and Struggling Second Graders," *Journal of Learning Disabilities* 42 (2009): 431–443.

declarative knowledge found that teachers' philosophy of how to teach reading is established early and is very difficult to change. In addition, much of the declarative knowledge that a teacher needs to master to become an expert reading teacher is elusive and cannot be acquired through experience alone.

Furthermore, teachers' natural instincts about how to teach children, especially those who struggle with reading, are often at odds with what actually works. Brady et al. found that teachers with a whole language orientation were less responsive to professional development (PD) in phonemic awareness, phonics, and spelling. And in another study in 2009 that examined teachers' preferences for teaching reading, Cunningham noted, "it appears that a philosophical orientation towards literature-based instruction tends to be more exclusive of other instructional approaches."

However, there is research to support the fact that deep knowledge transfers to student learning. For example, the more nitty-gritty knowledge teachers have about the structure of language, the better able they are to make informed instructional decisions for students who need more explicit, code-based instruction. A study conducted by Piasta and her colleagues showed that for students of more knowledgeable teachers, more time spent in explicit instruction predicted stronger word-reading gains. [58]

What Is (or Isn't) Happening in Higher Education?

Although we know what prospective teachers should (but don't) know, they aren't learning this information in their undergraduate programs. Several studies have been conducted to determine what colleges of education cover in their teacher prep programs. The National Council on Teacher Quality (NCTQ, 2006) released its findings in *What Education Schools Aren't Teaching about Reading and What Elementary Teachers Aren't Learning*. Two hundred and twenty-two reading course syllabi from seventy-two institutions were analyzed along with a number of reading textbooks. The results of

---

[58] S. B. Piasta, C. M. Connor, B. J. Fishman, and F. J. Morrison, "Teachers' Knowledge of Literacy Concepts, Classroom Practices, and Student Reading Growth," *Scientific Studies of Reading* 13 (2009): 224–248.

these analyses confirmed the fact that the vast majority (85 percent) of the programs studied ignored the scientific research on reading. Only four of the 226 textbooks examined obtained an "acceptable" rating for incorporating the relevant reading research. Another study that looked at course syllabi from Connecticut colleges and universities replicated these findings.[59] Teaching candidates are not being prepared to assess or instruct students, particularly those who may need additional tiers of instruction to reach their full potential.

Current Reading Policy and Legislation

Several states, including Colorado, Connecticut, Florida, Indiana, Kentucky, Louisiana, Minnesota, Ohio, Oklahoma, Texas, Wisconsin, and Washington, have various versions of literacy legislative components dedicated to preventing reading failure. This literacy legislation ranges from third-grade retention for students not reading on grade level, a test for certified teachers measuring their knowledge of how to teach reading, to federally funded reading initiatives. A handful of states include language in their bills that defines dyslexia and describes the necessary qualifications of dyslexia specialists to include training consistent with the knowledge and practice standards.

Other states are requiring individual reading plans for failing students. However, while the laws state that students must demonstrate proficiency in reading at the end of each formative grade, they do not articulate what teachers must know and be able to do to help their students become reading proficient. An obvious and major flaw!

In part 3 and the appendices of this book, you will find a comprehensive body of model legislation synthesized from an extensive evidence base, ranging from cross-sectional regression studies to quasi-experimental matched comparison studies to fully randomized treatment-control trials. Conducted over the last two decades and funded by federal grants totaling over several hundred million

---

[59] J. McCombes-Tolis and L. Spear-Swerling, "The Preparation of Pre-service Elementary Educators in Understanding and Applying the Terms, Concepts, and Practices Associated with Response to Intervention in Early Reading Contexts," *Journal of School Leadership* 21 (2011): 360–389.

dollars, these studies have investigated multiple aspects of students' learning and the best methods of improving reading acquisition and development. The model state literacy legislation reflected in literacy policy leverages the findings from this scientific knowledge and the cumulative achievement data in order to inform our work on the present template and also to provide a data-driven context for solving America's reading crisis. We have a sufficiently sophisticated knowledge base at this point to translate it into practice.

Conclusion and Recommendations

A Two-Pronged Approach:

1. Preservice Teacher Training
   Teacher of Reading Certification
2. In-service Teacher Training
   Teacher of Reading Certification and Licensure
   (Continuing Education Units for Accountability)

(Note: More detailed information is found in appendix B of the book. Teachers in grades K-3 (both preservice and in-service) will become certified teachers of reading who are required to pass an advanced reading instruction competence assessment. As well, all pre-and in-service content-area teachers will pass the subject-specific licensure and the basic reading instruction competence assessment.)

As a nation, we must increase the academic quality and declarative knowledge of our teaching force. In order to address the inadequacies of both teacher preparation programs and in-service professional development for current teachers, a two-pronged approach is needed. First, prospective teachers of reading must master the disciplinary knowledge described above and then be mentored by master teachers to ensure that they can apply that knowledge in real-life situations. And, second, until all of our teacher preparation programs equip would-be teachers with this prerequisite knowledge and opportunities to apply the knowledge, our current practicing teachers should be required to demonstrate mastery of the same pedagogical content knowledge required of their novice counterparts.

What Would This Look Like?

Teachers would have to take and pass the same dedicated reading test as described in the last chapter, an advanced reading instruction competence assessment for teachers of reading in grades K-3 and all teachers in Title I, ELL, and special education, along with teaching specialists. In addition, all content-area teachers would have to take and pass the basic reading instruction competency assessment. If they didn't pass, in order to maintain their teaching licenses, teachers would be required to take continuing education courses tailored (i.e., differentiated) to their demonstrated need(s). Currently, most of our teachers sit in seats, sign an attendance sheet, and receive certificates stating that they showed up for professional development workshops—as opposed to demonstrating mastery of rigorous content described above. In order to make the best use of teachers' certification requirements, state departments of education should ensure that the required courses target specific content that teachers' data (i.e., how their students perform on reading assessments) indicate a need for.

As states around the country are reevaluating their teacher tenure and evaluation systems, now is the perfect time to take a close look at how to better qualify and support teachers in their jobs. We must not settle for anything less than the most well-trained reading teachers for our children!

CHAPTER SEVEN

ACTIONS OF THE POTENTATE

Success depends upon previous preparation, and without such preparation there is sure to be failure.

—Confucius

Words Matter

THIS CHAPTER WILL help you to craft your messages and to better understand the psyche of the American people—the people you need to get behind your state movement.

State literacy law and the Standards are all about the students and their achievement. If your state movement is to be successful, all of your communications must begin and end with the students themselves. Ignore this and nothing else matters.

Polls tell us that most Americans think that education reform is unattainable and for good reason:

> Decisions on educational policy and the use of resources for education are made by literally thousands of different entities, including 16,000 separate school districts, 3,300 colleges and universities, 50 state governments, several agencies of the federal government, and the courts at every level.[60]

---

[60] J. Rutherford and A. Ahlgren, *Science for All Americans* (New York: Oxford University Press, 2013).

No one group is in sole possession of power, transformation, or wisdom, and few can agree on the essentials needed for reform. So even though the American people may be unhappy with educational outcomes, we might go so far as to say they are "disgusted" with the status quo; the average citizen has little hope that change is possible.

So that is your first challenge—proving that change is possible. The good news in overcoming this objection or malaise is that there is wide agreement that student literacy is critical.

The second challenge is this: people must understand exactly what you are proposing (literacy law for your state's students) and how it directly affects the students' success. Therefore, to lead your state's literacy movement, to be the potentate, to build the critical mass, you need to drive change; you must make everything personal and real and tell how it affects students—every example, every statement, every fact, every advertisement must be about students.

This chapter is your workbook. It is here you will learn how to develop your lines and practice them with your teams. We are going to teach you how to set language priorities and establish arguments that work best to reach people and get them to support you. We will also warn you about what language should be avoided at all costs. You will learn how to best use stories and emotions to support your facts. Stories, emotions, facts—these are the ingredients for successful communication.

Have our leaders always, or generally, worked for the benefit of human beings, to increase the prosperity of all the people, to give each some opportunity of living decently and bringing up his children well? [61]

—*Theodore Roosevelt, 1912*

Potentate?

Recently I was in New York at a conference in which I heard a series of panel discussions and lectures centered on startling statistics that speak to the descent of America as the world leader in many

---

[61] "The Rights of the People to Rule," speech delivered by Theodore Roosevelt, March 20, 1912, accessed March 13, 2012, http://teachingamericanhistory.org/library/index.asp?document=1125.

CINTHIA COLETTI

arenas. The word "potentate" was bounced around for several days, and I must admit that it was not a word with which I was familiar. The second or third time I heard the word, I grabbed my iPad to check its meaning. A "potentate" is one who possesses great power as a sovereign, monarch, or ruler; one who dominates or leads a group or an endeavor. America has led the world as a potentate of individual freedoms secured by a Constitution and a Bill of Rights:

> *The development of the ideal of freedom and its translation into the everyday life of the people in great areas of the earth is the product of the efforts of many peoples. It is the fruit of a long tradition of vigorous thinking and courageous action. No one race and one people can claim to have done all the work to achieve greater dignity for human beings and great freedom to develop human personality. In each generation and in each country there must be a continuation of the struggle and new steps forward must be taken since this is preeminently a field in which to stand still is to retreat.*
>
> —*Eleanor Roosevelt, 1948*

In all we do and say, it is important to remember who we are as a nation of people. Our focus groups have highlighted that, as a people, Americans want this country to be "special" in every aspect. Whether

> . . . unalienable Rights, that among these are Life, Liberty and the pursuit of Happiness.
> —United States Declaration of Independence, 1776

we are extreme liberals, radical conservatives, or somewhere in the middle, history shows that the principles of liberty protected by our founders in our Declaration of Independence, and later in the United States Constitution and Bill of Rights, has led us to an inconceivable level of prosperity, safety, and happiness. To this end, our collective will and action inspire us to embrace the principle of "opportunity." The American principles of liberty that led to self-reliance, equity, and social justice in our young country will help enact new state literacy policies so that all young people will have the opportunity to participate in modern society.

As we move forward in efforts to be the world's "education potentate," we should be mindful that good communication does not attack or accuse but rather provides hope, a solution, and a solid plan backed up by science. There are three primary goals that must be accomplished in every successful call to action:

- First, it is important to be effective in showing positive, results-driven outcomes for students. Our desired outcome is for all students to become literate and earn an education. This is what the pundits call "American equity."
- Second, it is important to motivate our community of friends, our social network followers, and like-minded people and organizations to become committed to our mutual goal: to make certain every student is literate and educated, able to become gainfully employed and contribute to society. This is what the pundits call "American self-reliance."
- Third, we must challenge our education communities to become student-centered by encouraging the pursuit of excellence for each student. This is what the pundits call "American social justice."

I believe we can do this. In state after state, I am a part of a growing effort—state teams that are starting movements and driving change! We, the country of opportunity, have plenty of experience and a great track record of doing big things, hard things, together. I believe that most American citizens want a world-class education system for their neighborhood schools. Start asking questions of your grocer, hairdresser, and neighbor, in all likelihood, they will tell you that education matters deeply to them. So this is why specialists say that in any "call to action," it is important to play the "America the great" card without hesitation.

> The bottom line is that we are Americans, everyday people who can unite across race and class to lead, to take action against the status quo of education today, and to regain the American dream through quality public education.

Earlier, I shared Ali's strongly worded concerns for America's loss of its former "ascendancy" because our children's educational aspirations were not being met. Ali's comments represent the feelings of many people whose energies and passions we can channel into positive change. What is wonderful in today's age of instant communication is that in short order, through social networking, a movement can communicate to millions of followers to drive positive, vital change simply by tweeting, posting on Facebook, Google+, Pinterest, and more.

I'm a great believer that any tool that enhances communication has profound effects in terms of how people can learn from each other and how they can achieve the kind of freedoms that they're interested in.

—*Bill Gates*

It's What People Hear

There are many things to remember about the creation of compelling communications. The first is easy. When communicating your call to action, nothing is more important than crystallizing your message into your goal: all students literate—no excuses, no exceptions; all teachers supported with deep knowledge and skill—no excuses, no exceptions. Right from the get-go of gathering your team of like-minded supporters, your message should be clear about whom the goal will affect: all children, all students first. Teachers, schools, and the economy are featured subsequently.

Second, the messaging needs to be crafted carefully using language that is inclusive—all children, all of us. Third is storytelling. Nothing relays facts better than a compelling story. In America today, many think tanks and organizations focus on the "achievement gap," difference between students of lower economic status and their more advantaged peers. However, for a decade, new analyses have highlighted a different "gap": an "education gap" that not only affects minorities and impoverished students but also includes middle-class kids of all races. This is an epidemic, and it is affecting all of us— affecting all kinds of students.

And finally, the message should never place blame on the teachers, for they too are the collateral damage of a broken system in which scientific knowledge is decades behind teacher preparation and schoolroom practice.

Personalize, Individualize—and Above All, Humanize

Most corporations, politicians, and organizations use focus groups to test "messages." Focus groups are a marketing research tool adapted for inquiry in many fields, including medicine, social sciences, politics, and business. The knowledge acquired is used to craft messages for a politician's constituents or for a corporation seeking to expand its market share. Anyone can conduct informal focus groups, and I encourage you to do so. For this book, I felt it was highly important to understand what education messages are most likely to get the attention of the public. To best support your efforts and our mutual goal, I needed to hear what the pros had to say.

The Word Doctors is a powerhouse firm in the profession of message creation. They have messaged for presidents and prime ministers, Fortune 100 CEOs, and Hollywood creative teams. For decades, they have researched, polled, and consulted worldwide, with proven results that withstand the test of time. Essentially, they do exactly what we need: test language

> The end goal is to use imagery to establish quick agreement with the messages you are conveying.

and find words that will help us focus public opinion on an issue. Our issue is education—we need to know what to say and how to say it so that people hear what we need them to hear. The Word Doctors have conducted focus groups to do just that, and they have provided us with education communications that have the most impact when we do three things with our words and messages: (1) elicit feelings, (2) emphasize equity, and (3) use powerful, proven images. So let's take them one at a time.

1. For your message to be heard, you must elicit "feelings" from your audience . . .

    The best way to do this is by eliciting "personal" feelings. The bottom line is that most people don't get involved unless an issue affects them. Messaging needs to be personal; it needs to be about them, their circle, or their community. Use words like "your kids," "my kids," "his kids," "her kids," "the kids who play in your neighborhood," or "our kids." Also, to elicit feeling, it is important to know that people respond more eagerly to a humanized message—one that is not about numbers and statistics, but rather about people, about children. It is important to give a sense of the "personal" touch in everything you do and say. So share your stories and ask about theirs.

2. For your message to be heard, you must emphasize "equality" to your audience . . .

   Your messaging needs to be about equality, motivating everyone to join in your efforts. Literacy and a good education are the "right" of every student, every family, every hometown, and every community. Your messages are not just about middle-class or poor kids or kids with dyslexia or English learners or inner-city kids; your messages are about every kid. It is important to give a sense that "equality" is inclusive for all.

3. For your message to be heard, you must use the right "images" with your audience . . .

Often, the most potent messages are communicated through imagery, both positive and negative. When this is done well, each person in the audience will engage his or her own imagination and draw personal experiences into the equation. Images that show what your generation's education looked like, compared to that of children today, are powerful. Positive images depict happy, engaged kids learning in a classroom; negative images portray forlorn-looking kids. You will want to be creative in mixing both visual stimuli with your words as we did in the Literate Nation movie (found on YouTube under *Literate Nation, Facing the Frightening Facts*). Eliciting feelings by communicating a sense of the personal and conveying equality is less tricky than evoking imagery. Here we need to be mindful of what images invoke and whether they enlist agreement or rejection. Focus groups have shown that a powerful, positive education image is seeing teenagers wearing caps and gowns, graduating from high school, ready for life's next step. This is especially powerful if the image is coupled with "equality" words such as "Every student. No exception." The image of caps and gowns allows the audience to agree with the theme and invokes in their imagination the student going off to college or into employment, or a combination of the two. There is a proud satisfaction generated, a feeling that a significant challenge has been completed successfully. Effective images elicit agreement with your message. Another positive image features young children in school, happily engaged with a teacher.

Negative imagery must clearly show what happens when we fail our children. In so doing, keep in mind that images of students failing are compelling and that failure images should never include teachers. These images divide our cause, because it is our belief that when teachers are provided data-validated, quality preparation, professional development and advancement, they will have the skills to ensure student academic success. Just as it is not a child's fault that he or she cannot read, it is not the teacher's fault that he or she was not prepared to teach the complexities of reading development and reading literacy to a diverse group of students.

When negative images were sampled by the focus group, strong imagery told the story best. For example, on a test sheet, a large, red *F* was circled in the top, right-hand side of the page. This elicited the highest "agreement response" from the focus groups. They agreed that a grade of F was not acceptable and that something needed to be done to change it. Further, the group had empathy for the student rather than disgust; they essentially blamed the "system."

The next most powerful image was of a fourth-grade boy sitting at his desk sadly, holding up his head, feeling powerless. This elicited the response that he needed help; he wanted to do his class work but could not—everyone wanted him supported. The third-best response was an image of a forlorn sixth-grade boy standing in front of a green board holding a paper with an *F* in red that had been angrily written on the top of the page. The focus group felt that he had studied and tried his hardest, yet failed. They felt that he needed help, that his failure wasn't his fault, and that he could succeed with proper support and instruction. These images all led to agreement within the focus groups that the message was correct: the current educational system is failing our kids—our kids are not failing the system. Visit www.literatenation. org to download images for your work.

Powerful communication will raise understanding of the reading problem and help everyone understand that there is a solution: Enacting comprehensive state literacy law.

Many exceptional documentaries also convey agreement about using negative images. I believe the title of Patrick Ireland's upcoming documentary, *Can't Read, Go to Jail,* says it all. Another strong image is the illiterate young man in prison, clearly unprepared for life, working hard to learn to read and achieve his GED. The idea is to lead thought: without a GED, what else was there for this youth other than crime? He couldn't read text, resulting in his inability to learn in any of his school subjects; for this reason, he could not graduate from high school, and once that happened, he could not read well enough to fill out a job application, follow directions, or write a coherent paragraph about himself. What is wrong with this picture?

Imagery, words, film, and infographics, if done well, capture the "personal" idea that these youths are our kids—America's future—and for too long, we have allowed them to be shuffled through a broken system. Every thoughtful citizen wants students to achieve the things they dream of rather than become downtrodden and angry because the school system didn't provide tools for opportunity. Good messaging can be this simple; it can elicit feeling and drive action. It can take the blame off the child and place it on a failing system: kids have not failed us, but rather their schools have failed them—you and I have failed them, and you and I must do something about it.

Your call to action will need to go viral—reach your local and state newspapers, television stations, and all your networks (neighborhoods, schools, churches, clubs, etc.). Additionally, working with local organization's LinkedIn, Twitter, and Facebook will attract new members to your grassroots campaign, making you more powerful. E-mails and correspondence with local newspaper and television editors remain one of the most important resources communities can use to draw attention to their cause. In chapter 12, "Tricks of the Trade," we have provided sample e-mails and letters for your perusal.

Another longstanding, successful tool is to get individuals and local businesses in your community to sign their names via digital signatures on petitions and through e-mail when it is time to flood the state capital with voices for change, which can easily be accomplished electronically. The Literate Nation team (***www.LiterateNation. org***) has engineered a digital web platform for each state group to use quickly and efficiently to reach your congressional leaders. Endorsements, alliances, and signatures from both small businesses and large industries in the state are powerful—they demand literate, career-ready employees that only quality education can give them. Politicians are greatly encouraged to pay attention when business voices rise in unison to demand change. Consider a list here:

- Gather varied alliance partners to join your movement by first creating a target list of organizations that are community oriented and then by contacting them with an invitation to meet to discuss a new movement for student success—specifically reach out not only to "equity groups" involved with education, poverty, and English learners certainly but also groups that help their communities, groups that support minorities, groups that help juvenile delinquents and the prison population, boys and girls clubs, and after school programs. Literacy failure affects them all.
- Start a spreadsheet with your lists of partners and their e-mail addresses and work affiliations. Store it on Google docs or your state's Literate Nation web space (call 415-789-5574 for assistance) so everyone in your movement can have access to materials, breaking news, and adding new partners.
- Help quickly bring folks and groups up to speed when they join your movement through fact sheets of knowledge and marketing materials. Here is another place the Literate Nation state-specific web space can assist. It has many marketing tools, including training videos, materials, and fact sheets. Personalizing a "new member orientation program" that is readily available and comfortable for you to use will be of great assistance as your team builds your state's movement.
- Reach out to your school district, schools, PTA, and local union organizations, for they too want their students literate and their teachers knowledgeable, supported, and advanced. They want the colleges of education to do a better job with preparing teachers.

Bottom line is that most people care about a literate nation, and almost no one will walk away from the work once they understand the ramifications for millions of students—maintaining the status quo or working to effect change.

Know Your Stuff

The first goal of any call to action by your movement is to tell people what the problem is and offer a solution by creating a goal, an action plan, and measurable objectives. One starting goal is finding out who the elected politicos are in your state. List them and get their e-mail and office addresses. This includes your governor, legislators, state education committee members, top mayors, state superintendent, district superintendents, union leaders, and state PTA. A strategic action plan could have you or one of your partners meet with these officials to explain the problem and the proposed solution, and ask for their support. Determine if your governor will sponsor literacy policy, and/or choose one or two top congressional officials to cosponsor. If you can convince either the governor or the chair of the education committee to sponsor the literacy law, your road to enact will bear fruit more quickly. With the other officials you meet, your goal is to educate, to answer questions, and to ask if they are ready to support the work.

Experts tell us time and again to practice our lines, so take heed. The most brilliant salespeople typically are CEOs who can tell an intriguing story to their investors, to Wall Street, as well as to their customers and employees. That is why they sit in the corner office. In education, we need to do the same with our lawmakers and partners. Making the story as personal and earnest as possible, especially in your opening lines, is most captivating to any audience. Some say that jokes have a good effect, but if you take this route, make a joke about education. Good storytellers weave in personal intensity to "elicit feeling from the listeners"; if accomplished quickly, this compels your audience to listen to the important call to action in the message. Here are three examples:

For so long we've heard about education reform. For *four* decades people have talked about the challenges of our schools, but no one has acted. The only people who are going to make the necessary changes and get it done for our children are the people in this room and people in rooms all across America. We are unwilling to accept the status quo—we demand more for our children *now*.

You know that *our* neighborhood kids cannot achieve our state Standards. Do you think they will be ready to work in or compete with today's twenty-first-century career demands? How does this make you feel?

It is critically important to enact Literacy Law because it is the only way to rapidly solve our huge educational problem: the majority of students today can't read or write well enough to meet career demands. Millions of young adults are dropping out of school and/or are unemployed. Why? Because our schools have not prepared them to succeed. What will they do?

Chapter 12, "Tricks of the Trade," highlights the focus group's favorite positive-response questions, and provides phrasing for you to practice and learn until it rolls right off your tongue.

Design your campaign thoughtfully and strategically. Dr. Rich Long's descriptions in chapter 11 shed further clarity on the lawmaking tasks—structure, protocol, what needs to be done, and why. Legislative experts tout that it is best to frame literacy law by asking questions, conjuring imagery, and using the words "why" and "how" around our request. Here is an example using questions and engaging imagery with NAEP statistics:

> Ask educational stakeholders if they understand that early reading development skills can mean the difference between a child going to college or going to jail; between America staying on top or America losing its ascendency.

Thought-provoking questions such as these that have the sense of the personal and use imagery are very powerful. Practice your message, learn your facts, ensure your mission is clear, follow your tactical plan, and enable and encourage your advocacy group to do the same. Get fired up!

Public Education: A Nation Is Fueled by It and Volatile without It

Let's take a minute to think about public education and its effect on our own communities. In part 1 of this book, we spoke about education and the economy, noting that across the world, there is no greater influence on a society than education. This is also true for education's effect on our own neighborhoods and especially on our poor neighborhoods. When we message our call to action, when we talk about the problem and the solution with our lawmakers, we can make it personal by using "neighborhood imagery" and "neighborhood equality" to elicit emotion that gets them to agree that our message is correct. Think of telling a story:

Poor neighborhoods are filled with folks who have not gone to good schools, and many are functionally illiterate and unable to meet the employment demands of today's world. Volatility is apparent in their homes, on their streets, and in their schools, and hope is so bleak for these students . . . More than half of the young men and women will have dropped out of high school, angry, as they should be, having been given no skills, even the basic literacy, to change their position. This isn't their fault. It is ours. We stole their dream when we passed over them in school.

"Congresswoman, did you know that 67 percent of our students today are *not* reading and writing at a level deemed "proficient?" (This invites a question to engage.)

Next, ask: "How does this make you feel? Do you think our state's schools should get a failing grade for this performance?"

Next, ask: "If you took an exam and only got 33 percent right, wouldn't this warrant a grade of *F*?"

Then add imagery to solidify your point by presenting a piece of paper with "33%" grade and a big red *F* circled.

Next, ask: "What do you think is the leading cause of high-school dropout rates in our state?"

Next, ask: "Can you explain to us how in the world our community will flourish in this fast-paced society if almost *seven out of ten* of our students *lack* proficient literacy skills, and 25 percent of our students drop out of school?" (Your state dropout percentages can be found at www.nces.ed.gov.)

The truth is that many of our poor neighborhoods have illiteracy rates as low as Somalia, Afghanistan, and Haiti.[62] It only takes a moment to understand and connect why turbulence exists in our own poor-hoods, just as turbulences exist in illiterate countries. There is no optimism, no skill, no opportunities without literacy. Don't you agree?

---

[62]   "Countries with the Lowest Literacy Rates," United Nations Educational, Scientific, and Cultural Organization, accessed August 2, 2011, http://www.sil.org/lingualinks/literacy/prepareforaliteracyprogram/countrieswiththelowestratesofl.htm.

There are advocates on every corner, and you will find them. Once you make it personal, about equity, self-reliance, and social justice, our movement is hard to ignore. Within this context, even strangers quickly become allies.

> Your advocacy—your literacy call to action—your movement must empower folks to want to be involved so the American dream can continue, especially in our poor neighborhoods.

Tools in Action

At social events, I am frequently asked what I am doing. With a honed skill, I flow easily into my concern and passion for a literate nation. Most people, especially those aware of my business background, are perplexed at first, expecting that I will launch into a topic about market trends or new innovation. So to get the conversation rolling, I ask questions that require them to share their "feelings," possibly elicit some fear, and play up "social justice." Then I drop little "knowledge bombs."

I might start out by chatting and asking those at the table some questions:

> "Did you know that we are losing a generation of American minds? Yes, only one in three of our eighth-grade children are reading proficiently. This means they can't read or write well enough to pass their classes by the time they reach high school, and this, in turn, results in more than 1.2 million students dropping out of high school each year. It is tragic. Worse, just ten years of high-school dropouts cost you and me—our society—more than $4 trillion dollars in lost income, taxes, and in social expenses." Then I ask those at the table what they think.

Then I'll take it to the next level and seek engagement and discussion:

> "Do you think our economy, and possibly even our democracy, can survive when our students aren't graduating able to read or write well enough to be employed in our companies?"

"If these kids are not literate, how in the world can they participate in the requirements of a democracy?"

"Do you know how our kids perform competing against other countries in earning high-school diplomas and college degrees?"

The answers are always so hopeful around the table. Then when I share the truths about our kids' inability to compete with the rest of the world, faces drop.

"Sadly you are all mistaken:
- sixteen countries have graduation rates higher than the United States;
- two countries have more than half of all their students earning a college degree, South Korea and Russia;
- twenty-two countries beat the United States in science literacy;
- thirty countries beat us in math literacy; and
- sixteen countries beat us in reading literacy.

Essentially, America earns a grade of *F* on public education at the moment because only 33 percent of *our* students graduate from college."

The *F* imagery sinks in and then comes the perfect lead-in to the need for a literacy movement:

"This is why I am involved in this movement—the United States is falling so far behind in educating our students that it certainly may affect your quality of life, and mine, and that this concerns me greatly.

"We have forty-six million folks living in poverty and most without even the basic literacy skills needed to support themselves. If we don't reform American education to ensure our students become literate and career-ready, most things our forefathers fought for will not exist for our grandchildren."

Practicing these little "questions and knowledge bombs" with friends prepares you for legislators and alliance partners. Knowledge bombs never fall short of fueling intelligent and impassioned conversation about the need for a world-class education system in the United States.

As with most projects involving the government and bureaucracies, people just don't know what to do. They are not pleased with the status quo, yet they are not quite resigned to failure. But when you give them tangible solutions to a complex problem, they are likely to be willing to join the movement to enact state literacy laws that support the Standards.

> In all you do for this cause, strive to build and empower an army of invested individuals and groups that will get folks fired up—emailing, tweeting, blogging, and visiting congressional leaders with the solution—state literacy laws that guarantee early reading and full literacy.

Ready, Set, Commit

Success in any endeavor requires commitment on many levels. An initial commitment is to learn the facts about the problems besetting our schools, to learn your lines, and to tell your story. We must also commit to patience and understanding. It is inevitable that there will be differences of opinion among those of us engaged in this work. We can commit to make this an opportunity rather than a problem. We can commit to personally engage and encourage others to build relationships of trust—both those who share views and those holding divergent positions in literacy policy. Commit to

- shaping a new goal, a goal for landmark law that can trump and bridge differences for the sake of all young people and for the sake of all teachers;
- building trust by allowing room to listen and learn from one another;
- the new ethos—all students learning to read, all teachers achieving professionalism in their trade.

Dr. Jim Lanich, who is passionately devoted to education and leads the Educational Results Partnership, says, "We know how to teach reading, but we don't. Do you want to know why? Because we don't have to!"

Dr. Lanich calls it the way he sees it, pulling no punches as he aches for the kids today, knowing a majority are doomed because of the educational system. This book is all about taking Jim's statement, "Because we don't have to!" and turning it around to say, "Let's have to!"

Political Action Requirement: Pressure

Recently I attended a conference to hear Dr. Frank Luntz, author of *Words That Work*. Luntz's genius is best summed up as political willpower: "We all know that deep down politicians don't act, don't move, don't actually do anything unless we put pressure on them. We have seen a lot of significant changes when people organize and force politicians to act."

I agree totally with Frank's sentiment, and I know that to enact the literacy law we desire, we must commit to pressuring our lawmakers.

Respectfully make the statement to your politician that you are unwilling to accept the status quo of literacy failure in our schools today. This is a clear demand for immediate action. As I mentioned earlier, I am working with and following a number of states that are making the journey toward literacy law. To date, more than twenty state grassroots teams are making legislative inroads both initiating and implementing new literacy laws. Many concerned citizens, including teachers whose message can be the most profound, have joined the movement.

Idaho's Teacher of the Year, first-grade teacher Erin Lenz, testified to her state lawmakers that the key to education is a focus on early reading skills:

> I am not going to talk about the hot topics in education today, not about education reform, not about teacher evaluation or performance pay, not about college or career readiness. What I share with you today has direct implications, though, for all of these issues, and I am absolutely passionate about it: making sure that every child learns to read . . . . It is imperative that we look at cost-effective means to make sure students are reading proficiently at grade level before they leave the primary grades.

In her first class as a student teacher, she recalled a young boy who was in the fifth grade but only read at a second-grade level; he inspired her to find ways to prevent that.

Lenz told the lawmakers that over time, the discrepancy between a struggling reader and his or her peers grows exponentially. I work daily with students who walk in the doors feeling defeated when their efforts to read go unrewarded. This is devastating.

Basically, Erin's call put pressure on the politicians to enact laws that demand that "we follow research that says 'intervene early.'" As a result of Lentz' efforts and changes in her entire school, 99 percent of students scored proficient or advanced in reading last year on the Idaho state tests—just as science has proven it's possible—even though nearly 65 percent of the school's kids are on free or reduced-price lunch. Lenz ended her plea by stating, "All schools need kindergarten and first-grade teachers who are experienced and effective in teaching reading."[63] And I add: no excuses, no exceptions.

Whether you are working with one legislative champion or a group of champions in your state, pressure creates a ripple effect with enough momentum to get the bill through legislation. Pressure begins early by calling for meetings and getting in touch with a champion(s). Elicit feeling right away, as Lenz did with her personal story of fifth-grade boy. Ask personal questions: "Surely the benefits of living among educated people resonate with you?" This invokes images of solid citizens and good neighbors—every politician's desire for his or her constituents.

"Surely you understand the consequences of living among the uneducated in society?" This imagery of consequences influences people, physically and emotionally.

"Surely you understand that crime, prison populations, high-school dropout rates, and people's need for social services are, more often than not, the direct or indirect result of functional illiteracy?" Not one politician in office can refute this. Share with him or her the literacy policy as Lenz did: "Research says to intervene early and we did . . . and 99 percent of [our] students scored proficient or advanced in reading last year . . ." And emphasize in your work literacy's importance in achieving Common Core State Standards, and that, as Lenz stated, "It is imperative that we look at cost-effective

---

[63] "Idaho Teacher of the Year: Focus on Early Reading," accessed March 13, 2012, http://www.spokesman.com/stories/2012/mar/12/idaho-teacher-year-focus-early-reading/.

means to make sure students are reading at grade level before they leave the primary grades."

Like us, American politicians are influenced by the concept of the American dream. They too want to depend on good schools to educate their children and students to become respectable citizens. Why? Because it leads to good property values, good jobs, good GSP (gross state product), and their reelection. However, they should not be reelected when more than 30 percent of public-school students can't graduate from high school. With confidence and pressure, stress that "their constituents" want school accountability, responsibility, and change, and the first step is to change the paradigm—enact literacy law. Pressure them on the moral issue: student literacy is a social right, a human right, and a moral imperative, without which students fail, and the burden of these individuals on society will become unbearable.

> *I like to see a man proud of the place in which he lives. I like to see a man live so that his place will be proud of him.*
> —*Abraham Lincoln*

Literacy Overhaul: Is it a Matter of Spending More Money or Spending Smart Money?

The best way to overcome questions of budgets and costs are to face them head on with the facts: literacy is a mandate; education is a societal obligation; and one does not happen without the other. The United States in 2010 spent more than $11,000 per elementary-school student, more than $12,000 per high-school student, and a total of about $15,171 per each young person in the educational system—the highest spending of any developed country, according to the Organization for Economic Cooperation and Development—and yet, we must correlate this with the fact that only 33 percent of students are reading at a level of "proficiency." In its 2013 annual report, the organization also states that novice and experienced teachers in the United States earn more than their peers in many other countries, though salaries in the United States are growing at a slower rate than those in some countries. [64]

---

[64] The 2013 Education at a Glance Report can be accessed online at http://www.oecd.org/edu/eag.htm.

In a nutshell, the United States

1. spent 7.3 percent of its gross domestic product on education in 2010, compared with the 6.3 percent average of other OECD countries;
2. spent $15,171 on each young person in the system—more than any other nation covered in the report; and yet
3. does not rank in the top ten OECD nations.[65]

"When people talk about other countries out-educating the United States, it needs to be remembered that those other nations are out-investing us in education as well," said by Randi Weingarten, president of the American Federation of Teachers labor union. In order for any country to be able to provide quality education, they need to invest in quality teachers. Adequate and equitable remuneration is a key factor in attracting well-qualified teachers to and retaining teachers in this lauded profession.

OECD further compares educational attainment to major impacts on employability: "Across OECD countries, only 4.8 percent of people with tertiary degrees were unemployed in 2011 as compared to 12.6 percent of people without an upper secondary education," thus, education is the best protection against a nation's unemployment. And so I argue that educational spending, particularly to prepare aspiring teachers and advance existing teachers, is a budget mandate, not an option. The socioeconomic benefits of a highly qualified population far exceed the costs and should be a particularly strong reason for state governments to invest in early literacy and education.

Preferences and Perspectives

Citizenship comes first today in our crowded world. No man can enjoy the privileges of education and thereafter with a clear conscience break his contract with society. To respect that contract is to be mature, to strengthen it is to be a good citizen, to do more than your share under it is noble.

—Isaiah Bowman

---

[65] Top Ten PISA OECD countries, III Forum Microsoft Educacion, Madrid (2012) can be accessed online at http://edutechassociates.net/page/2/.

Don't be surprised to learn that politics is said to be the visible clash of preferences and perspectives. Preferences guide politicians in seeking favorable publicity for reelection plans, or benefits for friends and supporters and organized interests pursuing goals. Perspectives determine the politicians' personality, background, and experience about what matters and what does not, what should be attended to and what should not. As education potentates, we must grasp that both influence the visible choices that politicians make and always involve personal biases that consciously or unconsciously drive the selection of the "next" issue for their attention.

> And this is why this chapter is important to your work—remember it is what they hear, not what you say.

Keep it personal by "eliciting feeling" from your politician, your champion. Make it "personal" about them, understanding their personalities, backgrounds, experiences, goals—personal biases. Make it about "equality" by tapping into their responsibility for their constituents, neighborhoods, all the state's kids, and teachers. Don't make it a Union issue; don't blame teachers; make it a budget mandate.

> Use all the beautiful social networking roads given to us in this century, for they are an amazingly expedient landscape in which to build support for your call to action, keep your teams informed, and inspire your politicians to accomplish your goal by getting on their agenda, making it their issue, and making them the champion.

Force the issue onto the political stage. Politicians do not make decisions in a vacuum, so bring in the troops of grassroots teams, tell stories, cite statistics, recount successes, use imagery, grow a coalition of political and stakeholder partners, and speak to them using digital force.

Build support digitally! There are more than four hundred social media and social networking sites today. Follow government officials on Twitter, Facebook, LinkedIn; write comments; gather supporters to do the same; and while going viral, continue to effectively communicate equality, imagery, and a sense of the personal; remember that your language should be visual, descriptive, and imaginative so they can "hear" you. Tell stories.

As I mentioned earlier in the book, Carolyn Cowen, a colleague, friend, and an education and research pundit, pushed me into social media. She spoke of the power of these social alliances, the potent information that came to her without effort, the awakening of perspective that she experienced on every outlet of information and opinion. She told me how thrilling this great shift in social communication is in its applicability as a force for social good; its return on investments is better than any IPO.

Because of Carolyn, I am proud to say that I began using Twitter in the early spring of 2012, and the connections I have forged since then have been a tremendous boon to the message I wish to send. Social networking is endless and fascinating, and I owe much of my progress this past year to Carolyn's push to get me involved. And she has intelligently and scholarly prepared the next chapter for you so you can engage thousands in your call to action. Enjoy!

CHAPTER EIGHT

LEVERAGE SOCIAL MEDIA TO DRIVE CHANGE!

Twitter Power for Literacy Educators and Activists
by Carolyn D. Cowen

DISCLOSURE: ABOUT TWO years ago, I knew almost zilch about social media. In fact, I am fairly technophobic. Really. Ask anyone who knows me. Only the largess of my tech-savvy family and occasional panicky interactions with "tech support" enable me to stumble along in the digital era with a modicum of competence. Recently, however, I embarked on a quest to explore social media. What I learned persuaded me that anyone seeking to improve the teaching-learning landscape must initiate his or her own quest to understand and leverage the power of social media. In this chapter, I hope to inspire you to do exactly that.

Confessions of a Closet Tweeter

When social media first began emerging as a game changer, I was dismissive. "That's for college kids," I thought. Despite being married to a new-media expert and early-adopter type, I was slow to recognize the power of social media, even as it began invading our household— long before "friend" became a verb.

Over time, I did succumb to environmental pressure. I acquired a Facebook page, joined LinkedIn, started a Twitter account, and even posted a few presentations on SlideShare.[66] I would trot out these social-media credentials when I was feeling the need to demonstrate I was not some hopeless digital illiterate. Truth be told, I wasn't very active on any of those platforms. For the most part, I was

1. Mystified—why is every news anchor on the planet suddenly talking about hashtags?
2. Skeptical—how can anyone say anything significant in 140 characters?
3. Busy—who has time to play around with social media?
4. Fearful—who knows what evil lurks beneath the benign-looking social media surface? (Stories about hackers and phishing scams seemed reason enough not to venture into those dangerous waters.[67])

Then I received an unlikely Christmas present—a bunch of books on social media. Imagine my enthusiasm. My gift-giver also made a point of challenging me on two fronts:

- As a mission-driven social entrepreneur and educator, isn't it time to learn how to leverage social media tools to achieve my goals?
- How can I be so concerned with education and print literacy and ignore new-media literacy and the imperative to prepare children to live in a world that will demand new-media competence?

Less than thrilled, I began reading and trying some of the strategies in the books. I started with LinkedIn because it seemed more professional and, well, more grown-up than Facebook. (Yes, I know Facebook is by far the most powerful platform on the web, but it just felt frivolous to me.) Next, I delved into SlideShare and Twitter because the first had obvious professional applications, and the latter

---

[66] SlideShare—a web-based slideshow-hosting service—is a dynamic social-media/education tool similar to YouTube, but for presentations.

[67] Phishing: Posing as a trustworthy entity to steal usernames, passwords, credit-card information.

seemed relatively uncomplicated and easy to incorporate into my busy life.

To my surprise, I began to like dabbling in social media and found myself venturing into its deeper waters. The small experiments I conducted began producing results, especially on Twitter. I was inspired.

But I was a closet tweeter. Most of my esteemed colleagues were not, heaven forbid, tweeting, and I was not ready to confess that I had crossed over. Not yet. Meanwhile, building on success and with scaffolding and support from my family and books, my learning accelerated. I witnessed the power of social media's tools and strategies in arenas where I had thought they had no relevance. Finally, tentatively, I emerged from the closet to share this power with colleagues.

There is nothing more irritating than the sanctimony of the newly converted, so I promise to temper my enthusiasm. You will hear no claims from me that social media will bring world peace, stop climate change, or even solve the thorny challenges we face in education. And hazards do indeed lurk in social media's waters.

I will, however, try to persuade you to test these waters and to learn to swim in them with some degree of competence. In a nutshell, here is why: to achieve your goals and for the sake of the children whose future you steward, you must begin to understand and tap the power of social media.

If you are reading this book, my assertion above almost certainly applies to you. Very likely, you too have been dismissive of social media and still are mystified by, cynical about, or fearful of its power. In fact, I am willing to bet that most readers of this book are not digital natives.[68] You are the audience for whom this chapter is written. My goal is to help so-called digital immigrants who are doing important work in education to venture into social media, understand its power, and begin learning how to leverage its tools and strategies.

---

[68] Digital native: Someone born after digital technology became mainstream and, presumably, with greater digital competence and comfort than a digital immigrant, someone born before digital technology became mainstream.

CINTHIA COLETTI

However, I will take you only so far. Why? Any Google search will yield plenty of social-media how-to books destined to become obsolete in six months. Things are happening that fast. Instead of providing nuts-and-bolts detail that may not be relevant in just months, I will drop a few breadcrumbs to help you get started on the path— particularly the Twitter path—and provide a little support to help you find success and feel inspired to persevere in a rapidly changing environment.

I know. You want me to tell you exactly how to do social media step-by-step. We non-digital natives like books and lean away from discovery learning, especially when it comes to technology. We want direct, systematic, explicit instruction. We want someone to break it down, make it multisensory, and provide guided practice. So go buy a book (several are listed at the end of this chapter). Go find a mentor. My goal is to motivate you to take such steps and to persist. Think of me as someone who traveled the road just a few steps ahead of you and has circled back to offer a few pointers about how and why to start down the path—to tell you about some of the awesome vistas ahead and to help you get oriented. Think of me as one who has not traveled far enough along the road to give you a comprehensive map. You must find your own map and guides. But I can help you begin. So let's start!

How Can Social Media Enhance Your Work?

The most important step in my own exploration of social media was to understand that I could use its tools and strategies to enhance my work. That epiphany was the starting gun that propelled me forward. Why should you, too, consider undertaking such an exploration? The answer is simple: social-media tools and strategies can be powerful in the hands of literacy educators and activists working to improve the teaching-learning landscape for children at risk for reading failure—the "SEEDS" children discussed in this book's first chapter. [69]

How? Social media can achieve important objectives under four broad categories: (1) WEB STRATEGY, (2) MESSAGING, (3) NETWORKING/

---

[69] SEEDS: Struggling readers from all backgrounds, Economically disadvantaged youngsters, English-language learners, and students with Dyslexia or Specific learning disabilities.

ACTION, and (4) PEDAGOGY. One or two of those categories may not be meaningful to you, so let's sharpen our focus and look at specific objectives for each category:

1. WEB STRATEGY OBJECTIVE: Enhance search engine optimization (SEO) strategies to improve search-engine visibility—more on this in a moment
2. MESSAGING OBJECTIVE: Listen, broadcast, and engage
3. NETWORKING/ACTION OBJECTIVES: Build personal learning networks (PLNs) and ignite social action
4. PEDAGOGY OBJECTIVE: Enrich/engage learning and differentiate teaching

If you are a literacy educator or activist, one or more of those objectives ties directly to your work and goals. All these objectives can be important elements in a comprehensive campaign to improve the teaching-learning landscape for children at risk for reading failure. Let's sharpen our focus still further to define terminology and concepts that may be new to you as we consider each of these categories and objectives through the lens of Twitter—a very powerful microblogging platform. [70]

How Does Twitter Advance Web Strategy?

Twitter advances web strategy (i.e., drives traffic to your website or blog) in at least three ways: (1) through messages that draw in targeted audiences, (2) by building a distribution network of followers who help convey your messages, and (3) by enhancing search engine optimization. We will examine each.

First, think of Twitter as an outpost or billboard that funnels traffic back to your blog or website (see figure 1).

---

[70] Microblogging, as the name suggests, falls under the broadcast medium of blogging, but differs from traditional blogging in that small elements of content are shared.

cdcowen Carolyn D Cowen
Carroll School—dyslexia/learning differences leader—hosts math
teacher-training bit.ly/zkNK2H #hsmath #mathchat #dyslexia
2 minutes ago ☆ Favorite ↰ Reply ☰ Delete

Figure 1. Example of a tweet (top) driving traffic to a website. In this case, the tweet first linked to a constant contact (not shown), which then linked to the website (above).

A good tweet is like a good headline; it captures attention and draws the reader in. With three hundred million tweets per day and climbing, how do you stand out in the cacophony of noise about the likes of Ashton Kutcher to capture anyone's attention, much less draw them in? [71] The answer: hashtags! A hashtag (#) preceding particular words in your Twitter message enables people to search for messages and conversation about those topics. Hashtags function something like

---

[71] According to *Wikipedia*, in 2011 over three hundred million users generated over three hundred million tweets and over 1.6 billion search queries per day. However, Twitter is reported to have a low retention rate (keeping those who join). Retrieved, 1/2/12.

zip codes; they allow you to target your messaging to people hanging out in certain "topical neighborhoods" following particular issues. Use hashtags strategically to reach specific audiences. Your message, intended audience, and goals should inform your use of hashtags (see figure 2). [72]

Figure 2. Example of a tweet using hashtags (#) to target specific audiences. Compare these hashtags to those used in figure 1.

Second, as you become more active on Twitter, you will acquire followers. These are people who have decided to follow you (at least for a while), which means your tweets show up in their Twitter feeds. This is good! Your followers are a select segment of your audience. They have decided to follow you because they agree or disagree with you, find you entertaining or informative, or reciprocated when you followed them. Think of your followers as your distribution network, the people most likely to retweet your tweets (i.e., pass along your information to others). You want to build your distribution network and populate it with people of influence. There are many tricks, strategies, and tools for acquiring followers, but the best method by far is to generate high-quality tweets on a regular basis linking to high-quality content related to your goals and work. In other words, to attract followers of value, you must provide value (see figure 3).

> **PosieAk** Posie Boggs
> Omg. Multi-sensory instruction! RT @TheBrainScience: Gestures improve language learning sns.mx/Yffvy0 #literatenation #dyslexia
> 6 Jan

---

[72] See SlideShare URL at the end of this chapter and view Twitter Tutorial: How-To Links to access links to lists of education-related hashtags.

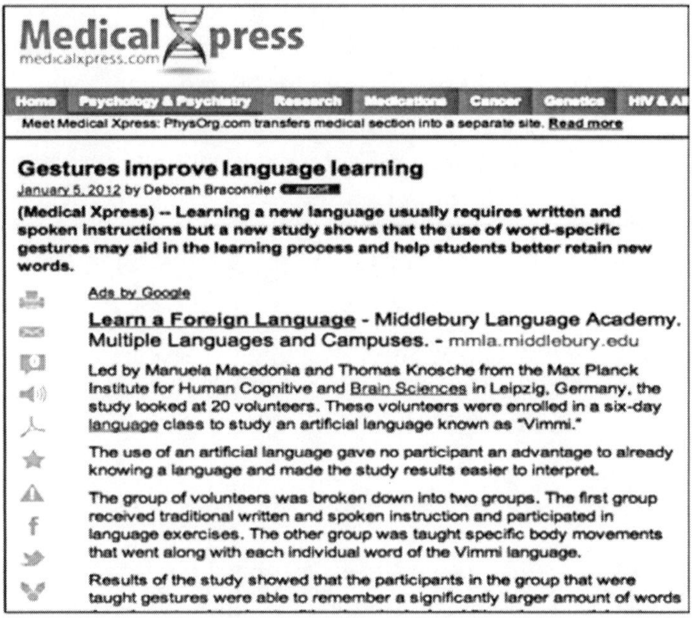

Medical Xpress
medicalxpress.com

Home | Psychology & Psychiatry | Research | Medications | Cancer | Genetics | HIV & AI

Meet Medical Xpress: PhysOrg.com transfers medical section into a separate site. Read more

Gestures improve language learning

January 5, 2012 by Deborah Braconnier

(Medical Xpress) -- Learning a new language usually requires written and spoken instructions but a new study shows that the use of word-specific gestures may aid in the learning process and help students better retain new words.

Ads by Google

Learn a Foreign Language - Middlebury Language Academy. Multiple Languages and Campuses. - mmla.middlebury.edu

Led by Manuela Macedonia and Thomas Knosche from the Max Planck Institute for Human Cognitive and Brain Sciences in Leipzig, Germany, the study looked at 20 volunteers. These volunteers were enrolled in a six-day language class to study an artificial language known as "Vimmi."

The use of an artificial language gave no participant an advantage to already knowing a language and made the study results easier to interpret.

The group of volunteers was broken down into two groups. The first group received traditional written and spoken instruction and participated in language exercises. The other group was taught specific body movements that went along with each individual word of the Vimmi language.

Results of the study showed that the participants in the group that were taught gestures were able to remember a significantly larger amount of words

Figure 3. Example of high-quality tweet—attention grabbing/conveys complete thought—linking to high-quality content. Note hashtag use and that the tweet is a retweet (RT) from @TheBrainScience. (For full article, see http://medicalxpress.com/news/2012-01-gestures-language.html).

Third, tweeting enhances search engine optimization (SEO). What is that? SEO improves the visibility of a website or webpage on a search engine, such as Google. SEO tactics seek to ensure that a given website or blog shows up near the top of a results page in response to a web search query. The higher on the results page, the better the odds people will click on the link to a site. (Few of us scroll beyond the first few items on a search results page.) So if, for example, your organization and website are all about literacy, you want to show up near the top of the results page on a search for literacy (or for similar words or topics, e.g., illiteracy, teaching literacy). An entire industry has grown up around the creation and use of sophisticated SEO tactics, but all you need to know for now is that through the simple act of tweeting, you can enhance SEO and page ranking, especially if you consistently and strategically use keywords and phrases that summarize or relate to your cause.[73]

[73] For now, anyway. SEO dynamics are fluid.

How does Twitter advance web strategy? *Branding Yourself* authors Erik Deckers and Kyle Lacy put it best: "Twitter allows the instantaneous sharing of your blog or website content, which means you have the opportunity to publish your opinions and ideas to a readership of millions" (2011, 88). How? Via tweets to hashtags and followers and through the power of SEO.

How Does Twitter Facilitate Messaging?

Twitter is a two-way communication channel that not only allows you to broadcast information to others but also brings information to you via your Twitter feed.

Twitter Feed: Source of Breaking News and Content

Your Twitter feed—tweets from people you follow—provides a steady stream of customized breaking news and content. As you follow people interested in issues that interest you, these "tweople" provide valuable links to information you might have missed otherwise. The people you follow determine the scope and quality of the content in your Twitter feed. Following people with diverse interests and perspectives yields wide-ranging content that can get overwhelming. Following people with similar interests and perspectives yields targeted content that can be too narrow. The trick is to find a balance that reflects your interests and needs and allows you to follow emerging information in your content niche.

How do you know whom to follow? There is a lot of buzz these days about analytics tools, such as Klout (klout.com), which seek to measure the strength of someone's online influence.[74] Theoretically, you want to follow people with influence and, presumably, those with high Klout scores. Keep in mind, though, this is just one measure, one many criticize as superficial. Twitter also offers regular "who-to-follow" suggestions. But if you are just starting out, it is important to look at Twitter profiles and tweets to assess for yourself if a prospect is "follow-worthy." In the process, you learn valuable lessons about

---

[74] See SlideShare URL at the end of this chapter and view Twitter Tutorial: How-To Links for links to discussions about Klout score pros/cons

effective tweeting and see who is tweeting and retweeting what in your areas of interest. You also can search hashtags in your Twitter search window (see figure 4) to find and follow people on your topics of interest, but you still should review their profiles and tweet history.

Figure 4. Example of results for #literacy search using Twitter search field (small white box, upper left). Tweet results are on left. People results are top right.

As you follow more people, your Twitter feed can explode with incoming tweets. If a daily tsunami of incoming e-mails and other data already swamps you, a hyperactive Twitter feed is not good. Fear not. You can and should unfollow people as your interests and priorities shift and as you learn more about who best meets your needs. You also can create lists within your Twitter feed to break down incoming tweets into categories to make monitoring groups of people and particular topics more manageable.

Another strategy for managing an active Twitter feed is to deploy a tool such as Paper.li (http://paper.li). Advertised as content curation, Paper.li is more topical aggregation (bundling) and too automated to be true content curation.[75] No matter. Paper.li's real value is in taking

---

[75]   Scoop.it! (http://blog.scoop.it/en) probably is closer to content curation and appears to be a promising tool.

links from people you follow and converting tweets into a digital "tweet-paper" for easy reading—far easier for busy digital immigrants to scan and digest than a highly active Twitter feed. Your Paper.li also can tweet itself when it is hot off the press, and you can tweet and retweet directly from your own paper.li or from other paper.lis to which you subscribe, making this a very valuable two-way communication tool.[76]

Is your head spinning? Not to worry. File some of this away under "Solutions for Future Problems," which, if you are just starting out, you will not need to think about for a while.

Twitter: A Broadcasting Medium

Broadcasting is one thing. Attracting, engaging, and keeping high-quality followers who act on or pass along your messages is another. Some influential tweeters have thousands of followers; if they retweet you, your message can go viral in seconds. There are all kinds of tricks and tools for acquiring followers (Google it), but attracting and keeping valuable followers is something else. Following and retweeting other quality tweeters are two effective strategies that often prompt people to check you out and follow or retweet back. This is good! You are looking for active retweeters with their own followers. But again, the single most effective strategy for attracting and keeping quality followers is to learn the art of a good tweet and to place it in hashtag neighborhoods your target audiences frequent. Your goal is strategic and engaging broadcasting of quality content, not scattershot self-indulgent drivel.

In 140 characters or less, effective tweets

1. post links to valuable content;
2. engage, interact, and build relationships; and
3. promote your cause—but not too much, interspersing your cause-related tweets with those of others, especially those with aligned causes and content.

As Deckers and Lacy say, "the more content-rich your tweets, the more people will read" (2011, 94). Content comes from linking to your blog, website, or other blogs and news sources, and by engaging

---

[76]   Paper.li also works with Facebook or Google+.

in conversation. Of course, if your tweets are well written and thought provoking, all the better (see figure 5).

Literate Nation @LiterateNation   25 Jan
2/3 of states SUE Feds over #K12 school funding cuts <$5.4b>
bit.ly/XBshrB | The US needs the #LEARN Act! #edchat @TIME
Expand ← Reply 🗑 Delete ★ Favorite ••• More

LiterateNation Literate Nation
What? 2 more years and 2011 Nation's Report Card shows US students had NO growth in reading literacy! 1.usa.gov/vWVHEu
#literacylaw
7 Dec ☆ Favorite ⇄ Retweet ↩ Reply

web20classroom Steven W. Anderson
@m_lula Thanks so much! Means a lot to me
10 hours ago ☆ Favorite ⇄ Retweet ↩ Reply

irasocol Ira Socol
Assuming - merely assuming - that I do not actually tie knots in my headphone cable, how do they get there?
3 hours ago ☆ Favorite ⇄ Undo Retweet ↩ Reply

1ScottRedmond Scott Redmond
Dyslexia Legislation Passed in Ohio! ow.ly/8endY #LITERACYLAW
30 Dec ☆ Favorite ⇄ Retweet ↩ Reply

psychcentral PsychCentral
Early Resilience Research Helps Now psych.ly/yBfMS4 #mhsm
#mentalhealth
53 seconds ago ☆ Favorite ⇄ Retweet ↩ Reply

Figure 5. Examples of effective tweets. Why? They have many of the following attributes: They convey complete thoughts, link to content, engage or interact (tweet 4 uses levity), leverage hashtags, or promote causes. Tweets 2 and 5 might have been even more effective by using additional hashtags to broaden the audience. Tweet 3 is interacting with an individual, so no need for a hashtag. Tweet 4: @irasocal already has a very large audience of followers.

There are no rigid rules when it comes to tweeting, but following a few common sense guidelines can ease your way and facilitate effective messaging. Do not promote yourself too much (bad manners), do not overdo quotes (boring),[77] do not lose track of time and spend all day tweeting (foolish), and do not forget that tweets are public (really foolish). Do be goal oriented and relevant (smart), do be active (shoot for five to ten tweets per day), and do embrace "givers gain" (Deckers and Lacy suggest one self-serving tweet for every nine about others).

A final quote from Deckers and Lacy: "When it comes to Twitter, you're expected to share others' content more than your own. When you share their content, they're more likely to share yours in return" (2011, 104). Being retweeted is a compliment that furthers your objectives. Retweeting is good form and builds your network (see figure 6).

ElennSteinberg Elenn
Great food for thought "The Future of Teacher Prep" on Vimeo:
vimeo.com/33322270 #edreform @LiterateNation
8 Dec ☆ Favorite ↻ Retweet ↩ Reply
↻ Retweeted by CatColetti

cdcowen Carolyn D Cowen
Wow. An awesome new site: Literate Nation --> bit.ly/vPPszz
#literacylaw #allchildrenreading #literacy #edreform #edchat #dyslexia
2 Dec ☆ Favorite ↩ Reply 🗑 Delete

---

[77] I have tweeted a quote once or twice in about five thousand tweets. I regard people who tweet daily quotes as "cheap tweeters" and do not follow them. Why clog up my Twitter feed? I can read a book of quotes or search online anytime I feel the need for an inspirational quote. But maybe that is just me.

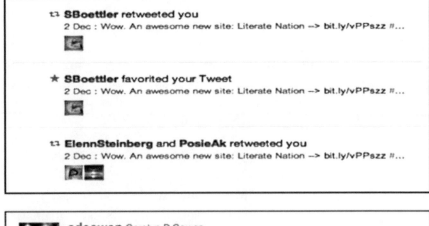

Figure 6. Retweet (RT) examples. Tweet 1: Retweeted by CatColetti (note circular arrows lower left). Tweet 2: Retweeted by SBoettler, ElennSteinberg, and PosieAk (appearing in my personal "@ feed," see tweets 3-5). Tweets 6 and 7: Twitter etiquette and networking—people often thank for retweets. The thank-you tweets (and "Kudos" to 1ScottRedmond) appeared in their own "@ feeds," which can be seen by all their followers by clicking on "View conversation." (Only people who follow each other can send private tweets, a.k.a. direct messages or DM.) Also note SBoettler's use of "favoriting" (gold star) in tweet 4 to indicate that she especially likes a tweet. Finally, in tweets 1, 6 and 7, note use of @, which is like saying "To: so-and-so." Using @ ensures the tweet will be seen by a particular person in their "@ Twitter feed."

Which brings us to this incredibly important point: Twitter's linking and sharing culture is a powerful asset for igniting change. Borrowing from Malcolm Gladwell's (2000) *The Tipping Point*, mavens (databanks), connectors (social glue), and salesmen (persuaders) all populate Twitter—a medium that further empowers them to do what they already do well. Twitter helps you enlist the talents of mavens, connectors, and salesmen to convey your messages.

A final point about Twitter's broadcasting power: Twitter gives you more control of your messaging and press. No longer must you rely exclusively on traditional press to tell your story. Social media enables you tell it yourself with accuracy and passion! And if you tell it well enough, traditional press sometimes follows.

How Does Twitter Promote Networking and Social Action?

Even if you know very little about Twitter, you probably have heard about the so-called Twitter revolutions.[78] You also may have encountered the term professional learning networks (PLNs). Both relate to what Twitter is exceptionally good at—building social networks and igniting social action. How do these relate to the work and goals of literacy educators and activists?

Twitter-Fueled PLNs: New Ways to Promote Professional Knowledge

Let's start with *professional learning networks*, which, according to Wikipedia, "have become prevalent in the field of education and rapidly are becoming adopted as centers for the dissemination of field-related information."[79] A key PLN concept is that it is learner-centered: "Learners create connections and develop a network that contributes to their professional development and knowledge."[80] The other defining feature of the PLN trend is its connection to social media.

We probably can anticipate that PLNs driven by social media will play an expanding role in twenty-first-century teacher preparation and professional development. Most literacy leaders of the "evidence-based persuasion" will feel varying degrees of discomfort with the learner-centric concept at the heart of PLNs and will worry about leaving too much responsibility for directing professional learning in

---

[78] Twitter was used to organize protests in Egypt, Tunisian, Iran, and Moldova.

[79] Accessed January 2, 2012, http://en.wikipedia.org/wiki/Personal_Learning_Networks.

[80] Accessed January 2, 2012, http://en.wikipedia.org/wiki/Personal_Learning_Networks.

the hands of those who may not know enough to know what they do not know, never mind how to acquire the deep knowledge they need. A concern, yes.

But imagine the synergistic power in a skillfully executed effort to organize PLNs for literacy educators in teacher preparation and professional development programs that embody, for example, the tenets of the International Dyslexia Association's Knowledge and Practice Standards for Teachers of Reading.[81] Imagine leveraging PLNs to organize a grassroots campaign to raise public awareness about the knowledge base required for skilled reading instruction. Imagine coordinating PLNs nationwide to share effective strategies for pushing for state literacy laws.

PLNs are not new. Throughout human history, formal and informal professional and grassroots networks have shared knowledge and information to advance social goals. Here is what is new: social media platforms like Twitter expand the power and reach of these learning networks profoundly.

Twitter: A Power Tool for Igniting Social Action

Social media also has the power to ignite social action for good and bad. Twitter is thought to have played a role in the United Kingdom civil unrest in the spring of 2011. Twitter was used to organize protests in Egypt during 2010-2011, Tunisia during 2009-2010, Iran in 2009, and Moldova in 2009. Twitter also helped launch the Occupy Movement (#OWS, 2011[82]). A pretty big impact for a social media platform launched as recently as 2006, no?

Twitter's power to galvanize and coordinate social action has been used closer to home as well. During the summer of 2011, a grassroots effort called Save Our Schools (SOS) organized a march in Washington, DC, to demand "(1) equitable funding for all public school communities; (2) an end to high-stakes testing used for the purpose of student, teacher, and school evaluation; (3) teacher, family, and community leadership in forming public school policies; and

---

[81] See http://www.interdys.org/standards.htm.
[82] Roughly one in every five hundred hashtags on Twitter worldwide was #OWS (http://en.wikipedia.org/wiki/Occupy_Wall_Street, accessed January 2, 2012).

(4) curriculum developed for and by local school communities" (see www.saveourschoolsmarch.org). [83]

Leaving aside how you may feel about these demands (some of which will worry parents, educators, and policy makers fighting for "evidenced-based practices"), the SOS movement offers important lessons in deploying social media to achieve social goals. SOS has been especially skillful in leveraging Twitter to

1. recruit new members and build community identity around shared frustrations;
2. tweet a barrage of headlines driving traffic to websites and blogs where prolific writers further articulated the cause;
3. sustain ongoing conversation around core talking points;
4. attract the attention of traditional press; and
5. focus attention on a call to action—a Washington march that further solidified everything above.

A few qualifiers: Twitter is not SOS's only organizing tool; there have been missteps, and to what extent this movement ultimately will be successful remains to be seen. But SOS (including its missteps) offers a great case study for literacy educators and activists seeking to tap the power of social media. SOS also offers a warning for those not yet deploying social media tools and strategies. Others are doing so, and they are honing their skills.

How Can Twitter Enrich/Engage Learning and Differentiate Teaching?

Twitter and other social media are at the heart of a freewheeling pedagogical frontier. Exploration, intuition, improvisation, and market forces will drive development of social media/education practices and interventions for a while. There will be risk taking, missteps, snake-oil salesmen, and brilliant innovation. It will take years for empirical research to catch up (if it ever does). Schools are struggling with online policies and access issues, but there is no closing this barn door. Educators already are experimenting with social media, such as Twitter,

---

[83]   See http://www.saveourschoolsmarch.org/.

to enrich and engage learning, to differentiate teaching, and for other pedagogical purposes.

Check out a sampling of high-profile education Tweeters to get a taste of the action:[84]

1. https://twitter.com/edutopia
2. https://twitter.com/rmbyrne
3. https://twitter.com/TeachPaperless
4. https://twitter.com/mbteach
5. https://twitter.com/Larryferlazzo
6. https://twitter.com/web20classroom
7. https://twitter.com/coolcatteacher
8. https://twitter.com/ShellTerrell
9. https://twitter.com/stumpteacher
10. https://twitter.com/NMHS_Principal
11. https://twitter.com/cybraryman
12. https://twitter.com/langwitches

This is uncharted territory. Shouldn't the people who know the most about the knowledge base required for skilled reading instruction be exploring this territory too? Given what we know about the reading brain and the science of teaching and learning, shouldn't we be out there as well helping to blaze the trails? If we worry about the erosion of "deep reading" skills in a digital environment—as cognitive neuroscientist Maryanne Wolf cautions (2010)—shouldn't we be lending our expertise to chart this new territory and to help ensure that one of civilization's greatest triumphs (deep reading/thinking skills) is not lost along the way? Just because something is technology based and powerful does not mean it delivers on its promise or is good. Our expertise is needed to help determine what is pedagogically promising in this free-wheeling social-media frontier and to meld these promising practices with the substantial body of multidisciplinary knowledge about effective reading instruction.

---

[84] Disclaimer: This is just a taste and by no means exhaustive—merely the result of an hour or so spent trolling my Twitter feed. These tweeters will lead you to others. (Inclusion on this list does not signify endorsement; omission does not signify the opposite.)

Finally, if we are dedicated to ensuring children are print-literate in order to function in a text-driven culture, shouldn't we also be dedicated to preparing children to live in a society that demands new-media literacy?[85] This last question may be the trickiest of all. What exactly is new-media literacy, how does it relate to print literacy, and how do schools based on industrial-era design impart new-media literacy skills? A complex ever-changing digital environment further complicates these questions.

It is not clear how to navigate the tricky waters of these and similar questions. What is clear is that we cannot learn to swim without getting in the water. So far, in my relatively brief but intense exploration of social media, I have been struck by the conspicuous absence of most literacy and learning differences experts. We have very little presence in this arena, especially on Twitter.

You may have noticed that other than offering a few leads, I did not actually answer the question that kicked off this section of this chapter: How can Twitter enrich/engage learning and differentiate teaching? After a few false starts, I realized that my answers would be far too preliminary. More to the point, better answers would come from literacy master practitioners and thought leaders partnering with new-media experts to explore the frontiers of social media's pedagogical applications and to identify promising practices. Of course, a new generation of rigorous translational research should follow. [86] Partnerships among educators, new-media experts, and researchers will be vital to exploring new media's teaching-learning applications and implications, which may indeed blaze pathways to solutions for longstanding education challenges and to exciting innovations for future generations of learners.

---

[85] An array of evolving new-media literacy definitions pulled from the web over the last two years share characteristics such as the ability to (1) analyze, evaluate, and communicate information in a complex ever-changing digital environment; (2) be both a critical thinker and creative producer of a range of messages using image, language, and sound; and (3) skillfully apply print literacy skills (decoding/encoding symbols and comprehending, synthesizing, analyzing, and producing messages) to media and technology messaging.

[86] Translational research: Practice-based research to enhance evidence-based practice.

Your Turn to Act

I have touched on Twitter's applications and possibilities related to (1) WEB STRATEGY, (2) MESSAGING, (3) NETWORKING/ACTION, and (4) PEDAGOGY. Will Twitter save the planet or, barring that, solve the pressing challenges most people agree we now face in education across the nation? Definitely not. Frederick Hess voiced a relevant caution in *The Same Thing Over and Over: How School Reformers Get Stuck in Yesterday's Ideas*: "The challenge is not to romanticize any given technological advance, but to ask how it might be used to solve problems in smarter ways" (2010, 26). To be sure, social media has plenty of downsides, some of which we probably cannot even glimpse at this early juncture. Twitter is just a social media tool. Like all tools, it has limitations. It is as good or bad as the humans who wield it.

With those important disclaimers and cautions underscored, I have no doubt that Twitter can be a power tool for literacy educators and activists. As Guy Kawasaki, author of *Enchantment: The Art of Changing Hearts, Minds, and Actions,* said, "Twitter is the most powerful enchantment tool I've used in my career" (2011, 126). Kawasaki is the former chief evangelist of Apple, so that is saying something.

Perhaps enchantment has been a missing ingredient in our decades-long campaign to bring skilled reading instruction to every child. We have tried the levers of research, policy, legislation, and accountability, but how well have we practiced the art of enchantment to change hearts, minds, and actions? To what extent might the current backlash of angry resistance to evidence-based efforts be because we have relied mostly on top-down strategies for creating change while neglecting to give bottom-up grassroots strategies our attention?

Twitter is a powerful tool for enchanting, for building grassroots support, and for igniting change. Twitter or future iterations of Twitter also may prove to be an especially valuable teaching-learning tool. Yes, using Twitter requires learning a few tricks and strategies, but it is not rocket science. Twitter is low-hanging fruit. Why not pluck it? Which brings us to two steps you can take now to begin sampling some of the fruits of social media:

STEP #1: If you have not done so already, start a Twitter account. It is free and not difficult to do. Go to Twitter.com and follow the prompts.

Once you start your account (or if you already are on Twitter but not active), here is your assignment:

1. Explore Twitter and get to know its various features. (Don't freak out if the layout changes. It happens now and then as Twitter improves its design. The basic features will remain intact.)
2. Follow fifteen new people each week for a month. (This is the best way to quickly understand what works and what does not and to build a valuable Twitter feed.)
3. Tweet at least once a day for a month. (This will help you build the habit and become fluent).

Here is a bit of scaffolding: If you check out the three resources below as you complete the assignments above, you will be well on your way.

- http://www.slideshare.net/carolyndcowen
  View Draft 3 Twitter Power 4 Literacy Educators and Activists and Draft 3 Twitter Power Tutorial: How-to Links (Introductory)
- http://mashable.com/guidebook/twitter/
  The Twitter Guide Book: How-To, Tips and Instructions (Basics to Advanced)
- http://socialtriggers.com/twitter-tips/
  How to Attract and Influence People on Twitter (The Ultimate Twitter Resource)

STEP #2: If I have inspired and empowered you to explore Twitter, I hope you will do the same for your colleagues. Pay it forward! Also, teaching is one of the best ways to consolidate your own learning.

This chapter focused on social media's *why* more than its *how*—hoping to entice, guide, and gently prod you to take the steps needed to learn how to engage in social media, especially Twitter. To avoid overwhelming those just venturing into this new environment, I limited detail to what is most needed to take those initial crucial steps. You do not need to master Twitter or other social media platforms overnight. Take it one step at a time. I hope you will! Social media tools will be powerful in the hands of literacy educators and activists working to improve the teaching-learning landscape in behalf of children at risk for reading failure. Come explore this frontier and learn powerful new ways to achieve your goals. You might even have fun!

What saves a man is to take a step. Then another step.
—C. S. Lewis

Disclaimers and Cautions

Like all social media platforms, Twitter periodically redesigns its layout and features, so what you see on your screen may not correspond exactly with the figures 1-6 in this chapter (captured at the time of publication). The fundamental elements, however, usually remain intact. A related caution: book production is a lengthy process, but things happen quickly in new media, especially social media. By the time this book is in your hands, Twitter may have evolved powerful new capabilities and other new social media tools may have emerged. That said, the general principles discussed in this chapter about how social media can enhance your work will continue to apply.

Finally, as always, use good judgment online, no matter what platform you are on, be it e-mail, Twitter, Facebook, or whatever. Spammers and hackers are there. On Twitter, be cautious about clicking on links in direct messages (DM), or in "@ messages," even from people you know. Until you learn to recognize bogus links (with time, you will), it is best to let something pass than to take a chance and click. Also, be careful about whom you follow. Be wary of the buxom young blonde or someone without a picture or profile who has very few followers but lots of similar tweets inviting you to click on links. Nothing good will come from following this person. Finally, remember to change your passwords often. With these cautions in mind, you can safely dabble in social media and begin to venture into its deeper waters with confidence.

Sidebar

Social media experiments: Here are two of several informal experiments I conducted that helped turn me from a social-media skeptic to cautious advocate. The results themselves are not huge, but provide insights into huge possibilities.

- Views of two of my presentations/documents on SlideShare jumped significantly after being featured briefly on SlideShare's homepage—one because it was "being tweeted more than anything else on SlideShare" (probably because of hashtags I used) and one because it was "popular" (probably because of keywords in the title). Taken together, these two presentations have had over 2,250 views. (As this book goes to press, the tally for all twelve of my public SlideShare presentations/documents is about 5,850 views). Take away: Hashtags and keywords are important, and Twitter and SlideShare can work synergistically to broadcast messages and reach audiences.
- For years, the International Dyslexia Association struggled to attract high-caliber proposals for its Multisensory Structured-Language Research Grant Program. Nine proposals were received from 2006 to 2010; one was accepted. In 2011, we experimented with a social-media call-for-proposals strategy (Twitter) that yielded five proposals (three from outside the United States), one of which was funded. Take away: Twitter reaches a wide range of audiences from around the world, including neuroscientists and cognition/education researchers.

Christmas (2010) books: I am often asked about the books I received. Keep in mind, I do not necessarily endorse these and, even though all have publishing dates between 2008 and 2011, their content may be dated already.

1. *Branding Yourself: How to Use Social Media to Invent or Reinvent Yourself,* by Erik Deckers and Kyle Lacy
2. *Content Rules: How to Create Killer Podcasts, Videos, Ebooks, Webinars and More,* by Ann Handley and C. C. Chapman
3. *Disrupting Class: How Disruptive Innovation Will Change the Way the World Learns,* by Clayton Christensen
4. *Facebook Marketing an Hour a Day,* by Chris Treadway and Mari Smith
5. *Grown Up Digital,* by Don Tapscott
6. *Inbound Marketing: Get Found Using Social Media, and Blogs,* by Brian Halligan and Dharmesh Shah

7. *The Young and the Digital: What the Migration to Social Network Sites, Games, and Anytime, Anywhere Media Means for Our Future*, by S. Craig Watkins

Here are three more I have since discovered and found relevant:

1. *Dragonfly Effect: Quick, Effective, and Powerful Ways to Use Social Media to Drive Change*, by Jennifer Aaker and Andy Smith
2. *Enchantment: The Art of Changing Hearts, Minds, and Actions*, by Guy Kawasaki
3. *Social Media for Social Good: A How-To Guide for Nonprofits*, by Heather Mansfield (I cannot recommend this one highly enough, especially since she periodically sends out e-updates on her book!)

Follow suggestions: Come find me on Twitter (https://twitter.com/cdcowen). Tell me about your Twitter adventures and send me an RT-worthy tweet! Also follow

LiterateNation (https://twitter.com/LiterateNation). Literate Nation: Working together across disciplines to ensure all students are reading literate and equipped with twenty-first-century skills to flourish in school, career, and life.

CHAPTER NINE

FIRST HELPING MY CHILD

> *Elenn Steinberg, like many passionate educational advocates, joined the cause first as the parent of a child who struggled. She took on the task of helping her son and, out of frustration with the lack of progress in his classroom or with outside intervention, became herself highly skilled as a reading interventionist. In short order, Elenn began advocating for children, supporting teacher training, and motivating Colorado's legislators to enact new literacy law with great success! Elenn is now working on the implementation of the Colorado literacy law. Her positive energy, intellect, and wisdom fuel this work, and I am grateful for her collegial endeavors and friendship.*

First Helping My Child, Then Creating Community Change
by Elenn Steinberg

THE TASK OF working to create systematic change in literacy may appear like too much of a challenge—especially when dealing with the day-to-day struggles of how to help our own children survive in an educational world that is based on the ability to read. As parents, we ourselves struggle to navigate a system that doesn't seem to understand what to do with children (SEEDS; see chapter 1 for definition) who have difficulty learning to read. While it is essential that we change these systems, often we are confronted with the overwhelming needs of our individual children.

While you instinctively know that the world of literacy must change, at this moment, your primary focus must be on procuring services for your child. Each child must successfully navigate through school and optimally thrive. However, we know that, generally speaking, when one child is not learning how to read, there are many more who are failing as well. Regardless of the various reasons for this, the job of the school is to teach all children to read, including the SEEDS students.

For the parent of the child who is struggling, the task of working with the school can be daunting. We may feel as if we are confronting our own past as we tuck ourselves into the desk or small chair we remember from years ago. In order to help our own children succeed, we must step outside of our school experience, build our own understanding of the system that now exists for our child, and press on. When working with a school, assume the best. Teachers genuinely want to teach children so that they may succeed in school and in life. However, teachers often don't know what they don't know, so it may be up to parents and guardians to help guide them.

Surviving the System

So where does a family member start to ensure that his or her child's needs are met at school?

The best place to start is at home. Spend time organizing your thoughts about your child's educational experience, successes, and challenges. Identify your concerns. Be specific and go into detail. Only you can know what goes on at home and when a child is struggling. A parent can bring insight to the situation that the school may be missing.

Details about reading may include the areas of language in which your child struggles. For example, if he is failing to sound out words, guessing words very slowly, or showing a lack of comprehension, make a note: this is the place to begin. Other examples that only you can know may include that your child spends an excessive amount of time on homework compared to his peers. Only you know that he or she cries at the end of the day, voicing his or her fears of being a failure, or whether he feigns illness to avoid turning in incomplete homework or feels unprepared to take an exam. You may know of a teacher who calls your child lazy or tells him to work harder—when you know that your child does work hard, but without success.

Take time to learn about dyslexia and how children learn to read so that you can go to school prepared with facts. Your collection can also include past assessment reports from teachers or other professionals, although these are not required. Furthermore, ready yourself with details on how your child is doing in other subjects, since writing and math can be equally troublesome for some kids.

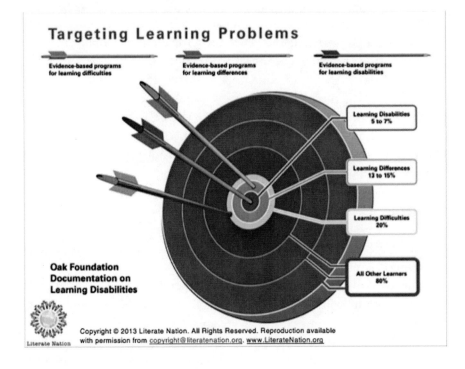

The Meeting

Request a meeting with your child's teacher. Identifying the goals that you want to accomplish at this meeting will help determine who should attend. Can the classroom teacher accomplish the goals, or do you need to include the principal, reading specialist, or special-education teacher? If the outcome you are seeking is an Individual Education Plan (IEP), then the special-education service administrators must provide you with the documents you need to sign to have various assessments completed. Your request and signature on the requisite form also puts your child's school, by law, on the clock to accomplish this evaluation task. Check your state department of education's website to determine the time frame for the evaluation to be completed, because while this falls under the Individuals with Disabilities Act (IDEA) special-education law and is mandatory, states can set their own timelines once the request for testing has been signed. More information on the American Disabilities Act (ADA) and Individuals with Disabilities Education Act (IDEA) federal law is available in the document Model State Literacy Law (available at ***www. literatenation.org***).

Once you have a meeting scheduled and everyone is around the table, you can start the conversation with your school personnel by simply saying, "My child doesn't seem to be reading (writing, spelling, doing math) very well." Provide the details you have prepared on what your child is struggling with: sounding out, reading words, reading text fluently, generally guesses at words, spends too much time on homework, dislikes reading, purports to "hate school," is depressed, compares him or herself to other students, or feels like a failure. Bring examples of his work to help demonstrate the marginal spelling or other academic struggles. Share the stories that your child brings home about being embarrassed by a teacher who singles him out for his challenges. Share anecdotes and stories that move the people in the room to feel compassionately for your child. And finally, ask if your child could possibly be a SEEDS student (Struggling readers, English language learners, Economically disadvantaged youngster, and students with Dyslexia and Specific learning disabilities). States, schools, and school districts use different nomenclature for kids who struggle with reading. The words "dyslexia" and "learning disability," however, are the terms used in federal law. Special-education law lists them as a specific learning disability (20 USC 1401 [30]). Be sure to state your goal—your child reading and succeeding—and then discuss what services the school might provide to accomplish this goal.

Being a SEEDS student or having dyslexia will not automatically qualify a child for special services. The qualifications for special-education services are defined by the district and require assessment data, which differs from state to state. At this time, most states have implemented an initiative that goes under two names: Multi-Tier System of Supports (MTSS) and Response to Intervention (RtI) (see more in the Model State Literacy Law). This MTSS initiative can be highly beneficial to your child, since it provides immediate services for any child who is determined to be at risk for learning problems. After initial screening, more customized educational support is then provided according to ongoing assessment data gathered in your child's class.

The classroom teacher is responsible for regular assessments, known as progress monitoring, to ensure that all students are learning at grade level and making progress throughout the school year. These assessments are standardized and are not conjecture on the part of the teacher. One popular and excellent assessment tool is called DIBELS Next, and it can be viewed online if you want to have an idea of what the assessment looks like. Children in older grades may receive outcome assessments (sometimes referred to as achievement tests and typically given at the end of the school year) that show where your child is in comparison to the standards for their grade, statewide or even nationally. While useful, this information may not tell you how your child is performing in the key components of reading— phonological awareness, phonics, comprehension, or vocabulary.

In addition to test scores, the school staff should have work samples that demonstrate the success and challenges your child faces. You may bring work samples (i.e., graded homework, tests) from home, as well.

It is important to keep in mind that you, as the parent, can still request an assessment for special-education services at any time if you feel your child is not making adequate progress even though an MTSS plan is in place at your child's school. As a parent, you have a legal right under the Individuals with Disabilities Act (IDEA) to request an educational or what might be called a psychoeducational evaluation at any time you feel your child is not making adequate progress. (Both MTSS and IDEA are discussed in length in appendix E.)

Over the course of the conversation in the meeting, you might want to ask these questions to assess if your school offers the tools your child will need:

- How do you teach reading in this school?
- Do you use any particular programs?
- Does the school have a core reading instruction program? Is it utilizing multicomponent, structured language instruction?
- How are you identifying and assessing students at risk?
- What is the intervention program and tiered supports the school is using to support SEEDS students?

- How are you identifying students at risk in your MTSS model? (See information below.)
- What type of professional development has the school been providing to the staff to educate them on teaching reading effectively?

Keep all the information you collect in a file so that if you need to follow up, you have documented all the information necessary to request more support for your child.

This then becomes a series of if/then scenarios. If they take your concerns seriously, then request a timeline so you can track what interventions are being provided and what results are being produced. Updates should be provided at least every two weeks and not longer than four.

I'd suggest e-mail if that is possible, as it is quick and easy for all involved. Report card grading periods are often not frequent enough!

If the services they provide your child work, then you applaud and continue to follow up with monitoring progress on a regular basis— it should not be longer than four weeks between reports, and gains should be strong and consistent. As you track the progress your child makes through teacher communication, it should be easy for you to see the educational growth your child is making through these tools and in the work you see at home. If your child is not making adequate gains, then you must request an assessment for special-education services. Do not wait longer than six weeks even if the school suggests a "wait and see approach"—your child is now six weeks further behind!

If the school is conducting assessment for special-education services, then you need to be given a timeline so you can be prepared for the follow-up meeting. Typically, the assessment must be completed and a meeting scheduled within forty-five to sixty days from the time you provided written permission to assess. Be sure to check your school system's website for the laws in your state. At that point, you need to understand what it takes to have your child become a grade-level reader. Four simple keys to ensuring reading literacy are discussed in the Model State Literacy Law (see part 3 of the book):

1. structured, systematic, multicomponent teaching;
2. a well-trained, highly skilled teacher of reading;
3. adequate time and support; and
4. intensity of instruction.

A Bit More

The Individuals with Disabilities Education Act (IDEA) protects the rights of all children under the law. You can request an assessment for special education for your child at any time, even within an MTSS

> However, special-education services do not guarantee that your child will be provided a highly skilled, certified teacher of reading who is able to teach him or her to read.

model. It is important to understand what it takes to catch a child up to where he or she needs to be to keep up with classmates.

If, after speaking with your child's teacher and principal, you feel you have not received a satisfactory response to your questions and a request for intervention, your next step is to go up the ladder, the chain of command. Contact your district or area's special-education director as listed on the district or state website and also research services for individuals or parental support organizations as listed below. Federal law mandates these advocacy offices in every state, and they are available free to you as a resource.

You are your child's best advocate. Keep pushing until you get the answers you need and your child gets the help that he or she is entitled to for a successful educational experience.

Can a Parent Influence Change in a School System?

Do not let what you cannot do interfere with what you can do.
—Ancient Chinese Proverb

Just as in Brownsville, Texas, (see chapter 10) parents have the ability to bring about major change in schools, even though it often does not appear possible. While one parent can create awareness, multiple parents can work together to move mountains. When change is needed in your school or district, talk to other parents, attend a PTA meeting, network, and gather people and resources you think will be useful.

Set up a meeting with the principal. In some cases, providing the principal with the facts you have gathered and a sample of the Model State Literacy Law will open the discussion. Emphasize and demonstrate how the changes you want for the school will benefit not just your child but all children. This valuable point could be just what it takes to bring about that necessary change. In other cases, you may face more of a challenge, so you need to be tenacious, engaged, and committed, as described in chapter 7, "Actions of the Potentate."

Here are some larger issues you may want to address. They are the primary reasons we ask everyone to join the call to action to enact literacy law in every state in the country:

a. How do you teach failing readers, all SEEDS kids?
b. How does your state certify teachers of reading? Does the exam include questions that address the phonological system of our language, fluency, comprehension, expressive vocabulary, semantics, and critical thinking skills?
c. What is your state doing about the high number of failing readers?
d. How does the state certify teachers of reading?
e. How does the state monitor teacher quality and student achievement?
f. How does the state monitor teacher education programs to ensure that graduates effectively teach reading to all students, including our SEEDS students?

Partnerships Are Important—Don't Go It Alone

You can form grassroots partnerships with others in your community, as described in chapter 5. Form these partnerships with those with similar concerns and work together. Groups to cultivate as allies include the following:

a. parents
b. teachers of reading
c. educators
d. administrators
e. psychologists
f. pediatricians
g. minority organizations
h. community associations—small business, youth, afterschool
i. state departments of education
j. school boards—national and state associations of school boards, principals, superintendents

k. parent-teacher associations—state PTA boards
l. schools for students with learning disabilities
m. education groups—special education, twice-exceptional
n. teachers' unions
o. International Reading Association chapter in your state
p. International Dyslexia Association branch in your community
q. Learning Disabilities Association
r. National Center for Learning Disabilities
s. university and college support services offices
t. gifted-student groups
u. CHADD—Children and Adults with Attention-Deficit/ Hyperactivity Disorder; attention-deficit support group
v. all the Literate Nation State Coalitions.

Excerpted from *The Power to Act: Transforming Literacy and Education*, by Cinthia Coletti Haan.

CHAPTER TEN

CHALLENGES BREED OPPORTUNITY

You Can Do This

A T THE CORE, this book is about an ambitious and far-reaching campaign to solve one of the most pervasive problems of life: who succeeds and who fails. And what can any of us do to steer an individual child—or a whole generation of children—away from failure and toward success. In this chapter, I would like us to stare down the hard facts about the conditions of life we face. And then I will share with you an incredible story of how an entire community—a challenged community—confronted the hardest of societal conditions to save their children's futures. How they used the tools of science to peel back the mysteries of failure and transcend their harsh reality.

Today's Challenges

It is often said that it is hard today to raise a family. Today's norm finds two working parents in most young family households; or one single, working parent scrambling to do it all; or one or two parents unemployed. For half a decade now, | Alarmingly, we find poor and homeless children to be the fastest-growing student population in our schools today.

since 2008, millions of Americans have been living in an economic nightmare with more than a half-million children homeless and suffering greatly—they are the victims of these tough times. They are the ones who most need skills to become literate, independent citizens.

Alarmingly, we find poor and homeless children the fastest-growing student population in our schools today. For the first time in our history, roughly 46.2 million people remain below the poverty line, unchanged since 2010: nearly one in every five children lives below the poverty line, the highest in the more than half a century since records have been kept.[87] And dare we think about the unemployment rates that may drive this number even higher? Well, let's do that—let's move from the heartbreak of children suffering and think about hard statistics.

If we take the number of unemployed as roughly thirteen million citizens, according to the 2012 Bureau of Labor statistics, and look at the labor force of roughly 160 million citizens, then the unemployment rate is close to 9 percent. Now you may recall earlier facts in the book that state corporations have three million open jobs today—jobs they cannot fill because there are no qualified workers to fill them. Therefore, on the bright side, this means employers could, almost overnight, employ three million workers if they could find them. This would immediately reduce deficit spending by easing the financial strain on social services. And most importantly, it would mean that the tearful waters in which these innocent underprivileged children are submerged would retreat as silently and mysteriously as they have risen. They would no longer be homeless because their parents could not earn a paycheck. But rather they would be able to see hope that they too would be employed and sustain a family.

Unfortunately, all too few of these families and children who live under great pressure are being met with the compassion they deserve until the waters of our economy calm. Within school walls, I have heard bureaucrats complaining that the parents don't do enough with their children: essentially, passing the blame to them, crafting excuses for why children aren't keeping up in school. To this I say, baloney.

In chapter 4, I reported on my visits to high-performing schools where poverty and homeless children are the norm. These children

---

87   "More Than 40 Million Now Use Food Stamps," *Boston Globe*, accessed March 13, 2012, http://www.boston.com/news/nation/articles/2010/06/03/more_than_40m_now_use_food_stamps/.

are blossoming in the expertise of knowledgeable school leaders who live by the mantra of no excuses, no exceptions. Perhaps if the young parents of these children had received a quality education, they would have the skills necessary to fill one or two of the three million open jobs in America today.

After having read part 1 of this book, I trust you agree that unemployment figures are closely related to educational achievement in our rapidly changing society. In this, the richest, most productive land in the world, we cannot boast of an educational structure that opens doors of opportunity to tens of millions of young citizens; rather we see instructional programs that have imprisoned their dreams, leaving them unprepared for college or career.

To help create jobs, industry is espousing the Reshoring Initiative—a gallant, national attempt to bring jobs to back to the North American shore. Harry Moser, the founder of the Reshoring Initiative, says it calls for "producing literate, career-ready citizens capable of joining the workforce and enabling industry to once again lead the innovation, designing, building, and exporting of quality American products and services around the globe."

Yes, industry is championing our mantra. Four hundred organizations and thousands of corporate representatives have signed onto the Initiative. However, the Initiative can only succeed when all schools are producing literate graduates. Industry can't fill the job openings they have today because potential workers lack the skills needed. However, if policy makers and school systems adhere to state literacy law and the Standards, the goals of Reshoring could be reached.

The challenges of reform can be met. Remember earlier in the book learning about China's educational initiatives? China made a huge education reform decision a decade ago, calling it the "2020 Vision for Universal High Schools and World-Class Universities," and in less than ten years' time, their major population centers are leading the world in all educational statistics. Singapore also did it by deciding to propel their economy from third world to first world through education reforms. Finland did it by deciding to become a modern society and economy, free from domination by larger powers.[88] Bottom

---

[88]   Vivian Stewart, *A World-Class Education: Lessons from International Models of Excellence and Innovation* (Virginia: ACSD, 2012).

line, we can do it too, but we can't fool ourselves that bold initiatives like Reshoring can begin in earnest until our education statistics compete with the world's trend.

Parents Breed Opportunity

So let me return to my point about parents and lead you into a magical story of what can happen when parents stand up and fight for their children. Overwhelmingly, the economic case mentioned above resonates with partners—especially with those unemployed. Those unemployed for more than a year know that with each month, the probability of getting a job is bleaker, and their skills are weakening. Even if they know the importance of lifelong learning, they have few opportunities to maintain or enhance their skills.

Working parents are grateful to be employed and will fight to do whatever it takes to remain employed, even if this means learning new, ever-evolving skills. Those who have had a solid education are fortunate that they have the literacy to do so. Elenn Steinberg in the last chapter demonstrates that parents understand that education, employment, and life style are tightly woven together. With this knowledge, you can attract parents and grandparents to work with you to transform education. More than anything, parents want their children to succeed. If you lead them, they will follow.

Why parent involvement? Parents do not perceive themselves as a constituency for children. They lack advocacy skills, but not the motivation or will to make change for children. The desire of parents to engage with purpose is impeded often by a lack of skill in how change comes about. Parents are rarely encouraged to get past barriers to leadership that are often seated in family history or haunted by class, race, and gender bias. Your call to action may be their first step in civic skills. The cornerstones of true parent leadership are respect, validation, and a belief that when the tools of democracy are understood, families will enter civic life.

—Elaine Zimmerman
Connecticut Commission on Children

Building a community advocacy of parents, grandparents, neighbors, and coworkers is the powerful force that can make possible any new law. When you read about the community of Brownsville, you will understand better the "Actions of the Potentate."

> *Culture does not change because we desire to change it. Culture changes when the organization is transformed; the culture reflects the realities of people working together every day.*
> —*Frances Hesselbein*
> *Leader to Leader*

One City's Tale—Brownsville, Texas

A Community's Quest to Turn Nonreaders into College-Bound Kids

Norma Garza's son, Alec, started having problems learning to read in first grade. By the age of ten, in fourth grade, he was still struggling to read. Desperate to get help for her son, Garza, who worked as a certified public accountant, sought diagnosis and guidance from a pediatric neurologist at the Texas Scottish Rite Hospital for Children in Dallas, Texas. It was the hospital staff who explained the importance of making education decisions based on science-based research as used in the medical field. Despite the fact that she had taken an analytical approach, read books on how children learned to read, and consulted national reading experts, Garza found that her son's public school was not only at a loss as to how to remedy the situation but also pushing back against her suggestions and efforts.

Garza joined forces with Elsa Cardenas-Hagen, a speech—language pathologist with a clinic for children with language and learning differences in Brownsville, Texas. Garza and Cardenas-Hagen discovered that students in Brownsville were not being taught with a balanced approach to literacy, which would include phonological awareness, phonics, fluency, vocabulary, and comprehension skills. The computerized program it offered did not meet state standards for a dyslexia intervention program.

Located on the US-Mexico border, the Brownsville school district faced major hurdles, including poverty and a student population that was 98 percent Latino with few native English speakers. Such populations tend to have high numbers of children who fail to learn to read, as well as large numbers of students who drop out altogether. In 1996, Garza and Cardenas-Hagen cofounded the Brownsville Reads Task Force, a nonprofit organization of community members and educators who joined together to promote research-based reading instruction in the public and private schools of Brownsville, with the overall goal of creating a more literate community.

Together they created a strategic plan for the district that was approved by the school board, and Elsa personally retrained all kindergarten through third-grade teachers in a balanced, systematic, and explicit approach for the development of Spanish literacy. Neuhaus Education Center in Houston, Texas, provided professional development in language enrichment (LE) via videoconferencing, as it was not economical for teachers to travel to Houston for training, nor feasible to send Neuhaus staff to Brownsville. For the last fifteen years, with the help of Neuhaus, new teachers have been trained, and refresher courses have been provided to current teachers. This professional development program has been maintained despite the district having had eight superintendents in the last fifteen years, and it has helped to ensure continuity and sustainability.

Brownsville Reads began the initiative by working with regular education teachers in kindergarten through third grade. They then used Academic 2000 Goals money to retrain all teachers of dyslexic students and Title I funds to retrain upper elementary, middle-school, and high-school reading teachers, as well as English-as-second-language teachers. The Texas Reading Initiative provided further training, and the No Child Left Behind Act helped initiate Reading First. As Cardenas-Hagen explains, "You see, we were already using this model in the late 1990s because we improved our regular education literacy instruction, and only those students who were not responding to this multisensory, structured reading instruction were given extra instruction. Having trained reading coaches and mentors has been extremely helpful. This was made possible with the Reading First Grant."

During this time, the Brownsville school district also participated in research initiatives sponsored by the National Institutes of Health and the Institute for Education Sciences, led by the University of Houston and the University of Texas at Austin. "It is due to the research that we have been conducting in this district and other districts across the nation that we have learned more about how to instruct English language learners and students who struggle with learning to read. Brownsville is on the cutting edge because it is the laboratory from which public policy will be set in the future," explains Cardenas-Hagen.

And the results speak for themselves. According to Neuhaus, after the first year of the initiative, a group of 522 second-grade students was identified. Half the students had been taught by teachers who had received the professional development; the other half had been taught by teachers who had not yet received the professional development. The achievement of the group on the state-mandated reading tests was followed from third through fifth grades. Students who had received LE instruction in second grade performed at statistically significantly higher levels of proficiency on the third-grade test than students in the other half of the group. Continued higher achievement of the students who had received LE in second grade was documented in an analysis of the fifth-grade test.

Cardenas-Hagen and Garza believe this success can be recreated elsewhere, and they offer the following checklist of must-haves:

1. a strategic plan of action
2. data-based decision-making practices and procedures
3. multitiered, data-validated intervention programs
4. a strategic, professional development plan for increasing teacher knowledge and skill
5. support from business and community leaders
6. research within the district
7. a plan for working with English language learners and students with reading difficulties (SEEDS)
8. mentors and coaches as supports for the teaching community
9. fidelity in implementation of the science
10. public policy at the local, state, and national level to support reading reform
11. financial resources
12. a leadership sustainability plan for community systemic reform and sustainability
13. a belief that all students can and will learn to become proficient readers

The community of SEEDS students can learn to read despite economic and language barriers; 90/90/90 schools continue to prove this all over the country. Brownsville is a stellar example of how concerned citizens and a very determined mother took charge, and of how grassroots efforts within a community can create a movement and succeed. Furthermore, in 2008, the Brownsville school district was awarded the Broad Prize for Urban Education, which offers $1 million in scholarships, allowing students the opportunity to go to college. Brownsville was able to successfully reverse the trend of illiteracy within one generation, truly leaving no child behind. More impressive, Brownsville's successes drove many more efforts in both Texas and around the country to ensure that students received science-based literacy instruction.

The Tactical Plan

When seeking to bring about change and improvement, how far do we need to go? To whom do we need to talk? What do we need to ask for? When have we achieved victory? It is these questions that we hope to answer in this chapter.

As with everything in life, skillful planning is key in education reform, and these tactics will help you work through the education bureaucracy to make an impact. Following these steps helped in the quest to improve reading instruction in Texas and to move higher education law in Minnesota, dyslexia law in Texas, mandates on dyslexia awareness in Ohio, and much more. This is the basic plan:

1. Know the problem. As we said in chapter 3, you are seeking to solve the problem that too many kids in the state can't read well enough to comprehend their grade-level textbooks, read, write, speak, and think at grade level. How is this possible? Know the statistics and get the facts for your state.

2. Focus on the solution: A new literacy law for all students to become literate—no exceptions, no excuses; knowledge, skill, and supports for all teachers of reading—no excuses, no exceptions. This could be playfully called "research is your friend." Do your homework. Understand the issues. Who is for or against fixing the literacy problem? What are their positions? Why? Know the data. Be confident that the state has made a

big mistake in how kids are taught to read and how teachers of reading are prepared to teach. This is not the students' fault; this is not the teachers' fault; it is the system's fault. There is an opportunity to correct it, but first, you need the state's bureaucracy to admit the problem; to be willing to enact law that drives change, and to spend the money necessary to carry it out. This won't be easy.

3. Use the power of information to support your case. After you have consumed the available information and data, feed it to those who can make the decisions. This information is a powerful tool to support your request for literacy law. Data shouldn't sit on a shelf; it should be used, interpreted to inform and guide policy and practical decision-making. Data-validated practices and professional development, instruction, and assessment are imperative for student success. As an example in California, despite the "best" core language curriculum available and a bevy of "trained" teachers, California students were almost at the bottom of the pack when it came to reading scores after phonics-based professional development and curricula were eliminated. The several hundred 90/90/90 California schools using well-prepared teachers and reading programs that are evidence-based continue to outperform these schools. Their results should encourage a powerful incentive for California to enact new literacy policy.

4. Insist on moving toward enacting each component within the model literacy legislation. If you can't get all components, enact a portion and then keep going back for more. The Minnesota team did not accept "no." They kept right on going until they enacted law for preparing emerging reading teachers in the universities and colleges of education. There is always a way to keep the discussion going or to move this issue closer into the spotlight. Use retailing: focus your selling point on the law to help it move toward reality. This is also the time to identify your allies and supporters and work with organizations and individuals who can help with the grassroots. A lone voice won't carry the day. You need more than a stack of papers, advice, and facts. You need to identify and recruit supporters in and out of politics.

5. Overcome obstacles. Change isn't easy. But if you prepare for your opponents, the naysayers, and the protectors of the status quo, you can confront the obstacles and overcome them. Remember, that which is worth changing often isn't easy to change.

6. Push with all your might against all parties fighting the adoption of new literacy legislation. Ask them why they are against these important practices when student achievement facts are so stark. Keep your antennae tuned to both state and federal reports. When the NAEP examination is administered and reveals the same poor test scores year after year, you will have the ears of those making the decisions and possibly be able to convert a few opponents. When the Common Core State Standards can't be met, you and your team will be in demand, and the research papers, once ignored, will be requested and read. They will listen to your experts. And unanimously, they will ratify the legislation desperately needed for each student to succeed.

7. Tell a story about your state. As an example, let's think again about the $14 billion per year that California wastes on remedial college education. Let's drill down further to the largest school district in the state and the second largest in the United States, Los Angeles Unified School District (LAUSD). Now let's look at LAUSD's high-school graduation rate.

Figures Can't Lie

Here is the story, and data do not lie. Since state records are public domain, it isn't difficult to find interesting information about any district, such as how much LAUSD spends per year per student:

> Knowledge-bomb: LAUSD spends more than $30,000 a year per student in grades K-12. Think about that.

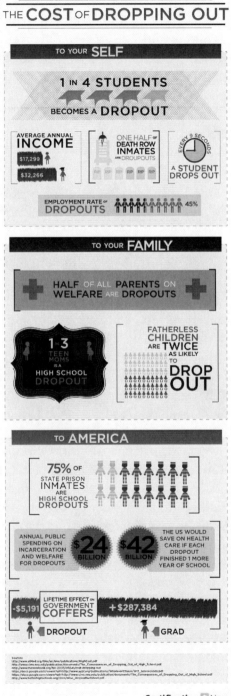

THE COST OF DROPPING OUT

TO YOUR SELF

1 IN 4 STUDENTS BECOMES A **DROPOUT**

AVERAGE ANNUAL **INCOME**
$17,299
$32,266

ONE HALF OF **DEATH ROW INMATES** ARE DROPOUTS

EVERY 9 SECONDS **A STUDENT DROPS OUT**

EMPLOYMENT RATE OF **DROPOUTS** 45%

TO YOUR FAMILY

HALF OF ALL **PARENTS** ON **WELFARE** ARE **DROPOUTS**

1 IN 3 TEEN MOMS IS A **HIGH SCHOOL DROPOUT**

FATHERLESS CHILDREN ARE **TWICE** AS LIKELY TO **DROP OUT**

TO AMERICA

75% OF STATE PRISON **INMATES** ARE HIGH SCHOOL **DROPOUTS**

ANNUAL PUBLIC SPENDING ON INCARCERATION AND WELFARE FOR DROPOUTS **$24 BILLION**

$42 BILLION THE US WOULD SAVE ON HEALTH CARE IF EACH DROPOUT FINISHED 1 MORE YEAR OF SCHOOL

LIFETIME EFFECT ON **GOVERNMENT COFFERS**
-$5,191 **DROPOUT**
+$287,384 **GRAD**

Sources:
http://www.all4ed.org/files/archive/publications/HighCost.pdf
http://www.nea.org/publication/docuemnts/The_Consequences_of_Dropping_Out_of_High_School.pdf
http://www.thenotebook.org/feb-2005/09564/strait-dropping-out
https://docs.google.com/viewer?url=http://www.aypf.org/publications/WhateverItTakes/WIT_InterimOdds.pdf
https://docs.google.com/viewer?url=http://www.cmu.nea.edu/publication/docuemnts/The_Consequences_of_Dropping_Out_of_High_School.pdf
http://www.betterhighschools.org/docs/tdrac_dropoutfactsheet.pdf

Certification Map
Teacher certification made simple

That is more money per student toward tuition than charged by the very best private elementary and secondary schools, and more in tuition than most colleges and universities. One would think that if a system is charging taxpayers $30,000 a year to educate each student, then the high-school graduation percentages should be off the charts. Wrong!

> Knowledge-bomb: The high-school graduation rate of LAUSD students is only 40.6 percent!

Yes, only four in ten students graduate with a high-school diploma. In other words, after spending $30,000 per student, per year, six out of every ten students will not graduate from high school. This also means that if a student in tenth grade drops out (six in ten kids), then it cost more than $330,000 for that student to drop out (grades K-10 cost for eleven years in school). I'm sorry, but this is criminal—someone should go to jail for harming these students for the rest of their lives, as well as for stealing taxpayers' hard-earned money!

Another good strategy to have in your pocket is combining the "national story" on the cost of our teenagers not graduating from high school with your state's story. We spoke of this previously, but it is good to address it again. According to the US Department of Education, the 1.23 million students who drop out of school, nationally each year, cost our country $319 billion in lost wages, taxes, and productivity over their lifetimes ($260,000 per student). We also established that LAUSD dropout-education costs are $330,000 per student (K-tenth grade). So if you add the losses together ($260,000 in lost wages, taxes, and productivity plus $330,000 in educational costs), it costs us $590,000 of taxpayers' dollars to produce a high-school dropout! Abandonment, malpractice, negligence, social injustice, inequity, discrimination—I don't care what we call it; it is immoral in my book.

These costs to society are showstoppers, but the story's real message is how much we are robbing our young people of opportunity, and what a burden we place on them psychologically and financially.

Like most things in life, these tactical plan steps seem much easier in theory than they are in practice. Getting folks to work together is not always easy, but once started, it can be overwhelmingly rewarding. You need to trust us here. Change can happen, and you can achieve it.

The economic tragedy is a powerful story to tell, as powerful as opportunity: the prison inmate who learns to read while incarcerated achieves a GED, works in the prison library, and moves back into society prepared for a job. Had this prisoner, the dropout, been afforded literacy skills and earned a high-school diploma, would he or she have been in prison to begin with?

In the next chapter, a friend and expert in this field, Dr. Richard Long, director of government relations for the International Reading Association, shares his experiences in moving legislation into a bill, securing the passage of law. Rich and I are colleagues working to enact the LEARN ACT with a team of alliance partners. The goal of LEARN is for the federal government to fund $2.35 billion to support states in implementing the components of the state literacy policy. Rich is a staunch supporter of reading teachers and the SEEDS community of children, working as the executive director for government relations for the National Title I Association. He is a unifier by nature, a great storyteller, and he is heavily involved in protecting students' rights to their education.

CHAPTER ELEVEN

NUTS AND BOLTS OF ENACTING LEGISLATION

By Richard Long, EdD

E VERY DAY, ALMOST fifty-four million children go to school. Some walk, some take the bus, some are driven. All arrive with a vast array of hopes, problems, challenges, assets, and potential, and as they move into their classrooms, they become part of a group. They are instructed as a group, yet it is as individuals that each one learns—this is especially the case when they are learning to read. Unfortunately, group reading instruction leaves many children behind. When the instruction is poor or based on outmoded thinking, the entire class suffers. Even when the instruction is effective for many children, others are lost. As has been stated earlier, strong legislation is needed in every state to maximize every child's potential to learn and succeed. In this chapter, we will explore how to create laws that will work to close the education gap, give teachers of reading the tools needed to be successful educators, and give every child the best chance to be well educated.

Form Your Idea

The first phase of an advocacy program, a call to action, is to develop an idea of what needs to be done; in this case, enacting a new state or local literacy law. With this goal in mind, finding a champion to push your bill through a legislature is important. Equally important is finding allies who will help your champion garner attention and win votes.

Your bill is critically important. The bill is the actual fix for the problem. It addresses a wrong that you want righted. What will make or break your advocacy program is whether or not the bill is appealing to more than a handful of people. When a problem is so highly defined that it is about just a very few people, it will be very hard to rally others to your cause. In your case, the problem is about kids and good literacy skills. Literacy failure needs to be defined so that others can develop a stake in the problem and become willing to help fix it. Clearly state your idea—literacy law so all kids read—or it won't attract any others to promote it. Your "fix" can also be stated like this: schools must use the best methods available to teach reading so that all children can learn. What makes your cause gather strength is that when others see their own children as having the same problem, it becomes personal. Clarifying this idea is important because it moves people from the problem to the solution.

In developing your idea for change into a proposed literacy law, be sure to research to find out how many children may be suffering with language problems and what happens to these children as a result. Seeking a legislative remedy may collapse when someone says, "Didn't we try to do something like this a few years ago?" or "Didn't we look into this a few years ago and find out that only a few people really have this problem?" Checking to see what data may be available in your state is critically important. How can you get this done?

First, an Internet search for your state is a good start. Second, find out if any literacy legislation has been introduced that has tried to deal with this problem, what was done as a result, and who were the organizers of the effort. Your members of Congress or their staff can help you locate the information. In addition, you can get help locally from teachers or administrators who will jump on your bandwagon because they want change too.

Find a Champion

Finding your politician, your champion, is more than just finding a friend who will listen and give advice. It means finding a state or local legislator and possibly a columnist who will take on the issue of literacy failure in public schools—the problem and the solution—as theirs. There are several ways to find a champion. One way is to meet with all the legislators who work on education in your state and see if there is any interest among the group. Another is to look into the backgrounds of all the legislators and see who has children or grandchildren in school. All parents, whether your next-door neighbors or members of Congress, want their children to do well in school and will get very frustrated when they aren't getting the information or help they need for them to be successful.

Now that the background information is in hand, ask the appropriate members for an appointment to meet with them. Do bring your personal story and information about your child/grandchild/friend's child—the problem, how many others it affects, and what needs to be done.

Sometimes a legislator is looking for an issue that will make him or her a leader in the eyes of his or her colleagues and the wider community, even if he or she doesn't have a personal stake in the issue. Often he or she needs a big issue for reelection. This is important, as rarely can a member of Congress be seen as the champion of too many causes, so he or she may "specialize" in some aspect of education and educational effects. Frequently, some of the best politicians are fairly new to the legislative arena and have served for only one or two terms, but they have learned that fellow legislators hold knowledgeable colleagues in high regard, and they want to build their reputations. Literacy is a great place for them to start.

> Finding a politician based on an idea that may be appealing to him or her requires a little work. You can find out which members have already taken up similar causes in education, reading, prisons, welfare, jobs, etc.

However, finding a champion isn't enough. You need to help your champion build allies, using your call to action. Sometimes the allies come before choosing the champion. To find allies, you need to talk to others—start with other parents and then talk to other community leaders and elected leaders. Don't be afraid to ask if they will help you. If they do not want to be your key leader or champion, they will say so. When this happens, the legislator might say, "I will help, but I have a lot of other things on my plate," and offer a different way of helping out. Ask if you can count on support for the bill if it comes up for a vote. Ask for advice about who in the legislative process is important for you to talk with. It is crucial to find out what the "natural" network is for your idea.

The Formal Process

In civics class, you may have learned how the government works. Unfortunately, since the 1960s, few states have required such courses. However, if you hope to influence legislation, you need to understand how the formal process operates and how to intervene in it. Voters elect representatives who vote in bodies—legislatures at the state level and councils at the city level. The sequence of steps is as follows: ideas are introduced in a bill, and then they are studied by a committee of the legislature, voted out of committee, and then voted on by one chamber (for example, the state's House, Assembly, or Senate) of a legislature. The next step is to work through the same sequence in the second chamber. After each chamber finishes a bill, the differences between the chambers then have to be resolved in what is called a conference committee. Finally, the bill is signed by the executive—the governor in a state or the president at the federal level. Simple.

One of the key links in this process is the agenda-setting role of the committee chairperson. The committee chairperson becomes the first filter in the formal legislative process. Once an idea is introduced and becomes a bill, the committee chairperson must decide if it will go forward. This decision is made based on the support the bill may have, as reflected by the members of the committee. You can help to get this crucial support by spending time briefing committee members to win their votes. This is done by setting up appointments and taking a copy of the draft legislation (www.LiterateNation.org), the literacy bill, with examples of how the problem affects the committee member's district, his or her constituents' schools, or any other information that will help connect the committee member to your issue. Remember—you can get support more easily if people are attracted to the issue.

Your goal is to have committee members cosponsor the legislation. This will send a signal to other members that there is strong support for the proposed literacy bill, because the more members who sign on as cosponsors, the more strength and importance the bill has. One of the keys to seeking support and cosponsorship is having members of both major political parties signed on as cosponsors. Having bipartisan cosponsors is one way of telling a committee chairperson that the literacy bill has the attention of the members.

Another way to get the chairperson's support is to ask for it directly. When a chairperson cosponsors a bill, this is a powerful sign that he or she is in favor of it. To do this effectively, you need to find the support of others in the chairperson's home district.

In summary, this is how a bill becomes a law:

1. Bill is introduced
2. Committee hearing
3. Floor action
4. Other chamber—bill introduced
5. Committee hearing
6. Floor action
7. Conference committee
8. Signed into law

The Informal Process

The informal process of taking an idea and making it a law includes all the elements of the formal process but with one addition— by mustering the energy, compassion, or attention of lawmakers at each level of government, you can kick the formal process into high gear. Sometimes the informal system pushes the formal system through compelling testimony by a parent at a committee hearing. Be ready to testify.

Members of the legislature are frequently captivated not only by information in a presentation but also by the pain with which parents talk about the needs of their children. This personal testimony that takes the issue to a human level makes a powerful impression and argument, as mentioned in the previous chapters, one that members will sometimes quote during formal consideration of a measure.

Visit Your Lawmaker's Office

Visits to a member's office also make a strong impression. Most legislators maintain offices in their home district and in the capital. To find out about them, check the website of your legislator or the online directory in the state government section. Call and ask for an appointment. Once the appointment is made, keep it, arrive on time, and bring information that is helpful to clarify your points on literacy failure in your/their schools. After saying hello, feel free to ask questions of your legislator with regard to his or her education knowledge (see chapter 7, "Actions of the Potentate," for messaging; and chapter 12, "Tricks of the Trade," for examples), then get quickly to the point and make it as clear as possible without making disparaging remarks. Engage them and let the facts speak for themselves and make them personal. After you have presented these facts, ask for questions and don't be surprised by the questions you get. Remember, you have been living with this issue, but the legislator may be just finding out about it. Always be polite, but ask for a commitment or for suggestions about what can be done.

Frequently, legislators will state that they will ask for clarification of the issue from the responsible governmental agency or individual, such as the state school board or state secretary of education. Since many children share the problem of learning to read, these agencies or individuals should play a role in proposing solutions. Ask for their thoughts.

Call Your Legislators into Action

Phone calls are another important tool for communicating with legislators, and the rules for communicating effectively hold here as well. Stay on task. Write down the points you want to make so you can follow them during the course of the conversation. You will be surprised that you can forget to ask for help or get caught up talking about some past hurt, or some person who has treated you badly, rather than staying focused on the problem at hand. Make sure you are polite and listen, but don't forget you are asking for their help.

Write and E-mail

You and your team may be unable to visit your legislator in person, but you can send a letter or an e-mail. Letters to members of a legislature need to hit several critical points. First, they need to be clear, state the problem (all children need to be taught to read), and make a request for action (we need a literacy law in our state). Don't send a letter with more than one issue in it. Don't threaten anyone. Threats rarely invite people to solve problems, and once you make a threat, any hope of discussion is over. Find the address of your legislator on the web or in a phone book. Address any elected official as "the Honorable" ("the Honorable Jill Smith," for example). Examples of letters are presented in chapter 11—"Tricks of the Trade." State who you are and why you are writing. Be specific as to what you want done—new state literacy law. Letters can also be a great way to communicate with more than one member of the legislature. They can provide individual lawmakers with background information about what the problem is and why your proposed solution makes sense. Don't hesitate to post on politicians' Facebook and Twitter accounts.

Letters to the Editor

Most political offices have staff members responsible for reviewing letters to the editor that appear in the lawmaker's hometown newspapers to get an advance warning of problems the constituents are facing. If you want to raise attention about your issue, consider writing a letter to the editor of your local paper that responds to an article that appeared very recently in the paper on a related topic such as education, illiteracy, high-school dropout rates, or prison populations. The letter should be brief and to the point, and either refute or agree with the points in the original article. Send your letter no more than two or three days after the original article, as it becomes old news after that time.

Don't Be Afraid to Compete

The legislative process is competitive. For every person who wants money spent one way, there are others who want it spent another way. And for each person who wants to change the status quo, there are others who want to keep things exactly as they are. Therefore, it is important to learn who may be opposed to literacy law and why.

The education field has a wide range of interest groups. Teachers, administrators, publishers, unions, politicians, and computer vendors all have their own special interests.

President Eisenhower had an interesting perspective on this. He never subscribed to the notion that those in opposition to his ideas were motivated by anything other than doing good. He avoided a lot of anger and focused on getting what he thought was the right thing done. He also did not give adversaries any fuel that could be used to complicate arguments to support his primary purpose. He talked about what needed to be done. You should do the same with literacy law.

But it's also important to understand the perspective of your opposition. For teachers, the change you want may add to the demands of their day, or they may not have access to the training or the textbooks to teach in a new way. They don't want to fail either. For administrators, a new requirement might mean that funds are going in a direction they can't control when they already have to cut back on spending. For others, it may mean that a book series they worked on for ten years could become outdated. While it is important to understand what the barriers are, it is not a reason to stop pushing for vital change in literacy attainment.

To be successful in advocating for literacy law for your child and others, you need to understand that the legislative process involves people. Just like you and your allies, the lawmakers had to start at the beginning to learn the process; and just like you, they are under many pressures. It is hard not to take every setback as a slap in the face, but the reality is that the process is designed to be complex. The reason for this is simple: our founding fathers did not want the government to pass laws too easily. They didn't trust government, so they wanted to make sure that it required a lot of agreement by many people to make a law. This is also why it is important to always be polite. You never know when the person saying no to you today might be able to help in a small way later on in the process—remembering you as polite, yet forceful, may pay off down the road.

First Steps

Several years ago, a mother begged her fourth-grade son's teacher, "Please, just teach him to read." The teacher didn't know what to do. The mother asked the principal of the school why her children and others were not learning to read. The principal said it was complicated. At that point, the mother went from pleading mother to advocate. This scene is played out in schools each day. Taking this step requires courage and conviction. It also requires persistence. It doesn't require lots of money, high-priced talent, or legions of movie stars standing in your corner. They are just tools. But you can use your voice and your determination to provide all children with the best possible education and enlist groups of other parents to help move mountains. Others have done so over the last thirty years, and the result has been federal laws that require all schools to provide a quality education in the Elementary and Secondary Education Act (ESEA); to allow children with disabilities to get a free, appropriate public education in the Education for All Handicapped Children Act (IDEA); and to help struggling parents of poor families gain special help through the Title I program. These parents took their problems and turned them into ideas, and they found and recruited champions and allies by writing letters and making visits. They told their stories and, in doing so, helped not only their own children but also millions of others. You can do the same for literacy in your state.

> When a parent is unable to achieve change in her child's school, she has two choices—to accept the limitations of the school and therefore sacrifice her child's future, or to seek a remedy elsewhere. And at this point, a parent steps into the role of state advocate. These are the folks you want on your team.

Just as women have redirected our medical research to address heart problems and breast cancer, and concerned parents have made a tremendous impact on drinking and driving laws, parents can also improve the reading education their children receive and, in doing so, help many others. If not parents, then who will speak for the children? Create your call to action, gather your allies, and get the job done. It will be worth it, and the next chapter guides you through it.

Excerpted from *The Power to Act: Transforming Literacy and Education*, by Cinthia Coletti Haan, and *Why Kids Can't Read: Challenging the Status Quo in Education*, edited by Phyllis Blaunstein and G. Reid Lyon

CHAPTER TWELVE

TRICKS OF THE TRADE

THIS CHAPTER WILL provide you with the tools and ingredients to embark upon your Call to Action. My colleagues and I have assembled key topics and the critical communication tools you will need. Here you will find sample communications and messaging, research, and statistics to use, as well as a script for engaging people in your grassroots movement.

One of the first "tricks of the trade" is current knowledge—know the buzz. Most states have signed onto the Standards, and schools are attempting to figure out what these Standards mean and how to attain them. Implementation of these Standards will make your call to action easier because these Standards, once viewed as superficial, are slowly becoming the mandate. What are these Standards (Common Core State Standards Initiative), and what do they mean?

The Standards set requirements not only for English language arts (ELA) but also for literacy in history, social studies, science, technology, and new-media subjects. The Standards are the culmination of an extended, broad-based effort to fulfill the charge issued by the states to create the next generation of K-12 standards in order to help ensure that all students are college and career-ready in literacy no later than the end of high school.[89]

---

89 "Introduction, Common Core State Standards," National Governors Association Center for Best Practices and the Council of Chief State School Officers, accessed September 12, 2011, http://www.corestandards.org/assets/CCSSI_ELA%20Standards.pdf.

Essentially, the Standards are stringent requirements to put American education back on track to compete with other countries for jobs by creating the human capital necessary to generate gross domestic product (GDP), which is needed to maintain our freedoms and quality of life. However, the elephant in the room is that the Standards' requirements are not likely to be achieved if students have not been taught to read in early elementary school. This muddy fact may be your ticket to fast-track literacy law.

Where Is the Leverage?

Before you can hope to persuade politicians or business and community leaders to take up your cause and join the movement, you must know who these people are and what they do—specifically, what they can do for you.

1. Learn about your state infrastructure and affiliation. Become knowledgeable about the structure and functions of your state legislature, and use this knowledge to find your champion for legislative action. Establish relationships with staff members who will take the time to inform you of the inner workings of your state government. Through your own research and in collaboration with others, determine what affiliations exist, what politics are at play, what laws affecting education have been passed, and who the key players are in lawmaking. When considering leadership party affiliation, ask yourself: Is there a mix of political persuasions? What are the politics at play? And consider the games and favors to make sure you are not simply working toward someone else's agenda. Maintain focus on your agenda—all students literate and educated. Find out the players, infrastructure, and key initiatives your state school board association and state teacher unions comprise. Is there a board of education or a board of teachers? Is your education/legislation leader, or are any of his or her family members

> From the governor to state senators and representatives or assemblymen, top mayors and chief state school officers, a great number of state officials have both the power and the interest to advance your cause, if you are willing to reach out to them.

experienced in working with SEEDS students, or do they indeed have any knowledge of this student demographic? Are they familiar with effective evidence- and science-based reading instruction?

2. Understand state and national educational agendas. On the small scale of your community or school district, there are issues around third-grade reading standards or scores, school and teacher accountability, and school choice. On a larger scale, at the state and federal level, there are education voucher programs, state and large urban literacy plans, Race to the Top activities, Multi-Tier System of Supports (MTSS), third-grade retention laws, parent trigger laws, and specific learning disability rules and laws to consider.

3. Know how other community organizations and leaders fit in. If you are starting small, working with school psychologists or local adult literacy providers, consider going to the state level for help from the reading association, school board association, principals' organization, superintendents' organization, teachers' union, and speech pathologists, all valuable and diverse human resources. Other places to look for support are minority groups (caucuses, the Urban League, Hispanic organizations), business groups such as metropolitan commerce/coalitions, university research centers outside of the school of education, and foundations with a focus on education. All of these organizations and their leaders approach the issues of literacy, education, and career-readiness in different ways, offering you unique perspectives on both the problem and its solutions.

4. Know the structure and reporting chain of the State Department of Education:

   1. teaching and/or reading specialists
   2. special-education teachers
   3. Title I teachers
   4. ELL teachers
   5. school psychologists
   6. speech and language pathologists
   7. licensure/credentialing requirements
   8. K-3 teachers of reading

9. Grades 4-12 content-area teachers of English language arts and other subjects
10. Department of Education (DOE) staff
11. Institutes of higher education (IHE), Colleges of Education teacher preparation programs
12. private and LD Schools with trained professionals and teachers
13. children dyslexia centers (Masons, Scottish Rite) and cultural centers
14. individual and program certification: AOGPE, ALTA, IMSLEC, Wilson, Lindamood Bell, and other centers

Understand that education is an industry with numerous stakeholders. Study the chart below so you can better understand the interdependencies and complexities of the system.

5. Learn about what bills are proceeding in your state with literacy and SEEDS legislation.

Each state has an online website or resource to track current legislation and bills. Your state team should first search "literacy legislation" on these sites. One thing you can't afford to do is silo your efforts into smaller student demographics. Remember the importance of "equity."

Once you discover the legislation under consideration, search for the bill's authors. Next, research these legislators/authors. They have a passion for literacy and/or for our SEEDS community of students. These legislators can become your champions. Go a step further and research the coauthors of the bills, identify the communities they are on, and then target (1) the most powerful leaders on their committees to become your champion(s) and (2) the legislator whose bill most closely matches your team's mission (e.g., K-3 teachers of reading certifications, universal screening, multitier supports in general-education classrooms, early childhood education). Drill as deep as you can.

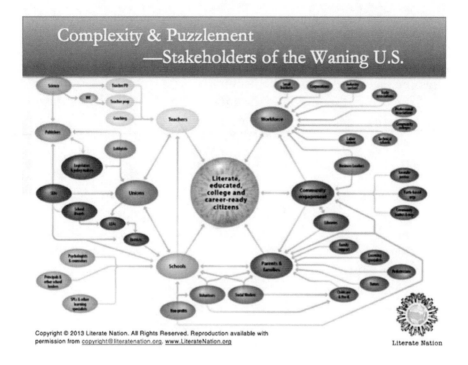

Complexity & Puzzlement
—Stakeholders of the Waning U.S.

Ask Questions and Build Political Relationships

Listen First:

It is important to know as much as possible about your local politicians before you meet with them. But don't be so busy learning that you don't get to the "doing." As Stephen Smith adeptly states in his book, *Stoking the Fire of Democracy*, "Instead of wondering what may persuade our [political] targets, we summoned the courage to ask them." So ask them:

1. What is your top priority and why it is important to you?
2. What legislation are you most proud of enacting?
3. What are your feelings about the state of education?

Listen intently. Legislators who are passionate about literacy, education, and closing the education gap will help you best understand their points of reference and will work with you to develop a dialogue on which you can build a deeper understanding and trust.

Listening will also prevent you from making the often-fatal mistake of a one-way feed of information. After initial conversations, you can move into a series of more personal questions before you present your ideas and facts, and request their support.

After you listen, focus groups have found the following conversational questions are powerful in engaging politicians and personalizing the literacy and SEEDS community of students' issues:

1. "Do you remember how your children (or grandchildren) learned to read? Have you ever known a young child who did not want to learn to read?" These questions summon the imagery of their children or grandchildren taking those necessary first big steps—steps that took work, steps that are not natural, steps that needed to be taught. And of course, all kids want to read and succeed in school. Remember to say that we fail to teach children to read; they don't fail us.

2. "Can you share with me what happens to the neighborhood students that drop out of high school, unable to read their textbooks, unable to pass their classes, with no ability to get a job?" Yes, they know the answer: characteristically, the recourse for these students is social services, crime, or both.

3. You can also ask curious questions for which they may not know the answers: "Did you know that only X percent of our state's kids read at grade level in the eighth grade? What do you think will happen to these local students who can't read at grade level? If these statistics continue and they drop out of high school, what will happen to our state's gross state product (GSP)?" Use the NAEP eighth-grade reading score for your state. Trust me, the scores won't be high and should instigate compelling recognition for why you are meeting with them. Small, concrete numbers can be very effective. For example, "Only three out of ten students in our state can read proficiently!"

4. And the last and most important question is "As our state representative, can you allow this crisis to continue for another day unchallenged?" At this point, they can identify with the problem and recognize that they can't allow it to continue. Next, they will want a solution.

These questions allow you to engage in conversation and gain your legislator's agreement that the literacy problem is serious and cannot continue. You have not come empty-handed but with solutions: politely ask them to help solve the problem by championing state literacy law . . . Ask for their commitment to adopt the issue of literacy failure as their own. Ask if they will work to get the issue on the next agenda, move the bill through the committee and make every effort to see that the bill is enacted into literacy law.

Once you have had your first meeting, feel proud. Recap the meeting with your team and get their feedback. Talk to them about how it felt to be in the room with your state assemblyman or woman. Share the answers given to your questions. Talk about what went well and what needs more work. Fine-tune your presentation after each and every meeting. Then prepare your next steps: follow-up letters, phone calls, e-mails, requests. Twitter and Facebook your meeting, ask your team to retweet you, send your legislator a tweet @GovJaneDoe asking for a response, and schedule your next series of meetings. Blog, e-mail, and listserv this information to everyone you can in the state. Get others to do the same. Our state representatives, I am assured, pay close attention to the "social voices" of their constituents. When you can get hundreds of "networkers" tweeting away, things happen very quickly. (For tweeting lessons, see chapter 8.)

Mastering the Art of Dialogue

Know the facts and ask engaging questions to turn the tide in your direction. A one-way feed seldom produces agreement. Use questions to get all parties involved, thinking, and responding. Whether meeting with legislators or their aids or with local school board members, with members of interested organizations, you will learn much by listening to their views. In such meetings, stick with the facts, make them as personal as possible, and use "sculpted language" that challenges the status quo. In all you do, remember it is about the children, about our future—a simple, unselfish goal.

Focus groups responded enthusiastically and positively on the following five statements and questions designed to lead to healthy dialogue. They found them thought provoking, and they could relate personally to the statistics because they elicited feelings, emphasized equality, used imagery, and played the "American card." You can arm yourself and your teams with this scripted dialogue. Practice will ensure you don't rush the process or end up just winging it.

This dialogue brings to mind children in his or her neighborhood—it makes the issue personal, shows inequality, and has good imagery.

YOUR STATEMENT: "The statistics show only three out of every ten of America's eighth-grade public-school students meet the NAEP standard of reading proficiency" (NCES, 2011).[90]

YOUR QUESTION: "If this is true, and I believe it is, what do you think it means for 70 percent of my neighborhood kids that I see walking to school each day?" Wait for the answer, then ask: "What do you think the future for these children looks like?" and "What does it mean for our country?"

This dialogue projects good vivid imagery of inequality, social failure, and sadness about feeling left behind in today's tech-driven society.

YOUR STATEMENT: "The statistics show an incomprehensible forty-two million Americans cannot read, write, or perform simple math. Another fifty million Americans cannot read past the fourth-grade level" (National Right to Read Foundation).[91]

YOUR QUESTION: "How do you think people support themselves and their families if they are functionally illiterate, unable to participate in modern society?" Wait for the answer, then ask: "Do you think it is more difficult to be functionally illiterate in today's advancing twenty-first century than in the past century?"

---

[90]   National Center for Educational Statistics, accessed, June 2012, http://nces.ed.gov.

[91]   National Right to Read Foundation, accessed January 2013, http://www.nrrf.org.

This dialogue inspires a sense of urgency while again stressing the inequality of the situation.

YOUR STATEMENT: "The statistics show about two in three prison inmates are high-school dropouts, and one in three were also juvenile offenders that read well below the fourth-grade level."[92]

YOUR QUESTION: "Did you know the local high-school district is only graduating X percent of my hometown kids?" Wait for the acknowledgement, then ask: "What will these kids do? Go on social services? Turn to crime? What do you think?"

This dialogue poses good imagery, gives a sense of the personal, establishes the need for equality, and calls for the politician to assume responsibility and take action.

YOUR STATEMENT: The statistics show "30 percent of all public school students do not graduate from high school"[93] and that "more than three out of four people on welfare are illiterate."[94]

YOUR QUESTION: "Can you tell me how we are going to support almost twenty million of our fifty-four million public-school children who will not graduate from high school?" Wait for the answer, then ask: "Does it astonish you?" Wait . . . "What does it mean—higher taxes, more prisons, drug cartels?" Wait . . . "What is your plan?"

---

[92] National Center for Educational Statistics, *Trends in High School Dropout and Completion Rates in the United States: 1972–2008* (Washington DC: 2008).

[93] National Center for Educational Statistics, accessed January 2012, http://nces.ed.gov.

[94] The Washington Literacy Council's research shows that more than three out of four of those on welfare, 85 percent of unwed mothers, and 68 percent of those arrested, are illiterate; three in five of America's prison inmates are illiterate (accessed June 2013, http://washingtonliteracycenter.org).

Amplify Researched Realities

This section provides reading research on third-grade literacy failure and its correlation to high-school dropout rates. Memorize these facts, if possible, or at least have them handy if you get nervous and are asked a question. Our goal is to have all incoming fourth-grade students reading literate so they can begin to learn subject or content material. Another way to think about it: kids must first learn to read, then read to learn! Numerous studies speak to the fact that grade-level reading proficiency by third grade is compulsory for educational attainment through postsecondary schooling.

During your meetings, continue to highlight for your legislators and grassroots teams that literacy is *vital*, and the earlier the better. But it is never too late for any student to become reading literate. Ultimately, share with your champion(s) that we know this requires a process of retraining, retooling, testing, certifying, and supporting our teachers of reading, reading specialists, and content-area teachers so they can best serve the diverse needs of their students. Support your goal by saying:

> This responsibility is made most clear when we focus on the correlation of third-grade reading skills and students who drop out of high school. Much of what these studies show is that future teen drug use and violence in high school points to the fact that these students are frustrated because they seriously struggle with reading and, thus, passing their classes. Psychologically they feel academically helpless. We are robbing them of their futures if we don't teach them to be reading literate.

Insist upon certified and qualified teachers of reading in every classroom. Every kindergarten to third-grade classroom teacher, school specialist in reading, English language learners (ELL), Title I, and special-education teacher in grades 4 through 12 must be certified as a teacher of reading, able to teach diverse student populations. In addition, all content-area teachers must pass a basic reading instruction competence examination so they are prepared for the requirements of literacy in the Standards.

CINTHIA COLETTI

The focus groups working for the development of this book found the two questions below and the associated research were powerful in getting citizens and parents to take action and to achieve community cohesiveness:

QUESTION 1: Is your child (grandchild) reading well?" "Did you know that students reading below the proficient range in third grade are not likely to graduate from high school?"

FACT: Students reading below or chronically below the proficient range in third grade are not likely to graduate from high school.

The research shows that a child's reading proficiency by third grade has a direct correlation to his or her success in high school and beyond. Effectively, reading does matter by the end of third grade, and there is a strong link between third-grade reading skill and high-school dropout rates.[95]

QUESTION 2: Do you know why reading is so important to your child's education?"

FACT: Research shows that if a child is reading poorly at the end of first grade, chances are high that he or she will read poorly at the end of fourth grade, and further, if he or she is still reading poorly in ninth grade, there is a high probability that he or she will drop out of high school.

Eighty-eight percent of youngsters who read poorly at the end of the first grade read poorly at the end of the fourth grade as well. Those students who have not caught up by nine years of age carry

---

[95] Christopher B. Swanson, *Cities in Crisis: A Special Analytic Report on High School Graduation* (2008); Anderson, Hiebert, Scott, and Wilkinson, *Becoming a Nation of Readers: The Report of the Commission on Reading* (1985); Francis, Shaywitz, Stuebing, Shaywitz, and Fletcher, "Developmental Lag versus Deficit Models of Early Reading Disability: A Longitudinal, Individual Growth Curves Analysis," *Journal of Educational Psychology* 88 (1996).

their limited reading skills into adulthood. Those students who have not learned to read by the ninth grade typically drop out of school at significantly higher rates than their classmates who read proficiently.[96]

Letters, Letters, Inspirational Letters

Dr. Long, in the previous chapter, referred to several ways you can call for action, starting with collecting all the information available about your legislators and other movers and shakers. He also referred to the power of the pen. You may be surprised that a well-thought-out letter is still one of the most effective methods we have at our disposal to influence politics—yes, even in the twenty-first century! Two politicians I know fly back and forth to Washington, DC, almost every week. They differ in age, gender, and political affiliation. Each shared with me that, without fail, they read letters sent from their constituents on these long plane rides. Many of us today use e-mail to communicate; however, do not underestimate the power of a signed letter from a constituent. If e-mail is easier, attach the letter to the e-mail as a document file.

The thing to remember when writing a letter is to keep it simple, personal, direct, and polite—one page, if possible. Let your politician know right away why you are writing—the problem—and who you are (include that you are a voter in his or her district, as well as your credentials and follow-up address). Provide factual details. If a legislative bill is involved, cite the correct title or number. Close your letter by asking for specific action on the legislator's part (for example, "I urge you to support state literacy law in our state.").

Discover the protocol for addressing your letters to members of your state legislative body. This information is readily available on the state's website. It is important to address the letter correctly: The Honorable [insert first and last name]. Make sure you specifically

---

[96] Alliance for Excellent Education, "The High Cost of School Dropouts" (2008); Evers, *What's Gone Wrong in America's Classrooms* (California: Hoover Institution Press); J. M. Fletcher and G. R. Lyon, "Reading: A Research-Based Approach" (1998); Snow, Burns, and Griffin, *Preventing Reading Difficulties in Young Children* (Washington DC: National Academy Press, 1998).

address the correct body of the legislature (for example, State Assembly or State Legislature) and use the correct salutation for your state representative depending on the office held (Dear Assemblyman [insert last name]. Other examples include Congresswoman, Senator, and Representative).

E-mail or Letters to a Legislator

December 23, 2013

The Honorable Trisha Gates
Nevada State Assembly
State Capitol, Room 401
Carson City, NV 89701

Dear Assemblywoman Gates,

I am writing to ask for your support to end literacy failure in our classrooms. As a citizen, I feel strongly that our schools should, at the very least, teach all students to be literate citizens—able to read and write with clarity. Recently, the newspaper reported that my school district is graduating only 60 percent of its high school students. This means that 40 percent of these students are dropping out of high school into our community with little or no opportunity for their future. I have learned that a leading cause of these children dropping out of school is their inability to read grade-level textbooks or write coherently, without which skills they cannot pass their classes. This has me worried for them, my family, my neighborhood, my town, and our state. We really can't allow this to happen, and we need your help and leadership to make a dramatic change to fix this problem.

I am a family man, a Nevada citizen, and a small business owner. Two of my three children are having a hard time reading and writing and are falling behind in their other subjects. So many others in their schools are suffering with the same problem. Based on the statistics, my wife and I are afraid they and hundreds of other students may drop out of school. We need your help.

I am writing to request that you do everything in your power to fix this literacy problem so our kids are capable of participating in the demanding 21st century workforce, so they can seize opportunities and follow their dreams. I have learned that there is a potential new Nevada law on literacy that will fix this problem. Please do all you can to pass this law for my children and our community's children.

Thank you for your consideration,

John McInerney Garcia
2401 Top Valley Road
Reno, NV 89503
JMG@gmail.com
(702) 555-3172

Letter to the Editor

Even in this day of digital communication explosion, don't underestimate the power of your local papers. Letters to the editor are best e-mailed but can also be mailed. Keep them to the point and be witty and succinct. As Dr. Long has already advised, it is best if you are responding to an article in the paper or magazine that involves education. If so, mention the article right away. Focus on your message by confining yourself to no more than two or three paragraphs. First, introduce your problem (literacy failure/high-school dropouts) and your objective (all students literate—first/new state literacy law). Support your view. Include your name, address, affiliation(s), e-mail address, and phone number so the publication can contact you to verify your authorship of the letter. You may ask that your information be withheld from publication.

Note: Please see chapter 13 for a more detailed and explanative letter to state lawmakers.

Dear Dayton Daily News:

Today's article in your paper, "Finding Qualified Employees," got my heart racing. How in the world can our schools graduate students who can't read, write, or spell? I recently traveled to Japan to stay with friends. Did you know that the majority of Japanese students graduate from college and become productive citizens, earning a paycheck and paying taxes? Do you think this is happening in the United States?

America is losing its grip competing with foreign countries, and in a few more generations may not be able to compete in the world's economy. If, according to the Organization for Economic and Cooperation Development (OECD), American fifteen-year-olds finished fifteenth out of twenty-one developed countries in literacy, it won't take too long before we reach the bottom. Then what?

I have heard that many states are enacting literacy laws that require teachers of reading to have deep knowledge and skill and learn the best methods of differentiated instruction to ensure all students learn to read, write, spell, and think critically about what they are reading. As so many other states are out-producing Ohio in literacy, maybe it is time for your paper to raise public awareness and make a push to enact new state literacy law for Ohio. This way we can graduate students who are able to enter the workforce and raise families without going on welfare.

Yours truly, wanting the best for our state and country,

Frank G. Morgan
Retired Naval Officer
2509 Seminary Drive
Akron, OH 44301
Email: oldcutter@aol.com
Phone: 330-572-8878

If you have already established a grassroots team and are embarking upon a movement, use everyone's signature on the letters. Include home cities and places of employment if possible. Also, use the "Informational" one-page document, for which a template can be found at *www.LiterateNation.org*, that outlines the nine major components of the literacy law and provides areas for you to customize state facts that surround functional illiteracy: state dropout rates, prison population, NAEP student scores, college remedial class costs, etc. This will become a tool that you use in all settings as your "leave behind" or "send ahead" document of information for people to consider.

Script to Gather the Flock

When you recruit folks to join your efforts, all the components of the part 2 of this book come into play. Being honest and transparent is always best. You are passionate about this cause for all the right reasons, making it easy to be direct, trustworthy, and forthright in your expression of your mission. Focus groups from across the country confirm the power of equality, imagery, and personal stories. You will be most effective if you present the problem not as a complaint about the system, but rather as the results-driven solution. The appreciation that action can solve the problem will motivate your colleagues and friends into working with you to end the status quo of a failing education system. Here is a sample script that has been used in telephone solicitations and town hall meetings.

These "Tricks of the Trade" may seem a bit cumbersome at this reading. It takes practice to thoroughly incorporate stories, imagery, equity, and ideas about humanizing the literacy problems while highlighting social reliance and social justice into your own sound bites. Know that the work is worth it—even the presidents of the United States practice and rehearse, over and over again, with professional teams in order to sway public opinion. It may be heartening to know that state grassroots teams all over the country are using these tools, and they are realizing milestones each day for the children. Read this several times and visit *www.LiterateNation.org* for more tools and templates to assist you to reach your goals.

Hello_____,

I want to talk to you about the reading crisis in our school. Did you know that more than 70 percent of our eighth-grade students can't read their textbooks with understanding?

We've embarked on a grassroots effort across the state to tackle this problem, this year. We've talked to teachers, principals, parents, children, and community and business leaders. In short, we have done our homework and have a plan to fix the problem of our kids not learning to read in our schools. This plan can have impact, starting in year one. What we are doing to our kids' future is immoral:

- Without the ability to read, our students drop out of high school and have nowhere to turn but crime, prison, drugs, and social dependency. We can change this, year one.
- We need genuine accountability so that every tax dollar goes to educate students, not support bureaucracies that are robbing our kids of a future through illiteracy. We can change this, year one.
- With a new state literacy law for our school, we can ensure that all kids learn to read and write. We can make it happen this year.

We don't need your money. But we need your commitment and a few minutes of your time.

Imagine how proud you will be, knowing that your grandkids and all the kids in your neighborhood can read well and excel in school and in life.

Imagine how proud you will be when schools across this state turn out kids who are taught to read and think critically, ready for college, ready for a career, ready for the challenges and opportunities of life in the twenty-first century.

Imagine how proud you will be when America once again has the best and brightest students because they can read and learn—and our country will not be listed more than halfway down the pack of developed countries in literacy and math.

You don't have to imagine; you can make it happen.

It is no secret that reading is the foundation for all of education, without which there is no education. New literacy law can fix this. Science has proven that we can teach all students to read; we know how, but we don't do it because we don't have to. Reading can make the difference between going to college and going to jail.

Just a few hours of your time can make a difference. Go to our website and sign up. Join the effort to ensure that all children learn to read.

We can't be silent and sit on the sidelines while this crisis threatens to take down our country. If you don't help, who will?

Will you join us?

Friends, as you go forward, it is wise to always explain that for any population of people in any country, literacy is not innate. To become fully literate, every person must receive foundational reading and writing instruction, speaking, listening, and language instruction for a range of subject areas. This affords the literate citizens of any country the opportunity to flourish and participate in society and to be capable of both critical analysis and reflective thinking across a wide range of areas necessary for the good of their society.

This is the final chapter of your Toolbox. In part 3, I will outline literacy science and the most comprehensive model of best practices and policies that has ever come before. I will also share my personal reflections along this journey that now we share together.

PART THREE

LITERACY SCIENCE

Providing Technical Recommendations and
Blueprint on Literacy Policy and Practices

Today's world demands a shift in the culture of the classroom, beginning in grade 4 to allow ready access to information via technology and limits the value of memorization. Students need to use information to sort, analyze, and critique it, make and defend arguments, solve problems, and incubate ideas. Students must learn to interact: to communicate and collaborate effectively for success in a rapidly changing world.

A unifying theme in literacy, science, and math, grades 4 through 8 is the need for a fundamental shift in the culture of the classroom where students do more of the thinking, sense-making, and explaining, and teachers do more listening, rephrasing, and advancing thought in subject areas. As in the workforce, students must be more active in their own learning and the learning of their classmates. Although teachers may appear to be doing less lecturing when students do more of the talking, they must actually work with greater expertise and nimbleness to accomplish learning outcomes.

Data collection via technology allows for efficient, routine collection of student thinking so that teachers can quickly understand which students are on a productive track and which are not, expanding the potential to engage in continuous improvement in student evaluation, curriculum assessment, and teacher collaboration.

Strategic Education Research Partnership
www.SERPinstitute.org
2013

To see how to improve student outcomes dramatically, go to: www.SERPInstitute.org

Important note: The methodical learning revealed in the lauded SERP middle school work cannot happen if students are not reading at grade level by third grade.

CHAPTER THIRTEEN

READING LITERACY BLUEPRINT
Advocates and Policy Makers

I N THIS CHAPTER and the appendices following, you will find a blueprint for action and policy. This will guide you step-by-step to reach fellow stakeholders and influence those in positions of power who can drive the changes we must bring to bear for our nation and our children.

On the Effort to Inform School District Leaders about Decisions Affecting the Future of Education—

The four key challenges identified in the report that all school district leaders need to face include (1) graduating all students college and career ready; (2) managing shrinking budgets; (3) training and supporting teachers; and (4) dealing with the growing technology needs of society and individual students, especially low-income students and students of color who are most at-risk of being left behind. By employing effective educational strategies that link and improve the "three Ts"—teaching, technology, and use of time—district leaders can create the conditions for whole-school reform and effective instruction, the report finds.

Alliance for Excellent Education
Report to Inform Education Leadership Challenges
11/15/2012

Transparency, Ingredients, and Results

As we venture into the technical and methodological recommendations that follow, it is important to point out that working toward and achieving the goals we need is a dynamic process and that it is a process that will continue to evolve as science builds more evidence to identify and support best instructional practices.

The blueprint for literacy is the result of a unique experiment that synthesized and curated more than four hundred research studies in the fields of

- reading, literacy, language and writing;
- teacher knowledge, skill, preparation, and professional development;
- leadership, compliance, and school administration;
- implementation and sustainability of practices;
- data systems, assessments, and screening;
- high-school dropout prevention;
- learning disabilities and dyslexia identification and instruction;
- Multi-Tier System of Supports in general education;
- early childhood and emergent literacy;
- elementary, middle, and high-school literacy; and
- institutes of higher education practices.

These culminate in a complete operational system designed to produce a positive seismic shift in our student literacy outcomes. The blueprint is intended to guide and advise all those who care about the state of literacy in America—parents, teachers, advocates, school boards, communities, businesses, policy makers. Employing this system will produce the educational changes that student success demands.

Literacy science betters the odds for our nation and for our children, and this blueprint embraces a bottom-up/top-down theory of change. It is a project designed and best implemented in whole and at the state level. However, you will discover that nine out of ten sections are self-organized and can be implemented as a subset in distinct settings.

Throughout this book, we have learned that "text" has become exponentially demanding in the twenty-first century's "wired" world, and so shall students' literacy skills and educators' teaching skills. Increasingly, full participation in society and opportunities for personal success demand dual-literacy competence—the ability to find and digest relevant information quickly *and* the ability to read critically and deeply for knowledge and understanding. The analysis of student achievement trends in this book indicates that these competencies depend on our schools, administrators, and teachers advancing with the times.

We have learned about the urgent need to accelerate teachers' pedagogical skills for working with a diverse student population; science confirms that highly skilled and knowledgeable teachers in grades kindergarten through third is a key to later student success. We have also learned the importance of assisting content-area teachers in defining a new identity for themselves—as language teachers in their discipline.

Premise

Our education policies, although well intended, have not been rigorously validated. Thus, we find ourselves in a crisis affecting each of us regardless of our personal level of education and social status. Identifying a common purpose is a critical first step. Next is mobilizing leaders and grassroots workers who can work together in supporting a state literacy initiative.

If your state acts now, everyone wins. Failure to enact perpetuates a system in which large numbers of students are condemned to failure.

The literacy blueprint that follows is your power tool for education transformation. To begin the process below, you will find:

1. A pocket guide for policy makers, their legislative committees, news and media groups, and community organizations. Quickly setting the stage, it cites compelling facts that address the issue of literacy failure head-on and can be tailored to statistics of your state. Please remember the "tricks of the trade" in chapter 11, and when you present the model legislation, weave the elements described there into your presentation.
2. A technical reference outline and the nine sections for literacy overhaul, designed to quickly apprise policy makers, educators, and, you, the advocates.
3. Appendices with complete methodology in each section to include an executive summary, a framework of key components of the science, a road map of procedural specifics, and model state legislative language.

> Today's generation is the least skilled, least educated, and most likely to become the least productive generation of our time.
>
> —Cinthia Coletti (Haan)
> Leveraging Literacy Legislation Conference
> Chicago, 2011

Policy Makers' Pocket Guide

To: State policy makers
Subject: The problem of inadequate literacy plagues the United States

Over the past several decades, the Nation's Report Card, National Assessment of Educational Progress, has shown little or no growth in students' reading and writing. [97]

Sixty-seven percent of our students are reading below grade-level proficiency, thus lacking the fundamental skill required for full participation in twenty-first-century society.

At the secondary level, the inability to read and comprehend complex text predicts that students may not graduate from high school and are unlikely to succeed in college. Not only the less advantaged—including racial and language minorities, students with learning differences, and those living in poverty—but also the great middle class appears stuck with mediocre achievement levels that compare unfavorably to the requirements of literacy in the labor market and modern society. This is a primary reason that within one generation, the United States has fallen in international rankings from first place to ninth place in the proportion of young people with college degrees. [98]

This is why we have taken an enormous amount of time, research, and energy to write to you with a plea for literacy and to support policy changes, which can be found in the appendices of this book.

---

[97] National Assessment of Educational Progress, *The Nation's Report Card* (Washington DC: 2011), http://nationsreportcard.gov/reading_2011/.

[98] Organisation for Economic Co-operation and Development, Program for International Student Assessment, accessed October 6, 2013, http://www.oecd.org/pisa/.

Education in the United States is entering a dangerous period in which a serious achievement gap is affecting more than half of our students. In dangerous times, there is no sin greater than inaction.

Scholars across the globe have found a direct correlation between literacy and levels of wealth, health, poverty, and general quality of life. Americans shall confront and reverse the downward spiral that is affecting all of us. State by state, we can outpace global competitors by investing in high-quality teachers, high-quality instruction, high-quality data systems, and the supportive contexts that will enable learning to take place. Legislators can take the reins and implement state literacy laws that are likely to increase the number of students who can achieve the Common Core State Standards and be prepared for college or career. It is time for all of us to drive policy that ensures the United States will lead the literate nations.[99]

We have attached for your inspection detailed information regarding the seriousness of our literacy problem and its effect on our productivity. We also provided evidence to support our call for enacting the literacy policy and the Common Core Standards as important steps in addressing this problem.

Birth to Career in a Literate Nation
Preparing our children for their future

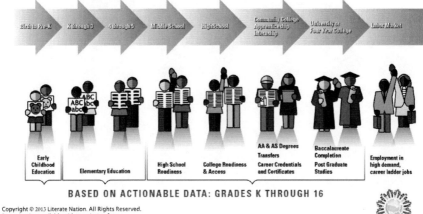

BASED ON ACTIONABLE DATA: GRADES K THROUGH 16

---

[99] Frank Luntz, *Words That Work: It's Not What You Say, It's What People Hear* (New York: Hyperion, 2007).

Facts and Knowledge that You and Every Policy Maker Need to Lead

In 2000, the Organisation for Economic Co-operation and Development (OECD) first implemented the Program for International Student Assessment (PISA). PISA tests fifteen-year-old students in three literacy domains: reading literacy, math literacy, and science literacy. The United States government considers PISA one of the most comprehensive measures available. Every three years, the test is produced and aims to measure student skills near the end of secondary school. [100] The 2012 study should stir concern for our future competitiveness: our students ranked in the bottom tier of the thirty-four OECD countries: thirty-second in math literacy, twenty-third in science literacy, and seventeenth in reading literacy. Our students scored behind their peers in Korea, Poland, and New Zealand. Worse, students from seventeen of these countries outperformed US students so drastically that the difference reached statistical significance.

---

[100] Organisation for Economic Co-operation and Development, Program for International Student Assessment, *PISA 2012 Results: What Students Know and Can Do* (Paris: 2012), accessed October 6, 2013, http://www.oecd.org/pisa/pisaproducts/48852548.pdf.

CINTHIA COLETTI

PISA — Program for International Student Assessment: 2009 Survey Results

READING

SHANGHAI, CHINA	556
SOUTH KOREA	539
FINLAND	536
HONG KONG, CHINA	533
SINGAPORE	526
CANADA	524
NEW ZEALAND	521
JAPAN	520
AUSTRALIA	515
NETHERLANDS	508
BELGIUM	506
NORWAY	503
ESTONIA	501
SWITZERLAND	501
POLAND	500
ICELAND	500
UNITED STATES	500
LICHTENSTEIN	499
SWEDEN	497
GERMANY	497
IRELAND	496
FRANCE	496
TAIWAN	495
DENMARK	495
UNITED KINGDOM	494
HUNGARY	494
PISA Average	493
PORTUGAL	489
MACAO, CHINA	487
ITALY	486
LATVIA	484

SCIENCES

SHANGHAI, CHINA	575
FINLAND	554
HONG KONG, CHINA	549
SINGAPORE	542
JAPAN	539
SOUTH KOREA	538
NEW ZEALAND	532
CANADA	529
ESTONIA	528
AUSTRALIA	527
NETHERLANDS	522
LICHTENSTEIN	520
GERMANY	520
TAIWAN	520
SWITZERLAND	517
UNITED KINGDOM	514
SLOVENIA	512
MACAO, CHINA	511
POLAND	508
IRELAND	508
BELGIUM	507
HUNGARY	503
UNITED STATES	502
PISA Average	500
NORWAY	500
CZECH REPUBLIC	500
DENMARK	499
FRANCE	498
ICELAND	496
SWEDEN	495
LATVIA	494

MATH

SHANGHAI, CHINA	600
SINGAPORE	562
HONG KONG, CHINA	555
SOUTH KOREA	546
TAIWAN	543
FINLAND	541
LICHTENSTEIN	536
SWITZERLAND	534
JAPAN	529
CANADA	527
NETHERLANDS	526
MACAO, CHINA	525
NEW ZEALAND	519
BELGIUM	515
AUSTRALIA	514
GERMANY	513
ESTONIA	512
ICELAND	507
DENMARK	503
SLOVENIA	501
NORWAY	498
FRANCE	497
SLOVAKIA	497
AUSTRIA	496
PISA Average	496
POLAND	495
SWEDEN	494
CZECH REPUBLIC	493
UNITED KINGDOM	492
HUNGARY	490
LUXEMBOURG	489

Throughout the twentieth century, the United States led the world in high-school graduation rates. Now it ranks twenty-first out of the twenty-six developed nations with competing economies (OECD); only five countries have lower high-school graduation rates than the United States. High-school dropout rates have tripled in the last thirty years, continuing a downward trend.[101] The United States has also fallen behind in the percentage of fifteen-year-olds who are enrolled in school, ranking third from bottom of the OECD countries, above only Mexico and Turkey.

The College Board reported that the 2012 college-bound seniors' scores on the SAT College and Career Readiness Benchmark were the lowest in forty years. Coincidentally, the overall educational attainment of the United States is declining as the aging workforce of the baby boom generation moves toward retirement. This better-educated, skilled workforce shall be replaced, but current trends are not reassuring, thus creating further fear for unemployment rates and GDP growth.

Moreover, the college board reported that our standing in college degrees awarded (as a percentage of twenty-five- to thirty-four-year-olds) has declined significantly—from first-place to a twelfth-place ranking among the most developed nations. South Korea, Ireland, Russia, Israel, Canada, Japan, New Zealand, Norway, France, China, Belgium, and Australia have all pulled ahead of the United States.

Just how great is our education problem? According to a report from the President's Council of Economic Advisers 2010, global spending on education is $3.9 trillion, or 5.6 percent of planetary GDP. America spends the most—about $1.3 trillion a year—and the most on a per student basis; yet the United States ranks in the bottom tier of the thirty-four OECD countries in mathematics, science, and reading. And as in so many other areas of American life, those averages obscure a deeper divide: The United States is the only

---

[101] College Board, "U.S. Must Ensure 55 Percent of Americans Earn Postsecondary Degree by 2025 or Risk World Standing: College Board Report," http://press.collegeboard.org/releases/2008/us-must-ensure-55-percent-americans-earn-postsecondary-degree-2025-or-risk-world-standing-co.

CINTHIA COLETTI

developed country to have high proportions of both top and bottom performers. About a third of American fifteen-year-olds do not have basic competence in science, can't use math in daily life, and do not read well enough to function in the workforce.

We can no longer wait to improve schools that deny children the opportunity for a world-class education. Low attainment on OECD literacy assessments—reading for knowledge and writing accurately and coherently—diminishes the earning power and standard of living for millions of our future citizens. Our children, and our country, need and deserve the best. Americans take real pride in the idea that our nation is exceptional. And it is true that our education has unique strengths—we have rich resources, an unmatched tradition of innovation, and a higher education system that is still the finest in the world. But this will not last if we do not raise our sights on prekindergarten through twelfth-grade education. It is time to acknowledge that our teacher-preparation programs are not exceptional, our reading development programs in kindergarten through grade 3 are failing, and our literacy and STEM programs in middle and high school are weak at best.

High-performing education systems set rigorous academic standards for student success. In state after state, our system lacks meaningful evaluation and incentives for the most effective teachers to teach the most challenged students. Too often we treat teachers as if they were interchangeable widgets in a school assembly line rather than professionals with deep knowledge and expertise. Many of our federal policies are moving in the right direction, but the practices of high-performing countries show clearly that we have much work to elevate the teaching profession, from the recruitment, training, credentialing, advancing, and support of teachers through meaningful evaluation, professional development, and incentives for the most effective teachers to teach the most challenged students.

The Common Core standards, the Race to the Top program, School Turnaround grants, Teacher Incentive Fund, all have potential to raise the tide. However, the first imperative is for all students to become reading literate. Without literate readers, no program can succeed. Thus, our lawmakers will have to work hard to initiate new, rigorous literacy laws in state after state and to ensure that they are implemented with fidelity and sustained within all school districts.

Why Do We Have This Literacy Problem?

One of the most misunderstood aspects of education is the fact that the human brain was never genetically programmed to learn to read. Reading is one of the most complex and demanding "new circuits" that the young brain has to learn.

Learning to read, write, and think critically about text, therefore, is neither easy nor natural for many of our students, and the teaching of reading and writing—particularly to children with diverse learning challenges—demands expert levels of knowledge from teachers. One of the biggest national challenges is to *attract, prepare, support, reward, retain, and advance high-quality teachers*, while at the same time requiring them to learn the demanding skills of literacy instruction. The students who are most at risk for underachievement in acquiring reading development skills are those who pose the greatest challenges to teachers, both because there are multiple reasons for their being at risk and because effective programs and methods require comprehensive, intensive, direct, systematic, differentiated, and informed teaching. Many teachers are underprepared for these varied challenges because their training has not given them mastery of the complexity of reading or understanding of the various reasons children fail to acquire it.

Reading involves a progression of skills that begins with understanding spoken language and culminates in the deep understanding of written words. To be effective with diverse learners, teachers should master a range of complex language underpinnings, including awareness of speech sounds, spelling patterns, word meanings, grammar, and patterns of word formation. With this mastery, they can give students a platform for reading fluency and comprehension. Once these skills are acquired, the reader can attain advanced literacy, including the ability to approach printed material with critical analysis, inference, and synthesis; to write with accuracy and coherence; and to use information and insights from text as the basis for information decisions and creative thought. Reading literacy unleashes each citizen's potential to make informed decisions, enriches his or her life, and allows full participation in society. Every teacher needs to understand both the complexities involved in reading development and the consequences for those who fail to become proficient.

CINTHIA COLETTI

In the past, student reading scores that ranked below proficient levels were most often associated with poverty, limited English proficiency, learning disabilities, and dyslexia. In the 2011 NAEP, however, 55 percent of the students who were below proficient in reading were not poor as measured by eligibility for free or reduced-price school lunch. This suggests, surprisingly, that children from middle- and upper-income families are also falling behind in literacy. In contrast to these trends, research funded by the National Institutes of Health and other agencies confirms that all but a small percent of first-graders can attain grade-level reading skills, and a large proportion of those who are below proficient in the other grades can also improve significantly.

What Can You Do As a Policy Maker?

Learn the facts. Become a champion for literacy and education. Help us pass new literacy legislation, now.

The education sector of our economy produces the human capital that drives a nation's accomplishments, innovations, and living standards. As other countries on the world stage begin to outpace the United States in several industries, the most serious consequence of a failed education system is failure to produce the workforce that drives our GDP. Today, more than two dozen countries are investing more wisely and with a far greater proportion of their resources, in their students' educations than we are. The critical question we shall ask is whether America is losing pace with itself, or whether dozens of other countries are simply outeducating us by driving higher standards of quality education. The answer is both—we are losing ground and being outeducated. Below you will find four key components to reverse this negative trend:

1. Let science guide decision making. Legislation, educational policies, standards, and implementation guidelines such as teacher preparation, teacher licensure and credentialing, curriculum frameworks, and program adoptions shall be guided by our best scientific research and shall be specific enough to discourage ineffective practices.
2. Employ data systems to direct student instruction. This includes early, universal screening to flag students at risk, and

continual monitoring of the progress of students so that they will perform at their highest levels of capability.

3. Build the leadership capabilities of principals and school-based leaders so that they can nurture, support, and evaluate the work of teachers.

4. Prepare all teachers to become literacy teachers regardless of their areas of expertise. More specifically, all kindergarten through third-grade teachers should be licensed reading specialists: "certified teachers of reading." A certified teacher of reading will have deep knowledge and the skill to differentiate instruction necessary for the range of diverse learners in their classes.

The legislative language in the body of this document is offered as a template for action on these issues.

Scholars across the globe have found a direct correlation between literacy and levels of wealth, health, poverty, and general quality of life. We shall confront and reverse the downward spiral that is affecting all of us. State by state, we can outpace global competitors by investing in high-quality teachers, high-quality instruction, high-quality data systems, and the supportive contexts that will enable learning to take place. Legislators can take the reins and implement state literacy laws that are likely to increase the number of students who can achieve the Common Core State Standards and be prepared for college or career. [102] It is time for all of us to drive policy that ensures the United States will lead the literate nations.

Success in the twenty-first century requires significant core competencies in reading, learning, and analytical thinking. Today's students tend to have several careers in their lifetimes, so for success in an increasingly interconnected and complex world, schooling must allow students to study, infer, analyze, communicate, collaborate, and create new knowledge. Thus, experts realize that building an environment of learning in which text and information flow, leading to ideas and discussion, is paramount to preparing the next generation for global world competition.

---

[102] National Governors Association Center for Best Practices and the Council of Chief State School Officers, "Common Core Standard State Standards," http://www.corestandards.org/.

CHAPTER FOURTEEN

ADVOCATES GESTALTS

Overhaul through Grassroots

A S WE WORK together toward the goal of literacy improvements, it is important to pledge ourselves in united voice: all young people of the state will become fully literate, graduate from high school, attend postsecondary school poised for a career, and able to fully participate as contributing citizens in twenty-first-century society. This is not happening for too many young people in our state, and indeed it can and it must.

The tenets of literacy policy, as outlined in the previous chapter, are based on an extensive and increasing science ranging from cross-sectional, regression studies to quasi-experimental matched comparison studies to fully randomized treatment-control trials. Conducted over the last two decades and funded by federal and private grants totaling a hundred million dollars, these studies have investigated multiple aspects of teaching, learning, cognitive neuroscience, data analysis, and the best validated methods of improving reading acquisition and full literacy across disciplines.

The knowledge and model policies synthesize and leverage the findings in order to inform, advise, and sustain solid practice in general-education classrooms. Each of the nine sections is segmented into various components that may be required for different audiences to inform and direct action and success.

2013 Data Confirms 5 Pillars from Best Practices

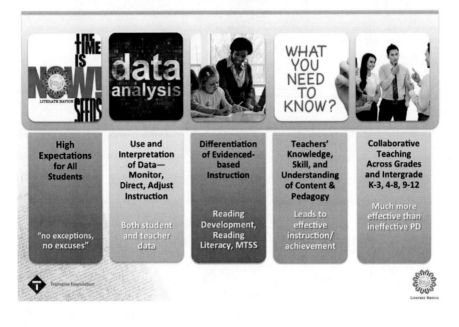

High Expectations for All Students	Use and Interpretation of Data— Monitor, Direct, Adjust Instruction	Differentiation of Evidenced-based Instruction	Teachers' Knowledge, Skill, and Understanding of Content & Pedagogy	Collaborative Teaching Across Grades and Intergrade K-3, 4-8, 9-12
		Reading Development, Reading Literacy, MTSS	Leads to effective instruction/ achievement	Much more effective than ineffective PD
"no exceptions, no excuses"	Both student and teacher data			

Literacy Policy Partner with the Common Core State Standards Initiative

Literacy Policy (Policy) is also a directive to realize the Common Core State Standards Initiative (Standards).[103] Teachers in grades 4 through 12 cannot meet the extensive objectives of the Standards *if* they obtain students who are unable to comprehend text, speak, and write at grade level. For content teachers of English language arts, science, math, and social studies to be successful, to accomplish and build upon their students' skills each year, literacy is a mandate. Today's classrooms dictate students be literate in order to engage in the dynamic learning of the Standards: debating, writing, thinking, and incubating ideas.

---

[103] National Governors Association Center for Best Practices and the Council of Chief State School Officers, "Common Core Standard State Standards," http://www.corestandards.org/.

CINTHIA COLETTI

Both the Policy and the Standards were developed in collaboration with teachers, school administrators, researchers, and field experts to provide a clear and consistent framework of effective models derived from scientific knowledge, as well as from cumulative data from states across the country and countries around the world. Fundamentally, both seek a level of student literacy competence that moves from the schoolroom to the workplace, to citizenship, to lifelong learning, and in so doing, fulfills or is central to achieving an individual's aspirations.

Policy and Standard criteria afford a clear understanding of what students are expected to learn. Unswerving Policy and Standards secure benchmarks for all students, regardless of where they live or what school they attend. Along with the imperative that each student read proficiently by the third grade, the Policy and Standards require both higher education and school cultures to recognize that every teacher—not just K-3—is a reading and writing teacher in every subject area. Such a vision requires an entire system to work collectively toward the highest levels of teacher knowledge, skill, and supports.

New approaches to school leadership, collaborative exchanges among teachers, and indeed a cultural change within schools will ensure that students meet their potential at every age. The Policy and Standards define that all teachers are teachers of reading and writing, language, and speaking and listening—in all subjects. This requires state, districts, and schools to acknowledge three capacities of teacher expertise and requirements:

1. teachers of reading—teaching in grades K-3;
2. teaching specialists—specializing in reading, ELL, Title I, and special-education instruction in grades K-12; and
3. content-area teachers—teaching in grades 4-12.

Teachers and teaching candidates should essentially be prepared for new licensure, relicensure, and certification by passing new basic-reading-instruction-competence examinations for content-area teachers K-12 and an advanced reading instruction competence assessment for teachers of reading K-3 and teaching specialists K-12. This new Policy will craft a road toward Standards success and teacher

The preparation of the twenty-first-century students requires a long view of literacy that stretches across all the content areas of study and deepens the students' abilities to use reading and writing to prepare for interaction with new knowledge.

success. By virtue of preparing for and passing the examinations and being awarded the certificate, teachers will more clearly be perceived as the professionals they are—acknowledged for their expertise in the more dynamic, interactive, and flexible classroom that learning demands.

While teacher effectiveness is crucial to student success and the Standards, it is still only one piece that is necessary for sustained improvement in student learning. Without exemplary, dedicated school-based leadership to establish, implement, and sustain the conditions under which optimal teaching, collaborations, and learning take place, the impact of effective teachers, evidence-based instructional programs, and robust data systems will be diluted. Just as reading and writing develop to incorporate the highest forms of critical thinking—from inferential and deductive reasoning to critical analysis and novel thought—so must be the teaching of literacy in our schools. Every teacher and every administrator is important to the success of every individual student within this view.

Challenges Met by Developing Specifications

Literacy Policy and Standards highlight specific detail that district and school personnel (teacher/faculty/leader) be provided. Along with a healthy dose of time for student progress monitoring and analysis, collaboration time, classroom supports, and training resources are necessary for systemic literacy overhaul. Both theoretical and technical knowledge concerning literacy science techniques and pedagogy is needed for teachers and school-based leadership growth and effectiveness. This is no small order, but the reality is that many school-based leaders are making decisions on instruction without either this knowledge or data on the past performance of their own students.

The Policy and Standards require a commitment from the state

- to form an achievement-oriented, data-based culture in districts and schools;
- to influence the stakeholders—parents, teachers, community leaders; and
- to hold accountable high-standard implementation that improves all levels of student achievement through high-school graduation.

To reverse US literacy trends, each school system should incubate specifications of the Policy for best outcomes, launching the full scope of the policies, data collection systems and technologies, certifications, and collaborations to influence student achievement. Of great importance are policies that quickly identify and provide systems of support for students who lag behind at any stage of reading development from acquisition through subject-matter literacy. The extensive research that directs the Policy has teased out that students who fail to learn cannot be considered casualties of socioeconomic classification, but rather these students comprise every racial, ethnic, social, and economic group.

The conclusion among many experts was to reclassify these students, as you learned in part 1 of the book, as a community of students not performing at grade level due to environment, weak or improper instruction, learning disabilities and/or dyslexia, and lack of school supports. We refer to these children as SEEDS (noun), an acronym that is positive in its vision to be both inclusive and specific, demonstrating that regardless of any classification, science confirms that each and every student can grow to become reading literate, be educated, and to contribute to society and culture as engaged citizens. The SEEDS community includes

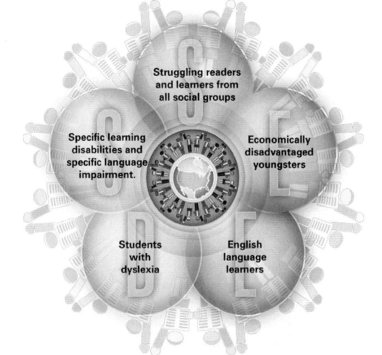

Struggling readers and learners from all social groups,
Economically disadvantaged youngsters,
English language learners, and students with
Dyslexia,
Specific learning disabilities, and language impairment.

Members of the SEEDS community of today's youth are all capable of lifelong success in every conceivable job: teachers; innovators; entrepreneurs; business people; community leaders; professionals in medicine, engineering, and Policy; skilled workers in health care, manufacturing, technology, communications, and media; contractors, developers, and builders; and many other vocations. It is up to us, their society, to ensure they have the tools and the support to maximize their potential in the present and the motivation to contribute these skills back to society in the future.

Ethos of the Literacy Policy and the Standards

Both the Policy and the Standards share the tenet that all students will graduate high school able to succeed in entry-level, credit-bearing academic college courses, and/or in workforce training programs. The Standards and Policy define the knowledge and skills that students must master within their K-12 education careers. Criteria

1. are aligned with college and work expectations;
2. are clear, understandable, and consistent;
3. include rigorous content and application of knowledge through high-order skills;
4. build upon strengths and lessons of current state standards;
5. are informed by other top-performing countries so that all students are prepared to succeed and compete in a global society; and
6. are data validated/evidence based.

To achieve the mutual criteria of the Policy and the Standards, it is understood that students meet or exceed grade-level reading development in grades K-3 and proficiency in literacy in all content subjects grades 4-12 (e.g., science literacy, math literacy, technology literacy, English language arts literacy).

To accomplish this goal, both the Policy and the Standards have directives for reading literacy development in the following areas:

1. Reading development foundational skills are directed toward fostering students' understanding and working knowledge of concepts of print, the alphabetic principle, and other basic conventions of the English writing system, and the way the English language works. Children should know that words are made of letters that represent sounds and that words convey rich layers of meaning that are encapsulated in their spelling. The richness of vocabulary and the growing complexity of grammar should be integrated into their knowledge. These foundational development skills are not an end in themselves; rather, they are the necessary and important components of an effective, comprehensive, foundational reading instruction program designed to develop proficient readers and writers with the capacity to comprehend and analyze texts across a range of types and disciplines.

2. The goal of all reading strategy is to produce fluent, thinking readers. Toward that end, instruction should be differentiated: good readers will need much less practice with these concepts than SEEDS students will. A Multi-Tier System of Supports (MTSS) will be integrated into general-education instruction. Teachers in general and special education will be unified in their commitment to producing fluent, thinking readers through a system of collaborative professional development. The goal throughout the system will be to teach students what they need to learn, to develop their highest capacities, and to work together to attain this.

3. Reading literacy skills offer a focus for instruction each year and help ensure that students gain adequate exposure to a range of academic language texts and tasks. Rigor is also infused through the requirement that students read increasingly complex texts through the grades and develop a strong academic vocabulary. Thus, grade-level reading literacy proficiency is required for each grade. Students advancing through the grades are expected to be proficient in each year's grade-specific standards and retain or further develop skills and knowledge mastered in preceding grades.

Writing skills offer a focus for instruction each year to help ensure that students gain adequate mastery of a range of writing skills and applications. Each year in their writing, students should demonstrate increasing sophistication in all aspects of language use, from vocabulary and syntax to the development and organization of ideas, and they should address increasingly demanding content and sources. Students advancing through the grades are expected to meet each year's grade-specific standards and to retain or further develop skills and knowledge mastered in preceding grades.

Speaking, listening, and language skills offer a focus for instruction each year to help ensure that students gain adequate mastery of a range of skills and applications. Students advancing through the grades are expected to meet each year's grade-specific standards and to retain or further develop skills and knowledge mastered in preceding grades.

Template for Policy Excellence and Success

Sections of Policy are offered as a transcript of model practice and literacy legislation, a template for each school and state to individualize with offered nomenclature. It is also prepared to augment existing policies, practices, and strategies in detail for rigorous upgrading within each of these domains.

Political climates in districts and states may require a more gradual, stepwise approach; however, for the best student learning outcomes, Policy is designed to be executed in its entirety. Policy sections are segmented into semi-independent areas of concern and are presented in the model template—separate, distinct, and individually potent:

1. Section 2: Policies of high standards for institutes of higher education and states in teacher selection, preparation, licensure, and certification for every teacher. With great emphasis on certifying teachers of reading in grades K-3, each new teacher needs to acquire state-of-the-art, evidence-based knowledge and solid skills. This is the only approximate of a guarantee that each student will develop foundational reading skills and become reading literate.

2. Section 3: Policies on data technology, data interpretation, and the use of data to direct and improve instruction, learning, and student thinking. This will ensure that shortfalls are

CINTHIA COLETTI

immediately identified, to include screening for learning disabilities and dyslexia, and are addressed so that both students and teachers can be successful. Data on the students and teachers represents the most powerful tool to guide progress.

3. Section 4: Policies on districts and schools instituting appropriate, evidenced-based, adequate, core reading development instruction in early grades to ensure student reading literacy before grade 4.

4. Section 5: Policies on K-12 classroom scaffolding systems of support for SEEDS in reading development and in all content-area literacy including English language arts, science, social studies, and math.

5. Section 6: Policies for early childhood education providers and child school readiness.

An important note in the context of current economic trends, the warnings issued by varied federal reports, and the ranking of colleges of education by US News and World Reports: [104] "According to the National Center for Teacher Quality, successful, high-performing schools are far outnumbered by those that fail to prepare their teaching candidates for the challenges of real classrooms . . . No school-based factor has more impact on our students' success than the quality of our teachers. The preparation teachers receive has a crucial impact on their performance in the classroom. We believe that having specific, actionable information about individual teacher preparation programs will enable us to take steps to improve the overall quality of our teacher workforce."

K-18 institutions across the nation are under more pressure than ever to improve—in terms of both the number of their students who graduate and the level of preparedness for their graduates. With such emphasis in place, it is inevitable that an upsurge in the varied uses of technology will guide much of the development in structures used to advance classroom learning. These technological additions may well bring a multitude of advantages to student learning; however,

---

[104] Information and full report can be found at http://www.nctq.org/siteHome.do.

they must be proven to be as evidence based as any other method before any assumption that they are the new magic bullets. Indeed, history has taught us there are no such things. Rather, the uses of technology, like any other pedagogical method, must be employed judiciously and appropriately and not lurched to yet another unproven pedagogical solution, which is what the SERP work mentioned earlier is confirming. The use of data systems and progress monitoring is the way to discover if a student is in need of additional tiers of teaching supports, and evidenced-based intervention systems by a certified teacher of reading will thwart reading failure so that student engagement can happen in every grade.

Systemic change will never be solved by any single stroke but by an entire society committed to the potential of its future constituents. Toward that end, this model legislation is a first and necessary step that will take us all to enact.

TECHNICAL SYNOPSIS OF LITERACY POLICY

It is first important to remember that for decades in the United States, public-education policy has not been rigorously validated—although well intentioned. Thus, as citizens, this book helps us to see the crisis we find ourselves in, that in a short period of time affects each of us regardless of our personal level of education and social status.

Each of the nine sections of Policy is written as model practice and legislation. You will find these sections in the appendices A-H. Each appendix defines a section of exemplary levels of Policy/practice that details a set of specific, science-based principles central to achieving the goal for literacy. Each section contains the following:

1. Introduction of importance and explanation as it relates to achieving reading literacy and the goals of the Standards;
2. Executive Summary (one page);
3. Key Components (grid);
4. Roadmap and Specifics for a State Literacy Handbook (detail); and
5. Model Literacy Law (language that will be reduced in the actual enactment of law but is intended to help support and educate your state's policy makers and education committees).

Important Note on Model Policy

The model legislation component found in the appendices is written in more detailed language than the actual bill and law language that will be submitted for vote. Model policy is shaped for state education committees, is filled with specifics, and is written in both legal language and as an "operations guide/state handbook" to assist the legislative committee's engineer language that is science based. It is imperative to note that each section will require fidelity of implementation to realize impressive student learning objectives.

Summary

Over the past decade, a committed group of distinguished educators, researchers, and policy makers have developed the detailed materials that follow in the appendices. It has been my pleasure and honor to have worked with them, and I would like to share with you some reflections about the journey I have traveled. Working together, we have maintained as our focus and our motivation all of the children who now struggle to master the essential skills of literacy.

CHAPTER FIFTEEN

PERSONAL REFLECTIONS

There's just three things I'd ever say:
If anything goes bad, I did it.
If anything goes semi-good, then we did it.
If anything goes real good, then you did it.
That's all it takes to get people to win football games for you.

—*Paul (Bear) Bryant*

T HERE HAS NEVER been a time in my career where I have found myself so in awe of the many people with whom I work. They inspire me, challenge me, delight me, guide me, and compel me to do more, better. Together we are shining the spotlight on the fact that student literacy seems to have fallen off both the state and federal radars.

To combat this fact, with amazing energy while having a lot of fun, an army of talented people started an innovative, nonprofit organization that could fuel a literacy *movement*. Its name is pertinent to the work and to this book, Literate Nation. Today it thrives with thousands of talented volunteers across the nation—a mere 18 months after inception. Yes, we all have other "jobs," families, friends, and hobbies; yet, we work day in and day out for student literacy. We work as hard as we have ever done in any job we have ever had. My friends often ask me why I labor so, having chosen to leave my life of business, adventure, and leisure. So I will use the closing of part 3 to share my personal purpose and the great joy I foresee in the future.

In the process of this humble journey, I continue to reflect on what led me to this point. Playing a robust role in the education of both of my children, I felt an enormous sense of relief when they each achieved good scholastic status. It gave me such peace to know that my children had the skills necessary to adapt to any occupation and interest in life they might choose. But realizing how much I had learned on their educational journey forced me to face the truth: all this knowledge only helped two children. That was it; no more, no less. With this truth, how could I ever find peace again knowing millions of children and their parents were feeling the exact sense of desperation, agony, and impotence that I once felt during my own children's educational journey?

I have never really been an activist. I have worked hard and met life's challenges. I grew up in an America that demanded I become a college-educated citizen and participate fully in society. Try as I might to stay in my old contented world with my sights focused on "my" future; try as I might to let others "who knew more" handle the challenges in America; try as I might, I am no longer comfortable. No longer can I ignore, dismiss, or escape the fact that our education is a travesty to diverse, capable minds. Nor can I overlook the treatment of our youth, the psychological damage our system is doing to tens of millions of individuals who cannot participate in modern society's call for lifelong learning.

Out of heartbreak and fear rather than desire, I must wear my new badge of "education-activist." My lifelong journeys brought me to this point. This is not a practice drill; this is a genuine call to action. Both on a large scale as lawmakers and on a smaller scale as individuals and volunteers, we must address the imperative of literacy for the vitality of our nation now.

A story that keeps me in this battle is that of a nameless, loving grandmother who once touched my arm and said to me, "I don't want my grandchild to be stupid because he can't read." Just as with my own children's struggles, neither will this moment leave me—the grandmother's solemn face, her caring, sad eyes, her emotional request for my help, and my utter feeling of helplessness. I was so ignorant about education that I didn't know how to guide her then, yet we were in sisterhood, searching to help our families. In retrospect, there is so much I could have done; I just didn't think I had the tools to do anything. To this very day, I wonder about her pain and what happened to her grandson.

And so I have come to realize that comfortable inaction is no longer an option for me or for any of us, really. We are united in the spirit of being moms and dads, aunts and uncles, neighbors, stewards of our communities. I have come to realize that inaction is immoral. I know it sounds harsh, but it is true. *When we know what to do, we* must *do it to save lives. Each life is a precious being—no exceptions, no excuses—each life worthy of opportunity.* Vision, leadership, high standards, and commitment to equity are crucial starting points to change lives by giving each child the gift of literacy.

Tiny slivers of change and demand for high standards are coming together to form a bigger picture, as witnessed in the acceptance of the Common Core State Standards Initiative and the growing number of states enacting components of a state literacy law. But unless and until they implement these policies, with fidelity, they won't bring about the momentous transformation needed to turn the tide.

If we want to see our children and grandchildren thrive, we must face the challenge of instituting a literacy mandate for all students—as a moral obligation that stands up through political cycles and leadership turnover. The more efficiently we work together as a cohesive community with a shared vision and commitment, the faster we will triumph in our goal for a booming, literate nation. Within three to five years, we could witness substantial transformation, as our international competitors have demonstrated is possible. Without question, this problem is so critical and compelling that our leaders *could* unite across the aisles; they *could* organize for the common goal—all children. And then I will buy the champagne!

Rinku Sen, author of *Stir It Up*, articulated well: "Organizing is essentially the process of creating politically active constituencies out of people with problems by focusing on the strengths and the solutions embedded in their experience." Accordingly, we can rally. Or we can remain resigned to the present condition—failing children, stealing dreams. It is a choice—to choose to live in a literate democracy or to choose to accept the status quo.

> At the moment, most folks are either unaware of the facts or choosing an illiterate society. But it is not too late to harness our will and create a literate nation. Frankly, there are no options in between.

Don't be too timid and squeamish about your actions. All life is an experiment.

—Ralph Waldo Emerson

How grateful I am to read every day of my life, for I understand that literacy is my gateway to independent learning and decision making; to critical thinking; to the escape and fantasy of fiction; and to participation in the explosion of new digital media. So, too, I am doubly blessed that both of my SEEDS children have flourished, and equally heartbroken that this is not true of all our children.

I want this for all Americans—the ability to invest in themselves and in society. My relentless travels around the world continue to awaken me to the ubiquitous erosion of our capital as a result of poor education. Like most of you, I intensely want the continuation of America's great democracy, innovation, culture, and arts. Like most of you, I understand that an uneducated populace puts democracy's survival at risk. Thus, for my children and grandchildren, as well as for yours, I am panicked into action, committed to change the fact that students are getting lost in the literacy abyss.

So well summarized by Michael Gecan in his book *Going Public*, "So leaders and organizers face a tough challenge . . . We are called to love, engage, and uphold our most cherished institutions, while watching them, questioning them, and pressing upon them to change, all at the same time." Plain, simple, and possible, we must invest in edu-transformation: "ReTrain, ReDesign and ReBuild" our teachers, school methodology, and education workforce.

There are risks and costs to a program of action. But they are far less than the long-range risks and costs of comfortable inaction.

—John F. Kennedy

Ultimately, we cannot decree change by talking and writing about it; rather, we must impress upon ourselves and our institutions the need to face the tough challenges, to become leaders of transformation, to step up to the plate of action. Our power must come in the "doing," moving forward, and sharing our unflinching conviction for America's future. The practice and policy solutions await you next, in the appendices of this book.

CINTHIA COLETTI

I hope these heartfelt reflections clarify my quest and that you will join me toward success.

—Cinthia Coletti

Current posts:

Founder and CEO, The Coletti Institute for Education and Career Achievement

Co-founder and Chairman, The Haan Foundation for Children

Founding Board of Directors, Chair and CEO, Literate Nation

President, Power4Kids Reading Initiative

Vice President, Board of Directors, Strategic Education Research Partnership Institute

Vice Chairman, Board of Directors, Dyslexic Advantage

Board of Directors, California Business for Education Excellence

Board of Directors, Harvard Medical School, Program in Education, Afterschool and Resiliency

Board of Directors, San Francisco RBI

Board of Advisors, Southern Methodists University, Department of Education Policy and Leadership

Board of Advisors, University of California, San Francisco, Neuroscience Initiative

LITERACY POLICY TECHNICAL OUTLINE AND GENERAL PROVISIONS OF LITERACY LAW

THIS FIRST APPENDIX provides you with a technical outline of the key beginning of new Policy that will require general provisions and definitions. The legislative committee with which you are working will guide you on the protocol of your state.

Policy's Technical Reference Outline

Components for Literacy Policy and Education System Overhaul

This appendix contains the framework and operational blueprint, based on scientific findings, to drive a seismic shift in student literacy outcomes through legislation.

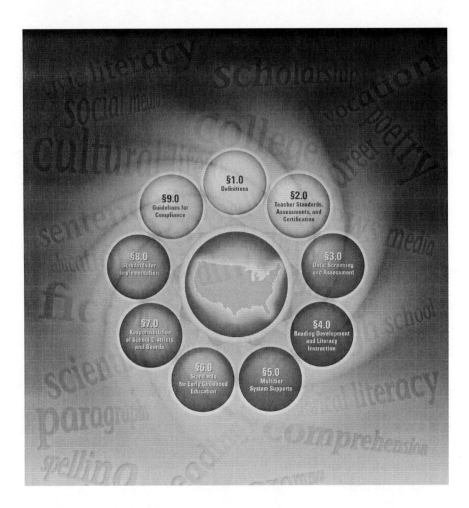

TECHNICAL COMPONENTS OF LITERACY POLICY

Technical Summary:

§1.0 Definitions;

§2.0 Standards, Certification, and Assessment for Teachers of Reading, Teaching Specialists, and Content-Area Teachers on Their Preparation, Professional Development, Knowledge, and Skill;

§3.0 Screening, Formal Assessment, Gathering Data, and Referral to Special Education; General Procedures

CINTHIA COLETTI

§4.0 General Education: Foundational Reading Development and Literacy Instruction; Speaking, Listening, and Language Instruction; Content-Area Reading Literacy Instruction; and Writing Literacy Instruction;

§5.0 Multi-Tier System of Supports in General-Education Classrooms (MTSS)

§6.0 Guidelines for Early Childhood Education

§7.0 Responsibilities of School Districts and Boards;

§8.0 Guidelines and Standards for the Implementation of the Policy; and

§9.0 Guidelines for Compliance with the Policy

Technical Reference Components of Literacy Policy:

Section One: Definitions Outline

> Reading Development, Reading Literacy, Full Literacy, Writing Literacy
> SEEDS Community of Students
> Economically Disadvantaged Youngsters
> English language learners (ELL) and/or Students with Limited English Proficiency (LEP)
> Dyslexia, Specific Learning Disabilities, Specific Language Impairment
> Teachers of Reading, Teaching Specialist, Content-Area Teachers

Section Two: Teacher Preparation, Assessment, and Certification

Certification Assessments are outlined:

1. Basic Reading Instruction Competence Assessment (BRICA)
    A. The foundations of reading portion of a BRICA shall cover the understanding of phonological and phonemic awareness, the understanding of concepts of print and the alphabetic principle, the role of phonics in promoting reading development, and the understanding of word analysis skills and strategies.
    B. The development of reading comprehension portion of a BRICA shall cover the understanding of vocabulary development, the understanding of how to apply reading comprehension skills and strategies to imaginative/literary texts, and the understanding of how to apply reading

comprehension skills and strategies to informational/expository texts.

C. The reading assessment and instruction portion of a BRICA shall cover the understanding of formal and informal methods for assessing reading development, and the understanding of multiple approaches to reading instruction.

D. The integration of knowledge and understanding portion of a BRICA shall consist of at least two open response questions requiring organized, developed analyses on topics related to foundations of reading development, development of reading comprehension, and/or reading assessment and instruction.

E. The passing score for a BRICA shall not be lower than 75 percent of the total possible points or 85 percent of the total possible points for prospective special-education teachers, reading teachers, and reading specialists.

F. Institutions of higher education are to provide free, approved remedial work as specified in this law for their candidates who fail a BRICA.

G. Results of a BRICA are to be reported and made public annually, with first-time passage rates and overall passage rates tied to specific institutions of higher education for initial and professional license candidates and to individual districts for out-of-state hires.

2. Advanced Reading Instruction Competence Assessment for Teachers of Reading Certification (ARICA)

A. The reading processes and development portion of an ARICA shall cover in depth the understanding of the connections among listening, speaking, reading, and writing; phonological and phonemic awareness; concepts of print and the alphabetic principle; the role of phonics knowledge in reading development; other word analysis skills and strategies; the development of vocabulary knowledge and skills; skills and strategies for comprehending literary/imaginative texts; and skills and strategies for comprehending expository and content-area text.

B. The reading assessment portion of an ARICA shall cover the understanding of test construction and the interpretation of test results; characteristics and uses of formal and informal reading and writing assessments; the role of assessment in promoting reading and writing development; and the screening and diagnosis of reading difficulties and disabilities.

C. The reading instruction portion of an ARICA shall cover the understanding of research-based instructional strategies, programs, and methodologies for promoting early reading and writing development; research-based instructional strategies, programs, and methodologies for consolidating and expanding reading, writing, and spelling skills; the differentiation of reading instruction to meet the needs of individual students; and characteristics and uses of reading resources, materials, and technologies.

D. The professional knowledge and roles of the teachers of reading, special-education teacher, Title I reading teacher, or ELL reading specialist (as appropriate to the candidate) portion of an ARICA shall cover the understanding of the interpretation, evaluation, and application of reading research; the multiple roles of the candidate's prospective position in planning and implementing reading instruction in collaboration with other members of the school community; and the understanding of the role of professional development in promoting the effectiveness of the candidate's prospective position and other educators.

Teacher preparation programs are outlined:
A. Board-approved teacher preparation programs for certifying teachers of reading in K-3 grade education
   1. Foundational concepts about oral and written language learning
   2. Knowledge of the structure of language
   3. Knowledge of SEEDS community and learning disorders
   4. Interpretation and administration of assessments for planning instruction
   5. Structured language teaching of phonology
   6. Structured language teaching of phonics and word recognition

7. Structured language teaching of fluent, automatic reading of text
8. Structured language teaching of vocabulary
9. Structured language teaching of text comprehension
10. Structured language teaching of handwriting, spelling, and written composition

Section Three: Use of Data to Achieve Literacy Outcomes

Screening and assessment procedures are outlined:

Screening Procedures: The goal of universal, early reading screening is to identify children at risk of future failure *before* that failure actually occurs. By doing so, we create the opportunity to intervene early when we are most likely to be more effective and efficient. Therefore, the key to effective screening is maximizing the ability to predict future difficulties. With the use of screening, teachers of reading can quickly assess if a child will experience reading difficulties and can provide early stage, targeted instruction by isolating the skills that need to be strengthened.

A. All entering kindergarten students will be universally screened during the first, early weeks of reading instruction, again before the fall break, and also in the spring to evaluate reading progress. If a student is falling behind his or her peers, common characteristics will be identifiable early in these screening assessments. A teacher of reading will use data analytics to provide Multi-Tier System of Supports in general-education classrooms to most quickly and assuredly ameliorate the areas of weakness. The school district, school, or charter school shall also implement tiers of support and a reading intervention (accelerated and/or intensive) that appropriately addresses students' reading difficulties and enables them to "catch up" to their typically performing peers.

B. If the screening tool determines that a student is at serious risk for literacy failure and/or a learning disability/dyslexia, a systematic assessment will be provided, and the school district, school, or charter school shall notify the student's parents/guardians within ten weeks of a student's demonstrating lack of progress achieving skills.

Assessments for reading literacy are outlined:

Progress monitoring is a critical function when directing instruction so all students develop full reading skills. Once a skill is identified as weak, implementing Multi-Tier System of Supports in general-education classrooms is mandated. Any assessment plan shall include progress monitoring and screeners that include a progress-monitoring component to direct tiers of student supports.

Assessments for reading literacy: All students in prekindergarten, kindergarten, and grades 1, 2, and 3 are to be systematically assessed for their reading development, progress, and comprehension grade-level skill attainment.

A. Every student in public school shall be assessed for grade-level reading attainment. Every student in grades 1, 2, and 3 shall be systematically assessed every two to three weeks during the year for grade-level reading skill attainment through to fluency and comprehension to ensure a successful skill progression to full literacy.

B. In doing such assessments, students receiving below grade-level scores shall be a top priority, and the student will be provided support within a week. When a student is identified and provided with systems of support, yet grade-level attainment is not accomplished within thirty days, then more intensive intervention is mandated.

C. Assessments shall have one or more of the following results:
   1. no indication of need for services;
   2. indication of need for MTSS (tier II) in general-education reading services to ameliorate SEEDS literacy failure;
   3. indication of need for assistance to improve the effect of general-education reading instruction through *intense* intervention services (MTSS-tier III); and
   4. referral for further formal diagnostic assessment for the existence of SEEDS factors and eligibility for the receipt of special-education services.

Formal assessment is outlined:

Formal assessment: Student's formal assessment diagnostic is dependent upon multiple factors including the student's reading performance, reading difficulties, poor response to supplemental scientifically based reading instruction/intervention supports, teachers' input, and input from the parents or guardians. Additionally, the appropriate time for assessing is early in a student's school career (pre-K-1); the earlier the better.

A. These procedures should be followed:
1. notify parents or guardians of proposal to perform a formal assessment diagnostic on a student;
2. inform parents or guardians of their rights;
3. obtain permission from the parent or guardian to assess the student; and
4. assess student, being sure that individuals/professionals who administer assessments have training in the evaluation of SEEDS.

B. The district, school, or charter school administers measures that are related to the student's educational needs. Depending upon the student's age and stage of reading and intellectual development, the following reading areas should be assessed:
1. reading real and nonsense words in isolation (decoding);
2. phonological awareness;
3. letter knowledge;
4. rapid naming;
5. reading fluency;
6. reading comprehension; and
7. written spelling.

Dyslexia and learning disability determination are outlined:

A. A district, school, or charter school team or committee of knowledgeable persons determines whether the student has a learning disability or dyslexia after reviewing all accumulated data, including the following areas:
1. observations of the teacher, district, charter school staff, and/or parent/guardian;
2. data gathered from the classroom (including student work and the results of classroom measures) and information found in the student's cumulative folder (including the developmental and academic history of the student);
3. data-based documentation of student progress during instruction/intervention;
4. results of administered assessments; and
5. all other accumulated data regarding the development of the student's learning and his or her educational needs.

Section Four: Reading, Writing, Listening and Language Instruction

Grades K-3 Foundational Reading Development Instruction is outlined:
  A. Foundational reading development instruction programs shall consist of specific program content and a defined delivery system in general-education classrooms. The programs shall be taught by certified teachers of reading and consist of the following components:
    1. Foundational Reading Development Instructional Content Components
       a. Language Based
       b. Phonological Awareness
       c. Phoneme-Grapheme Correspondence Knowledge
       d. Syllable Instruction
       e. Linguistics
       f. Meaning-Based Instruction
       g. Reading Fluency Instruction
       h. Phonics
    2. Instructional delivery that uses a simultaneous combination of internal learning pathways (visual, auditory, kinesthetic, and tactile) to achieve proficiency in language processing.
    3. Synthetic to analytic phonics delivery that teaches students the sounds of the letters first and then combines or blends these sounds to create words. Analytic phonics requires prior knowledge of letters and their corresponding sounds to decode and form new words.
    4. Synthetic phonics methodology teaches students the sounds of the letters first and then combines or blends these sounds to create words. It is delivered to students
       a. systematically,
       b. sequentially,
       c. cumulatively, and
       d. individually.

Grades K-5 speaking, listening, and language instruction is outlined:
  Speaking and listening skills of increasing difficulty by grade level will be taught to students in grades K-5 for academic and lifelong expression, comprehension, cooperation, and collaboration.

A. comprehension and collaboration in discussion with increased difficulty by grade level;
B. expression and presentation of knowledge and ideas in discussion with increased difficulty by grade level;
C. conventions of standard English in speaking and writing with increased difficulty by grade level;
D. knowledge of language with increased difficulty by grade level; and
E. vocabulary acquisition and use with increased difficulty by grade level.

Grades 4-12 reading literacy instruction in content areas is outlined:

Reading literacy skills will be provided to all students by content area and English language arts as determined by the Standards to define college and career readiness expectations.
A. key ideas and details in content-area reading literacy with increased difficulty by grade level;
B. craft and structure content-area reading literacy with increased difficulty by grade level;
C. integration of knowledge and ideas in content-area reading literacy with increased difficulty by grade level; and
D. range of reading and level of text complexity for reading literacy with increased difficulty by grade level.

Section Five: General-Education Classroom, Multi-Tier System of Supports for Literacy Attainment

Multi-Tier System of Supports (MTSS) are outlined:

Grades K-3

The term "MTSS" means a comprehensive system of differentiated supports that includes evidence-based instruction, universal screening, progress monitoring, formative assessments, summative assessments, research-based interventions matched to student's needs, and educational decision making using academic progress over time.
A. Principles of Multi-Tier System of Supports
1. Assumption and belief that *all* students can learn to read and write;
2. Early intervention for students who demonstrate risk for literacy failure;

3. Use of a multitier model of service delivery (to achieve high rates of student success; instruction may be differentiated in both nature and intensity);
4. Use of a problem-solving or standard-protocol method to make decisions within a multitier model;
5. Use of research-based, scientifically validated interventions/instruction to the extent of existing valid research;
6. Monitoring of student progress to inform instruction; and
7. Use of data to make decisions.

B. The process described is for general-education MTSS for SEEDS who struggle in the area of reading:
1. Tier I—Foundational reading instruction should involve (1) the use of a scientifically based instructional program for all students taught by a certified teacher of reading, (2) ongoing assessment of progress and monitoring of reading achievement gains, and (3) teachers of reading using flexible grouping to target specific skills and differentiate instruction for all students.
2. Tier II—MTSS intervention is designed to meet the needs of SEEDS who do not respond quickly to foundational reading instruction.
3. Tier III—MTSS intensive instruction involves a small percentage of students who have received tier II intervention in general education and continue to show marked difficulty in acquiring necessary reading development to reach grade-level attainment. These students necessitate intensive instruction that is more explicit and specifically designed to meet their individual needs. If this intensive instruction does not yield marked gains within ten weeks, the child will be referred for formal assessment in K-1 grades.

Grades 4-12

In middle and high school, it is important to establish a school culture that recognizes that every content-area teacher is a reading teacher because reading is involved in every subject area. Therefore, reading strategies will be implemented as a school-wide program in connection with a school culture and vision that works toward high levels of student achievement in reading literacy. Specific interventions and strategies will be provided to support SEEDS who have struggled to learn to read and are performing below grade level in reading. Schools will provide every opportunity for students to read, practice their strategies in every subject, every day, to enhance their development of the reading skills they need to become better readers and, ultimately, reading literate.

A. Each school will provide intensive reading interventions to SEEDS in grades 4-12 with reading problems. Research supports identification and MTSS to help with the following:

1. Identify students who are more than one grade level behind in reading and provide daily reading intervention. Using a dedicated period each day with a certified teacher-of-reading professional, students who have reading difficulties that are one or more grade levels below expectations are provided with daily reading instruction, approximately forty to fifty minutes per day, focused specifically on their instructional needs.

2. Target instruction for each student by providing systems of support in three tiers with an outline of assessments of skill accomplishments and a timeline for stages of support.

3. During tier I intervention for grades 4-12 students who need intervention in word study, a certified teacher of reading provides students with approximately twenty-five lessons taught over seven to eight weeks depending on student mastery.

4. During tier II intervention, the instruction emphasis is on vocabulary and comprehension with additional instruction and practice provided for applying the word study and fluency skills and strategies learned in tier I intervention.

5. Tier III intervention continues the instructional emphasis on vocabulary and comprehension with more time spent on independent student application of skills and strategies.

B. Each content-area teacher will identify key content subject words for each student to learn and teach at least two new words every day and review one from the previous day.

C. Teachers should ask students to ask questions while they read and after they listen to the teacher read while they are following the text so that they will monitor comprehension and learning.

D. Teachers shall teach word-meaning strategies within content-area classes.
E. Teachers should instruct students how to activate and build appropriate background knowledge for understanding text content.
F. Teachers should teach students to use reading comprehension strategies while reading complex text.
G. Teachers should guide and engage students in activities that are text related.
H. Teachers should maximize all opportunities for students to read printed material.
I. Teachers should organize students into collaborative groups for reading tasks.

Section Six: Early Education

Early care and education requirements are outlined:
A. Board-approved provider, educator, and teacher preparation programs shall certify early care educators and providers in preliteracy birth to age five.
  1. The program or collection of practices for early care and education providers in preliteracy birth to age five shall include, at a minimum, instruction in and application of the following five areas of foundational preliteracy:
     a. early literacy research;
     b. language development;
     c. shared book reading with an emphasis on vocabulary;
     d. phonological awareness; and
     e. the speech-to-print connection with an emphasis on alphabet knowledge.
B. The program or collection of practices for early care and education providers shall take into account the variables representing early or precursor literacy skills.
  1. Strong predictors of early literacy success include
     a. alphabet knowledge;
     b. phonological awareness;
     c. rapid automatic naming (RAN) of letters or digits;
     d. rapid automatic naming (RAN) of objects or colors;
     e. reading or writing name; and
     f. phonological memory.

2. Strategies for promoting early literacy include
   a. shared book reading;
   b. phonological awareness activities; and
   c. connecting speech to print.
C. Given the research-proven link between the major elements of spoken and written language development (listening, speaking, reading, and writing), early care and education providers shall know how these language skills interrelate and contribute toward full literacy.

Important elements of language to be incorporated into preliteracy education include
1. phonology;
2. vocabulary;
3. morphology;
4. syntax; and
5. pragmatics.
D. Shared book reading (reading with children, rather than to children) with an emphasis on vocabulary is a critical step in preparing children for the development of language skills and reading literacy. This activity
1. builds oral language and print awareness;
2. builds vocabulary by introducing high-frequency words for mature language users; and
3. can be adapted for other shared book reading strategies.
E. The program or collection of practices for early care and education providers shall include an understanding of phonological awareness.
F. The program or collection of practices for early care and education providers shall include speech-to-print connection with an emphasis on alphabet knowledge.
G. Early care providers will assess students for dyslexia and learning disabilities should a child display difficulty with speech, sounds, and identifying symbols.
H. Early care providers will assist children in learning to experience print in the following contexts:
1. recognizing print in their surroundings;
2. understanding that print carries meaning;
3. knowing that print is used for many purposes; and
4. generating print through exploratory writing.

CINTHIA COLETTI

Section Seven: School Districts Responsibilities for Literate Students

School board and district requirements are outlined:

Each board of education can:
- A. ensure that procedures for using data systems and assessments to identifying a SEEDS student are implemented in the district and MTSS to bring all students to reading proficiency;
- B. ensure that procedures for providing appropriate instructional services and accommodations or modifications for the student are fully implemented in the district; and
- C. ensure that the district or school complies with all applicable requirements of state educational programs.

Each school district can assist schools to
- A. administer K-3 universal screening at least three times during the kindergarten year;
- B. provide early identification, intervention, and support;
- C. apply results of early assessment instruments to instruction and report to the district;
- D. implement procedures according to the state board of education;
- E. provide annual training of certified teachers of reading, staff, and paraprofessionals about SEEDS students;
- F. ensure the procedures for identification, instruction, and communication are in place;
- G. ensure the individuals responsible for administering and interpreting the necessary testing receive ongoing professional development in the assessments used;
- H. test for SEEDS students at appropriate times, as needed and in all grades;
- I. provide appropriate instruction, tier of supports, and accommodations for SEEDS and IEP students;
- J. purchase or develop programs that include descriptors listed in the state handbook;
- K. notify parents in writing before an assessment or identification procedure is used with an individual student;
- L. inform parents of all services and options available to eligible students;

M. provide students with services of a teacher of reading and/or a teaching specialist certified and skilled in methods appropriate for SEEDS students' success;

N. provide MTSS for students requiring specialized instruction;

O. provide a parent education program; and

P. provide appropriate progress monitoring.

Section Eight: Implementation Objectives

For all students to reach full literacy, it is important for states and districts to create state literacy implementation teams to ensure that core features of the blueprint for literacy success are put into practice. These teams will

A. identify and define all aspects of research-defined reading literacy instruction, data use, and supports;

B. provide training for state, regional, and local implementation teams to build implementation capacity for program and school administrators that will include core components of implementation science;

C. provide preservice and professional development training so that all content-areas teachers and teachers of reading have the skills and knowledge to pass basic and/or advanced reading instruction competence teaching assessment;

D. develop a system of oversight of teacher preparation programs in order to align such programs with state certification exams;

E. provide training for teacher preparation personnel; and

F. develop a communication protocol to help align policies and systems and to remove barriers to effective implementation.

Section Nine: Guidelines for Compliance

Each school district, school, and charter school shall

A. provide to parents, teachers, school administrators, staff, and all interested parties public notice regarding the school system's specific implementation plan;

B. ensure that teachers and administrators are aware of the state regulations regarding literacy failure; the characteristics of SEEDS; and licensure or credentialing requirements of teachers;

C. ensure that teachers and principals have the capacity to implement core components for literacy success;

D. implement a program for universal screening for K-1 students and assessment for all grade pre-K-3 students and those students displaying characteristics of SEEDS;

E. provide tier I instruction through a data-validated and evidence-based foundational reading instruction program;

F. provide tier II of the MTSS within thirty days of screening or assessment if a SEEDS is found;

G. provide tier III of the MTSS within ten days of tier II instruction should the SEEDS student not make adequate progress;

H. provide tier III of the MTSS within ten days of tier II instruction should the SEEDS student not make adequate progress;

I. initiate referral for special education under timelines specified under state and IDEA law to SEEDS students who have not responded to MTSS in regular education;

J. initiate procedures for evaluation of eligibility under §504/ADAAA if the student is not found to be eligible for special education; and

K. initiate procedures to implement the Standards for reading and writing literacy and for speaking, listening, and language skills.

STATE LITERACY LAW

General Provisions Of Literacy Law

BE IT ENACTED BY THE LEGISLATOR OF THE STATE OF [insert state name] ON [insert date] THE LITERACY LAW. The Law warrants literacy proficiency for all students in the state of [insert name] and hereby requires that each college and university school of education, school district, school, local school board, and local education agency provide in general education all components of literacy science to include teacher preparation, development and certification, classroom foundational reading development and reading literacy instruction, use of data to inform instruction that includes screening, assessments, strategies, and Multi-Tier System of Supports to achieve reading and writing literacy for all students.

[Insert state name] Literacy Law is hereby enacted in the following:

§1.0 Definitions
    1.1. Reading Development
    1.2. Reading Literacy
    1.3. Writing Literacy
    1.4. Full Literacy
    1.5. SEEDS Community of Students
    1.6. Economically Disadvantaged Youngsters
    1.7. English Language Learners (ELL) and/or Students with Limited English Proficiency (LEP)
    1.8. Dyslexia
    1.9. Specific Learning Disabilities
    1.10. Teachers of Reading

1.11. Teaching Specialist

1.12. Content-area Teachers

1.13. Specific Language Impairment

§2.0 Standards, Certification, and Assessment for Teachers of Reading, Teaching Specialists, and Content-Area Teachers on Their Preparation, Professional Development, Knowledge and Skill;

2.1. All Education Professionals, Teachers of Reading, and Support Personnel Qualifications

2.2. Requirements for All College and University Teacher Preparation Programs

2.3. Reading Instruction Competence Teaching Assessments

2.4. Reading Instruction Competence Teaching Assessment Reporting and Support

2.5. Pretest and Grant for Candidates in an Approved Teacher Preparation Program

2.6. Passing Score on a Reading Instruction Competence Teaching Assessment

§3.0 Screening, Formal Assessment, Gathering Data, and Referral to Special Education; General Procedures

3.1. General Procedures

3.2. Screening Procedures

3.3. Assessments for Reading Development and Literacy

3.4. Literacy Failure Diagnosis

3.5. Data Gathering

3.6. Formal Assessment

3.7. English Language Learners (ELL)/Limited English Proficiency (LEP)

3.8. Dyslexia/Learning disabilities/Language impairment

3.9. Referral to Special Education

§4.0 General Education: Foundational Reading Development and Literacy Instruction; Speaking, Listening, and Language Instruction; Content-Area Reading Literacy Instruction; and Writing Literacy Instruction;

4.1. Foundational Reading Development Instruction in Grades K-3

4.2. Speaking, Listening, and Language Instruction in Grades K-5

4.3. Reading Literacy Instruction in Grades 4-12 Content Areas

MODEL LEGISLATION LANGUAGE DEFINITIONS

Section §1 Definitions

§BE IT ENACTED BY THE LEGISLATURE OF THE STATE OF
[insert state name] the following definitions for the literacy law:

1.1   **Reading development** involves a progression of skills that begins with the ability to understand spoken words and culminates in the deep understanding of text. Reading development involves a range of complex language underpinnings including awareness of speech sounds (phonology), spelling patterns (orthography), word meaning (semantics), grammar (syntax), and patterns of word formation (morphology), all of which provide a necessary platform for reading fluency and comprehension. Attaining English literacy depends on the successful acquisition of these skills.

1.2   **Reading literacy** represents the lifelong, intellectual process of gaining meaning from print. It includes the ability to approach printed material with critical analysis, inference, and synthesis; to write with accuracy and coherence; and to use information and insights from text as the basis for informed decisions and creative thought. "Reading literacy" is a term that has evolved over time with changes in our society, economy, and culture. It goes beyond the development of reading's active and interactive skills and beyond comprehension of rich text. Reading literacy implies that there is a capacity for reflection on written material that initiates personal experiences as well as cognitive function. It moves from the schoolroom to the workplace, to citizenship, to lifelong learning. It affords the reader a set of linguistic tools that are increasingly important in modern society, from communication with peers and communities to interactions with large bureaucracies and complex legal systems. To attain reading literacy, individuals must be taught to utilize a wide range of reading and literacy skills that will develop into subject matter literacy—such as science or math literacy, and eventually to vocational literacy. Reading literacy is the foundation from which readers seek, use, and understand all textual matter; it unleashes the potential to enrich and extend one's personal life and empowers one to participate fully in society.

1.3 **Writing literacy** is a term that has evolved and increased with the demands of a text-driven society. It has multiple components of discipline that reflect requirements to accurately write informative and explanatory texts. Writing literacy affords opportunity to convey ideas, concepts, and information clearly and accurately through the effective selection, organization, and analysis of content. Writing literacy implies that there is capacity for writing narratives to develop real or imagined experiences or events using effective technique, well-chosen details, and well-structured event sequences.

1.4 **Full literacy** is the ability to identify, understand, interpret, create, communicate, and compute using language and printed, written, and digital materials associated with varying contexts. Full literacy involves a continuum of learning in enabling individuals to achieve their goals, to develop their knowledge and potential, and to participate fully in their community and wider society.

1.5 **SEEDS** is an acronym (noun) that represents a community of students not performing at grade-level reading proficiency due to weak or improper instruction and lack of school supports. A term positive in its vision, which is both inclusive and specific, of a community of students who make up 67 percent of the student population according to National Assessment of Education Progress. The SEEDS community includes **S**truggling learners and readers encompassing *all* groups in society, **E**conomically disadvantaged youngsters, **E**nglish language learners, and students with **D**yslexia and **S**pecific learning disabilities and language impairment. Members of the **SEEDS** community are capable of achieving academic and lifelong success with multitier systems of reading development and reading literacy instruction and supports.

1.6 **Economically disadvantaged youngsters** are the students who often enter school significantly behind and less prepared than their more well-to-do peers. Their academic disadvantage is witnessed in everything from impoverished language input in early childhood (letter awareness and spoken vocabulary) to number awareness and self-control. If they are victims of poor quality or inappropriate reading instruction, these students can be even further behind their peers in language skills by the middle of second grade. Students in this category will require Multi-Tier System of Supports appropriate to their literacy needs beginning in pre-K through third grade. Many of these students are "Title I Eligible" and receive "Free and/or Reduced Lunch," meaning the federal Elementary and Secondary Act provide financial assistance to local educational agencies and schools with high numbers or high percentages of children from low-income families to help ensure that all children meet challenging state academic standards.

1.7 **English language learners (ELL) and/or students with limited English proficiency (LEP)** are students who have recently come to the United States from another country, have parents that speak a foreign language in their homes, or are older students of poor instruction often due to cultural-linguistic perception differences. ELL and LEP students are becoming the majority minority in many public schools. With more immigrants having arrived in the United States during the 1990s than any other single decade, the number of public school students in need of additional language instruction has increased dramatically in recent years (Bureau of US Citizenship and Immigration Services, 2001). A survey of state education agencies found that, in 2004, more than 5.5 million students with limited proficiency in English were enrolled in public schools across the nation, making up almost 10 percent of the total K-twelfth-grade public school enrollment. The population of students who are ELL has grown 105 percent, while the general school population has grown only 12 percent since the 1990-91 school year. States report more than 460 languages spoken by students with limited proficiency in English (Kindler, 2002) with 80 percent of the students speaking Spanish. These burgeoning numbers pose unique challenges for educators striving to ensure that language-minority students achieve to high levels. Achievement data suggest that students with LEP lag far behind their peers. Nationwide, only 7 percent of these students scored "at or above proficient" in reading on the National Assessment of

Educational Progress, compared to about 33 percent of students overall. Results in fourth-grade math as well as eighth-grade reading and math were similar. Findings support that limited oral language proficiency does not constrain a student's emergent reading and writing development. Limited English language students are capable of making sense of written input while they are working on becoming fluent speakers of English. This research orientation maintains that just as speaking, reading, and writing are interrelated in the emerging literacy of native speakers, they are equally related in the emerging literacy of second-language students.

1.8 **Dyslexia** is neurobiological in origin. It is characterized by difficulties with accurate or fluent word recognition and by poor spelling and decoding abilities. These difficulties typically result from a deficit in the phonological component of language that is often unexpected in relation to other cognitive abilities and the provision of effective classroom instruction. Secondary consequences may include problems in reading comprehension and reduced reading experience that can impede the growth of vocabulary and background knowledge (National Institutes of Child Health and Human Development and the International Dyslexia Association). Dyslexia is usually characterized by early difficulties with accurate or fluent word recognition and poor spelling, and by later difficulties with text-level fluency, leading to problems with written comprehension and sometimes writing. Students with dyslexia represent a continuum of underlying difficulties, typically beginning with weaknesses in the phonological component of language and in the speed of processing multiple, language-related components of reading. These difficulties can be found singly or, more typically, together. It is important to note that they are largely unexpected in relation to other often-strong cognitive abilities in the student and the provision of otherwise effective instruction. Some students who have both decoding and fluency issues and who receive effective decoding instruction go on to have only fluency-based issues that affect comprehension and the quality of their reading and how much they read. Whatever the pathway, reduced reading can impede the growth of all language capacities, particularly vocabulary and grammar, which then can

CINTHIA COLETTI

impede the development of background knowledge necessary for advances in learning. Further characteristics of students with dyslexia are often witnessed in rote math calculations, speech, word retrieval, and processing speed. Appropriate interventions can change the course of these students' academic careers. Dyslexia and specific learning disabilities represent approximately one-third of all literacy failure groups and may require intensive, appropriately matched intervention as early as possible. Kindergarten screening most often will identify these students early, so foundational reading instruction and systems of support can lead to good reading skills through life.

1.9 **Specific learning disability,** as defined by the Individuals with Disabilities Education Act of 2004, is a disorder in one or more of the basic psychological processes involved in understanding or using language, spoken or written, that may manifest itself in difficulty with listening, thinking, speaking, reading, writing, spelling, or doing mathematical calculations, and conditions such as perceptual disabilities, brain injury, minimal brain dysfunction, dyslexia, and developmental aphasia. Specific learning disability does not include learning problems or intellectual disabilities that create limitations in mental functioning that are mostly dealt with in special-education environments and are primarily the result of visual, hearing, or motor disabilities, mental retardation, or emotional disturbance. Specific learning disabilities can include metacognitive strategy development and self-regulation such as those with attention deficit and hyperactivity disorders and those with dysgraphia, both of whom display written expression problems. Research provides six clear classifications of learning disabilities: word reading (dyslexia), reading fluency, reading comprehension, written expression, mathematics calculation (dyscalculia), and mathematics problem solving. Each of these disabilities has a distinct cognitive correlate for which there is specific evidence-based intervention.

1.10 **Teachers of reading** are defined as educational professionals who have mastered the foundations of reading development and the use of formative data analysis to direct individual instruction that is required for teaching diverse student populations to read in grades K-3. Certified teachers of reading are essential to every student's academic foundation. They have received high-quality teacher preparation, professional development, advancement, and certification that warrants he or she has mastered the complexity of teaching reading, reading and writing literacy, speaking, listening, and language skills to all students. Teachers of reading will have passed the state's *advanced* reading instruction competence assessment, earning certification and demonstrating expertise in all aspects of reading literacy instruction; data analysis, interpretation, use, screening, monitoring, assessments, and strategies; and the Multi-Tier System of Supports necessary for all students to achieve grade-level reading literacy on or before third grade.

1.11 **Teaching specialists** (also known as literacy coaches, reading specialists, literacy specialists, and learning specialists) are teachers in elementary, middle school, and high school who specialize in reading/literacy instruction, English language learner instruction, Title I student instruction, and special-education instruction. Reading specialists, along with K-3 teachers of reading, are also certified as teachers of reading, passing the advanced reading instruction competence assessment. Teachers with a certificate are considered to be advanced and highly important as a group of teachers within a school because they teach the foundational skills necessary for all educational attainment. Passing the advanced reading instruction competence assessment requires a solid knowledge base of a skilled expert in all aspects of reading instruction, data analysis and interpretation, screening, assessments, strategies, Multi-Tier System of Supports and interventions for all students to achieve grade-level reading literacy proficiency.

1.12 **Content-area teachers** are teachers of subject matter required in the state curricula and across curricula. Every teacher, regardless of content, is a reading and writing teacher because both are involved in every subject area. Reading and writing strategies and instruction should be implemented in all teacher preparation programs, professional development, and as a school-wide program in connection with school culture and vision that works toward high levels of student achievement in reading literacy. All requirements of the Literacy Policy and Standards highlight that all teachers and schools will provide every opportunity for students to read and practice their strategies in every subject, every day, to enhance their development of the literacy skills that are needed to become better readers and writers and, ultimately, reading and writing literate.

1.13 **Specific language impairment** (SLI) is characterized by difficulty with language that is not caused by known neurological, sensory, intellectual, or emotional deficit. It can affect the development of vocabulary, grammar, and discourse skills, with evidence that certain morphemes may be especially difficult to acquire (including past tense, copula be, third person singular). Children with SLI may be intelligent and healthy in all regards except in the difficulty they have with language. They may in fact be extraordinarily bright and have high nonverbal IQs.

TRANSFORMING COLLEGES OF EDUCATION, TEACHER PREPARATION, PROFESSIONAL DEVELOPMENT AND NEW CERTIFICATIONS

IN EDUCATION, THE foundation lies at the top: in the institutes of higher learning, which prepare teachers and school-based leaders to take on responsibility for the knowledge and prospects of the next generation. We cannot have effective students without effective teachers, and the only way to ensure teacher effectiveness is to take an active approach to creating and expanding preparation programs that are based on science-validated practices. This chapter will not only serve as a comprehensive outline for enhancing teacher knowledge and skill but also demonstrate how a teacher's expertise in the area of reading development and reading literacy has an enormous impact on how quickly and effectively his or her students will grasp the concepts of subjects.

In this appendix, we present you five tools to assist you in adopting state Literacy Policy on preparation, certification, and professional development: **§2.0 Standards, Certification, and Assessment for Teachers of Reading, Teaching Specialists, and Content-Area Teachers on Preparation, Professional Development, Knowledge, and Skill.**

Included in this section of the Policy are these tools to assist your work: An Executive Summary of the goals describes effective teacher preparation and how they are to be achieved; Key Components present a structured look at the makeup of a preparation program; the Roadmap and Specifics delve into the details of such a program; and the Model Legislation for colleges of education is designed to help you and your community bring these changes to fruition in your own state and district with the help of your legislators.

Also included at the end of this appendix is a section for colleges of education on the advanced knowledge necessary to become a certified teacher of reading. This provides a content framework for courses and course sequences, and delineates proficiency requirements for practical application of reading development instruction in all contexts what teachers of reading should know and be able to do, ethical standards for the profession, guidelines for the practical teaching skills necessary for teaching SEEDS students, teacher collaborations, and supervised practice opportunities to be successful. All this is necessary to pass the advanced reading instruction competence assessment that this Policy requires for all teachers of reading from kindergarten through third grade. Learning to teach reading, language, and writing is a complex undertaking. The competence and expertise of teachers can be nourished with training that emphasizes the study of reading development, language, and individual differences.

The goal of this chapter is to provide material to ensure that all teachers are better prepared so the impact of reading difficulties will be lessened and many more students will receive the instruction and support that they require to reach their potential. We owe them no less. It is incumbent upon the colleges of education and the state education boards to prepare all teaching professionals with the knowledge necessary to pass new, stringent examinations. This must occur before teachers are assigned the responsibility of teaching children to read and develop subject-matter literacy.

Executive Summary
for Transforming Colleges of Education

Teacher effectiveness starts with effective preparation programs: Colleges of education play a key role in literacy, education, and the workforce. It is incumbent upon the universities and colleges of education to prepare all teaching professionals to pass new, stringent examinations before being assigned the responsibility of teaching children to read and become subject-matter literate.

Issue:

Approximately one-third of students read on grade level; two-thirds do not. Often this is due to a lack of teacher preparation in teaching reading development skills. The 2013 NCTQ Teachers Preparation Rankings show that four out of five universities in the review of the undergraduate and graduate programs cannot even agree upon the core skills and knowledge an elementary teacher should process, a striking confirmation that teacher preparation programs must change. Student achievement can only improve if every teacher becomes a teacher of literacy. Teaching reading literacy is a complex skill that requires specialized training.

Why this is important:

1. Teacher quality is the *number-one* predictor of a student's success.
2. Teachers' impact is additive and cumulative.
3. Up through third grade, children learn to read; after third grade, they read to learn. However, two-thirds of students leave third grade not reading on grade level; and without intervention, the gap grows.

Goals of section:

1. To improve requirements of *teacher preparation programs* regarding reading instruction to enhance all teachers'.

CINTHIA COLETTI

2. To incorporate *three levels of teacher certification* to earn a teacher of reading certification.
3. To require a *basic or advanced* reading instruction competence teaching assessment for all teachers.

How to achieve these goals:

1. Universities and colleges of education should prepare all teaching professionals with the skills to be reading literacy instructors.
2. Teacher preparation programs should equip their candidates with the knowledge and skills to take responsibility for students' reading development and literacy attainment.
3. Once certified, teachers should adapt their knowledge and evolving experience to the challenges of teaching diverse student populations.

Key points:

Teachers of reading are qualified to ensure that all but a small percentage of students for whom they are responsible will thrive and become fluent readers who can read well, write well, and think well.

Studies indicate that when teacher preparation programs and professional development programs leave out essential reading development instruction methods and knowledge, their students will not be adequately prepared to teach reading in a way that will provide full literacy to all of their students. When preparation programs include these essentials, their graduates will be more successful in teaching reading to all students.

Key Components
for Transforming Colleges of Education

Teacher Preparation Programs

Institutes of Higher Educations' (IHE) teacher preparation programs must		
1. follow procedures to attract, prepare, support, remediate, and advance high-quality teaching candidates	2. ensure that professors instructing teaching candidates are knowledgeable in scientifically based reading, writing, literacy, language, speaking, and listening acquisition knowledge	3. develop, retain, and advance high-quality teachers
Understanding the forms of evidenced-based reading development and reading literacy instruction required for students to reach their potential and the development of these programs must be the charge of all teacher preparation programs, professional development programs, and school-wide programs.		
Teachers must be trained in the following effective methods for achieving student reading literacy proficiency:		
1. Teaching complex data-validated, differentiated reading development and reading and writing literacy strategies to a diverse student population	2. Screening, assessment, and data instruments to direct instruction and advance student literacy skills	3. Foundational data-validated reading development and reading literacy instruction in the classroom
4. SEEDS community reading instruction in general education	5. Multi-Tier System of Supports and classroom implementation strategies in general education	6. Student accommodations to assess knowledge attainment
It is incumbent that universities and colleges of education prepare all teaching professionals to pass new, stringent examinations before being assigned the responsibility of teaching children to read and become subject-matter literate: advanced and basic reading instruction competence assessment.		
Scientifically discredited notions of reading acquisition and instructional practices that are incompatible with science or inhibit student progress, such as using picture and context cues for decoding rather than self-monitoring and comprehension shall not be promoted in teacher preparation programs.		

Every teacher can be trained to become a teacher of reading literacy, writing, and language—in every subject.

Practicum *for all teachers* of reading certification shall include

1. lesson planning
2. supervised practice both in teaching foundational reading development and reading literacy instruction to whole classrooms and differentiated students groupings, and in delivering intervention to individuals or small groups of SEEDS.

In addition, practicum for teaching specialists—special-education teachers, Title I instructors, and ELL instructors, reading specialists— shall include

1. documenting student progress with formal and informal assessments
2. completing an educational assessment of a student with a suspected reading disability who needs diagnostic assessment for special-education support services.

Road Map and Specifics for a State Handbook Transforming Colleges of Education

The Overview:

Academic success requires a ground shift for both higher education and school cultures: if our achievable goal is to have every student to learn to read at their highest potential, then every teacher must become a teacher of reading and writing. Reading literacy can no longer be seen as merely the purview of early English language arts teachers. Reading acquisition is the beginning of a long, tightly interwoven arc of literacy development, where the prefatory skills of early literacy prepare the child in grade 4 for subject matter literacy that, in turn, guides secondary and tertiary education as well as supports the goals of the Common Core State Standards Initiative. Without both, the foundational and the developmental evolution of reading skills that transition from the proverbial "learning to read" to "reading to learn" stages of literacy, students will never attain their full educational potential.

The Charge:

Understanding what underlies the development of reading across time and also what forms of evidence-based reading instruction are required by an individual student to reach his or her potential must be the charge of all teacher preparation programs, professional development programs, and school-wide programs. A new school culture with a vision that propels students toward their highest levels of achievement is demanded, and the first stepping-stone toward such a culture is the recognition that "full literacy" requires the full participation of all the teachers in a school across all years of schooling. Every teacher, every area contributes to the student's ability to use text to read, write, and think with increasing sophistication over time. The development of a future society of citizens who can use highly honed thinking skills—from inference and critical analysis to novel thought and creativity—depends on such a vision for the present schools.

Toward these ends, teachers and schools must

1. provide every opportunity for students to read, write, and practice their strategies in every subject, every day;
2. help students enhance their development of reading, writing, and thinking skills needed for reading fluency and comprehension;
3. ultimately provide support structures that ensure that each student achieves full English literacy.

Specifically, this means that students must be able to approach printed material with critical analysis, inference, and synthesis; to write with accuracy and coherence; and to use information and insights from text as the basis for informed decisions and creative thought.

The Foundation:

These requirements are informed by ongoing clinical research that documents how teachers of reading—using the particular approach to knowledge about reading that is provided in their teacher preparation and professional development programs—can either help or hinder a class of individual and diverse students in learning to read well. More specifically, there is extensive evidence that successful, expert teachers come from comprehensive teacher preparation and professional development programs that include rigorous training and evaluation. The training includes the linguistic, cognitive, and social-emotional aspects of reading development over time; the use of various reading methods that are empirically proven, evidence based, and engaging; the use and translation of assessment procedures and data; the ability to match tailored instruction and known strategies to individual profiles of students (typical and SEEDS); and finally, an understanding of how data can be analyzed and used to chronicle student progress under these methods and strategies.

These studies show that only "expert" teachers of reading are qualified to ensure that the great majority of students for whom they are responsible will thrive and become fluent readers who can read well, write well, and think well. Conversely, the same studies indicate that when teacher preparation programs and professional development programs leave out essential reading instruction methods and knowledge, these teachers will not be adequately prepared to teach reading in a way that will provide full literacy to all their students, especially students in the SEEDS community.

The Responsibility:

Teaching candidates, who will become responsible for the early reading development of students in grades K-3 along with those specializing in reading, ELL, Title I, and special education, must pass an *advanced* reading instruction competence assessment (ARICA). A passing score on this examination earns the teaching candidate a teacher of reading certification. Content-area teachers in grades 4-12 must pass a *basic* reading instruction competence assessment (BRICA) in order to instruct their students in how to become reading and writing literate in their subject areas.

To achieve these goals, key professionals and candidates in the field of education—especially those who are responsible for teaching reading and English language arts—need and deserve to have the most comprehensive knowledge about reading and language development, about empirically proven methods of teaching, about differences in reading development among children, and about how to use assessment data to chronicle and refine individual progress in reading development. These professionals need the highest-quality instruction and substantive support to become skilled teachers of reading and writing. The specific requirements for three capacities of teachers, their respective reading instruction competence teaching assessments, and the required knowledge and skills in each capacity are as follows:

1. "Teachers of reading" are certified by the state and are hereby defined as highly skilled experts in foundational reading and writing development; reading and writing literacy; and speaking, listening, and language skills. Teachers of reading are qualified educational professionals who, having passed a teaching *advanced* reading instruction competence assessment (ARICA), are permitted to teach foundational reading development skills to all children in grades K-3.

2. "Teaching specialists" are certified by the state and are hereby defined as highly skilled experts in foundational reading and writing development; reading and writing literacy; and speaking, listening, and language skills, along with the specialty licensure English language learners, Title I, and special education in grades K-12. Teaching specialists must pass a teaching *advanced* reading instruction competence teaching assessment (ARICA) to become certified as teachers of reading. The assessment ensures that these teachers are highly skilled and knowledgeable in the integration of knowledge and understanding of reading literacy, writing, speaking, listening, and language skills for their field of students.

3. "Content-area teachers" are grades 4-12 subject teachers who are licensed by the state in their area of expertise. These teachers must be knowledgeable in the foundations of reading, writing, language, speaking and listening development, and comprehension and integration of knowledge so that their students may become literate in their content areas.

Content-area teachers will take exams to receive content-area licensure and are required to pass a *basic* reading instruction teaching assessment (BRICA).

Teachers who pass the assessments should be respected and honored as true professionals, able to use their knowledge, expertise, and evolving experience in dynamic and flexible ways during daily interactions with diverse student populations, thereby ensuring that all students achieve reading literacy and become lifelong learners.

The teacher knowledge and skills required to pass an ARICA include ten areas of expertise.

Foundational concepts about oral and written language learning includes

1. understanding and explaining the language processing requirements of proficient reading and writing, including phonological (speech sound), orthographic (print), semantic (meaning), syntactic (sentence level), and discourse (connected text level) processing;
2. understanding and explaining other aspects of cognition and behavior that affect reading and writing, including attention, executive function, memory, processing speed, and graphomotor control;
3. defining and identifying environmental, cultural, and social factors that contribute to literacy development, including language spoken at home, language and literacy experiences, and cultural values;
4. knowing and identifying phases in the typical developmental progression of oral language (semantic, syntactic, and pragmatic), phonological skill, printed word recognition, spelling, reading fluency, reading comprehension, and written expression;
5. understanding and explaining the known causal relationships among phonological skill, phonic decoding, spelling, accurate and automatic word recognition, text-reading fluency, background knowledge, verbal reasoning skill, vocabulary, reading comprehension, and writing;

6. knowing and explaining how the relationships among the major components of literacy development change with reading development (i.e., changes in oral language, including phonological awareness, phonics and word recognition, spelling, reading and writing fluency, vocabulary, reading comprehension skills and strategies, and written expression);
7. knowing reasonable goals and expectations for learners at various stages of reading and writing development;
8. understanding first- and second-language acquisition stages, the impact of culture on student performance, bilingual education and English as a second language programming and teaching methods, results of students' oral language proficiency in relation to the results of tests measuring academic achievement and cognitive processes, and results of similar or parallel tests given in more than one language.

Knowledge of the structure of language includes

1. phonology (the sound system)—how to identify, pronounce, classify, and compare the consonant and vowel phonemes of English
2. orthography (the spelling system)—understanding the broad outline of historical influences on English spelling patterns, especially Anglo-Saxon, Latin (Romance), and Greek; defining "grapheme" as a functional correspondence unit or representation of a phoneme; recognizing and explaining common orthographic rules and patterns in English; knowing the difference between high-frequency and irregular words; and identifying, explaining, and categorizing six basic syllable types in English spelling
3. morphology—identifying and categorizing common morphemes in English such as Anglo-Saxon compounds; inflectional and derivational suffixes; Latin-based prefixes, roots, and derivational suffixes; and Greek-based combining forms
4. semantics—understanding and identifying examples of meaningful word relationships or semantic organization
5. syntax—defining and distinguishing among phrases, dependent clauses, and independent clauses in sentence structures and identifying the parts of speech and the grammatical role of a word in a sentence

6. discourse organization—explaining the major differences between narrative and expository discourse; identifying and constructing expository paragraphs of varying logical structures (e.g., classification, reason, sequence); and identifying cohesive devices in text and inferential gaps in the surface language of text.

Structured language teaching of phonology includes

1. identifying the general and specific goals of phonological skill instruction
2. knowing the progression of phonological skill development (i.e., rhyme, syllable, onset-rime, phoneme differentiation)
3. identifying the differences among various phonological manipulations, including identifying, matching, blending, segmenting, substituting, and deleting sounds
4. understanding the principles of phonological skill instruction (e.g., brief, multicomponent, conceptual, and auditory-verbal)
5. understanding the reciprocal relationships among phonological processing, reading, spelling, and vocabulary
6. understanding the phonological features of a second language, such as Spanish, and how they interfere with English pronunciations and phonics.

Structured language teaching of phonics and word recognition includes

1. knowing or recognizing how to order phonics concepts from easier to more difficult
2. understanding principles of explicit and direct teaching: model, lead, give guided practice, and review
3. stating the rationale for multicomponent and multimodal techniques
4. knowing the routines of a complete lesson format, from the introduction of a word recognition concept to fluent application in meaningful reading and writing
5. understanding research-based adaptations of instruction for students with weaknesses in working memory, attention, executive function, or processing speed.

Structured language teaching of fluent, automatic reading of text includes

1. understanding the role of fluency in word recognition, oral reading, silent reading, comprehension of written discourse, and motivation to read
2. understanding reading fluency as a stage of normal reading development, as the primary factor in some reading disorders, and as a consequence of practice and instruction
3. defining and identifying examples of text at a student's frustration, instructional, and independent reading level
4. knowing sources of activities for building fluency in component reading skills
5. knowing which instructional activities and approaches are most likely to improve fluency outcomes
6. understanding techniques to enhance students' motivation to read
7. understanding appropriate uses of assistive technology for students with serious limitations in reading fluency.

Structured language teaching of vocabulary includes

1. understanding the role of vocabulary development and vocabulary knowledge in comprehension
2. understanding the role and characteristics of direct and indirect (contextual) methods of vocabulary instruction
3. knowing varied techniques for vocabulary instruction before, during, and after reading
4. understanding that word knowledge is multifaceted
5. understanding the sources of wide differences in students' vocabularies.

Structured language teaching of text comprehension includes

1. being familiar with teaching strategies that are appropriate before, during, and after reading and that promote reflective reading
2. contrasting the characteristics of major text genres, including narration, exposition, and argumentation

3. understanding the similarities and differences between written composition and text comprehension, and the usefulness of writing in building comprehension
4. identifying in any text the phrases, clauses, sentences, paragraphs, and academic language that could be a source of miscomprehension
5. understanding levels of comprehension including the surface code, text base, and mental model (situation model)
6. understanding factors that contribute to deep comprehension, including background knowledge, vocabulary, verbal reasoning ability, knowledge of literary structures and conventions, and use of skills and strategies for close reading of text.

Structured teaching of handwriting, spelling, and written composition includes

1. knowing research-based principles for teaching letter naming and letter formation, both manuscript and cursive
2. knowing techniques for teaching handwriting fluency
3. recognizing and explaining the relationship between transcription skills and written expression
4. identifying students' levels of spelling development and orthographic knowledge
5. recognizing and explaining the influences of phonological, orthographic, and morphemic knowledge on spelling
6. understanding the major components and processes of written expression and how they interact (e.g., basic writing/transcription skills versus text generation)
7. knowing grade and developmental expectations for students' writing in the following areas: mechanics and conventions of writing, composition, revision, and editing processes
8. understanding appropriate uses of assistive technology in written expression.

Knowledge of dyslexia and other learning and language disorders includes

1. understanding the most common intrinsic differences between good and poor readers (i.e., cognitive, neurobiological,

and linguistic); recognizing the tenets of the NICHD/IDA definition of dyslexia
2. recognizing that dyslexia and other reading difficulties exist on a continuum of severity
3. identifying the distinguishing characteristics of dyslexia and related reading disorders (including developmental language comprehension disorder, attention deficit hyperactivity disorder, disorders of written expression or dysgraphia, mathematics learning disorder, nonverbal learning disorder, etc.)
4. identifying how symptoms of reading difficulty may change over time in response to development and instruction
5. understanding federal and state laws that pertain to learning disabilities, reading disabilities, and dyslexia.

Interpretation and administration of assessments for planning instruction includes

1. understanding the differences among screening, diagnostic, outcome, and progress-monitoring assessments
2. understanding basic principles of test construction, including reliability, validity, and norm-referencing, and knowing the best-validated screening tests designed to identify students at risk for reading difficulties
3. understanding the principles of progress monitoring and the use of graphs to indicate progress
4. knowing the range of skills typically assessed by diagnostic surveys of phonological skills, decoding skills, oral reading skills, spelling, and writing
5. recognizing the content and purposes of the most common diagnostic tests used by psychologists and educational evaluators
6. interpreting measures of reading comprehension and written expression in relation to an individual child's component profile.

The Oversight Duty of the State to the IHE, Colleges of Education:

To ensure ongoing success, these guidelines shall be written to mandate rigor in the study of reading development. This shall be accomplished in consultation with an oversight panel consisting of persons with demonstrated mastery of the knowledge.

The state department of education, in consultation with an oversight panel of persons with demonstrated mastery of knowledge in literacy, must approve (1) a minor in reading and (2) ensure that the courses required in the reading minor of any teacher preparation program cover in depth the knowledge contained in these guidelines. Doing so will ensure that teaching candidates involved in any such program attain certification to become an ARICA certified teacher of reading.

Changes in syllabi are to be approved by the state department of education in consultation with an oversight panel of persons with demonstrated mastery of the knowledge of reading development and reading literacy, and experts in evaluation of the content and quality of teacher preparation programs who have conducted such reviews in other states.

The state department of education shall designate funding for a higher education collaborative to provide professional development for reading administrators and instructors in institutions of higher education. The collaborative shall meet a minimum of three times per year. In addition, it shall feature national reading experts as presenters on topics related to the knowledge of literacy and to preparing teacher candidates to become certified teachers of reading equipped with knowledge in all foundational reading skills.

MODEL LEGISLATION LANGUAGE TRANSFORMING COLLEGES OF EDUCATION

Literacy Law for Teacher Preparation, Professional Development, and Advancement Programs

---

§BE IT ENACTED BY THE LEGISLATURE OF THE STATE OF [insert state name] that all institutes of higher education's (IHE) teacher preparation programs must follow procedures to attract, prepare, support, remediate, and advance high-quality teaching candidates; all IHEs must ensure the professors instructing teaching candidates are knowledgeable in scientifically based reading, writing, literacy, language, speaking and listening acquisition knowledge; and all school systems must develop, retain, and advance high-quality teachers. Teachers must be trained in the following areas of effective methods for achieving student reading literacy proficiency:

1. teaching complex data-validated reading development and reading and writing literacy strategies to a diverse student population;
2. screening, assessment, and data instruments to direct and advance student literacy skills;
3. foundational reading instruction in the classroom that is data validated;
4. SEEDS community reading instruction in general education;
5. Multi-Tier System of Supports and classroom implementation strategies; and
6. student accommodations to assess knowledge attainment.

As a part of effective methods for achieving student reading literacy, these educational goals should be achieved by designing and implementing ongoing, quality instruction for teaching candidates, and quality professional development and advancement, or remedial support for all in-service teachers: K-third-grade teachers of reading, reading specialists, and content-area teachers.

§2.1. New Qualifications, Licenses, and Certifications for All Education Professionals

The state must issue licenses and certain certification(s) under its jurisdiction to persons qualified and competent for their respective positions in education.

A. The board requires a teaching candidate to successfully complete a basic reading instruction competence teaching assessment before being granted an initial teaching license to teach content areas in grades 4-12 to any and all pupils.
B. The board must require a teaching candidate to successfully complete an advanced reading instruction competence teaching assessment to receive a teacher of reading certification before being granted approval to provide instruction to any students in grades K-3, for all reading specialists in elementary and secondary schools, and teachers in ELL, Title I, and special-education programs.

C. The board must require colleges and universities offering a board-approved teacher preparation program to provide remedial assistance, including a formal diagnostic component, to teaching candidates who wish to become K-3 classroom teachers and teaching specialist grades K-12, to persons enrolled in their institution who did not achieve a qualifying score on the advanced reading instruction competence teaching assessment to earn a teacher of reading certificate, and including those for whom English is a second language.

D. The colleges and universities must provide assistance in the specific academic areas of deficiency in which the person did not achieve a qualifying score.

E. Districts and schools must provide similar, appropriate, and timely remedial assistance that includes a formal diagnostic component and mentoring to those persons employed by the district/school who completed their teacher education program both in and outside the state, received a one-year license to teach in the state, and did not achieve a qualifying score on the advanced reading instruction competence teaching assessment to earn a certification, including those persons for whom English is a second language.

F. Districts and schools shall report annually to the state on the total number of teacher candidates during the most recent school year taking the basic reading instruction competence teaching assessment, and the teacher of reading/teaching specialists taking the advanced reading instruction competence teaching assessment; the number who achieve a qualifying score on the examination(s); the number who do not achieve a qualifying score on the examination(s); the distribution of all candidates' scores; the number of candidates who have taken the examination(s) at least once before; and the number of candidates who have taken the examination(s) at least once before and achieved a qualifying score.

G. A person who has completed an approved teacher preparation program and obtained a one-year license to teach but has not successfully completed the skills basic reading instruction competence teaching assessment or the teacher of reading/teaching specialists advanced reading instruction competence teaching assessment may renew the license for additional one-year periods, contingent upon the licensee

1. providing evidence of participating in an approved remedial assistance program provided by a school district or postsecondary institution that includes a formal diagnostic component in the specific areas in which the licensee did not obtain qualifying scores; and

2. attempting to successfully complete the skills reading instruction competence teaching assessment(s) during the period of the one-year extended license.

H. The state will grant continuing licenses only to those persons who have met board criteria for granting a continuing license, which includes successfully completing the basic reading instruction competence teaching assessment in reading, writing, and mathematics and, for teachers of reading, the teachers of reading certification as witnessed successfully passing the advanced reading instruction competence teaching assessment.

I. All colleges and universities approved by the state to prepare persons for teacher licensure must include in their teacher preparation programs a common core of teaching knowledge and skills to be acquired by all persons recommended for teacher licensure. These common core standards shall meet the standards developed by the National Governors Association model standards for beginning teacher licensing and development.

J. Districts and schools shall report annually to the state on the performance of teacher candidates: for teachers of reading report on student reading achievement; for content teachers, report on common core assessments of knowledge and skills under this paragraph during the most recent school year.

§2.2 Requirements for All College and University Teacher Preparation Programs

Reading and writing literacy strategies at all colleges and universities to prepare persons for content-area classroom teacher licensure must be approved by the state and include research-based best practices in reading and writing, consistent with Statutes, Section 4.0 of this law, that enable the licensure candidate to know how to teach reading and writing literacy in the candidate's content areas and prepare the licensure candidate for the basic reading instruction teaching assessment.

Teachers of reading preparation for grade K-3 teachers and Title I, special education, ELL, and teaching specialist grades K-12 will implement instruction in research-based, best practices in reading and writing development, consistent with Statutes, Section 4.0 of this law, that enable the candidate to know how to teach reading, writing, speaking, listening, and language to each student using foundational knowledge, practices, and strategies so that all students will achieve continuous progress. To become a certified teacher of reading, teachers and specialists will pass the advanced reading instruction teaching assessment through the implementation of

A. Board-approved teacher preparation programs for certifying teachers of reading in K-3 grade education. The program will require instruction in the application of comprehensive, foundational reading and instruction programs from Statutes, Section 4.0 of this law to include a program or collection of instructional practices that is based on valid, replicated evidence showing that when these programs or practices are used, diverse student populations can be expected to achieve, at a minimum, literacy and satisfactory reading progress.

The program or collection of practices for teachers of reading must include, at a minimum, instruction in ten areas of foundational reading instruction (Statutes, Section 4.0.A of this law), to include foundation concepts about oral and written language learning; knowledge of the structure of language; knowledge of SEEDS community and learning disorders; interpretation and administration of assessments for planning instruction; and structured language teaching of phonology, phonics, and word study, fluent automatic reading of text, vocabulary, text comprehension, and handwriting, spelling, and written expression. All certified teachers of reading must be effectively prepared and proficient in the following areas:

1. Foundational concepts about oral and written language learning that includes
   a. understanding and explaining the language processing requirements of proficient reading and writing, including phonological (speech sound) processing, orthographic (print) processing, semantic (meaning) processing, syntactic (sentence level) processing, and discourse (connected text level) processing;
   b. understanding and explaining other aspects of cognition and behavior that affect reading and writing, including attention, executive function, memory, processing speed, and graphomotor control;
   c. defining and identifying environmental, cultural, and social factors that contribute to literacy development, including language spoken at home, language and literacy experiences, and cultural values;
   d. knowing and identifying phases in the typical developmental progression of oral language (semantic, syntactic, and pragmatic), phonological skill, printed word recognition, spelling, reading fluency, reading comprehension, and written expression;
   e. understanding and explaining the known causal relationships among phonological skill, phonic decoding, spelling, accurate and automatic word recognition, text reading fluency, background knowledge, verbal reasoning skill, vocabulary, reading comprehension, and writing;
   f. knowing and explaining how the relationships among the major components of literacy development change with reading development (i.e., changes in oral language, including phonological awareness, phonics and word recognition, spelling, reading and writing fluency, vocabulary, reading comprehension skills and strategies, and written expression);
   g. knowing reasonable goals and expectations for learners at various stages of reading and writing development; and
   h. understanding first- and second-language acquisition stages, the impact of culture on student performance, knowledge regarding bilingual education and English

CINTHIA COLETTI

as a second language programming and teaching methods, knowledge of how to interpret results of students' oral language proficiency in relation to the results of tests measuring academic achievement and cognitive processes, and understanding how to interpret results of similar or parallel tests given in more than one language.

2. Knowledge of the structure of language includes

   a. phonology (the sound system), including how to identify, pronounce, classify, and compare the consonant and vowel phonemes of English;

   b. orthography (the spelling system), including understanding the broad outline of historical influences on English spelling patterns, especially Anglo-Saxon, Latin (Romance), and Greek; defining "grapheme" as a functional correspondence unit or representation of a phoneme; recognizing and explaining common orthographic rules and patterns in English; knowing the difference between high frequency and irregular words; and identifying, explaining, and categorizing six basic syllable types in English spelling;

   c. morphology, including identifying and categorizing common morphemes in English, for example, Anglo-Saxon compounds, inflectional and derivational suffixes, Latin-based prefixes, roots, and derivational suffixes, and Greek-based combining forms;

   d. semantics, including understanding and identifying examples of meaningful word relationships or semantic organization;

   e. syntax, including defining and distinguishing among phrases, dependent clauses, and independent clauses in sentence structures; and identifying the parts of speech and the grammatical role of a word in a sentence; and

   f. discourse organization, including explaining the major differences between narrative and expository discourse; identifying and constructing expository paragraphs of varying logical structures (e.g., classification, reason, sequence); and identifying cohesive devices in text and inferential gaps in the surface language of text.

3. Knowledge of dyslexia and other learning disorders includes
   a. understanding the most common intrinsic differences between good and poor readers (i.e., cognitive, neurobiological, and linguistic);
   b. recognizing the tenets of the NICHD and IDA definition of dyslexia;
   c. recognizing that dyslexia and other reading difficulties exist on a continuum of severity;
   d. identifying the distinguishing characteristics of dyslexia and related reading disorders (including developmental language comprehension disorder, specific language impairment, attention deficit hyperactivity disorder, disorders of written expression or dysgraphia, mathematics learning disorder, nonverbal learning disorder, etc.);
   e. identifying how symptoms of reading difficulty may change over time in response to development and instruction; and
   f. understanding federal and state laws that pertain to learning disabilities, especially reading disabilities and dyslexia.
4. Interpretation and administration of assessments for planning instruction includes
   a. understanding the differences among screening, diagnostic, outcome, and progress-monitoring assessments;
   b. understanding basic principles of test construction, including reliability, validity, and norm-referencing, and knowing the most well-validated screening tests designed to identify students at risk for reading difficulties;
   c. understanding the principles of progress monitoring and the use of graphs to indicate progress;
   d. knowing the range of skills typically assessed by diagnostic surveys of phonological skills, decoding skills, oral reading skills, spelling, and writing;
   e. recognizing the content and purposes of the most common diagnostic tests used by psychologists and educational evaluators; and
   f. interpreting measures of reading comprehension and written expression in relation to an individual child's component profile.

5. Structured language teaching of phonology includes
   a. identifying the general and specific goals of phonological skill instruction;
   b. knowing the progression of phonological skill development (i.e., rhyme, syllable, onset-rime, phoneme differentiation);
   c. identifying the differences among various phonological manipulations, including identifying, matching, blending, segmenting, substituting, and deleting sounds;
   d. understanding the principles of phonological skill instruction: brief, multicomponent, conceptual, and auditory-verbal;
   e. understanding the reciprocal relationships among phonological processing, reading, spelling, and vocabulary; and
   f. understanding the phonological features of a second language, such as Spanish, and how they interfere with English pronunciations and phonics.

6. Structured language teaching of phonics and word recognition includes
   a. knowing or recognizing how to order phonics concepts from easier to more difficult;
   b. understanding principles of explicit and direct teaching: model, lead, give guided practice, and review;
   c. stating the rationale for multicomponent and multimodal techniques;
   d. knowing the routines of a complete lesson format, from the introduction of a word recognition concept to fluent application in meaningful reading and writing; and
   e. understanding research-based adaptations of instruction for students with weaknesses in working memory, attention, executive function, or processing speed.

7. Structured language teaching of fluent, automatic reading of text includes
   a. understanding the role of fluency in word recognition, oral reading, silent reading, comprehension of written discourse, and motivation to read;
   b. understanding reading fluency as a stage of normal reading development, as the primary symptom of some

reading disorders, and as a consequence of practice and instruction;

 c. defining and identifying examples of text at a student's frustration, instructional, and independent reading level;

 d. knowing sources of activities for building fluency in component reading skills;

 e. knowing which instructional activities and approaches are most likely to improve fluency outcomes;

 f. understanding techniques to enhance student motivation to read; and

 g. understanding appropriate uses of assistive technology for students with serious limitations in reading fluency.

8. Structured language teaching of vocabulary includes

 a. understanding the role of vocabulary development and vocabulary knowledge in comprehension;

 b. understanding the role and characteristics of direct and indirect (contextual) methods of vocabulary instruction;

 c. knowing varied techniques for vocabulary instruction before, during, and after reading;

 d. understanding that word knowledge is multifaceted; and

 e. understanding the sources of wide differences in students' vocabularies.

9. Structured language teaching of text comprehension includes

 a. being familiar with teaching strategies that are appropriate before, during, and after reading and that promote reflective reading;

 b. contrasting the characteristics of major text genres, including narration, exposition, and argumentation;

 c. understanding the similarities and differences between written composition and text comprehension, and the usefulness of writing in building comprehension;

 d. identifying in any text the phrases, clauses, sentences, paragraphs, and academic language that could be a source of miscomprehension;

 e. understanding levels of comprehension including the surface code, text base, and mental model (situation model); and

 f. understanding factors that contribute to deep comprehension, including background knowledge, vocabulary, verbal reasoning ability, knowledge of literary structures and conventions, and use of skills and strategies for close reading of text.

10. Structured language teacher of handwriting, spelling, and written composition includes

    a. knowing research-based principles for teaching letter naming and letter formation, both manuscript and cursive;

    b. knowing techniques for teaching handwriting fluency;

    c. recognizing and explaining the relationship between transcription skills and written expression;

    d. identifying levels of students spelling development and orthographic knowledge;

    e. recognizing and explaining the influences of phonological, orthographic, and morphemic knowledge on spelling;

    f. understanding the major components and processes of written expression and how they interact (e.g., basic writing/transcription skills versus text generation);

    g. knowing grade and developmental expectations for students' writing in the following areas: mechanics and conventions of writing, composition, revision, and editing processes; and

    h. understanding appropriate uses of assistive technology in written expression.

B. The program or collection of teacher of reading practices must also include and integrate instructional strategies for continuously interpreting and administering student assessments and evaluations (Statutes, Section 3.0 of this law), and communicating the student's reading progress and needs to design and implement ongoing interventions (Statutes, Section 4.0 of this law) so that students of all ages and proficiency levels can read and comprehend text and apply higher-level thinking skills.

C. Practicum for all teachers of reading certification shall include lesson planning and supervised practice both in teaching foundational reading instruction to whole classrooms and in delivering intervention to individuals or small groups of SEEDS. In addition, practicum for teaching specialists— special-education teachers, Title I instructors, and ELL instructors shall include documenting student progress with formal and informal assessments and completing an educational assessment of a student's progress.

D. Scientifically discredited notions of reading acquisition and instructional practices that are incompatible with science or inhibit student progress, such as using picture and context cues for decoding rather than self-monitoring and comprehension shall not be promoted in teacher preparation programs.

E. The guidelines shall be rewritten to mandate rigor in the study of reading development to (include phonics) comply with this legislation. This shall be accomplished in consultation with an oversight panel consisting of persons with demonstrated mastery of the knowledge.

F. The [insert name state department of education], in consultation with an oversight panel consisting of persons with demonstrated mastery of knowledge in literacy approve a minor in reading, and ensure that the courses required in the reading minor of any teacher preparation program cover in depth the knowledge set forth in this legislation so as to ensure attaining a certificate to become a teacher of reading.

G. Syllabi changes are to be approved by the [insert name state department of education] in consultation with an oversight panel consisting of persons with demonstrated mastery of the knowledge of reading development and reading literacy, and experts in evaluation of the content and quality of teacher preparation programs who have conducted such reviews in other states.

H. The [insert name state department of education] shall designate funding for a higher education collaborative to provide professional development for reading administrators and instructors in institutions of higher education. The collaborative shall meet a minimum of three times per year and feature national reading experts as presenters on topics related to the knowledge of literacy and to preparing teacher candidates to become certified teachers of reading equipped with knowledge in all foundational reading skills.

§2.3 Reading Instruction Competence Teaching Assessment

The [insert state name] reading instruction competence teaching assessment examination must measure the knowledge, skill, and ability of kindergarten, elementary, secondary, ELL, Title I, and special-education teachers of reading in comprehensive, foundational reading and instructions, and Multi-Tier System of Supports as defined in Statutes, Section 4.0 of this law. The teaching-assessment examination must have been data validated and previously administered in another state for over five years (example: MTEL90 for BRICA and MTEL08 for ARICA) and be composed of multiple-choice and constructed-response questions designed to measure reading instruction knowledge and skills. Test content areas must assess foundations of reading development, development of reading comprehension, reading assessment and instruction, and integration of knowledge and understanding for reading literacy.

1. Basic Reading Instruction Competence Teaching Assessment
    Beginning (insert start date), all candidates for initial educator or professional educator licensure in Early Childhood Level Education (approximate ages birth through eight), Early Childhood through Middle Childhood Level Education (approximate ages birth through eleven), Middle Childhood through Early Adolescent Level Education (approximate ages six through twelve or thirteen), and Special Education, and all persons entering or pursuing an approved certification as a teacher of reading as defined earlier shall pass a new exam covering basic knowledge of the foundations of reading development, development of reading comprehension, reading instruction and assessment, and integration of knowledge and understanding.
    A. A basic reading instruction competence teaching assessment (BRICA) must have at least one hundred multiple-choice questions, worth 80 percent of the total possible points, and at least two open-response questions, worth 20 percent of the total possible points, and must have been previously administered in another state for over five years.
    B. If this BRICA is embedded in a comprehensive, multi-subject licensure exam, there must be at least one hundred multiple-choice and two open-response reading questions, and there shall be a separate passing score for the reading portion of the exam.

C. The foundations of reading portion of a BRICA shall be worth 35 percent of the total possible points and consist of multiple-choice questions covering the understanding of phonological and phonemic awareness, the understanding of concepts of print and the alphabetic principle, the role of phonics in promoting reading development, and the understanding of word analysis skills and strategies.

D. The development of reading comprehension portion of a BRICA shall be worth 27 percent of the total possible points and consist of multiple-choice questions covering the understanding of vocabulary development, the understanding of how to apply reading comprehension skills and strategies to imaginative/literary texts, and the understanding of how to apply reading comprehension skills and strategies to informational/expository texts.

E. The reading assessment and instruction portion of a BRICA shall be worth 18 percent of the total possible points and consist of multiple-choice questions covering the understanding of formal and informal methods for assessing reading development, and the understanding of multiple approaches to reading instruction.

F. The integration of knowledge and understanding portion of a BRICA shall be worth 20 percent of the total possible points and consist of at least two open-response questions requiring organized, developed analyses on topics related to foundations of reading development, development of reading comprehension, and/or reading assessment and instruction.

G. The Department of Public Instruction, in consultation with an oversight panel consisting of persons with demonstrated mastery of the knowledge set forth, shall select a BRICA and make a practice exam available by [insert date].

H. The passing score for a BRICA shall not be lower than 75 percent of the total possible points or 85 percent of the total possible points for prospective special-education teachers, reading teachers, and reading specialists. Persons entering or pursuing an approved program leading to certification as a reading teacher or reading specialist, who have previously passed a BRICA with a score of at least 85 percent, will not be required to retake the exam.

I. The Department of Public Instruction may grant a provisional license for up to a one-year term after failure and before retaking a BRICA if the individual candidate is actively involved in an approved remedial class or approved professional development as preparation for retaking the exam. No person shall be accepted into or continue in a program teaching grades pre-K-3 students, leading to certification as a teacher of reading or reading specialist without passing a BRICA.

J. Institutions of higher education are to provide free, approved remedial work as specified in for their candidates who fail a BRICA.

K. Districts are to provide free, approved professional development as specified for new out-of-state hires who fail a BRICA. The Department of Public Instruction shall require districts to earmark a specific amount of funds annually for professional development in reading, based on the number of new out-of-state hires who have not yet passed a BRICA.

L. Providers of the remedial work and professional development in subsections J and K must be approved by the Department of Public Instruction after consultation with an oversight panel consisting of persons with demonstrated mastery of the knowledge set forth in this legislation.

M. Results of a BRICA are to be reported and made public annually, with first-time passage rates and overall passage rates tied to specific institutions of higher education for initial and professional license candidates and to individual districts for out-of-state hires.

N. Individuals who are certified in reading remediation or language therapy by a nationally recognized professional organization, have demonstrated success for at least two years in teaching SEEDS, and who pass a BRICA, plus an ARICA in Section 2.3.2 below with scores of at least 85 percent, may be hired by districts to provide professional development to teachers or administrators, or to work individually with SEEDS, or may be hired by parents to work with their own children in schools during school hours.

2. Advanced Reading Instruction Competence Teaching Assessment for Teachers of Reading Certification

In addition to the requirements of Section 2.3.1 of the basic reading instruction competence teaching assessment of this legislation, candidates for initial educator or professional educator certified as a teacher of reading, special-education teacher, Title I reading teacher, or ELL reading specialist shall pass a new advanced level exam covering reading processes and development, reading assessment, reading instruction, reading support systems, professional knowledge and roles of the teachers of reading, special-education teacher, Title I reading teacher, or ELL reading specialist (as appropriate to the candidate), and integration of knowledge and understanding. This examination is required for all in-service and preservice teachers in grades K-3, teachers of reading in all grades, special-education teachers, Title I reading teachers, and ELL reading specialists (as appropriate to the candidate).

A. An advanced reading instruction competence teaching assessment (ARICA) must have at least one hundred multiple-choice questions, worth 80 percent of the total possible points; at least two open-response questions, worth 20 percent of the total possible points; and have been previously administered in another state for over five years.

B. The reading processes and development portion of an ARICA shall be worth 32 percent of the total possible points and consist of multiple-choice questions covering in depth the understanding of the connections among listening, speaking, reading, and writing; phonological and phonemic awareness; concepts of print and the alphabetic principle; the role of phonics knowledge in reading development; other words analysis skills and strategies; the development of vocabulary knowledge and skills; skills and strategies for comprehending literary/imaginative texts; and skills and strategies for comprehending expository and content-area texts.

C. The reading assessment portion of an ARICA shall be worth 16 percent of the total possible points and consist of multiple-choice questions covering the understanding of test construction and the interpretation of test results; characteristics and uses of formal and informal reading and writing assessments; the role of assessment in promoting reading and writing development; and the screening and diagnosis of reading difficulties and disabilities.

D. The reading instruction portion of an ARICA shall be worth 16 percent of the total possible points and consist of multiple-choice questions covering the understanding of research-based instructional strategies, programs, and methodologies for promoting early reading and writing development; research-based instructional strategies, programs, and methodologies for consolidating and expending reading, writing, and spelling skills; the differentiation of reading instruction to meet the needs of individual students; and characteristics and uses of reading resources, materials, and technologies.

E. The professional knowledge and roles of the teachers of reading, special-education teacher, Title I reading teacher, or ELL reading specialist (as appropriate to the candidate) portion of an ARICA shall be worth 16 percent of the total possible points and consist of multiple-choice questions covering the understanding of the interpretation, evaluation, and application of reading research; the multiple roles of the candidate's prospective position in planning and implementing reading instruction in collaboration with other members of the school community; and the understanding of the role of professional development in promoting the effectiveness of the candidate's prospective position and other educators.

F. The integration of knowledge and understanding portion of an ARICA shall be worth 20 percent of the total possible points and consist of at least two open-response questions requiring organized, developed analyses on topics related to reading processes and development, reading assessment, reading instruction, and/or the professional knowledge and roles of the teachers of reading, special-education teacher, Title I reading teacher, and ELL reading specialist (as appropriate to the candidate).

G. The Department of Public Instruction, in consultation with an oversight panel consisting of persons with demonstrated mastery of the knowledge set forth, shall select an ARICA and make a practice exam available by [insert date].

H. The passing score for an ARICA shall not be lower than 85 percent of the total possible points.

I. The Department of Public Instruction may grant a provisional license for up to a one-year term after failure and before retaking an ARICA if the individual candidate is actively involved in an approved remedial class or approved professional development as preparation for retaking the exam.

J. Institutions of higher education are to provide free, approved remedial work for their candidates who fail an ARICA.

K. Districts are to provide free, approved professional development for in-service teachers and new out-of-state hires who fail an ARICA. The Department of Public Instruction shall require districts to earmark a specific amount of funds annually for professional development in reading, based on the number of employees who have not yet passed an ARICA.

L. Providers of the remedial work and professional development in subsection N must be approved by the Department of Public Instruction after consultation with an oversight panel consisting of persons with demonstrated mastery of the knowledge set forth in this legislation.

M. Results of an ARICA are to be reported and made public annually, with first-time passage rates and overall passage rates tied to specific institutions of higher education for initial license candidates and to individual districts for out-of-state hires.

N. Individuals who are certified in reading remediation or language therapy by a nationally recognized professional organization, have demonstrated success for at least two years in teaching SEEDS, and who pass an ARICA, plus a BRICA in Section 2.3.1 with scores of at least 85 percent, may be hired by districts to provide professional development to teachers or administrators or to work individually with struggling readers, or may be hired by parents to work with their own children in schools during school hours.

§2.4 Reading Instruction Competence Teaching Assessment Reporting and Support

[Insert name of state board of education], no later than [insert date], shall adopt a reading instruction competence teacher assessment for all kindergarten, elementary, and secondary teachers; teachers of reading; special-education teachers; Title I reading teachers; and ELL reading specialists consistent with Statutes, Sections 2.0, 3.0, and 4.0 of this law.

A. [Insert name of state board of education] shall report to the Senate and House of Representatives committees having jurisdiction over prekindergarten through grade 12 education policy by [insert date], on the basic and advanced reading instruction competence teacher assessment that was adopted.

B. [Insert name of state board of education], in consultation with members of the professional reading community, shall establish an approved list of reading instruction program centers that offer staff development and remedial training necessary for all existing prekindergarten through 12 educators in reading and literacy to successfully pass either the basic or advanced reading instruction competence teacher assessment of this law (as appropriate to the candidate).

§2.5 Pretest and Grant for Candidates in an Approved Teacher Preparation Program

[Insert name of state board of education] shall provide teaching candidates and existing teachers reading instruction grants to improve their knowledge of teaching reading with the goal of passing the advanced reading instruction competence teacher assessment and becoming certified as a teacher of reading. A candidate taking the pretest is eligible for a grant to attend an approved reading instruction program if the candidate has successfully completed an examination of skills in reading, writing, mathematics, and reading literacy ([insert state name] Statutes, Section 2.1 of the law), commits to attend and complete an approved comprehension reading instruction program of his or her choosing, and commits to take both the basic and advanced reading instruction competence examination.

A. At the completion of the reading instruction program, no later than [insert date], a candidate enrolled in the final year of an approved teacher preparation program in kindergarten, elementary, secondary, or special education may apply to [insert name of state board of education] to take a [insert state name] reading instruction competence teaching-assessment pretest.

B. No later than [insert date], schools providing instruction in kindergarten through grade 6 may apply to the [insert name of state board of education] in a manner prescribed by the [insert name of state board of education] for their teachers to take the [insert state name] reading instruction competence teaching assessment pretest.

C. A school is eligible for a grant for kindergarten, elementary, secondary, and special-education teachers to attend an approved reading instruction program if the teachers

1. take the pretest;
2. commit to attending and completing an approved reading instruction program of their choosing;
3. take the basic and/or advanced reading instruction competence teaching assessment as determined by [insert state name] Statutes, Section 2.3 under this law.

§2.6 Passing Score on the [insert state name] Reading Instruction Competence Teaching Assessment

The [insert name of state board of education], in cooperation with the testing contractor providing the basic and advanced reading instruction competence teaching assessment, must use the reading instruction competence teaching assessment results on the pretest and posttest to determine a passing score on the [insert state name] reading instruction competence teaching assessment by [insert date].

§EFFECTIVE DATE. This section is effective [insert date].

HIGHER EDUCATION TEACHER PREPARATION REQUIREMENTS

A Blueprint for Literacy Success in the Classroom
Teachers of Reading Preparation
The Knowledge and Skills Required to Pass an Advanced Reading
Instruction Competence Assessment

Introduction:

In 2000, the National Reading Panel, under the auspices of the National Institutes of Health and the US Department of Education, issued a report that identified the five component reading skills necessary to become a successful reader: phonemic awareness, phonics, fluency, vocabulary, and comprehension. Although the report cited the need for highly qualified teachers, it did not spell out the required knowledge and skills necessary to be considered "highly qualified."

In 2011, I had the honor of becoming the Vice President of the Board of Directors for the International Dyslexia Association (IDA). This organization published a seminal report on the knowledge and practice standards for teachers of reading that addressed an unfilled need in the field. Below you will find the complete report: IDA *Knowledge and Practice Standards for Teachers of Reading (KPS)*. The KPS is a resource for teachers, schools, and especially for colleges of education's teacher preparation programs. The KPS, like the Literacy Policy, is filled with essential knowledge for helping to ensure all teachers are prepared to teach all children to read. It is my pleasure to reproduce this lauded work on IDA's behalf.

The
International
DYSLE✗IA
Association®

Knowledge and Practice Standards for Teachers of Reading

International Dyslexia Association,
Professional Standards and Practices Committee
2010

Louisa Moats, Committee Chair
Suzanne Carreker
Rosalie Davis
Phyllis Meisel
Louise Spear-Swerling
Barbara Wilson

Purpose of These Standards

The International Dyslexia Association (IDA) offers these standards to guide the preparation, certification, and professional development of those who teach reading and related literacy skills in classroom, remedial, and clinical settings. The term *teacher* is used throughout this document to refer to any person whose responsibilities include reading instruction. The standards aim to specify what any individual responsible for teaching reading should know and be able to do so that reading difficulties, including dyslexia, may be prevented, alleviated, or remediated. In addition, the standards seek to differentiate classroom teachers from therapists or specialists who are qualified to work with the most challenging students.

Although programs that certify or support teachers, clinicians, or specialists differ in their preparation methodologies, teaching approaches, and organizational purposes, they should ascribe to a common set of professional standards for the benefit of the students they serve. Compliance with these standards should assure the public that individuals who teach in public and private schools, as well as those who teach in clinics, are prepared to implement scientifically based and clinically proven practices.

Background: Why These Standards Are Necessary

Reading difficulties are the most common cause of academic failure and underachievement. The National Assessment of Educational Progress consistently finds that about 36 percent of all fourth-graders read at a level described as "below basic." Between 15 and 20 percent of young students demonstrate significant weaknesses with language processes, including but not limited to phonological processing, that are the root cause of dyslexia and related learning difficulties. Of those who are referred to special-education services in public schools, approximately 85 percent are referred because of their problems with language, reading, and/or writing. Informed and effective classroom instruction, especially in the early grades, can prevent and relieve the severity of many of these problems. For those students with dyslexia who need specialized instruction outside of the regular class, competent intervention from a specialist can lessen the impact of the disorder and help the student overcome the most debilitating symptoms.

Teaching reading effectively, especially to students experiencing difficulty, requires considerable knowledge and skill. Regrettably, current licensing and professional development practices endorsed by many states are insufficient for the preparation and support of teachers and specialists. Researchers are finding that those with reading specialist and special-education licenses often know no more about research-based, effective practices than those with a general-education teaching license. The majority of practitioners at all levels have not been prepared in sufficient depth to recognize early signs of risk, to prevent reading problems, or to teach students with dyslexia and related learning disabilities successfully. Inquiries into teacher preparation in reading have a revealed a pervasive absence of substantive content and academic rigor in many courses that lead to certification of teachers and specialists. Analyses of teacher licensing tests show that typically, very few are aligned with current research on effective instruction for students at risk. To address these gaps, IDA has adopted these standards for knowledge, practice, and ethical conduct.

Research-Based Assumptions about Dyslexia and Other Reading Difficulties

These standards are broadly constructed to address the knowledge and skill base for teaching reading in preventive, intervention, and remedial settings. Underlying the standards are assumptions about the nature, prevalence, manifestations, and treatments for dyslexia that are supported by research and by accepted diagnostic guidelines. These assumptions characterize dyslexia in relation to other reading problems and learning difficulties, as follows:

- Dyslexia is a language-based disorder of learning to read and write originating from a core or basic problem with phonological processing intrinsic to the individual. Its primary symptoms are inaccurate and/or slow printed word recognition and poor spelling—problems that in turn affect reading fluency and comprehension and written expression. Other types of reading disabilities include specific difficulties with reading comprehension and/or speed of processing (reading fluency). These problems may exist in relative isolation or may overlap extensively in individuals with reading difficulties.
- Dyslexia often exists in individuals with aptitudes, talents, and abilities that enable them to be successful in many domains.
- Dyslexia often coexists with other developmental difficulties and disabilities, including problems with attention, memory, and executive function.
- Dyslexia exists on a continuum. Many students with milder forms of dyslexia are never officially diagnosed and are not eligible for special-education services. They deserve appropriate instruction in the regular classroom and through other intervention programs.

- Appropriate recognition and treatment of dyslexia is the responsibility of all educators and support personnel in a school system, not just the reading or special-education teacher.
- Although early intervention is the most effective approach, individuals with dyslexia and other reading difficulties can be helped at any age.

How to Use These Standards

The standards outline the 1) content knowledge necessary to teach reading and writing to students with dyslexia or related disorders or who are at risk for reading difficulty; 2) practices of effective instruction; and 3) ethical conduct expected of professional educators and clinicians. Regular classroom teachers should also have the foundational knowledge of language, literacy development, and individual differences because they share responsibility for preventing and ameliorating reading problems.

The standards may be used for several purposes, including but not limited to

- course design within teacher certification programs;
- practicum requirements within certification programs;
- criteria for membership in IDA's coalition of organizations that provide training and supervision of teachers, tutors, and specialists (note that additional requirements for membership are to be determined);
- criteria for the preparation of those professionals receiving referrals through IDA offices; and
- a content framework for the development of licensing or certification examinations.

How to Read the Standards

The Standards include two major sections. Section I addresses foundation concepts, knowledge of language structure, knowledge of dyslexia and other learning disorders, administration and interpretation of assessments, the principles of structured language teaching, and ethical standards for the profession. Section II addresses skills to be demonstrated in supervised practice. In section I, standards A, B, C, and E are presented in two columns. The column on the left refers to content knowledge that can be learned and tested independent of observed teaching competency. The column on the right delineates the practical skills of teaching that depend on or that are driven by content knowledge. The exception to this format is standard D. It includes a third column on the right that specifies in greater detail what the teacher or specialist should be able to do.

Many of the standards are followed by the designation of (level 1) or (level 2). These designations indicate whether the standard should be met by novice teachers in training (level 1) or by specialists with more experience and greater expertise (level 2). In section II, the recommended standards for preparation of teachers and specialists are distinguished by these two levels.

References for this section are available at www.interdys.org/standards.htm

The International DYSLEXIA Association®

SECTION I: KNOWLEDGE AND PRACTICE STANDARDS

A. Foundation Concepts about Oral and Written Learning

Content Knowledge	Application
1. Understand and explain the language processing requirements of proficient reading and writing • Phonological (speech sound) processing • Orthographic (print) processing • Semantic (meaning) processing • Syntactic (sentence level) processing • Discourse (connected text level) processing	1. a. Explain the domains of language and their importance to proficient reading and writing (level 1). b. Explain a scientifically valid model of the language processes underlying reading and writing (level 2).
2. Understand and explain other aspects of cognition and behavior that affect reading and writing • Attention • Executive function • Memory • Processing speed • Graphomotor control	2. a. Recognize that reading difficulties coexist with other cognitive and behavioral problems (level 1). b. Explain a scientifically valid model of other cognitive influences on reading and writing, and explain major research findings regarding the contribution of linguistic and cognitive factors to the prediction of literacy outcomes (level 2).
3. Define and identify environmental, cultural, and social factors that contribute to literacy development (e.g., language spoken at home, language and literacy experiences, cultural values)	3. Identify (level 1) or explain (level 2) major research findings regarding the contribution of environmental factors to literacy outcomes.

4. Know and identify phases in the typical developmental progression of • Oral language (semantic, syntactic, pragmatic) • Phonological skill • Printed word recognition • Spelling • Reading fluency • Reading comprehension • Written expression	4. Match examples of student responses and learning behavior to phases in language and literacy development (level 1).
5. Understand and explain the known causal relationships among phonological skill, phonic decoding, spelling, accurate and automatic word recognition, text reading fluency, background knowledge, verbal reasoning skill, vocabulary, reading comprehension, and writing.	5. Explain how a weakness in each component skill of oral language, reading, and writing may affect other related skills and processes across time (level 2).
6. Know and explain how the relationships among the major components of literacy development change with reading development (i.e., changes in oral language, including phonological awareness; phonics and word recognition; spelling; reading and writing fluency; vocabulary; reading comprehension skills and strategies; written expression).	6. Identify the most salient instructional needs of students who are at different points of reading and writing development (level 2).
7. Know reasonable goals and expectations for learners at various stages of reading and writing development.	7. Given case study material, explain why a student is/is not meeting goals and expectations in reading or writing for his or her age/grade (level 1).

Explanatory Notes

An extensive research base exists on the abilities that are important in learning to read and write, including how these abilities interact with each other, how they are influenced by experience, and how they change across development. Teachers' knowledge of this research base is an essential foundation for the competencies and skills described in subsequent sections of this document.

References for this section are available at www.interdys.org/standards.htm

The
International
DYSLEXIA
Association®

B. Knowledge of the Structure of Language

Content Knowledge	Application
Phonology (The Speech Sound System) 1. Identify, pronounce, classify, and compare the consonant and vowel phonemes of English.	1. a. Identify similar or contrasting features among phonemes (level 1). b. Reconstruct the consonant and vowel phoneme inventories and identify the feature differences between and among phonemes (level 2).
Orthography (The Spelling System) 2. Understand the broad outline of historical influences on English spelling patterns, especially Anglo-Saxon, Latin (Romance), and Greek.	2. Recognize typical words from the historical layers of English (Anglo-Saxon, Latin/Romance, Greek) (level 1).
3. Define *grapheme* as a functional correspondence unit or representation of a phoneme.	3. Accurately map graphemes to phonemes in any English word (level 1).
4. Recognize and explain common orthographic rules and patterns in English.	4. Sort words by orthographic "choice" pattern; analyze words by suffix ending patterns and apply suffix ending rules.
5. Know the difference between "high frequency" and "irregular" words.	5. Identify printed words that are the exception to regular patterns and spelling principles; sort high frequency words into regular and exception words (level 1).
6. Identify, explain, and categorize six basic syllable types in English spelling.	6. Sort, pronounce, and combine regular written syllables and apply the most productive syllable division principles (level 1).

Morphology

7. Identify and categorize common morphemes in English, including Anglo-Saxon compounds, inflectional suffixes, and derivational suffixes; Latin-based prefixes, roots, and derivational suffixes; and Greek-based combining forms.

7. a. Recognize the most common prefixes, roots, suffixes, and combining forms in English content words, and analyze words at both the syllable and morpheme levels (level 1).
   b. Recognize advanced morphemes (e.g., chameleon prefixes) (level 2).

Semantics

8. Understand and identify examples of meaningful word relationships or semantic organization.

8. Match or identify examples of word associations, antonyms, synonyms, multiple meanings and uses, semantic overlap, and semantic feature analysis (level 1).

Syntax

9. Define and distinguish among phrases, dependent clauses, and independent clauses in sentence structure.

9. Construct and deconstruct simple, complex, and compound sentences (level 1).

10. Identify the parts of speech and the grammatical role of a word in a sentence.

10. a. Identify the basic parts of speech and classify words by their grammatical role in a sentence (level 1).
    b. Identify advanced grammatical concepts (e.g., infinitives, gerunds) (level 2).

Discourse Organization

11. Explain the major differences between narrative and expository discourse.

11. Classify text by genre; identify features that are characteristic of each genre, and identify graphic organizers that characterize typical structures (level 1).

12. Identify and construct expository paragraphs of varying logical structures (e.g., classification, reason, sequence).

12. Identify main idea sentences, connecting words, and topics that fit each type of expository paragraph organization (level 2).

13. Identify cohesive devices in text and inferential gaps in the surface language of text.

13. Analyze text for the purpose of identifying the inferences that students must make to comprehend (level 2).

Explanatory Notes

Formal knowledge about the structure of language—recognizing, for example, whether words are phonetically regular or irregular; common morphemes in words; and common sentence structures in English—is not an automatic consequence of high levels of adult literacy. However, without this kind of knowledge, teachers may have difficulty interpreting assessments correctly or may provide unintentionally confusing instruction to students. For instance, struggling readers are likely to be confused if they are encouraged to sound out a word that is phonetically irregular (e.g., *some*), or if irregular words, such as *come* and *have*, are used as examples of a syllable type such as "silent *e*." Similarly, to teach spelling and writing effectively, teachers need a knowledge base about language structure, including sentence and discourse structure. Research suggests that acquiring an understanding of language structure often requires explicit teaching of this information and more than superficial coverage in teacher preparation and professional development.

References for this section are available at www.interdys.org/standards.htm

C. Knowledge of Dyslexia and Other Learning Disorders

Content Knowledge	Application
1. Understand the most common intrinsic differences between good and poor readers (i.e., cognitive, neurobiological, and linguistic).	1. a. Recognize scientifically accepted characteristics of individuals with poor word recognition (e.g., overdependence on context to aid word recognition; inaccurate nonword reading) (level 1). b. Identify student learning behaviors and test profiles typical of students with dyslexia and related learning difficulties (level 2).
2. Recognize the tenets of the NICHD/IDA definition of dyslexia.	2. Explain the reasoning or evidence behind the main points in the definition (level 1).
3. Recognize that dyslexia and other reading difficulties exist on a continuum of severity.	3. Recognize levels of instructional intensity, duration, and scope appropriate for mild, moderate, and severe reading disabilities (level 1).
4. Identify the distinguishing characteristics of dyslexia and related reading and learning disabilities (including developmental language comprehension disorder, attention deficit hyperactivity disorder, disorders of written expression or dysgraphia, mathematics learning disorder, nonverbal learning disorders, etc.).	4. Match symptoms of the major subgroups of poor readers as established by research, including those with dyslexia, and identify typical case study profiles of those individuals (level 2).
5. Identify how symptoms of reading difficulty may change over time in response to development and instruction.	5. Identify predictable ways that symptoms might change as students move through the grades (level 2).

CINTHIA COLETTI

6. Understand federal and state laws that pertain to learning disabilities, especially reading disabilities and dyslexia.	6. a. Explain the most fundamental provisions of federal and state laws pertaining to the rights of students with disabilities, especially students' rights to a free, appropriate public education, an individualized educational plan, services in the least restrictive environment, and due process (level 1). b. Appropriately implement federal and state laws in identifying and serving students with learning disabilities, reading disabilities, and dyslexia (level 2).

Explanatory Notes

To identify children with dyslexia and other learning disabilities, teachers must understand and recognize the key symptoms of these disorders, as well as how the disorders differ from each other. In order to plan instruction and detect older students with learning disabilities who may have been overlooked in the early grades, teachers also should understand how students' difficulties may change over time, based on developmental patterns, experience, and instruction, as well as on increases in expectations across grades.

References for this section are available at www.interdys.org/standards.htm

D. Interpretation and Administration of Assessments for Planning Instruction

Content Knowledge	Application	Observable Competencies for Teaching Students with Dyslexia and Related Difficulties
1. Understand the differences among screening, diagnostic, outcome, and progress-monitoring assessments.	1. Match each type of assessment and its purpose (level 1).	1. Administer screenings and progress monitoring assessments (level 1)
2. Understand basic principles of test construction, including reliability, validity, and norm-referencing, and know the most well-validated screening tests designed to identify students at risk for reading difficulties.	2. Match examples of technically adequate, well-validated screening, diagnostic, outcome, and progress-monitoring assessments (level 1).	2. Explain why individual students are or are not at risk in reading based on their performance on screening assessments (level 1).
3. Understand the principles of progress monitoring and the use of graphs to indicate progress.	3. Using case study data, accurately interpret progress-monitoring graphs to decide whether or not a student is making adequate progress (level 1).	3. Display progress-monitoring data in graphs that are understandable to students and parents (level 1).

CINTHIA COLETTI

4. Know the range of skills typically assessed by diagnostic surveys of phonological skills, decoding skills, oral reading skills, spelling, and writing.	4. Using case study data, accurately interpret subtest scores from diagnostic surveys to describe a student's patterns of strengths and weaknesses and instructional needs (level 2).	4. Administer educational diagnostic assessments using standardized procedures (level 2).
5. Recognize the content and purposes of the most common diagnostic tests used by psychologists and educational evaluators.	5. Find and interpret appropriate print and electronic resources for evaluating tests (level 1).	5. Write reports that clearly and accurately summarize a student's current skills in important component areas of reading and reading comprehension (level 2).
6. Interpret measures of reading comprehension and written expression in relation to an individual child's component profile.	6. Using case study data, accurately interpret a student's performance on reading comprehension or written expression measures and make appropriate instructional recommendations.	6. Write appropriate, specific recommendations for instruction and educational programming based on assessment data (level 2).

Explanatory Notes

Teachers' ability to administer and interpret assessments accurately is essential both to early identification of students' learning problems and to planning effective instruction. Appropriate assessments enable teachers to recognize early signs that a child may be at risk for dyslexia or other learning disabilities, and the assessments permit teachers to target instruction to meet individual student's needs. Teachers should understand that there are different types of assessments for different purposes (e.g., brief but frequent assessments to monitor progress versus more lengthy, comprehensive assessments to provide detailed diagnostic information), as well as recognize which type of assessment is called for in a particular situation. Teachers need to know where to find unbiased information about the adequacy of published tests, and to interpret this information correctly, they require an understanding of basic principles of test construction and concepts such as reliability and validity. They also should understand how an individual student's component profile may influence his or her performance on a particular test, especially on broad measures of reading comprehension and written expression. For example, a child with very slow reading is likely to perform better on an untimed measure of reading comprehension than on a stringently timed measure; a child with writing problems may perform especially poorly on a reading comprehension test that requires lengthy written responses to open-ended questions.

References for this section are available at www.interdys.org/standards.htm

E-1. Structured Language Teaching: Phonology

Content Knowledge	Observable Competencies for Teaching Students with Dyslexia and Related Difficulties
1. Identify the general and specific goals of phonological skill instruction.	1. Explicitly state the goal of any phonological awareness teaching activity (level 1).
2. Know the progression of phonological skill development (i.e., rhyme, syllable, onset-rime, phoneme differentiation).	2. a. Select and implement activities that match a student's developmental level of phonological skill (level 1). b. Design and justify the implementation of activities that match a student's developmental level of phonological skill (level 2).
3. Identify the differences among various phonological manipulations, including identifying, matching, blending, segmenting, substituting, and deleting sounds.	3. Demonstrate instructional activities that identify, match, blend, segment, substitute, and delete sounds (level 1).
4. Understand the principles of phonological skill instruction: brief, multisensory, conceptual, and auditory-verbal.	4. a. Successfully produce vowel and consonant phonemes (level 1). b. Teach articulatory features of phonemes and words; use minimally contrasting pairs of sounds and words in instruction; support instruction with manipulative materials and movement (level 2).

5. Understand the reciprocal relationships among phonological processing, reading, spelling, and vocabulary.	5. a. Direct students' attention to speech sounds during reading, spelling, and vocabulary instruction using a mirror, discussion of articulatory features, and so on as scripted or prompted (level 1).
	b. Direct students' attention to speech sounds during reading, spelling, and vocabulary instruction without scripting or prompting (level 2).
6. Understand the phonological features of a second language, such as Spanish, and how they interfere with English pronunciation and phonics.	6. Explicitly contrast first and second language phonological systems, as appropriate, to anticipate which sounds may be most challenging for the second language learner (level 2).

Explanatory Notes

Phonological awareness, basic print concepts, and knowledge of letter sounds are foundational areas of literacy. Without early, research-based intervention, children who struggle in these areas are likely to continue to have reading difficulties. Furthermore, poor phonological awareness is a core weakness in dyslexia. Ample research exists to inform teaching of phonological awareness, including research on the phonological skills to emphasize in instruction, appropriate sequencing of instruction, and integrating instruction in phonological awareness with instruction in alphabet knowledge. Teachers who understand how to teach these foundational skills effectively can prevent or ameliorate many children's reading problems, including those of students with dyslexia.

References for this section are available at www.interdys.org/standards.htm

E-2. Structured Language Teaching: Phonics and Word Recognition

Content Knowledge	Observable Competencies for Teaching Students with Dyslexia and Related Difficulties
1. Know or recognize how to order phonics concepts from easier to more difficult.	1. Plan lessons with a cumulative progression of word recognition skills that build one on another (level 1).
2. Understand principles of explicit and direct teaching: model, lead, give guided practice, and review.	2. Explicitly and effectively teach (e.g., information taught is correct, students are attentive, teacher checks for understanding, teacher scaffolds students' learning) concepts of word recognition and phonics; apply concepts to reading single words, phrases, and connected text (level 1).
3. State the rationale for multisensory and multimodal techniques.	3. Demonstrate the simultaneous use of two or three learning modalities (to include listening, speaking, movement, touch, reading, and/or writing) to increase engagement and enhance memory (level 1).
4. Know the routines of a complete lesson format, from the introduction of a word recognition concept to fluent application in meaningful reading and writing.	4. Plan and effectively teach all steps in a decoding lesson, including single-word reading and connected text that is read fluently, accurately, and with appropriate intonation and expression (level 1).
5. Understand research-based adaptations of instruction for students with weaknesses in working memory, attention, executive function, or processing speed.	5. Adapt the pace, format, content, strategy, or emphasis of instruction according to students' pattern of response (level 2).

Explanatory Notes

The development of accurate word decoding skills—that is, the ability to read unfamiliar words by applying phonics knowledge—is an essential foundation for reading comprehension in all students. Decoding skills often are a central weakness for students with learning disabilities in reading, especially those with dyslexia. Teachers' abilities to provide explicit, systematic, appropriately sequenced instruction in phonics is indispensable to meet the needs of this population, as well as to help prevent reading problems in all beginning readers. Teachers should also understand the usefulness of multisensory, multimodal techniques in focusing students' attention on printed words, engaging students, and enhancing memory.

References for this section are available at www.interdys.org/standards.htm

The International DYSLEXIA Association®

E-3. Structured Language Teaching: Fluent, Automatic Reading of Text

Content Knowledge	Observable Competencies for Teaching Students with Dyslexia and Related Difficulties
1. Understand the role of fluency in word recognition, oral reading, silent reading, comprehension of written discourse, and motivation to read.	1. Assess students' fluency rate and determine reasonable expectations for reading fluency at various stages of reading development, using research-based guidelines and appropriate state and local standards and benchmarks (level 1).
2. Understand reading fluency as a stage of normal reading development, as the primary symptom of some reading disorders, and as a consequence of practice and instruction.	2. Determine which students need a fluency-oriented approach to instruction, using screening, diagnostic, and progress-monitoring assessments (level 2).
3. Define and identify examples of text at a student's frustration, instructional, and independent reading level.	3. Match students with appropriate texts as informed by fluency rate to promote ample independent oral and silent reading (level 1).
4. Know sources of activities for building fluency in component reading skills.	4. Design lesson plans that incorporate fluency-building activities into instruction at subword and word levels (level 1).
5. Know which instructional activities and approaches are most likely to improve fluency outcomes.	5. Design lesson plans with a variety of techniques to build reading fluency, such as repeated readings of passages, alternate oral reading with a partner, reading with a tape, or rereading the same passage up to three times (level 1).

6. Understand techniques to enhance student motivation to read.	6. Identify student interests and needs to motivate independent reading (level 1).
7. Understand appropriate uses of assistive technology for students with serious limitations in reading fluency.	7. Make appropriate recommendations for use of assistive technology in general-education classes for students with different reading profiles (e.g., dyslexia versus language disabilities) (level 2).

Explanatory Notes

Reading fluency is the ability to read text effortlessly and quickly as well as accurately. Fluency develops among typical readers in the primary grades. Because fluency is a useful predictor of overall reading competence, especially in elementary-aged students, a variety of fluency tasks have been developed for use in screening and progress-monitoring measures. Furthermore, poor reading fluency is a very common symptom of dyslexia and other reading disabilities; problems with reading fluency can linger even when students' accuracy in word decoding has been improved through effective phonics intervention. Although fluency difficulties may sometimes be associated with processing weaknesses, considerable research supports the role of practice, wide exposure to printed words, and focused instruction in the development and remediation of fluency. To address students' fluency needs, teachers must have a range of competencies, including the ability to interpret fluency-based measures appropriately, to place students in appropriate types and levels of texts for reading instruction, to stimulate students' independent reading, and to provide systematic fluency interventions for students who require them. Assistive technology (e.g., text-to-speech software) is often employed to help students with serious fluency difficulties function in general-education settings. Therefore, teachers, and particularly specialists, require knowledge about the appropriate uses of this technology.

References for this section are available at www.interdys.org/standards.htm

E-4. Structured Language Teaching: Vocabulary

Content Knowledge	Observable Competencies for Teaching Students with Dyslexia and Related Difficulties
1. Understand the role of vocabulary development and vocabulary knowledge in comprehension.	1. Teach word meanings directly using contextual examples, structural (morpheme) analysis, antonyms and synonyms, definitions, connotations, multiple meanings, and semantic feature analysis (levels 1 and 2).
2. Understand the role and characteristics of direct and indirect (contextual) methods of vocabulary instruction.	2. Lesson planning reflects: A. Selection of material for read-alouds and independent reading that will expand students' vocabulary.
3. Know varied techniques for vocabulary instruction before, during, and after reading.	B. Identification of words necessary for direct teaching that should be known before the passage is read.
4. Understand that word knowledge is multifaceted.	C. Repeated encounters with new words and multiple opportunities to use new words orally and in writing.
5. Understand the sources of wide differences in students' vocabularies.	D. Recurring practice and opportunities to use new words in writing and speaking.

Explanatory Notes

Vocabulary, or knowledge of word meanings, plays a key role in reading comprehension. Knowledge of words is multifaceted, ranging from partial recognition of the meaning of a word to deep knowledge and the ability to use the word effectively in speech or writing. Research supports both explicit, systematic teaching of word meanings and indirect methods of instruction such as those involving inferring meanings of words from sentence context or from word parts (e.g., common roots and affixes). Teachers should know how to develop students' vocabulary knowledge through both direct and indirect methods. They also should understand the importance of wide exposure to words, both orally and through reading, in students' vocabulary development. For example, although oral vocabulary knowledge frequently is a strength for students with dyslexia, over time, low volume of reading may tend to reduce these students' exposure to rich vocabulary relative to their typical peers; explicit teaching of word meanings and encouragement of wide independent reading in appropriate texts are two ways to help increase this exposure.

References for this section are available at www.interdys.org/standards.htm

E-5. Structured Language Teaching: Text Comprehension

Content Knowledge	Observable Competencies for Teaching Students with Dyslexia and Related Difficulties
1. Be familiar with teaching strategies that are appropriate before, during, and after reading and that promote reflective reading.	1. a. State purpose for reading, elicit or provide background knowledge, and explore key vocabulary (level 1). b. Query during text reading to foster attention to detail, inference making, and mental model construction (level 1). c. Use graphic organizers, note-taking strategies, retelling and summarizing, and cross-text comparisons (level 1).
2. Contrast the characteristics of major text genres, including narration, exposition, and argumentation.	2. Lesson plans reflect a range of genres, with emphasis on narrative and expository texts (level 1).
3. Understand the similarities and differences between written composition and text comprehension, and the usefulness of writing in building comprehension.	3. Model, practice, and share written responses to text; foster explicit connections between new learning and what was already known (level 1).
4. Identify in any text the phrases, clauses, sentences, paragraphs, and "academic language" that could be a source of miscomprehension.	4. Anticipate confusions and teach comprehension of figurative language, complex sentence forms, cohesive devices, and unfamiliar features of text (level 2).
5. Understand levels of comprehension including the surface code, text base, and mental model (situation model).	5. Plan lessons to foster comprehension of the surface code (the language), the text base (the underlying ideas), and a mental model (the larger context for the ideas) (level 2).

6. Understand factors that contribute to deep comprehension, including background knowledge, vocabulary, verbal reasoning ability, knowledge of literary structures and conventions, and use of skills and strategies for close reading of text.	6. Adjust the emphasis of lessons to accommodate learners' strengths and weaknesses and pace of learning (level 2).

Explanatory Notes

Good reading comprehension is the ultimate goal of reading instruction. Reading comprehension depends not only upon the component abilities discussed in previous sections but also upon other factors, such as background knowledge and knowledge of text structure. In order to plan effective instruction and intervention in reading comprehension, teachers must understand the array of abilities that contribute to reading comprehension and use assessments to help pinpoint students' weaknesses. For instance, a typical student with dyslexia, whose reading comprehension problems are associated mainly with poor decoding and dysfluent reading, will need different emphases in intervention than will a poor comprehender whose problems revolve around broad weaknesses in vocabulary and oral comprehension. In addition, teachers must be able to model and teach research-based comprehension strategies, such as summarization and the use of graphic organizers, as well as use methods that promote reflective reading and engagement. Oral comprehension and reading comprehension have a reciprocal relationship; good oral comprehension facilitates reading comprehension, but wide reading also contributes to the development of oral comprehension, especially in older students. Teachers should understand the relationships among oral language, reading comprehension, and written expression, and they should be able to use appropriate writing activities to build students' comprehension.

References for this section are available at www.interdys.org/standards.htm

E-6. Structured Language Teaching: Handwriting, Spelling, and Written Expression

Content Knowledge	Observable Competencies for Teaching Students with Dyslexia and Related Difficulties
Handwriting 1. Know research-based principles for teaching letter naming and letter formation, both manuscript and cursive. 2. Know techniques for teaching handwriting fluency.	**Handwriting** 1. Use multisensory techniques to teach letter naming and letter formation in manuscript and cursive forms (level 1). 2. Implement strategies to build fluency in letter formation, and copying and transcription of written language (level 1).
Spelling 1. Recognize and explain the relationship between transcription skills and written expression. 2. Identify students' levels of spelling development and orthographic knowledge. 3. Recognize and explain the influences of phonological, orthographic, and morphemic knowledge on spelling.	**Spelling** 1. Explicitly and effectively teach (e.g., information taught is correct, students are attentive, teacher checks for understanding, teacher scaffolds students' learning) concepts related to spelling (e.g., a rule for adding suffixes to base words) (level 1). 2. Select materials and/or create lessons that address students' skill levels (level 1). 3. Analyze a student's spelling errors to determine his or her instructional needs (e.g., development of phonological skills versus learning spelling rules versus application of orthographic or morphemic knowledge in spelling) (level 2).

Written Expression	Written Expression
1. Understand the major components and processes of written expression and how they interact (e.g., basic writing/transcription skills versus text generation).	1. Integrate basic skill instruction with composition in writing lessons.
2. Know grade and developmental expectations for students' writing in the following areas: mechanics and conventions of writing, composition, revision, and editing processes.	2. a. Select and design activities to teach important components of writing, including mechanics/conventions of writing, composition, and revision and editing processes. b. Analyze students' writing to determine specific instructional needs. c. Provide specific, constructive feedback to students targeted to students' most critical needs in writing. d. Teach research-based writing strategies such as those for planning, revising, and editing text. e. Teach writing (discourse) knowledge, such as the importance of writing for the intended audience, use of formal versus informal language, and various schemas for writing (e.g., reports versus narratives versus arguments).
3. Understand appropriate uses of assistive technology in written expression.	3. Make appropriate written recommendations for the use of assistive technology in writing.

Explanatory Notes

Just as teachers need to understand the component abilities that contribute to reading comprehension, they also need a componential view of written expression. Important component abilities in writing include basic writing (transcription) skills such as handwriting, keyboarding, spelling, capitalization, punctuation, and grammatical sentence structure; text generation (composition) processes that involve translating ideas into language, such as appropriate word choice, writing clear sentences, and developing an idea across multiple sentences and paragraphs; and planning, revision and editing processes. Effective instruction and intervention in written expression depend on pinpointing an individual student's specific weaknesses in these different component areas of writing, as well as on teachers' abilities to provide explicit, systematic teaching in each area. Teachers must also be able to teach research-based strategies in written expression, such as those involving strategies for planning and revising compositions, and they should understand the utility of multisensory methods in both handwriting and spelling instruction. Assistive technology can be especially helpful for students with writing difficulties. Teachers should recognize the appropriate uses of technology in writing (e.g., spell-checkers can be valuable but do not replace spelling instruction and have limited utility for students whose misspellings are not recognizable). Specialists should have even greater levels of knowledge about technology.

References for this section are available at www.interdys.org/standards.htm

F. Follow Ethical Standards for the Profession

Ethical Principles for Service Providers, Conference Exhibitors, and Advertisers

These principles are to be used by employees, board members, and branch officers of the International Dyslexia Association (IDA) in deciding whether members, conference exhibitors, conference or workshop presenters, and/or advertisers in IDA publications are serving the best interest of the public. These principles are intended to safeguard and promote the well-being of individuals with dyslexia and related learning difficulties, to promote the dissemination of reliable and helpful information, and to ensure that standards of best practice are upheld by the organization and its activities.

Practitioners, publishers, presenters, exhibitors, advertisers, and any others who provide services to individuals with dyslexia and related difficulties

1. strive to do no harm and to act in the best interests of those individuals;
2. maintain the public trust by providing accurate information about currently accepted and scientifically supported best practices in the field;
3. avoid misrepresentation of the efficacy of educational or other treatments or the proof for or against those treatments;
4. respect objectivity by reporting assessment and treatment results accurately, honestly, and truthfully;
5. avoid making unfounded claims of any kind regarding the training, experience, credentials, affiliations, and degrees of those providing services;
6. respect the training requirements of established credentialing and accreditation organizations supported by IDA;
7. engage in fair competition;
8. avoid conflicts of interest when possible and acknowledge conflicts of interest when they occur;
9. support just treatment of individuals with dyslexia and related learning difficulties;
10. respect confidentiality of students or clients; and
11. respect the intellectual property of others.

SECTION II: GUIDELINES PERTAINING TO SUPERVISED PRACTICE OF TEACHERS OF STUDENTS WITH DOCUMENTED READING DISABILITIES OR DYSLEXIA WHO WORK IN SCHOOL, CLINICAL, OR PRIVATE PRACTICE SETTINGS[105]

Training programs for individuals who are learning to work with challenging students often distinguish levels of expertise by the skills and experience of the individual and the amount of supervised practice required for certification. These levels are labeled differently by various programs and are distinguished here by the designation of "Level I" and "Level II."

A.   Level I individuals are practitioners with basic knowledge who:

1.   demonstrate proficiency to instruct individuals with a documented reading disability or dyslexia;
2.   implement an appropriate program with fidelity; and
3.   formulate and implement an appropriate lesson plan.

B.   Level II individuals are specialists with advanced knowledge who:

1.   may work in private practice settings, clinics, or schools;
2.   demonstrate proficiency in assessment and instruction of students with documented reading disabilities or dyslexia;
3.   implement and adapt research-based programs to meet the needs of individuals.

To attain Level I status, an individual must:

- pass an approved basic knowledge proficiency exam;
- complete a one-to-one practicum with a student or small group of one to three well-matched students who have a documented reading disability. A recognized, certified instructor* provides consistent oversight and observations of instruction delivered to the same student(s) over time, and the practicum continues until expected proficiency is reached.**
- demonstrate (over time) instructional proficiency in all Level 1 areas outlined on IDA Knowledge and Practice Standards, Section I that is responsive to student needs.
- Document significant student progress with formal and informal assessments as a result of the instruction.

---

[105]   Tier 3 in an RTI/MTSS system; students who may be eligible for special education or intensive intervention; students referred for clinical services because of learning difficulties; or students who qualify for dyslexia intervention services where available.

To attain Level II status, an individual must:

- Pass an approved advanced knowledge proficiency exam
- Complete a 1:1 practicum with a student or small group of well-matched students (1-3) who have a documented reading disability. A recognized, certified instructor* provides consistent oversight and observations of instruction delivered to the same student(s) over time, and the practicum continues until expected proficiency is reached.**

  > * A recognized or certified instructor is an individual who has met all of the requirements of the level they supervise but who has additional content knowledge and experience in implementing and observing instruction for students with dyslexia and other reading difficulties in varied settings. A recognized instructor has been recommended by or certified by an approved trainer mentorship program that meets these standards. The trainer mentorship program has been reviewed by and approved by the IDA Standards and Practices Committee.
  > ** Documentation of proficiency must be 1) completed by a recognized/ certified instructor providing oversight in the specified program; 2) completed during full (not partial) lesson observations; and 3) must occur at various intervals throughout the instructional period with student.

- Demonstrate (over time) diagnostic instructional proficiency in all Level 1 and 2 areas outlined on IDA Standards document, Section I.
- Provide successful instruction to several individuals with dyslexia who demonstrate varying needs and document significant student progress with formal and informal assessments as a result of the instruction.
- Complete an approved educational assessment of a student with dyslexia and/or language-based reading disability, including student history and comprehensive recommendations.

DATA POLICIES, USE AND SYSTEMS' ROLE TO GUIDE STUDENT AND TEACHER READING LITERACY SUCCESS

Data's Use, Analysis, and Interpretation in Screening, Assessment, Progress Monitoring, Formative Assessment, Formal Assessment, and Directing Student and Classroom Instruction

EFFECTIVE TEACHING IS both a science and an art. While many educators certainly have a natural aptitude for engaging their students and conducting a class, no school district or state should neglect the importance of data systems in student instruction and intervention, or in classroom operation and control. Embracing this scientific side of education allows for the measurement and tracking of aspects of literacy that are objective but not typically quantifiable. In this way, the application of evidence-based systems to a more intuitive teaching method adds both complexity and specificity, which will ultimately boost the effectiveness of the classroom environment.

The Policy requires that data implementation replace hunches and hypotheses with facts by utilizing data rather than symptoms to identify the areas of weakness in a student's reading. Districts, schools, and teachers should collect, analyze, interpret, and use data to determine each student's needs and target resources to achieve grade-level proficiency. Data should also be used to track the impact of staff development efforts.

In this section, §3.0 Enactment of Data Use and Systems, are tools to assist your work: An Executive Summary of the goals, uses and benefits of data systems to drive both classroom and student achievement; the Key Components structure of these data systems by student needs; the Roadmap and Specifics filled with applications of various types of data and intended charge for the practitioner and for a state handbook; and the model state legislation designed to help you and your community introduce a scientific component to your own state and school district.

It is critically important to realize that data-driven decisions must be considered an ongoing process than a one-time occurrence. Leadership and teachers must work collaboratively to develop a long-term implementation strategy for data driven decisions to be part of a continuous improvement objective. The following model policy represents the essential components of a goal-setting process with student reading literacy achievement at its core. It is critical that leaders understand *all* of these components are essential and should be integrated into a coherent and practical goal setting process. Each component is essential but not sufficient in its own right.

Data use is significantly related to student outcomes. School-based leaders need to maintain a focus on continually analyzing data to improve classroom instruction. The school leaders, in collaboration with classroom teachers, should develop observation strategies and data collection instruments for formative assessment that drive instructional practices that support SEEDS students' success. Teachers must be provided with immediate and informed feedback related to leadership's observations and data's role in directing instruction that aligns to grade-level student performance.

Teacher, student, and classroom data will further allow for school leadership to provide professional development practices contingent upon a basic understanding of each teacher's area of expertise and his or her ability to provide instructional Multi-Tier System of Supports by student. Systemic data collection, analysis, and use is a mandate to continue the professional training and advanced skills of each teacher. Without such data-collection concepts, little will be achieved in reaching the goal of directing instruction to student and classroom needs.

To be credible in guiding teachers and staff in the selection and implementation of evidence-based data tools and practices in all grades and across all content areas, leadership must be cognizant of what students need to learn, why they need to learn it, and the research-based instructional strategies that are most beneficial in reaching academic goals. The principal, in particular, should (1) spend a great deal of time in classrooms observing teachers, (2) model good teaching practice, (3) coach teachers on best researched-based instructional routines, and (4) closely monitor teachers to make sure that practices are implemented and sustained. It is important to point out that data guides both instructional leadership and collaborative leadership, which combine to influence individual student achievement. Teacher learning communities are the best practice for elevating knowledge and skill development. Good school-based leadership should carve out significant amounts of time, scheduled regularly for teachers to collaborate and advance together.

Executive Summary
for Data Use and Systems' Role

It is compulsory for schools to utilize data to improve student outcomes. The analysis of student data must be a priority of all educators, in all schools and districts. Data use through screening, progress monitoring, and formative assessments assist classroom teachers in identifying areas of weakness in student learning and then directing instruction for best learning outcomes.

Issue:

Approximately one-third of students read on grade level. The reading gap has increased in the SEEDS student populations, and this crosses the socioeconomic spectrum. Student achievement can only improve if every district, school, and education staff becomes familiar with data analysis, data interpretation, and data use to inform plans of actions and instruction that assist individual students in achieving grade-level reading proficiency.

Why this is important:

1. Without the use of data, students do not progress as far as they should when data drives differentiated instruction.

2. Data will also be used to track the impact of staff development efforts and student learning to ensure students are on track for postsecondary or workforce success.
3. Up through third grade, children learn to read; after third grade, they read to learn. However, two-thirds of students leave third grade not reading on grade level. Using data along the continuum will help to ensure that more students are reading on grade level.

Goals of section:

1. That all districts, schools, and education staff use data to ensure that all students achieve grade-level proficiency in literacy.
2. To ensure that all students enrolling in a public school are screened and assessed for literacy attainment.
3. To identify students who are not at grade level, and intervene immediately.

How to achieve these goals:

1. All students enrolling in public school must be screened and assessed for literacy attainment.
2. To ensure that students are reading for knowledge by the end of third grade, appropriate supports must be provided until grade-level reading skills are secured.
3. All screenings must be conducted by a trained specialist.

Key points:

1. Data-driven identification of students from their initial assessment will help to ensure that more students receive the services they need in a timely fashion.
2. Without the use of data, too many students go unidentified for the services and interventions they need.
3. All adults within a school need to know how to use data to improve student outcomes.
4. School systems should place immediate and particular emphasis on school, teacher, and student data so that there are mechanisms in place in every school to analyze the effectiveness of each program or system for each individual student's achievement.

Key Components
for Data Use and Systems' Role

The Goal: Schools need to use data to improve student outcomes by identifying student needs and directing instruction:

Screening Procedures: The goal of universal, early reading screening is to identify children at risk of future failure before that failure actually occurs. By doing so, we create the opportunity to intervene early when we are most likely to be more effective and efficient. Therefore, the key to effective screening is maximizing the ability to predict future difficulties. With the use of screening, teachers of reading can quickly assess if a child will experience reading difficulties and can provide early stage, targeted instruction by isolating the skills that need to be strengthened.

Assessments Procedures: Progress monitoring and formative assessments are critical functions when directing instruction so every student develops full reading skills. Once a skill is identified as weak, implementing Multi-Tier System of Supports in general-education classrooms is mandated. Any assessment plan shall include progress monitoring and formative assessments that include a progress monitoring to direct tiers of student supports.

The analysis of student data should be a priority of all educators, in all schools and districts. The continued success of students is best achieved through a sustainable assessment and implementation system that chronicles students (as individuals and as members of particular groups) in their ongoing attainment of specific reading, language, writing, and other learning skills.

Data-driven decision-making and instruction

All districts, schools, and education staff should become familiar with data analysis, data interpretation, and data use to inform plans of actions and instruction that assist individual students in achieving grade-level reading proficiency.

By using concrete data to guide instructional decisions, districts, schools, and teachers will be able to determine the changing needs of their students and to target specific resources needed to achieve grade-level proficiency for each student.

Data will also be used to track the impact of staff development efforts and student learning to ensure that students are on track for postsecondary or workforce success.

States shall require that all districts, schools, and education staff become familiar with state data systems, requirements, and analysis:			
1. Collecting and interpreting both school and student data to include screening and systematic assessments of progress	2. Data sharing	3. Framing questions from analysis of multiple sets of data reports	4. Creating plans to assist individual student achievement.

States shall require that all districts and schools			
1. Establish a school-wide data use plan and an ongoing review of implementation of that plan to monitor student progress toward goals	2. Guide and support teachers in use of data for instructional improvement to meet the needs of students and to support students in reaching their goals	3. Support and lead both students and their parents to be on track for postsecondary success by selecting goals and monitoring their progress toward those goals	4. Ensure that student- and school-level data needs are incorporated in the planning and implementation of district-wide data management systems.

Data shall continuously be used to identify root causes of student learning and improve student outcomes. Using data, all districts, schools, and teachers will collect, analyze, and require				
1. Clear assessment of students' needs	2. The expertise to target resources to address students' needs	3. The ability to set students' goals	4. The aptitude to determine whether the goals are being reached	5. The ability to track the impact of staff development efforts

Student Screening

To ensure that every student is ready and able to read for knowledge (reading literate) by grade 3, early intervention with SEEDS is essential.

1. All students pre-K-12, enrolled or enrolling in public schools, shall be screened and assessed for literacy attainment.
2. Appropriate supports shall be provided until proficient grade-level reading skills are secured.

Districts, schools, and charter schools must establish		
1. Written procedures for screening, assessing, and recommending students at risk for literacy failure within general-education settings	2. Internal procedures that address the needs of their student populations	
Frequency of Screening:		
All entering kindergarten students will be screened for potential characteristics of SEEDS during the first, early weeks of reading instruction, again before the winter break, and also in the spring to evaluate reading progress.	Every student in grades 1, 2, and 3 shall be systematically assessed every two to three weeks during reading development stages of instruction to ensure that they are making appropriate gains in achievement of grade-level reading.	Parents, guardians, students, school nurses, classroom teachers, or other school personnel who have data to support that a student has a need for diagnostic testing in any grade may request such screening. The assessment shall be conducted within thirty days.
Students Not at Grade Level:		
Students receiving below grade-level scores shall be provided intervention support within a week. When interventions do not yield grade-level results within thirty days, more intensive intervention shall be implemented.	If a student is found to be at serious risk for literacy failure, the school district, school, or charter school must notify the student's parent or guardian and implement MTSS until they are reading at grade level.	If a student continues to struggle with one or more components of reading and/or experiences literacy failure, districts, schools, and charter schools must collect additional information about the student.

Additional Data Collection Requirements for Underperforming Students:		
1. Vision screening	2. Hearing screening	3. Samples of schoolwork
4. Basal reading series assessment	5. Accommodations provided by classroom teachers	6. Academic progress reports (report cards)
7. Teacher reports of classroom concerns	8. Parent conferences	9. Speech and language screening through a referral

Assessment Diagnosis Results:			
No indication of need for services	Indication of need for MTSS (tier II) in general-education reading services	Indication of need for assistance to improve the effect of general-education reading instruction through intense intervention services (MTSS-tier III)	Referral for further formal diagnostic assessment for the existence of SEEDS factors and eligibility for the receipt of special-education services

The district office shall

report to the district-level committee the results of the assessment and reading instruments for each student

report, in writing, to a student's parent or guardian the student's results on the assessment and reading instrument

Screening Assessment Specialists

All screening assessments must be done directly by trained specialists (certified teachers of reading, guidance counselors, pupil appraisal personnel, or any other professional employees of the school system).

The number of hours of training in each assessment must be documented. Retraining is not necessary if any previous training can be documented within the last three years. See ***www.literatenation. org*** for approved screening/assessment instruments.

CINTHIA COLETTI

Screening Assessment Specialist Training Requirements:		
1. Identification and knowledge of SEEDS Characteristics of ADD and HD Characteristics of social, cultural, and emotional at-risk literacy failure factors Characteristics of gifted SEEDS	2. Use of appropriate screening instruments	3. Administration and interpretation of selected screening instruments
4. Operation and procedures of school building level committee	5. Selection of appropriate classroom strategies, accommodations, and modifications	6. Child advocacy

Road Map and Specifics for a State Handbook Data Use and Systems' Role

The Overview

The continued success of students toward successful job and career outcomes is best achieved through a sustainable, formative assessment, and an implementation system that chronicles students (as individuals and as members of particular groups) in their ongoing attainment of specific reading, language, writing, and other learning skills. This system necessarily involves considerable teacher supports for ensuring initial and continuous screening, assessment, and evaluation for, and organized planning and communication about, their students' progress.

In many schools and districts, student data analysis has not been viewed as a high priority. To reverse this trend, school systems (districts) must place immediate and particular emphasis on school, teacher, and student data so that there are mechanisms in place in every school to analyze the effectiveness of each program or system for individual students. Only in this way can data be gathered systematically to guide students' educational successes (or struggles) from year to year. School leadership and staff should become familiar with data analysis, data interpretation, and data use to inform plans of action and instruction that assist teachers with each individual students in his or her achievement of grade-level reading proficiency.

The Charge:

Using data implementation, schools and teachers can move from unsubstantiated observations and hypotheses to facts about their students' reading development and literacy attainment. By using concrete data to guide instructional decisions, principals and curriculum directors will be able to understand the changing needs of their students and teachers. They will have firm data to target specific resources needed to achieve grade-level proficiency for each student. Data is also used to track the impact of staff development efforts and student learning to ensure that students are on track for postsecondary and employment success. Overall, data use and interpretation systems provide the basis for a far more comprehensive and targeted approach to overcoming barriers to school learning and to providing instructional methods and strategies with a greater chance of school success.

Data Systems and Use:

The student screenings and assessments required shall be done directly by appropriately trained specialists (certified teachers of reading, guidance counselors, pupil appraisal personnel, or any other professional employees of the school system), all of whom shall operate as advocates for the students identified as needing services or assistance to reach grade-level achievement. Persons who have not been trained to do such screenings or assessments may not carry them out.

Screening/assessment specialists must be professional employees of the school system who have received training in the following: state-approved kindergarten screening instrument(s) to determine developmental strengths and needs, social/emotional factors at risk checklist, informal reading/language inventories, rapid automatic naming tests, written language samples, informal mathematical assessment, and norm-referenced tests.

The schools will adhere to administration and interpretation of selected screening instruments by training personnel to administer instruments and interpret screening results. All results will be documented, and if necessary multitier supports administered by teachers in the general-education classroom to include appropriate classroom strategies, accommodations, and modifications.

The parents or guardians of a student can request a private assessment. The school or district may take into account the assessment, administer additional assessments, or provide intervention based on the private assessment.

The federal ESEA requires annual testing of all students in reading and math in grades 3-8. Science recommends that testing begin in kindergarten and continue until grade-level reading is attained and sustained. Once in high school, all students must meet state-set proficiency standards, thus compelling the state to encourage ongoing assessment and progress monitoring of reading achievement gains for all students. Additionally, the most recent reauthorization of the IDEA 2004 is consistent with ESEA in emphasizing quality of instruction and documentation of student progress.[106] A process based on the student's response to scientifically validated, research-based intervention is one of the criteria included in IDEA 2004 that states may use in determining whether a student has a specific learning disability, including dyslexia. Regardless of the process in place, the parents or guardians always have the right to request a referral for assessment at any time. This right needs to be clearly communicated to the parent/guardian.

The IDEA 2004 also allows local education agencies (LEAs) to use up to 15 percent of their special-education funds for Early Intervening Services (EIS) to support prevention and early identification of SEEDS in general education, to minimize overidentification for and unnecessary referrals to special education. EIS is intended to provide academic and behavioral supports and professional development regarding early literacy and behavior especially in grades pre-K-3. LEAs

---

[106] The Individuals with Disabilities Education Act, which provides intervention and education services to disabled children across America.

with a disproportionate number of minority students identified for special-education services are required to implement a program with EIS funds.

Research indicates that students with dyslexia may demonstrate unexpected difficulties in the areas of reading, writing, and math despite the provision of effective foundational reading instruction; screening and assessment will therefore identify and accelerate MTSS. Additionally, students with dyslexia and learning disabilities may be gifted and their difficulties more difficult to appreciate because of their intellect. Formal assessment and diagnostics are necessary to understand these difficulties and their relationship to the student's cognitive abilities, reading fluency, writing, and mathematical skill.

Universal Screening of All Kindergarten Children:

Kindergarten entry screening should be used to measure the child's ability to acquire skills. There are many well-regarded readiness assessments to gauge children's skills through teacher observation. With observational screening assessments, teachers are trained in such areas as identifying signs of preliteracy sounds-letter and language development, and gathering a body of information on children over time. The information can then be compiled and used in the classroom to direct instruction and Multi-Tier System of Supports or shared with school administrators.

The goal of universal, early reading screening is to identify children at risk of future failure before that failure actually occurs. By doing so, we create the opportunity to intervene early when we are most likely to be more effective and efficient. Therefore, the key to effective screening is maximizing the ability to predict future difficulties. With the use of screening, teachers of reading can quickly assess if a child will experience reading difficulties and can provide early stage, targeted instruction by isolating the skills that need to be strengthened.

Good kindergarten-entry assessments measure children's learning and development across all the essential domains—especially language and literacy readiness, identifying potential learning disabilities, and also social skills, physical health, and emotional well-being. The kindergarten-entry assessments should align with academic standards in later grades and be used to guide teachers in talking to families about the skills their children have learned or still need to work on.

States vary widely in how—or if—they assess the skills and learning status of kindergartners. Research working on a multistate partnership has coordinated programs for young children and their families and examples are as follows:

In Maryland:
Type of Test: Work Sampling System

Developer: Pearson Education

How Used: Teachers are given "observational criteria" in seven different domains, including personal and social development, language and literacy, scientific thinking, and physical development. Teachers also collect portfolios of pupils' work.

In Washington:
Type of test: Teaching Strategies GOLD

Developer: Teaching Strategies LLC

How Used: Teachers observe children's skills in six areas, such as social-emotional, language, and cognitive. The program also includes connections to family, and the results inform statewide policy decisions.

In Connecticut:
Type of test: Observational Assessment

Developer: State-developed

How Used: The state's "kindergarten-entrance inventory" is administered in October. Teachers evaluate children on a variety of skills, such as counting to ten, holding a book and turning pages from front to back, and following classroom routines. An "exit inventory" also measures pupils' skills as they prepare to leave kindergarten.

In Ohio:

Type of test: Language and Literacy

Developer: State-developed

How Used: The state department of education's "Kindergarten Readiness Assessment-Literacy" measures skill areas needed to become a successful reader. The test helps teachers plan lessons that encourage reading.

Data Gathering:

If at any time (from kindergarten through grade 12) a student continues to struggle with one or more components of reading development and/or experiences grade-level reading literacy failure, school leadership must collect additional information about the student. This information shall be used to evaluate the student's underachievement and to determine what actions are needed to improve the student's academic performance. Some of the information that the district or charter school collects is in the student's cumulative folder; other data is available from teachers and parents/guardians.

To ensure that underachievement of the community of SEEDS students is not due to lack of appropriate instruction in reading development, other criteria should be considered. This information includes data demonstrating that the student received appropriate instruction as well as data-based documentation of repeated formal assessments of student achievement at reasonable intervals (progress monitoring). Additional information to be considered includes the results from some or all of the following: vision screening, hearing screening, teacher reports of classroom concerns, basal reading series assessment, accommodations provided by classroom teachers, academic progress reports (report cards), samples of schoolwork, parent conferences, and speech and language screening through a referral process.

One of the actions that the district, school, or charter school has available is to recommend that SEEDS be administered a diagnostic assessment if the student demonstrates poor performance in one or more areas of reading and/or the related area of spelling that is unexpected for the student's age, grade, or intellectual development.

When the district, school, or charter school recommends formal assessment for a student, the following procedures should be adhered to.

Formal Assessment:

A student's formal assessment diagnostic is dependent upon multiple factors, including the student's reading performance and skill, response to supplemental scientifically based reading instruction and Multi-Tier System of Supports, input from teachers, and input from the parents or guardians. Additionally, the appropriate time for assessment is early in a student's school career. While earlier is better, SEEDS should be recommended for assessment even if the reading difficulties appear in later grades.

These procedures must be followed: notify parents or guardians of the proposal to perform a formal assessment diagnostic on a student; inform parents or guardians of their rights; obtain permission from the parents or guardians to assess the student; and assess the student, ensuring that the professionals who administer the assessments have been trained in the evaluation of SEEDS. The notices and consent must be provided in the native language of the parent or guardian or by another mode of communication used by the parent or guardian, unless it is clearly not feasible to do so.

Tests, assessments, diagnostics, and other evaluation materials must be validated for the specific purpose for which they are used; include materials tailored to assess specific areas of educational need and not merely materials designed to provide a single general intelligence quotient; be selected and administered so as to ensure that, when a test is given to a student with impaired sensory, manual, or speaking skills, the results accurately reflect the student's aptitude or achievement level (or whatever other factor the test purports to measure) rather than these impaired skills; include multiple measures of a student's reading abilities, such as informal assessment information (e.g., anecdotal records, lists of books the student has read, audio recordings of the student's oral reading); and be administered by trained personnel in accordance with the instructions provided by the producer of the evaluation materials.

The school leadership should oversee the administration measures that are related to the student's educational needs. Depending on the student's age and stage of reading and intellectual development, the following reading areas should be assessed: reading real and nonsense words in isolation (decoding), phonological awareness, letter knowledge (name and associated sound), rapid naming ability, reading fluency (rate and accuracy), reading comprehension, and written spelling of age appropriate words. Based on the student's individual academic difficulties and characteristics, additional areas that can be assessed include vocabulary, written expression, handwriting, and mathematics.

English Language Learners (ELL)/Limited English Proficiency (LEP):

Much diversity exists among English language learners (ELLs). The identification and service delivery process for SEEDS must be in step with the student's linguistic environment and educational background, and the involvement of a language proficiency assessment committee is recommended. Additional data gathering may be required to produce language proficiency documentation that includes or addresses the following: home language survey, assessment related to identification for limited English proficiency (oral language proficiency tests and norm-referenced tests), linguistic environment and second-language acquisition development, previous schooling in and outside of the United States, and comprehensive oral language proficiency testing in English and in the student's native language whenever possible.

These data-gathering procedures are important in determining whether the student's current classroom setting is appropriate given his or her language abilities, appropriate languages in which to assess the student's academic achievement and cognitive processing, the degree to which language proficiency in both the first and second language influences or explains the student's test performance on the academic achievement and cognitive processing measures, and whether the student's difficulties in reading are the result of a disability or a reflection of the normal process of second language acquisition.

Additionally, personnel involved in the evaluation process of ELL for SEEDS need to be trained in bilingual assessment and interpretation procedures. It is strongly recommended that personnel involved in the assessment and interpretation of assessment results have the following knowledge: understanding of first and second language acquisition stages, impact of culture on student performance, knowledge regarding bilingual education and English as a second language programming and MTSS teaching methods, knowledge in interpreting the results of a student's oral language proficiency in relation to the results of the test measuring academic achievement and cognitive processes, and understanding of how to interpret the results of similar or parallel tests given in more than one language.

To appropriately understand data/test results, the examiner(s) or a committee of knowledgeable persons must interpret them in light of the student's language development (in both English and the student's native language), educational history, linguistic background, socioeconomic issues, and any other pertinent factors that affect learning.

SEEDS Determination:

The school leadership team or committee of knowledgeable persons determines whether the student is a SEEDS, after reviewing all accumulated data, including the following areas: observations of the teacher and classroom, data gathered from the classroom (including student work and the results of classroom measures) and information found in the student's cumulative folder (including his or her developmental and academic history), data-based documentation of student progress during instruction/intervention, results of administered assessments, and all other accumulated data regarding the development of the student's learning and his or her educational needs.

Difficulties in the area of reading development will reflect unexpectedly low performance for the student's age and educational level in the following areas: reading real words in isolation, decoding nonsense words, reading fluency (both rate and accuracy), and written spelling. Unexpectedly low reading performance, including poor reading fluency, will result from a deficit in phonological processing. Many SEEDS will have difficulty with the secondary characteristics of literacy, including reading comprehension, language, written composition, spelling, grammar, and rote math skills.

A committee of knowledgeable persons must also incorporate the following guidelines into its determination: the student has received MTSS instruction in his or her general-education classroom; the student has an unexpected lack of appropriate academic progress (in the areas of reading and spelling) relative to their age/grade/intellectual development; the student has adequate intelligence (an average ability to learn in the absence of print or in other academic areas); the student exhibits characteristics associated with SEEDS; the student's lack of progress is not due to sociocultural factors such as language differences, irregular attendance, or lack of experiential background.

Based on the above information and guidelines, the committee of knowledgeable persons determines and identifies SEEDS and determines whether the student has a disability under federal policy. A student is considered to have a disability if the condition substantially limits the student's learning. Students with additional factors that complicate SEEDS may require additional support or referral to special education.

Referral to Special Education:

At any time during the assessment for reading failure identification in grades K-3 or during content instruction in grades 4-12, students may be referred for evaluation for special education. At times, students will display additional factors complicating their instruction and requiring more support than what is available through Multi-Tier System of Supports in the general-education classroom. At other times, students with severe at-risk characteristics or related disorders will be unable to make appropriate academic progress within any of the programs described in the procedures related to SEEDS. In such cases, a referral to special education for evaluation and possible identification as a child with a disability within the meaning of the IDEA 2004, Section 504 of the federal Rehabilitation Act of 1973, and the 2008 ADAAA should be made as needed. [107, 108]

If a SEEDS student is found eligible for special education in the area of reading, the school district must include appropriate reading instruction on the student's Individualized Education Program (IEP). If a SEEDS is referred for special education, districts and charter schools must follow the Individuals with Disabilities Education Act (IDEA). In IDEA 2004 (due for reauthorization), students will be considered one of a variety of etiological foundations of "specific learning disability." This refers to a disorder in one or more of the basic psychological processes involved in understanding or using spoken or written language that may manifest in an imperfect ability to listen, think, speak, read, write, spell, or do mathematical calculations. The

---

[107] Congressional amendment to the Americans with Disabilities Act and other nondiscrimination laws.

[108] Section 504 provides greater opportunities to children with disabilities by accommodating their specific educational needs.

term includes such conditions as perceptual disability, brain injury, minimal brain dysfunction, dyslexia, and developmental aphasia. It does not apply to students who have learning problems that are primarily the result of visual, hearing, or motor disabilities; of mental retardation; of emotional disturbance; or of environmental, cultural, or economic disadvantage.

Note on federal law: IDEA 2004 indicates that states must permit the use of a process based on a student's response to scientific, research-based intervention as one of the criteria for determining whether a child has a learning disorder. Currently, the research base for a MTSS model is strongest at the elementary level, where large-scale implementation has been occurring for many years. Within IDEA 2004 exists the category of specific learning disability students, who need to qualify under state and federal requirements to receive these services as a special-education service. Currently, in most states, over 50 percent of students qualified for special education are in this category. There are significant numbers of students who fall below qualifying for this designation, yet fail to learn to read appropriately by national and state standards. The adoption of a MTSS model in compliance with IDEA 2004 will proactively address the beginning signs of reading and other academic struggles among SEEDS students.

MODEL LEGISLATION LANGUAGE FOR DATA USE AND SYSTEMS' ROLE TO GUIDE READING LITERACY ACHIEVEMENT

Enactment of Data Use and Systems in Schools to Ensure Student Reading Literacy Achievement

---

§BE IT ENACTED BY THE LEGISLATURE OF THE STATE OF [insert state name] a requirement that all districts, schools, and education staff become familiar with state data systems, requirements and analysis:

1. collecting and interpreting both school and student data to include screening and systematic assessments of progress,

2. sharing data,
3. framing questions from analysis of multiple sets of data reports, and
4. creating plans to assist individual student achievement.

It is ratified that each district and school in the state of [insert name state] will

1. establish a school-wide data use plan and ongoing review of implementation of that plan to monitor student progress toward goals;
2. guide and support teachers in use of data for instructional improvement to meet the needs of students and to support students in reaching their goals;
3. support and lead both students and their parents to be on track for postsecondary success by selecting goals and monitoring their progress toward those goals; and
4. ensure that school-level and student data needs are incorporated in district-wide data management systems planning and implementation.

It is adopted by [insert state name] that data be continuously utilized to provide new insights into student learning and how to improve it. This process is implemented so that facts, based on data, are utilized to identify the root causes of student learning problems, not just the symptoms.

With data, all districts, schools, and teachers will collect, analyze, and require

1. clear assessment on students' needs;
2. the expertise to target resources to address students' needs;
3. the ability to set students' goals;
4. the aptitude to determine whether the goals are being reached; and
5. the ability to track the impact of staff development efforts.

This Policy implements and provides for the application of a data use plan under which students, pre-K-12 enrolled or enrolling in public schools in [insert state name], are screened and assessed for literacy failure or grade-level reading attainment as may be necessary, and are provided appropriate supports dependent on multiple factors and at multiple times until proficient grade-level reading skills are secured.

§3.1 General Procedures

Districts, schools, and charter schools must establish written procedures for screening, assessing, and recommending students at risk for literacy failure within general-education settings. The state can no longer wait for these students to fail; all SEEDS will be provided with a systematic structure to learn. While districts, schools, and charter schools must follow federal and state guidelines, they must also develop internal procedures that address the needs of their student populations.

A. All entering kindergarten students will be screened for potential characteristics of SEEDS that could inhibit reading development. Kindergarten screening shall happen at least twice in the first semester of the year and once in the second semester.

B. Every student in grades 1, 2, and 3 shall be systematically assessed every two to three weeks during reading development stages of instruction to ensure they are reaching appropriate gains to achieve grade-level reading.

C. The Policy shall provide that, upon the request of a parent/guardian, student, school nurse, classroom teacher, or other school personnel who have data to support that a student has a need for diagnostic testing in any grade, such testing will be conducted within thirty days.

§3.2 Screening Procedures

[Insert state name] is committed to data-driven instruction. State Policy requires universal screening. With the use of screening, teachers of reading can quickly assess if a child will experience reading difficulties and can provide early stage, targeted instruction by isolating the skills that need to be strengthened. Both research and practice support that these at-risk students, identified early through screening and provided a systemic process of a continuous cycle of assessment, data analysis, ongoing progress monitoring, and informed instruction, are most often aptly prepared to enter first grade on target for grade-level reading requirements and beyond.

A. All entering kindergarten students will be universally screened during the first early weeks of reading instruction, again before the fall break, and also in the spring to evaluate reading progress. If a student is falling behind his or her peers, common characteristics will be identifiable early in these screening assessments. A teacher of reading will provide MTSS to most quickly and assuredly ameliorate the areas of weakness.

B. If a student is found to be at serious risk for literacy failure, a systematic assessment will be provided, and the school district, school, or charter school must notify the student's parents/guardians. The school district, school, or charter school must also implement a MTSS and a reading program (accelerated and/or intensive) that appropriately addresses students' reading difficulties and enables them to "catch up" with their typically performing peers.

§3.3 Assessments for Reading Literacy

All students in prekindergarten, kindergarten, and grades 1, 2, and 3 are to be systematically assessed for their reading development and comprehension grade-level skill attainment. The Policy acknowledges that early identification preferably happens in grades K-1, and that support systems will greatly improve every student's chances to realize reading literacy. It is understood that all students can be taught reading and literacy skills and perform at grade level. The purpose of this section is to ensure early intervention with SEEDS, with the goal of a successful school experience, and to bring to bear all resources that can be made available in a school setting to address any difficulty a student may have so that each student is ready and able to read for knowledge by grade 3. The following are requirements pursuant to this Policy:

A. Every student in public school shall be assessed for grade-level reading attainment. Every student in grades 1, 2, and 3 shall be systematically assessed, every two to three weeks during the year for grade-level reading skill attainment to ensure a successful skill progression.

B. In doing such assessments, students receiving below grade-level scores shall be a top priority, and the student will be provided support within a week (as defined in [insert state name] Statute, Section 4.0). When a student is identified and provided with systems of support, yet grade-level attainment is not accomplished within thirty days, then more intensive intervention is mandated (as defined in [insert state name] Statute, Section 4.0).

C. Assessments as required by [insert state name] Literacy, LD and Dyslexia Policy shall have one or more of the following results:
    1. No indication of need for services;
    2. Indication of need for MTSS (tier II) in general-education reading services to ameliorate SEEDS literacy failure, [insert state name] Statute, Section 4 of this Policy;
    3. Indication of need for assistance to improve the effect of general-education reading instruction through intense intervention services (MTSS-tier III); and
    4. Referral for further formal diagnostic assessment for the existence of SEEDS factors and eligibility for the receipt of special education services.

D. If the student has not made adequate progress, the student shall receive a diagnostic assessment for all other issues of learning disorders such as seeking identification of dyslexia and specific learning disabilities as defined in [insert state name] Statute, Sections 1.8, 1.9, and 1.12 of this Policy, and/or social, cultural, and environmental factors that put a child at risk for literacy failure as that term has been defined in [insert state name] Statute, Section 1.2.

E. Students in need of services and/or assistance shall have it provided to them. Services shall be provided in accordance with [insert state name] state and federal Policy, [insert state name] Statute, Section 1.12 of the Policy.

F. New students enrolling in public schools shall be screened and assessed, if needed, for at-risk reading attainment at appropriate times in accordance with content-area subject teacher request, request of parents or guardians, or poor school progress.

G. [Name of state department of education and/or name of board of trustees of each school district board] shall provide for the treatment of any SEEDS determination or learning disorders, [insert state name] Statute, Section 3 of this Policy, and shall adopt any rules and standards necessary to administer this section.

H. The screenings/assessments required shall be done directly by specialists (certified teachers of reading, guidance counselors, pupil appraisal personnel, or any other professional employees of the school system) who have been appropriately trained, all of whom shall operate as advocates for the students identified as needing services or assistance. Persons who have not been trained to do such screenings/assessments shall do no screenings/assessments, consistent with the requirements established for such training by [insert state name]'s Literacy, LD and Dyslexia Policy. Screening/assessment specialists shall be professional employees of the school system who have been appropriately trained, all of whom shall have met the following requirements:

1. Screening/Assessment Specialists Training Requirements
   a. Identification and knowledge of the following
      i. SEEDS pursuant to [insert state name] Statute, Section 1, of this Policy;
      ii. Characteristics of ADD and HD;
      iii. Characteristics of social, cultural, and emotional at risk literacy failure factors; and
      iv. Characteristics of gifted SEEDS (or twice exceptional in many states).
   b. Use of appropriate screening instruments:
      Kindergarten screening instrument(s) state approved/to determine developmental strengths and needs (see www.literatenation.org for instruments for SEEDS identification and screening/assessment checklist:
      i. social/emotional factors at risk checklist;
      ii. informal reading/language inventories;
      iii. rapid automatic naming tests;
      iv. written language samples;
      v. informal mathematical assessment; and
      vi. norm-referenced tests.

    c. Administration and interpretation of selected screening instruments
      i. Training of personnel to administer instruments; and
      ii. Interpret screening results.
    d. Operation and procedures of school building level committee
      i. membership;
      ii. referral process;
      iii. interventions in the classroom;
      iv. documentation; and
      v. decision-making process.
    e. Selection of appropriate classroom strategies, accommodations, and modifications
    f. Child advocacy

2. The number of hours in each must be documented. Retraining is not necessary if any previous training can be documented within the last three years.

I. A private assessment can be obtained by the parents/guardian of the student. The school or district may take into account the assessment, administer additional assessments, or provide intervention based on the private assessment.

J. The federal ESEA requires annual testing of all students in reading and math in grades 3-8. Once in high school, all students must meet state-set proficiency standards, thus the state is compelled to ensure that ongoing assessment and progress monitoring of reading achievement gains are encouraged for all students. Additionally, the most recent reauthorization of the IDEA 2004 is consistent with ESEA in emphasizing quality of instruction and documentation of student progress. A process based on the student's response to scientific, research-based intervention (*scientifically validated*) is one of the criteria included in IDEA 2004 that states may use in determining whether a student has a specific learning disability, including dyslexia.

Regardless of the process in place, the parents or guardians always have the right to request a referral for assessment at any time. This right needs to be clearly communicated to the parent/guardian.

The IDEA 2004 also allows local education agencies (LEAs) to use up to 15 percent of their special-education funds for Early Intervening Services (EIS) to support prevention and early identification of SEEDS in general education, to minimize overidentification for special-education eligibility and reduce unnecessary referrals to special education. EIS is intended to provide academic and behavioral supports and professional development regarding early literacy and behavior especially in grades pre-K-3. LEAs identified as having a disproportionate number of minority students identified for special-education services are required to implement a program with EIS funds.

K. Research indicates that there may be unexpected difficulties that students with dyslexia demonstrate in the area of reading, writing, and math despite the provision of effective foundational reading instruction and, thus, screening and assessment will identify and accelerate MTSS. Additionally, students with dyslexia and learning disabilities may be gifted and their difficulties more difficult to appreciate because of their intellect. The state of [insert state name] acknowledges formal assessment and diagnostics are necessary to understand these difficulties and the relationship to the student's cognitive abilities, reading fluency, writing, and math.

§3.4 Literacy Failure Diagnosis

A district-level committee may adopt a list of assessments/reading instruments for use in the district in addition to the assessments/reading instruments on the state's list based on data-validated research concerning reading skills development and reading comprehension (see www.literatenation.org for a state approved list of foundational reading instruction programs). A list of assessments/reading instruments adopted under this subsection must provide for diagnosing the reading development, fluency, and comprehension of students participating in a program.

Districts, schools, and charter schools must follow federal and state guidelines; they must also develop the following standards and procedures:

A. Schools administer assessments/reading instruments to diagnose student reading development, fluency, and comprehension;
B. Schools train specific educators in administering the assessments/reading instruments;
C. Schools apply the results of the assessments/reading instruments to the instructional program;
D. Schools adopt a list of assessments/reading instruments that a school district may use to diagnose student reading development and comprehension;
E. Districts shall administer, at the kindergarten level and in grades 1, 2, and 3, an assessment/reading instrument on the list adopted by the district-level committee. The district shall administer the assessment/reading instrument in accordance with the state's recommendations;
F. District office shall:
   1. report to the district-level committee the results of the assessment/reading instruments for each student;
   2. report, in writing, to a student's parent or guardian the student's results on the assessment/reading instrument;
G. Districts shall notify the parent or guardian of each student in kindergarten and grades 1, 2, and 3 who is determined, on the basis of assessment/reading instrument results, to be a SEEDS. The district shall implement accelerated MTSS [insert state name] Statutes, Sections 4.2 and 4.3 of this Policy that provides reading instruction and strategies that address reading deficiencies in students;
H. Districts shall make a good faith effort to ensure that the notice required under this section is provided either in person or by regular mail, that the notice is clear and easy to understand, and is written in English and in the parent or guardian's native language.

§3.5 Data Gathering

At any time (from kindergarten through grade 12) that a student continues to struggle with one or more components of reading development and/or experiences reading literacy failure, districts, schools, and charter schools must collect additional information about the student. This information shall be analyzed and used to evaluate the student's underachievement and to determine what actions are needed to ensure the student's improved academic performance. Some of the information that the district or charter school collects is in the student's cumulative folder; other data is available from teachers and parents/guardians. Data collection is as follows:

A. To ensure that under achievement in SEEDS is not due to lack of appropriate instruction in reading, other criteria should be considered. This information should include data that demonstrates the student was provided appropriate instruction and data-based documentation of repeated assessments of achievement at reasonable intervals (progress monitoring), reflecting formal assessment of student progress during instruction. Additional information to be considered includes the results from some or all of the following:
   1. Vision screening;
   2. Hearing screening;
   3. Teacher reports of classroom concerns;
   4. Basal reading series assessment;
   5. Accommodations provided by classroom teachers;
   6. Academic progress reports (report cards);
   7. Samples of schoolwork;
   8. Parent conferences; and
   9. Speech and language screening through a referral process.
B. One of the actions that the district, school, or charter school has available is to recommend that SEEDS be administered a diagnostic assessment if the student demonstrates poor performance in one or more areas of reading and/or the related area of spelling that is unexpected for the student's age, grade, or intellectual development;
C. When the district, school, or charter school recommends a student be formally assessed, the following procedures for assessment must be adhered to as determined by [insert state name] Statute, Section 3.6 of this Policy.

§3.6 Formal Assessment

Student's formal assessment diagnostic is dependent upon multiple factors including the student's reading performance, reading difficulties, poor response to supplemental scientifically based reading instruction (MTSS), teachers' input, and input from the parents or guardians. Additionally, the appropriate time for assessing is early in a student's school career; the earlier the better. While earlier is better, SEEDS should be recommended for assessment even if the reading difficulties appear later in a student's school career. (See www.literatenation.org for a list of formal assessment instruments.)

A. These procedures must be followed:
    1. Notify parents or guardians of proposal to perform a formal assessment diagnostic on a student;
    2. Inform parents or guardians of their rights;
    3. Obtain permission from the parent or guardian to assess the student; and
    4. Assess student, being sure that individuals/professionals who administer assessments have training in the evaluation of SEEDS, [insert state name] Statute, Section 3.3 of this Policy.
B. The notices and consent must be provided in the native language of the parent or guardian or other mode of communication used by the parent or guardian, unless it is clearly not feasible to do so.
C. Tests, assessments, diagnostics, and other evaluation materials must
    1. be validated for the specific purpose for which the tests, assessments, and other evaluation materials are used;
    2. include material tailored to assess specific areas of educational need and not merely materials that are designed to provide a single general intelligence quotient;
    3. be selected and administered so as to ensure that when a test is given to a student with impaired sensory, manual, or speaking skills, the test results accurately reflect the student's aptitude or achievement level, or whatever other factor the test purports to measure, rather than reflecting the student's impaired sensory, manual, or speaking skills;
    4. include multiple measures of a student's reading abilities, such as informal assessment information (e.g., anecdotal

records, lists of books the student has read, audio recordings of the student's oral reading); and

5. be administered by trained personnel and in conformance with the instructions provided by the producer of the evaluation materials.

D. The district, school, or charter school administers measures that are related to the student's educational needs. Depending upon the student's age and stage of reading and intellectual development, the following reading areas should be assessed:

1. Reading real and nonsense words in isolation (decoding);
2. Phonological awareness;
3. Letter knowledge (name and associated sound);
4. Rapid naming;
5. Reading fluency (rate and accuracy);
6. Reading comprehension; and
7. Written spelling.

E. Based on the student's individual academic difficulties and characteristics, additional areas that can be assessed include vocabulary, written expression, handwriting, and mathematics.

§3.7 English Language Learners (ELL)/Limited English Proficiency (LEP)

Much diversity exists among English language learners (ELLs). The identification and service delivery process for SEEDS must be in step with the student's linguistic environment and educational background. Involvement of a language proficiency assessment committee is recommended.

A. Additional data gathering may be required to include language proficiency documentation that includes the following:

1. Home language survey;
2. Assessment related to identification for limited English proficiency (oral language proficiency tests and norm-referenced tests);
3. Linguistic environment and second-language acquisition development;
4. Previous schooling in and outside of the United States; and
5. Comprehensive oral language proficiency testing in English and the student's native language whenever possible.

B. These data gathering procedures are important to determine the following:
   1. Whether the student's current classroom setting is appropriate given his or her language abilities;
   2. The appropriate languages for assessing the student's academic achievement and cognitive processing;
   3. The degree to which language proficiency in both the first and second language influences or explains the student's test performance on the academic achievement and cognitive processing measures; and
   4. Whether the student's difficulties in reading are the result of a disability or a reflection of the normal process of second language acquisition.
C. Additionally, personnel involved in the evaluation process of ELLs for SEEDS needs to be trained in bilingual assessment and interpretation procedures. It is strongly recommended that personnel involved in the assessment and interpretation of assessment results have the following knowledge:
   1. Understanding of first and second language acquisition stages;
   2. Impact of culture on student performance;
   3. Knowledge regarding bilingual education and English as a second language programming and MTSS teaching methods;
   4. Knowledge in how to interpret results of student's oral language proficiency in relation to the results of the test measuring academic achievement and cognitive processes; and
   5. Understanding of how to interpret results of similar or parallel tests given in more than one language.
D. To appropriately understand test results, the examiner(s)/committee of knowledgeable persons must interpret test results in light of the student's language development (in both English and the student's native language), educational history, linguistic background, socioeconomic issues, and any other pertinent factors that affect learning.

§3.8 SEEDS Determination

A. A district, school, or charter school team or committee of knowledgeable persons determines whether the student is a SEEDS, after reviewing all accumulated data, including the following areas:
   1. Observations of the teacher, district, charter school staff, and/or parent/guardian;
   2. Data gathered from the classroom (including student work and the results of classroom measures) and information found in the student's cumulative folder (including the developmental and academic history of the student);
   3. Data-based documentation of student progress during instruction/intervention;
   4. Results of administered assessments; and
   5. All other accumulated data regarding the development of the student's learning and his or her educational needs.
B. Difficulties in the area of reading for SEEDS will reflect unexpectedly low performance for the student's age and educational level in the following areas:
   1. Reading real words in isolation;
   2. Decoding nonsense words;
   3. Reading fluency (both rate and accuracy); and
   4. Written spelling.
C. Unexpectedly low reading performance, including reading fluency, will be the result of a deficit in phonological processing, including the following:
   1. Phonological awareness,
   2. Rapid naming, and
   3. Phonological memory.
D. Many SEEDS will have difficulty with the secondary characteristics of literacy, including reading comprehension, written composition, spelling, grammar, and rote math skills.
E. A committee of knowledgeable persons must also incorporate the following guidelines as authorized by this state Policy:
   1. The student has received MTSS instruction, [insert state name] Statute, Section 4 of this Policy;

2. The student has an unexpected lack of appropriate academic progress (in the areas of reading and spelling) relative to their age/grade/intellectual development;

3. The student has adequate intelligence (an average ability to learn in the absence of print or in other academic areas);

4. The student exhibits characteristics associated with SEEDS; and

5. The student's lack of progress is not due to sociocultural factors such as language differences, irregular attendance, or lack of experiential background.

F. Based on the above information and guidelines, the committee of knowledgeable persons determines and identifies SEEDS and the committee of knowledgeable persons also determines whether the student has a disability under the federal Rehabilitation Act of 1973, §504 and the 2008 ADAAA. A student is considered to have a disability under §504 if the condition substantially limits the student's learning. Students with additional factors that complicate SEEDS may require additional support or referral to special education.

§3.9 Referral to Special Education

A. At any time during the assessment for reading failure identification process or instruction, students may be referred for evaluation for special education. At times, students will display additional factors or areas complicating their instruction and requiring more support than what is available through instruction (MTSS). At other times, students with severe at-risk characteristics or related disorders will be unable to make appropriate academic progress within any of the programs described in the procedures related to SEEDS. In such cases, a referral to special education for evaluation and possible identification as a child with a disability within the meaning of the IDEA 2004 (20 USC section 1400 et seq.), the federal Rehabilitation Act of 1973, §504, and the 2008 ADAAA should be made as needed. See [insert state name] Statute, Section 1.5 of this Policy.

B. If a SEEDS is found eligible for special education in the area of reading, the school district must include appropriate reading instruction on the student's Individualized Education Program (IEP). Appropriate reading instruction includes the descriptors listed at www.literatenation.org.

C. If a SEEDS is referred for special education, districts and charter schools must follow the Individuals with Disabilities Education Act (IDEA). In IDEA 2004, §1401 (30), SEEDS is considered one of a variety of etiological foundations for "specific learning disability." 34 CFR 300.8(c)(10) states that a "specific learning disability" means a disorder in one or more of the basic psychological processes involved in understanding or in using language, spoken or written, that may manifest in an imperfect ability to listen, think, speak, read, write, spell, or do mathematical calculations. The term includes such conditions as perceptual disability, brain injury, minimal brain dysfunction, dyslexia, and developmental aphasia. The term does not apply to students who have learning problems that are primarily the result of visual, hearing, or motor disabilities; of mental retardation; of emotional disturbance; or of environmental, cultural, or economic disadvantage.

EFFECTIVE DATE. This section is effective [insert date].

READING DEVELOPMENT AND READING LITERACY

Classroom Instruction in General Education

Key Role In Education, The Workforce, And Society

IN THE MODERN world, literacy is more than a necessary skill set; it is a way of life. Without the ability to read critically and write with sophistication and clarity, education is frustrating and unfulfilling, and pursuing a rewarding employment path is nearly impossible. With these abilities, however, the possibilities are endless: high achievement in secondary and postsecondary education, recognition as an accomplished student and worker, success at each level of the professional world, and much more. These are opportunities that should be available to anyone who works for them—and yet for over half of our students, it will be a struggle to reach this point.

The current educational system is neither ambitious nor dynamic enough to address the unique difficulties and challenges of each child who fails to achieve full literacy, instead cementing the fate of these students by treating them as a challenged whole and allowing them to fall further behind. However, these students have everything they need to become literate and successful; they simply need the right tools, the right instruction, and the right knowledge provided to their teachers and schools.

In this appendix, we present you four tools to assist you in adopting state Literacy Policy on §General Education: Foundational Reading Development Instruction; Speaking, Listening, And Language Instruction; Content-Area Reading Literacy Instruction; And Writing Literacy Instruction

Included in this Section of the Policy are tools to assist your work: the Executive Summary explains the basics of reading development and reading literacy, and its attainment; the Key Components will organize the related concepts by their goals and results; the Roadmap and Specifics will provide the details of implementation; and the model state legislation is designed to help you and your community effect positive change in your own state and district.

Executive Summary
For Reading Development And Reading Literacy

Reading development and literacy instruction in general education must be acquired through systematic, explicit, multitiered, and balanced instruction.

Issue:

Reading and writing are an unavoidable part of our daily lives, thanks to ubiquitous digital technologies such as e-mail, texting, social media, etc. In fact, we communicate through written text more today than at any time in the history of mankind. This fact makes the ability to read and write imperative for success in today's schools and in the workplace. Reading literacy acquisition is not an easy process for more than half of all children; thus, only 33 percent of students today read proficiently. In order for all diverse student populations to attain grade-level reading proficiency, they need tiered reading instruction delivered by skilled and knowledgeable teachers in grades K-3. Additionally, student achievement can only improve if content-area teachers in grades 4-12 are committed to incorporating reading literacy into their instruction, allowing the students to become subject-matter literate (i.e., science literate).

Why this is important:

1. In grades K-1, a student learns to read. In grades 2 and 3, a student learns to understand (comprehend) what they are reading and write about the material. By grade 4, students need to enter a different phase of reading with the connected purposes of "reading for knowledge" (reading literacy) and of writing and speaking with structure and thought.
2. Up through grade 3, students concentrate on fluency attainment and text comprehension.
3. By grade 4, students continue their work toward full literacy through writing, speaking, language, and listening instruction in content-area subjects, which, in turn, leads to subject-area literacy. Students must be able to pick up a science text and fully comprehend what it is saying.
4. If a student has not received quality instruction preparing them for grade 4 and beyond, intense and increased instructional supports must be provided immediately, for as long as it takes the student to acquire grade-level reading, writing, speaking, and listening skills.

Goals of instruction:

1. Literacy policy is enacted to produce literate, career-ready citizens.
2. To provide students in grades K-3 with quality foundational reading, writing, speaking, and listening instruction to ensure that they are grade-level proficient. For students who are not at grade level at any stage during K-3, intervene immediately and continuously until grade level is attained.
3. To ensure that all students by grade 4 are capable of reading with both critical analysis and reflective thinking across a wide range of subjects. Ready to become subject-literate in grades 4-12 (i.e., math literate).

How skilled teachers, high-quality instruction, and assessments achieve these goals:

1. All K-3 teachers are certified teachers of reading capable of ensuring that all students reach grade-level proficiency. All

subject-area teachers are also skilled as reading teachers to ensure that students are capable of reading grade-level text with critical analysis and reflective thinking across multiple subject areas.

2. All students must regularly be assessed so that identification of needed interventions can happen immediately and throughout school depending on grade-level demands, K through high-school graduation.

Key points:

Reading literacy acquisition is attained through a complex development progression.

All reading instruction must be data validated by science and consist of foundational reading development and language instruction, speaking and listening instruction, and writing literacy instruction.

Key Components
For Reading Development And Reading Literacy

Students have everything they need to become literate and successful; they simply need the right tools, the right instruction, and the right knowledge provided to their teachers and schools.

The Scientific Principle:

Systematic, explicit, and balanced reading development and literacy instruction allow students to develop a sequenced progression of complex skills that build upon one another. In time, these skills progress, interact with each other, and lead to a deep understanding of print. To become fully literate, a student must receive foundational and advanced reading literacy, writing, speaking, listening, and language instruction for a range of subject areas.

The Progression:

To achieve student academic success, all reading literacy instruction must be data validated by science and consist of foundational reading

CINTHIA COLETTI

literacy and language instruction, speaking and listening instruction, and writing literacy instruction.

1. Reading literacy acquisition is attained through a complex development progression.
2. Speaking, listening, and language skills are taught in grades K-5 for academic and lifelong expression, comprehension, and collaboration.
3. Reading and writing literacy skills are taught in grades 4-12 by content-area teachers that will provide instructional supports so all students attain grade-level reading proficiency and subject matter literacy.

The Key Components:

Grades K-3 Reading Development Instruction

Foundational Reading Development Instruction shall consist of specific program content including the following components:			
1. Language-based instruction	2. Phonological awareness	3. Phoneme—grapheme correspondence knowledge	4. Syllable instruction
5. Linguistics	6. Meaning-based instruction	7. Reading fluency instruction	8. Phonics
Instructional Methodology and Delivery of Foundational Reading Development Content			
1. Foundational reading instruction with student-teacher interaction shall be delivered as follows:			

A. Systematic (structured), sequential, and cumulative instruction	B. Individualized instruction that meets the specific learning needs of each SEEDS in a small group setting	C. Intensive, highly concentrated instruction that maximizes student engagement	D. Meaning-based instruction that is directed toward purposeful reading and writing	E. Instruction that incorporates the simultaneous use of two or more sensory pathways during teacher presentations and student practice

2. To achieve proficiency in language processing, instructional delivery must simultaneously combine visual, auditory, kinesthetic, and tactile instruction.			
3. Synthetic to analytic phonics delivery that teaches students the sounds of the letters first and then combines or blends these sounds to create words. Analytic phonics uses prior knowledge of letters and their corresponding sounds to decode and form new words.			
4. Synthetic phonics methodology teaches students the sounds of the letters first and then combines or blends these sounds to create words. It is delivered to students as follows:			
A. Systematically	B. Sequentially	C. Cumulatively	D. Individualized
5. Automaticity of student reading performance requires a fluent processing of printed material.			
The implementation of the Foundational Reading Development Instruction is to be routinely provided to students within the regular school day for a specific amount of time (dependent on state Policy).			

Grades K-5 Speaking, Listening, and Language Instruction

For comprehension and collaboration in discussion, with increased difficulty by grade level, students will learn to		
1. Engage effectively in a range of collaborative discussions		
2. Come to discussions prepared, having read or studied required material		
A. Follow agreed-upon rules for discussions and carry out assigned roles	B. Pose and respond to specific questions by making comments that contribute to the discussion and elaborate on the remarks of others	C. Review the key ideas expressed and draw conclusions in light of information and knowledge gained from the discussions
3. Summarize a written text, read aloud, or present information using diverse media and formats		
4. Summarize speaker presentation and explain how each claim is supported by reasons and evidence		

For expression and presentation of knowledge and ideas in discussion, with increased difficulty by grade level, students will				
1. Report on a topic or text or present an opinion; sequence ideas logically and use appropriate facts and relevant, descriptive details to support main ideas or themes; and speak clearly at an understandable pace				
2. Include multimedia components and visual displays in their presentation to enhance the development of main ideas or themes				
3. Learn to adapt speech to a variety of contexts and tasks, using formal English when appropriate				
For conventions of standard English in speaking and writing, with increased difficulty by grade level, student will learn				
1. To command conventions of standard English grammar and usage when writing or speaking	2. The function of conjunctions, prepositions, and interjections in general and their function in particular sentences	3. To use the perfect verb tenses	4. To use verb tense to convey various times, sequences, states, and conditions	5. To recognize and correct inappropriate shifts in verb tense
For command of the conventions of standard English in writing, with increased difficulty by grade level, student will learn to				
1. Use punctuation to separate items in a series	2. Use a comma to separate an introductory element from the rest of the sentence	3. Use a comma to set off the words "yes" and "no," to set off a tag question from the rest of the sentence, and to indicate direct address	4. Use underlining, quotation marks, or italics to indicate titles of works	5. Spell grade-appropriate words correctly, consulting references as needed

For knowledge of language, with increased difficulty by grade level, student will learn to		
1. Use knowledge of language and its conventions when writing, speaking, reading, or listening	2. Expand, combine, and reduce sentences for meaning, reader and listener interest, and style	3. Compare and contrast the varieties of English used in stories, dramas, and poems

For vocabulary acquisition and use, with increased difficulty by grade level, student will learn to		
1. Determine or clarify the meaning of unknown and multiple-meaning words and phrases based on grade 5 reading and content, choosing flexibly from a range of strategies	2. Use context as a clue to the meaning of a word or phrase	3. Use common, grade-appropriate Greek and Latin affixes and roots as clues to the meaning of a word
4. Consult reference materials (e.g., dictionaries, glossaries, thesauruses), both print and digital, to find the pronunciation and determine or clarify the precise meaning of key words and phrases.	5. Demonstrate understanding of figurative language, word relationships, and nuances in word meaning	6. Interpret figurative language, including similes and metaphors in context
7. Recognize and explain the meaning of common idioms, adages, and proverbs	8. Use the relationship between particular words (e.g., synonyms, antonyms, homographs) to better understand each of the words	9. Acquire and use accurately grade-appropriate general academic and domain-specific words and phrases, including those that signal contrast, addition, and other logical relationships

Grades 4-12 Reading Literacy Instruction in Content Areas

Reading literacy instruction will be provided to all students, with increased difficulty by grade level, to fulfill the college- and career-readiness expectations provided by the Standards by teachers of all content areas, including English/language arts. Based on the instruction provided, students will learn

1. Key ideas and details in all content areas. Reading literacy will be determined by a student's ability to

A. Read closely to determine what the text says explicitly and to make logical inferences from it; cite specific textual evidence when writing or speaking to support conclusions drawn from the text	B. Determine central ideas or themes of a text and analyze their development; summarize the key supporting details and ideas	C. Analyze how and why individuals, events, and ideas develop and interact over the course of a text

2. Craft and structure of text in all content areas. Reading literacy will be determined by a student's ability to

A. Interpret words and phrases as they are used in a text, including determining technical, connotative, and figurative meanings, and analyze how specific word choices shape meaning or tone	B. Analyze the structure of texts, including how specific sentences, paragraphs, and larger portions of the text relate to each other and the whole	C. Assess how point of view or purpose shapes the content and style of a text

3. Integration of knowledge and ideas in all content areas. Reading literacy will be determined by a student's ability to

A. Integrate and evaluate content presented in diverse formats and media	B. Delineate and evaluate the argument and specific claims in a text	C. Analyze how two or more texts address similar themes or topics to build knowledge or to compare author approaches

4. Analyze and structure with complex textual literature that requires increased comprehension proficiency and encourages independent analysis.

Grades 4-8 Writing Literacy Instruction

Writing literacy instruction will be provided to all students, with increased difficulty by grade level, to fulfill the college- and career-readiness expectations provided by the Standards by teachers of all content areas, including English/language arts. Based on the instruction provided, students will master the skills of

1. Writing opinion pieces on topics or texts, supporting a point of view with reasons and information that increase in complexity by

A. Introducing a topic or text clearly, stating an opinion, and creating an organizational structure in which related ideas are grouped to support the writer's purpose	B. Providing reasons that are supported by facts and details	C. Linking opinions and reasons using words and phrases	D. Providing a concluding statement or section related to the opinion presented

2. Writing arguments to support claims in an analysis of substantive topics or texts, using valid reasoning and relevant and sufficient evidence including

A. Introducing precise, knowledgeable claim(s), establishing the significance of the claim(s), distinguishing the claim(s) from alternate or opposing claims, and creating an organization that logically sequences claim(s), counterclaims, reasons, and evidence	B. Developing claim(s) and counterclaims fairly and thoroughly, supplying the most relevant evidence for each while pointing out the strengths and limitations of both in a manner that anticipates the audience's knowledge level, concerns, values, and possible biases	C. Using words, phrases, and clauses as well as varied syntax to link the major sections of the text, create cohesion, and clarify the relationships between claim(s) and reasons, between reasons and evidence, and between claim(s) and counterclaims	D. Establishing and maintaining a formal style and objective tone while attending to the norms and conventions of the discipline in which they are writing	E. Providing a concluding statement or section that follows from and supports the argument presented

3. Writing narratives to develop real or imagined experiences or events using effective technique, descriptive details, and clear event sequences including

A. Orienting the reader by establishing a situation and introducing a narrator and/or characters; organizing an event sequence that unfolds naturally	B. Using dialogue and description to develop experiences and events or to show the responses of characters to situations	C. Using a variety of transitional words and phrases to manage the sequence of events	D. Using concrete words and phrases and sensory details to convey experiences and events precisely	E. Providing a conclusion that follows from the narrated experiences or events

4. The production and distribution of writing including:

A. Producing clear and coherent writing in which the development and organization are appropriate to task, purpose, and audience	B. With guidance and support from peers and teachers, developing and strengthening writing as needed by planning, revising, and editing	C. With some guidance and support from teachers, using technology, including the Internet, to produce and publish writing as well as to interact and collaborate with others; demonstrating sufficient command of keyboarding skills

5. Using research to build and present knowledge including:

A. Conducting short research projects that build knowledge through investigation of different aspects of a topic	B. Recalling relevant information from experiences or gathering relevant information from print and digital sources; taking notes and categorizing information; and providing a list of sources	C. Drawing evidence from literary or informational texts to support analysis, reflection, and research

Road Map and Specifics for a State Handbook
Reading Development And Literacy Instruction In General Education

In order to produce literate, career-ready citizens able to seize opportunity, schools must lay the foundation for education success and lifelong learning accomplishments. Comprehensive Reading Development and Literacy Instruction in General Education requires that students achieve a level of reading fluency that leads to deep comprehension skills—considered "full literacy." To become fully literate, a student must receive foundational reading and writing instruction and speaking, listening, and language instruction for a range of subject areas. Put simply, full literacy affords students the opportunity to flourish and participate in society, and to be capable of both critical analysis and reflective thinking across a wide range of areas necessary for societal good.

For some children, reading literacy is achieved through almost any reliable method of instruction. For many others, however, including most of our SEEDS community, reading must be acquired through systematic and explicit instruction. This instruction allows the students to develop a sequenced progression of complex skills that build upon and interact with one another, leading over time to a deep understanding of print. The intellectual processes involved in learning to gain ever greater meaning from text become, in turn, the basis of both more generalized coherent thinking and the evolving capacity to write and expand one's thoughts and ideas.

Extensive research has documented that not all children progress in reading acquisition in the same way. In order to ensure that all children learn in a way best tailored to their individual profiles of strengths and weaknesses, the use and interpretation of data regarding these learning profiles must drive instruction, not the other way around. It is well understood by now from the many studies conducted that foundational reading development skills are best taught by knowledgeable, skilled, and well-supported professional/certified teachers of reading/reading specialists, who not only have mastered reading, literacy, and language instruction and the Multi-Tier System of Supports, but can also interpret the results of data to tailor instruction to their students' specific needs. In other words, it is essential to have teachers know both which methodologies work best and how and when to implement them with students at particular levels of skills and needs.

For example, when teaching to a student in the SEEDS community, there exists substantial evidence that the amount of instruction time, its intensity, and the amount of exposure and repetition necessary to develop basic foundational reading skills will vary among individuals. It is by now well known that some SEED students with developmental dyslexia require very different amounts of exposure and practice to master particular foundational skills if they are to connect the multiple pathways in the brain's circuit for reading. For other students, such as those who may only need concentrated language enrichment, reading may come easily after the initial vocabulary is learned. Regardless, all but a few percent of students will become proficient readers when taught using data-validated and evidenced-based instruction by certified teachers of reading.

All educators must share this essential goal: for students in grades K-2 to receive quality foundational reading, speaking, and listening instruction. By grade 3, students move toward an emphasis on text comprehension and fluency attainment; this allows them to enter a different phase of reading with the connected purposes of "reading for knowledge" (reading literacy) and writing and speaking with structure and thought. By grade 4, students continue their work toward full literacy through writing, speaking, language, and listening instruction in content-area subjects, which, in turn, leads to subject-area literacy. A caveat is critical at this point: if a student has not received quality instruction in the early grades, then intense and increased instructional supports with a certified teacher of reading are necessary now, regardless of a student's grade level, and for as long as it takes to acquire grade-level reading, writing, speaking, and listening proficiency skills.

Specifics of Foundational Reading Development Instruction in Grades K-3

Foundational Reading Instruction programs shall consist of specific program content and a defined delivery system. The programs shall be taught by certified teachers of reading. There are eight Foundational

Reading Instructional Content Components: a program that provides instruction integrating all aspects of language, from the receptive (listening and reading) and expressive (oral expression such as word finding and sequencing) aspects to written expression (spelling, mechanics, coherence) and handwriting; a language program that explicitly supports that words are made up of individual speech sounds and that those sounds can be manipulated. This component includes rhyming; recognition of initial, final, and medial sounds; recognition of vowel sounds; recognition and identification of the number of syllables in a word; blending of phonemes (sounds) in words and detached syllables; phoneme segmentation of real words and detached syllables; and phoneme manipulation; a program that provides instruction on the system by which written symbols represent sounds. This encourages accurate pronunciation of each phoneme represented by a given grapheme (symbol to sound), writing the graphemes that represent each given phoneme (sound to symbol), and blending of rules; a program that provides instruction in syllables and their application to reading, as either a word or part of a word containing one sounded vowel; a program that involves the science of language, including phonology, morphology, syntax, and semantics (the study of the structure of a language and its relationship to other languages); a program that provides instruction, through words and sentences, in extraction of meaning; isolated letter-sound correspondence; morphology, from identification of morphemes to their functional use in written and spoken words; syntax, including sentence construction, combination, and expansion in narrative and expository text; semantics, including vocabulary acquisition, idioms, and figurative language; and comprehension of narrative and expository text; a program that provides instruction in the imperative of reading fluency, including accuracy; appropriate use of pitch, juncture, and stress; text phrasing; and the rate at which one reads. Instruction will provide for substantial practice and continual application of word recognition and decoding to work toward automaticity. It will also offer opportunities for reading large amounts of text to achieve independent, grade-level reading with 95 percent accuracy and will give students specific practice in the skills they are learning; and a program that provides instructional practices to emphasize the systematic ways in which spellings relate to speech sounds.

Instructional Methodology and Delivery of Foundational Reading
Development Instructional Content Grades K-3

All teachers of reading shall be prepared to use the following techniques and strategies with a diverse student population in the classrooms. The Literacy Policy requires teachers of reading and teaching specialists to pass the advanced reading instruction competence assessment (ARICA) to show knowledge and expertise in foundational reading development instruction. Student-teacher interaction shall be delivered as follows:

1. Systematic (structured), sequential, and cumulative instruction that is organized and presented in a way that follows a logical, sequential plan, fits the nature of language (alphabetic principle) with no assumption of prior skills or language knowledge, and maximizes student engagement. This instruction proceeds at a rate commensurate with students' needs, ability levels, and demonstration of progress.

2. Individualized instruction that meets the specific learning needs of each SEEDS in a small group setting, including a reading curriculum that matches each student's individual ability level.

3. Intensive, highly concentrated instruction that maximizes student engagement, uses specialized methods and materials, and produces results.

4. Meaning-based instruction directed toward purposeful reading and writing, with an emphasis on comprehension and composition and on independent thinking.

5. Instruction and instructional delivery that uses a simultaneous combination of internal learning pathways and incorporates the simultaneous use of two or more sensory pathways (auditory, visual, kinesthetic, tactile) during teacher presentations and student practice to achieve proficiency in language processing.

6. Synthetic to analytic phonics delivery that first teaches students the letters and their corresponding sounds and then combines or blends these sounds to decode and create words.

Synthetic phonics methodology is delivered to students as follows:

Systematically, the material is organized and taught in a way that is logical and fits the nature of our language. This characteristic of the methodology refers to the way a system of rules governs how sounds combine to form words and words combine to form sentences to represent knowledge;

Sequentially, the learner moves step-by-step from simple, well-learned material to that which is more complex, as he or she masters the necessary body of language skills; Cumulatively each step is incremental and based on those skills already learned;

Individualized, teaching is planned to meet the differing needs of learners who are similar to each other but never exactly alike; and

Automaticity, student reading performance requires a fluent processing of printed material. The goal is that the process requires little effort or attention, as in sight word recognition. Adequate student practice with decodable text is provided for mastery of automaticity skills and application of concepts.

A quick note on phonics. Learning to read is a complex task for beginners. They must coordinate many cognitive processes to read accurately and fluently. Readers must be able to apply their alphabetic knowledge to decode unfamiliar words and to remember how to read words they have read before. When reading connected text, they must construct sentence meanings and retain them in memory as they move on to new sentences. At the same time, they must monitor their word recognition to make sure that the words activated in their minds fit with the meaning of the context. In addition, they must link new information to what they have already read, as well as to their background knowledge, and use this to anticipate forthcoming information. When one stops to take stock of all the processes that readers perform when they read and comprehend text, one is reminded how amazing the act of reading is and how much there is for beginners to learn.

In teaching phonics explicitly and systematically, several different instructional approaches have been used. These include synthetic phonics, analytic phonics, embedded phonics, analogy phonics, onset-rime phonics, and phonics through spelling. Although these explicit and systematic phonics approaches all use a planned, sequential introduction of a set of phonic elements with teaching and practice of those elements, they differ across a number of other features. Thus, deep teacher knowledge and skill is required to address the needs of each child as they reach different developmental phases on his or her path to reading fluency, comprehension, and literacy attainment.

The Foundational Reading Development Instruction Program is routinely implemented within the regular school day for a defined amount of time per week or per day. The most successful model includes ninety minutes of early reading instruction each school day. The instruction is scheduled in two segments for students as follows: regular class instruction, out-of-class instruction, individual or small group instruction, a combination of these options, or any additional arrangements that may be developed by the committee.

Grades K-5 Speaking, Listening, and Language Instruction

Speaking and listening skills of increasing difficulty by grade level will be taught to students in grades K-5 for academic and lifelong expression, comprehension, cooperation, and collaboration.

Comprehension and collaboration in discussion with increased difficulty by grade level: (1) students will learn to engage effectively in a range of collaborative discussions (one-on-one, in groups, and teacher-led) with diverse partners on grade-level topics and texts, building on others' ideas and expressing their own ideas clearly; (2) students will learn to come to discussions prepared, having read or studied required material, and to draw explicitly on that preparation and other information known about the topic to explore ideas under discussion by following agreed-upon rules for discussions and carrying out assigned roles; posing and responding to specific questions by making comments that contribute to the discussion and elaborating on the remarks of others; and reviewing the key ideas expressed and drawing conclusions in light of information and knowledge gained from the discussions; (3) students will learn to summarize a written text read aloud or information presented in diverse media and formats, including visually, quantitatively, and orally; and (4) students will learn to summarize the points a speaker makes and explain how each claim is supported by reasons and evidence.

Expression and presentation of knowledge and ideas in discussion with increased difficulty by grade level: (1) Students will report on a topic or text or present an opinion; sequence ideas logically and use appropriate facts and relevant, descriptive details to support main ideas or themes; and speak clearly at an understandable pace. (2) Students will include multimedia components (e.g., graphics, sound) and visual displays in presentations when appropriate to enhance the development of main ideas or themes. (3) Students will learn to adapt speech to a variety of contexts and tasks, using formal English when appropriate to task and situation.

Conventions of standard English in speaking and writing with increased difficulty by grade level: (1) Students will learn and demonstrate command of the conventions of standard English grammar and usage when writing or speaking. (2) Students will learn and explain the function of conjunctions, prepositions, and interjections in general and in particular sentences. (3) Students will learn to use the perfect verb tenses (e.g., I had walked; I have walked; I will have walked). (4) Students will learn to use verb tense to convey various times, sequences, states, and conditions. (5) Students will learn to recognize and correct inappropriate shifts in verb tense (e.g., either/or, neither/nor).

Command of the conventions of standard English—capitalization, punctuation, and spelling—when writing with increased difficulty by grade level: (1) Students will learn to use punctuation to separate items in a series. (2) Students will learn to use a comma to separate an introductory element from the rest of the sentence. (3) Students will learn to use a comma to set off the words "yes" and "no" (e.g., Yes, thank you), to set off a tag question from the rest of the sentence (e.g., It's true, isn't it?), and to indicate direct address (e.g., Is that you, Steve?). (4) Students will learn to use underlining, quotation marks, or italics to indicate titles of works. (5) Students will learn to spell grade-appropriate words correctly, consulting references as needed.

Knowledge of language with increased difficulty by grade level: (1) Students will learn to use knowledge of language and its conventions when writing, speaking, reading, or listening. (2) Students will learn to expand, combine, and reduce sentences for meaning, reader and listener interest, and style. (3) Students will learn to compare and contrast the varieties of English (e.g., dialects, registers) used in stories, dramas, and poems.

Vocabulary acquisition and use with increased difficulty by grade level: (1) Students will learn to determine or clarify the meaning of unknown and multiple-meaning words and phrases based on grade 5 reading and content, choosing flexibly from a range of strategies. (2)

Students will learn to use context (e.g., cause/effect relationships and comparisons in text) as a clue to the meaning of a word or phrase. (3) Students will learn to use common, grade-appropriate Greek and Latin affixes and roots as clues to the meaning of a word (e.g., photograph, photosynthesis). (4) Students will learn to consult reference materials (e.g., dictionaries, glossaries, thesauruses), both print and digital, to find the pronunciation and determine or clarify the precise meaning of key words and phrases. (5) Students will learn to demonstrate understanding of figurative language, word relationships, and nuances in word meaning. (6) Students will learn to interpret figurative language, including similes and metaphors, in context. (7) Students will learn to recognize and explain the meaning of common idioms, adages, and proverbs. (8) Students will learn to use the relationships between particular words (e.g., synonyms, antonyms, homographs) to better understand each of the words. (9) Students will learn to acquire and accurately use grade-appropriate general academic and domain-specific words and phrases, including those that signal contrast, addition, and other logical relationships (e.g., however, although, nevertheless, similarly, moreover, in addition).

Grades 4-12 Reading Literacy Instruction in Content Areas

Reading literacy skills will be provided to all students by content area and English language arts teachers as determined by the Standards to define college- and career-readiness expectations.

Learning and identifying the key ideas and details in content-area reading literacy with increased difficulty by grade level: (1) Read closely to determine the explicit meaning of the text and to make logical inferences from it; cite specific textual evidence when writing or speaking to support conclusions drawn from the text. (2) Determine central ideas or themes of a text and analyze their development; summarize the key supporting details and ideas. (3) Analyze how and why individuals, events, and ideas develop and interact over the course of a text. (4) Craft and structure content-area reading literacy with increased difficulty by grade level: (a) Interpret words and phrases as they are used in a text, determining technical, connotative, and figurative meanings; and analyze how specific word choices shape meaning or tone. (b) Analyze the structure of texts, including how specific sentences, paragraphs, and larger portions of the text (e.g., a section, chapter, scene, or stanza) relate to each other and to the whole. (c) Assess how point of view or purpose shapes the content and style of a text.

Integration of knowledge and ideas in content-area reading literacy with increased difficulty by grade level: (1) Integrate and evaluate content presented in diverse formats and media, including visually, quantitatively, and in words. (2) Delineate and evaluate the argument and specific claims in a text, including the validity of the reasoning as well as the relevance and sufficiency of the evidence. (3) Analyze how two or more texts address similar themes or topics to build knowledge or to compare author approaches. (4) Range of reading and level of text complexity for reading literacy must increase by grade level. Instruction is based upon complex textual literature that requires increased comprehension and encourages independent analysis.

Grades 4-8 Writing Literacy Instruction

Writing literacy skills are provided to all students by teachers of content-areas subjects and English language arts as determined by the Standards, to define college- and career-readiness expectations. The Literacy Policy provides for all content-area teachers to pass the basic reading instruction competence assessment (BRICA) to ensure that his or her skill in teaching core subject literacy (reading for knowledge and writing in a clear and coherent form) is adequate to accomplish the following instructional components.

In grades 4-8, with increased difficulty by grade level, students will learn and master the skill of writing opinion pieces on topics or texts, supporting a point of view with reasons and information that increase in complexity: (1) Introduce a topic or text clearly, state an opinion, and organize the piece by grouping related ideas to support the purpose. (2) Provide reasons supported by facts and details. (3) Link opinion and reasons using words and phrases. (4) Provide a concluding statement or section related to the opinion presented.

With increased difficulty by grade, students will learn and master the skill of writing arguments to support claims in an analysis of substantive topics or texts, using valid reasoning and relevant and sufficient evidence to (1) introduce one or more precise, knowledgeable claim(s), establish the significance of the claim(s), distinguish the claim(s) from alternate or opposing claims, and create an organization that logically sequences the claim(s), counterclaims, reasons, and evidence; (2) develop the claim(s) and counterclaims fairly and thoroughly, supplying the most relevant evidence for each while pointing out the strengths and limitations of both in a manner that anticipates the audience's knowledge, concerns, values, and possible biases; (3) use words, phrases, and clauses as well as varied syntax to link the major sections of the text, create cohesion, and clarify the relationships between claim(s) and reasons, between reasons and evidence, and between claim(s) and counterclaims; (4) establish and maintain a formal style and objective tone while abiding by the norms and conventions of the discipline in which they are writing; and (5) provide a concluding statement or section that follows from and supports the argument presented.

With increased difficulty by grade level, students will learn and master the skill of writing narratives to develop real or imagined experiences or events using effective technique, descriptive details, and clear event sequences: (1) Orient the reader by establishing a situation and introducing a narrator and/or characters; organize an event sequence that unfolds naturally. (2) Use dialogue and description to develop experiences and events or to show the responses of characters to situations. (3) Use a variety of transitional words and phrases to manage the sequence of events. (4) Use concrete words and phrases and sensory details to precisely convey experiences and events. (5) Provide a conclusion that follows from the narrated experiences or events.

With increased difficulty by grade, students will learn and master the skills of the production and distribution of writing: (1) Produce clear and coherent writing in which the development and organization are appropriate to task, purpose, and audience. (2) With guidance and support from peers and teachers, develop and strengthen writing as needed by planning, revising, and editing. (3) With some guidance and support from teachers, use technology, including the Internet, to produce and publish writing and to interact and collaborate with others; demonstrate sufficient command of keyboarding skills.

With increased difficulty by grade level, students will learn and master the writing skill of using research to build and present knowledge: (1) Conduct short research projects that build knowledge through investigation of different aspects of a topic. (2) Recall relevant information from experiences or gather relevant information from print and digital sources; take notes and categorize information; and provide a list of sources. (3) Draw evidence from literary or informational texts to support analysis, reflection, and research.

Grades 9-12 Writing Literacy Instruction

Writing literacy skills will be provided to all students by content area and English language arts teachers as determined by the Standards to define college- and career-readiness expectations.

In grades 9-12, with increased difficulty by grade level, students will learn and master the skill of writing informative and explanatory texts to examine and convey complex ideas, concepts, and information clearly and accurately. They will accomplish this through the effective selection, organization, and analysis of content. Students must introduce a topic; organize complex ideas, concepts, and information so that each new element builds on that which precedes it to create a unified whole; and include formatting (e.g., headings), graphics (e.g., figures, tables), and multimedia to aid comprehension. Mastery of these skills requires that students consistently do the following: (1) Develop the topic thoroughly by selecting the most significant and relevant facts, extended definitions, concrete details, quotations, or other information and examples appropriate to the audience's knowledge of the topic. (2) Use appropriate and varied transitions and syntax to link the major sections of the text, create cohesion, and clarify the relationships among complex ideas and concepts. (3). Use precise language, domain-specific vocabulary, and techniques such as metaphor, simile, and analogy to manage the complexity of the topic. (4) Establish and maintain a formal style and objective tone while abiding by the norms and conventions of the discipline in which students are writing. (5) Provide a concluding statement or section that follows from and supports the information or explanation presented (e.g., articulating the implications or significance of the topic).

With increased difficulty by grade level, students will learn and master the skill of writing narratives to develop real or imagined experiences or events using effective technique, well-chosen details, and well-structured event sequences: (1) Engage and orient the reader by setting out a problem, situation, or observation and its significance, establishing one or multiple point(s) of view, and introducing a narrator and/or characters; create a smooth progression of experiences or events. (2) Use narrative techniques, such as dialogue, pacing, description, reflection, and multiple plot lines, to develop experiences, events, and characters. (3) Sequence events using a variety of techniques that build on one another to create a coherent whole and a particular tone and outcome (e.g., a sense of mystery, suspense, growth, or resolution). (4) Use precise words and phrases, telling details, and sensory language to convey a vivid picture of the experiences, events, setting, and characters. (5) Provide a conclusion that follows from and reflects on what is experienced, observed, or resolved over the course of the narrative.

With increased difficulty by grade level, students will learn and master the skills of production and distribution of writing: (1) Produce clear and coherent writing in which the development, organization, and style are appropriate to task, purpose, and audience. (2) Develop and strengthen writing as needed by planning, revising, editing, rewriting, or trying a new approach. Focus on addressing what is most significant for a specific purpose and audience. (3) Use technology, including the Internet, to produce, publish, and update individual or shared writing products in response to ongoing feedback, including new arguments or information.

In grades 9-12, with increased difficulty by grade level, students will learn and master the writing skill of using research to build and present knowledge: (1) Conduct short as well as more sustained research projects to answer a question (including a self-generated question) or solve a problem; narrow or broaden the inquiry when appropriate; synthesize multiple sources on the subject, demonstrating an understanding of the subject under investigation. (2) Gather relevant information from multiple authoritative print and digital sources, using advanced searches effectively; assess the strengths and limitations of each source in terms of the task, purpose, and audience; integrate information into the text selectively to maintain the flow of ideas, while avoiding plagiarism and overreliance on any one source and while following a standard format for citation. (3) Draw evidence from literary or informational texts to support analysis, reflection, and research.

MODEL STATE LEGISLATION LANGUAGE FOR READING DEVELOPMENT AND LITERACY

Enactment of Foundational Reading Development and Literacy Instruction in General Education

§4 General Education: Foundational Reading Instruction; Speaking, Listening, And Language Instruction; Content-Area Reading Literacy Instruction; And Writing Literacy Instruction

---

BE IT ENACTED BY THE LEGISLATURE OF THE STATE OF [insert state name] that all reading programs adopted by either districts or schools be data validated by science and consist of foundational reading and language instruction, speaking and listening instruction and writing literacy instruction. It is understood that reading literacy acquisition is attained through a complex development progression best taught by highly skilled and well-trained professional teachers of reading, accomplished in delivering reading and language instruction and MTSS to diverse student populations. It is further understood that speaking, listening, and language skills will be taught in grades K-5 for academic and lifelong expression, comprehension, and collaboration. It is further understood that all content-area teachers in grades 4-12 are teachers of reading and writing literacy and will provide instruction supports so all students attain grade-level proficiency.

§4.1 Foundational Reading Development Instruction in Grades K-3:

A. Foundational Reading Development Instruction programs shall consist of specific program content and a defined delivery system. The programs shall be taught by certified teachers of reading as defined in [insert state name] Statute, Section 2.0 of the Policy. The programs content shall consist of the following components:
  1. Foundational Reading Development Instructional Content Components
     a. Language-based—A program that provides instruction that integrates all aspects of language: receptive

(listening and reading); expressive (oral expression to include word finding and sequencing); written expression (spelling, mechanics, coherence); and handwriting.

b. Phonological awareness—A language program that explicitly supports that words are made up of individual speech sounds and that those sounds can be manipulated: rhyming; recognition of initial, final, and medial sounds; recognition of vowel sounds; recognition and identification of the number of syllables in a word; sound blending of phonemes (sounds) in words and detached syllables; phoneme segmentation of real words and detached syllables; and phoneme manipulation.

c. Phoneme-grapheme correspondence knowledge—A program that provides instruction on the system by which symbols represent sounds in a writing system: accurately pronouncing each phoneme represented by a given grapheme (symbol to sound); writing the graphemes that represent each given phoneme (sound to symbol); and blending rules.

d. Syllable instruction—A program that provides instruction in syllables and their application to reading both as a word or part of a word that contains one sounded vowel.

e. Linguistics—A program providing the science of language that includes phonology, morphology, syntax, and semantics; the study of the structure of a language and its relationship to other languages.

f. Meaning-based instruction—A program that provides instruction, through words and sentences, on how to best extract meaning in addition to teaching isolated letter-sound correspondence; instruction in morphology, which includes identification of morphemes and their functional use in written and spoken words; instruction of syntax to include sentence construction, combining, and expansion in both narrative and expository text; instruction of semantics to include vocabulary acquisition, idioms, and figurative language; and instruction in comprehension of narrative and expository text.

g. Reading fluency instruction—A program that provides instruction on the imperative of reading fluency to include accuracy; appropriate use of pitch, juncture, and stress; text phrasing; and the rate at which one reads. Instruction will provide for substantial practice and continual application of decoding and word recognition to work toward automaticity; and also opportunities for reading large amounts of text to achieve independent reading at grade-level with 95 percent accuracy and specific practices in skills being learned.

h. Phonics—A program that provides instructional practices that emphasize how spellings are related to speech sounds in systematic ways.

B. Instructional Methodology and Delivery of Foundational Reading Instructional Content

1. All teachers of reading shall be prepared to utilize the following techniques and strategies with a diverse student population in the classrooms. Foundational reading instruction with student-teacher interaction shall be delivered as follows:

a. Systematic (structured), sequential, and cumulative instruction that is organized and presented in a way that follows a logical sequential plan, fits the nature of language (alphabetic principle) with no assumption of prior skills or language knowledge, and maximizes student engagement. This instruction proceeds at a rate commensurate with students' needs, ability levels, and demonstration of progress;

b. Individualized instruction that meets the specific learning needs of each SEEDS in a small group setting to include a reading curriculum that matches each student's individual ability level;

c. Intensive, highly concentrated instruction that maximizes student engagement, uses specialized methods and materials, and produces results;

d. Meaning-based instruction that is directed toward purposeful reading and writing, with an emphasis on comprehension and composition, and independent thinking;

e. Instruction that incorporates the simultaneous use of two or more sensory pathways (auditory, visual, kinesthetic, tactile) during teacher presentations and student practice.

2. Instructional delivery that uses a simultaneous combination of internal learning pathways, visual, auditory, kinesthetic, and tactile to achieve proficiency in language processing.

3. Synthetic to analytic phonics delivery that teaches students the sounds of the letters first and then combines or blends these sounds to create words. Analytic phonics uses prior knowledge of letters and their corresponding sounds to decode and form new words.

4. Synthetic phonics methodology teaches students the sounds of the letters first and then combines or blends these sounds to create words. It is delivered to students as follows:

a. Systematically. The material is organized and taught in a way that is logical and fits the nature of our language. This characteristic of the methodology refers to the way a system of rules governs how sounds combine to form words and words combine to form sentences to represent knowledge.

b. Sequentially. The learner moves step-by-step, in order, from simple, well-learned material to that which is more complex, as he or she masters the necessary body of language skills.

c. Cumulatively. Each step is incremental and based on those skills already learned.

d. Individualized. Teaching is planned to meet the differing needs of learners who are similar to each other, but not ever exactly alike.

5. Automaticity of student reading performance requires a fluent processing of printed material. The goal is for the process to require little effort or attention, as in sight word recognition. Adequate student practice with decodable text is to be provided for mastery of automaticity skills and applications of concepts.

C. Implementation of the Foundational Reading Instruction Program is to be routinely provided to students within the regular school day for a minimum of [Insert state requirements (200-250)] minutes per week or a minimum of [Insert state requirements (40-50)] minutes each day. The instruction will be scheduled in two segments for students as follows: regular class instruction, out-of-class instruction, individual or small group instruction, a combination of these options, or any additional arrangements that may be developed by the committee.

§4.2 Grades K-5 Speaking, Listening, and Language Instruction
Speaking and Listening skills of increasing difficulty by grade level will be taught to students in grades K-5 for academic and lifelong expression, comprehension, cooperation, and collaboration.

A. Comprehension and collaboration in discussion with increased difficulty by grade level:
1. Students will learn to engage effectively in a range of collaborative discussions (one-on-one, in groups, and teacher-led) with diverse partners on grade-level topics and texts, building on others' ideas, and expressing their own ideas clearly.
2. Students will learn to come to discussions prepared, having read or studied required material; explicitly draw on that preparation and other information known about the topic to explore ideas under discussion:
   a. Follow agreed-upon rules for discussions and carry out assigned roles.
   b. Pose and respond to specific questions by making comments that contribute to the discussion and elaborate on the remarks of others.
   c. Review the key ideas expressed and draw conclusions in light of information and knowledge gained from the discussions.
3. Students will learn to summarize a written text read aloud or information presented in diverse media and formats, including visually, quantitatively, and orally.
4. Students will learn to summarize the points a speaker makes and explain how each claim is supported by reasons and evidence.

B. Expression and presentation of knowledge and ideas in discussion with increased difficulty by grade level:
   1. Students will report on a topic or text or present an opinion; sequence ideas logically and use appropriate facts and relevant, descriptive details to support main ideas or themes; and speak clearly at an understandable pace.
   2. Students will include multimedia components (e.g., graphics, sound) and visual displays in presentations when appropriate to enhance the development of main ideas or themes.
   3. Students will learn to adapt speech to a variety of contexts and tasks, using formal English when appropriate to task and situation.
C. Conventions of standard English in speaking and writing with increased difficulty by grade level:
   1. Students will learn and demonstrate command of the conventions of standard English grammar and usage when writing or speaking.
   2. Students will learn and explain the function of conjunctions, prepositions, and interjections in general and their function in particular sentences.
   3. Students will learn to use the perfect verb tenses (e.g., I had walked; I have walked; I will have walked).
   4. Students will learn to use verb tense to convey various times, sequences, states, and conditions.
   5. Students will learn to recognize and correct inappropriate shifts in verb tense (e.g., either/or, neither/nor).
D. Command of the conventions of standard English— capitalization, punctuation, and spelling when writing with increased difficulty by grade level:
   1. Students will learn to use punctuation to separate items in a series.
   2. Students will learn to use a comma to separate an introductory element from the rest of the sentence.
   3. Students will learn to use a comma to set off the words "yes" and "no" (e.g., Yes, thank you), to set off a tag question from the rest of the sentence (e.g., It's true, isn't it?), and to indicate direct address (e.g., Is that you, Steve?).

4. Students will learn to use underlining, quotation marks, or italics to indicate titles of works.
5. Students will learn to spell grade-appropriate words correctly, consulting references as needed.

E. Knowledge of language with increased difficulty by grade level:
1. Students will learn to use knowledge of language and its conventions when writing, speaking, reading, or listening.
2. Students will learn to expand, combine, and reduce sentences for meaning, reader and listener interest, and style.
3. Students will learn to compare and contrast the varieties of English (e.g., dialects, registers) used in stories, dramas, and poems.

F. Vocabulary acquisition and use with increased difficulty by grade level:
1. Students will learn to determine or clarify the meaning of unknown and multiple-meaning words and phrases based on grade 5 reading and content, choosing flexibly from a range of strategies.
2. Students will learn to use context (e.g., cause/effect relationships and comparisons in text) as a clue to the meaning of a word or phrase.
3. Students will learn to use common, grade-appropriate Greek and Latin affixes and roots as clues to the meaning of a word (e.g., photograph, photosynthesis).
4. Students will learn to consult reference materials (e.g., dictionaries, glossaries, thesauruses), both print and digital, to find the pronunciation and determine or clarify the precise meaning of key words and phrases.
5. Students will learn to demonstrate understanding of figurative language, word relationships, and nuances in word meaning.
6. Students will learn to interpret figurative language, including similes and metaphors, in context.
7. Students will learn to recognize and explain the meaning of common idioms, adages, and proverbs.
8. Students will learn to use the relationship between particular words (e.g., synonyms, antonyms, homographs) to better understand each of the words.

9. Students will learn to acquire and use accurately grade-appropriate general academic and domain-specific words and phrases, including those that signal contrast, addition, and other logical relationships (e.g., however, although, nevertheless, similarly, moreover, in addition).

§4.3 Grades 4-12 Reading Literacy Instruction in Content Areas

Reading literacy skills will be provided to all students by content area and English language arts as determined by the Standards to define college and career readiness expectations.

A. Key ideas and details in content-area reading literacy with increased difficulty by grade level:
  1. Read closely to determine what the text says explicitly and to make logical inferences from it; cite specific textual evidence when writing or speaking to support conclusions drawn from the text.
  2. Determine central ideas or themes of a text and analyze their development; summarize the key supporting details and ideas.
  3. Analyze how and why individuals, events, and ideas develop and interact over the course of a text.
B. Craft and structure content-area reading literacy with increased difficulty by grade level:
  1. Interpret words and phrases as they are used in a text, including determining technical, connotative, and figurative meanings, and analyze how specific word choices shape meaning or tone.
  2. Analyze the structure of texts, including how specific sentences, paragraphs, and larger portions of the text (e.g., a section, chapter, scene, or stanza) relate to each other and the whole.
  3. Assess how point of view or purpose shapes the content and style of a text.
C. Integration of knowledge and ideas in content-area reading literacy with increased difficulty by grade level:
  1. Integrate and evaluate content presented in diverse formats and media, including visually and quantitatively, as well as in words.

2. Delineate and evaluate the argument and specific claims in a text, including the validity of the reasoning as well as the relevance and sufficiency of the evidence.
3. Analyze how two or more texts address similar themes or topics to build knowledge or to compare author approaches.
D. Range of reading and level of text complexity for reading literacy with increased difficulty by grade level. Analyze and structure instruction with complex textual literature that requires increased comprehension proficiency and encourages independent analysis.

§4.4 Grades 4-8 Writing Literacy Instruction

Writing literacy skills will be provided to all students by teachers of content areas and English language arts as determined by the Standards, to define college- and career-readiness expectations.

A. In grades 4-8, with increased difficulty by grade level, students will be instructed on and master the skill of writing opinion pieces on topics or texts, supporting a point of view with reasons and information that increase in complexity:
1. Introduce a topic or text clearly, state an opinion, and create an organizational structure in which related ideas are grouped to support the writer's purpose.
2. Provide reasons that are supported by facts and details.
3. Link opinion and reasons using words and phrases.
4. Provide a concluding statement or section related to the opinion presented.
B. In grades 4-8, with increased difficulty by grade, students will be instructed on and master the skill of writing arguments to support claims in an analysis of substantive topics or texts, using valid reasoning and relevant and sufficient evidence:
1. Introduce precise, knowledgeable claim(s), establish the significance of the claim(s), distinguish the claim(s) from alternate or opposing claims, and create an organization that logically sequences claim(s), counterclaims, reasons, and evidence.
2. Develop claim(s) and counterclaims fairly and thoroughly, supplying the most relevant evidence for each while

pointing out the strengths and limitations of both in a manner that anticipates the audience's knowledge level, concerns, values, and possible biases.

3. Use words, phrases, and clauses as well as varied syntax to link the major sections of the text, create cohesion, and clarify the relationships between claim(s) and reasons, between reasons and evidence, and between claim(s) and counterclaims.

4. Establish and maintain a formal style and objective tone while attending to the norms and conventions of the discipline in which they are writing.

5. Provide a concluding statement or section that follows from and supports the argument presented.

C. In grades 4-8, with increased difficulty by grade level, students will be instructed on and will master the skill of writing narratives to develop real or imagined experiences or events using effective technique, descriptive details, and clear event sequences:

1. Orient the reader by establishing a situation and introducing a narrator and/or characters; organize an event sequence that unfolds naturally.

2. Use dialogue and description to develop experiences and events or show the responses of characters to situations.

3. Use a variety of transitional words and phrases to manage the sequence of events.

4. Use concrete words and phrases and sensory details to convey experiences and events precisely.

5. Provide a conclusion that follows from the narrated experiences or events.

D. In grades 4-8, with increased difficulty by grade, students will be instructed on and will master the skill of the production and distribution of writing:

1. Produce clear and coherent writing in which the development and organization are appropriate to task, purpose, and audience.

2. With guidance and support from peers and teachers, develop and strengthen writing as needed by planning, revising, and editing.

3. With some guidance and support from teachers, use technology, including the Internet, to produce and publish writing as well as to interact and collaborate with others; demonstrate sufficient command of keyboarding skills.

E. In grades 4-8, with increased difficulty by grade level, students will be instructed on and master the writing skill of using research to build and present knowledge:

1. Conduct short research projects that build knowledge through investigation of different aspects of a topic.

2. Recall relevant information from experiences or gather relevant information from print and digital sources; take notes and categorize information; and provide a list of sources.

3. Draw evidence from literary or informational texts to support analysis, reflection, and research.

§4.5 Grades 9-12 Writing Literacy Instruction

Writing literacy skills will be provided to all students by content area and English language arts teachers as determined by the Standards to define college- and career-readiness expectations.

A. In grades 9-12, with increased difficulty by grade level, students will be instructed on and master the skill of writing informative/explanatory texts to examine and convey complex ideas, concepts, and information clearly and accurately through the effective selection, organization, and analysis of content.

1. Introduce a topic; organize complex ideas, concepts, and information so that each new element builds on that which precedes it to create a unified whole; include formatting (e.g., headings), graphics (e.g., figures, tables), and multimedia to aid comprehension:

2. Develop the topic thoroughly by selecting the most significant and relevant facts, extended definitions, concrete details, quotations, or other information and examples appropriate to the audience's knowledge of the topic.

3. Use appropriate and varied transitions and syntax to link the major sections of the text, create cohesion, and clarify the relationships among complex ideas and concepts.

4. Use precise language, domain-specific vocabulary, and techniques such as metaphor, simile, and analogy to manage the complexity of the topic.
5. Establish and maintain a formal style and objective tone while attending to the norms and conventions of the discipline in which they are writing.
6. Provide a concluding statement or section that follows from and supports the information or explanation presented (e.g., articulating implications or the significance of the topic).

B. In grades 9-12, with increased difficulty by grade level, students will be instructed on and master the skill of writing narratives to develop real or imagined experiences or events using effective technique, well-chosen details, and well-structured event sequences:

1. Engage and orient the reader by setting out a problem, situation, or observation and its significance, establishing one or multiple point(s) of view, and introducing a narrator and/or characters; create a smooth progression of experiences or events.
2. Use narrative techniques, such as dialogue, pacing, description, reflection, and multiple plot lines, to develop experiences, events, and characters.
3. Use a variety of techniques to sequence events so that they build on one another to create a coherent whole and build toward a particular tone and outcome (e.g., a sense of mystery, suspense, growth, or resolution).
4. Use precise words and phrases, telling details, and sensory language to convey a vivid picture of the experiences, events, setting, and characters.
5. Provide a conclusion that follows from and reflects on what is experienced, observed, or resolved over the course of the narrative.

C. In grades 9-12, with increased difficulty by grade level, students will be instructed on and master the skill of production and distribution of writing:

1. Produce clear and coherent writing in which the development, organization, and style are appropriate to task, purpose, and audience.

2. Develop and strengthen writing as needed by planning, revising, editing, rewriting, or trying a new approach, focusing on addressing what is most significant for a specific purpose and audience.
3. Use technology, including the Internet, to produce, publish, and update individual or shared writing products in response to ongoing feedback, including new arguments or information.

D. In grades 9-12, with increased difficulty by grade level, students will be instructed on and master the writing skill of using research to build and present knowledge:

1. Conduct short as well as more sustained research projects to answer a question (including a self-generated question) or solve a problem; narrow or broaden the inquiry when appropriate; synthesize multiple sources on the subject, demonstrating an understanding of the subject under investigation.
2. Gather relevant information from multiple authoritative print and digital sources, using advanced searches effectively; assess the strengths and limitations of each source in terms of the task, purpose, and audience; integrate information into the text selectively to maintain the flow of ideas, while avoiding plagiarism and overreliance on any one source and following a standard format for citation.
3. Draw evidence from literary or informational texts to support analysis, reflection, and research.

§**EFFECTIVE DATE.** This section is effective [insert date].

MULTI-TIER SYSTEM OF SUPPORTS OF READING INTERVENTION IN GENERAL EDUCATION

General-Education System Supports For Students Who Struggle In Reading Development And Literacy Attainment—Grades Kindergarten through 12

WHILE NEARLY EVERY student is capable of achieving full literacy, no two students learn at the same pace or come from the same environments. In diverse student classrooms, multiple supports are necessary to bring students' skills to grade level. This is where knowledgeable teachers of reading and teaching specialists can provide Multi-Tier System of Supports (MTSS), also known as Response to Intervention (RtI), to foster student reading success.

Sadly today, too many students fall seriously behind grade-level reading in the early years and never catch up. According to research, these capable students often are relegated to special education with a slim chance of reintegration into general-education classrooms. The rationale behind all aspects of literacy law is for all students to become literate, educated, and career-ready young citizens—no excuses, no exception. For this is the goal of public education. To accomplish this, every aspect of the model legislation is important: teacher preparation, new reading certifications, teachers of reading in every K-third-grade classroom, student data systems, Multi-Tier System of Supports, and solid implementation by school leadership. Today's classrooms are filled with students who are functionally illiterate and have already been left behind with a dim view of happiness and success in their future. Multi-Tier System of Supports can help all of these students become competent, twenty-first-century readers.

The US Data Accountability Center that monitors students served under the Individuals with Disabilities Education Act indicates that 40.7 percent of students served have specific learning disabilities, and 80 percent of these students have their primary difficulty in the area of reading. Within a year, substantially fewer students will enter special education, and millions across the country will become proficient readers when these systems of multitiered instruction and intervention are implemented in the general-education classrooms Additionally, academic achievement levels will soar as content-area teachers dedicate less time closing a learning gap and the time with students learning skills for life's success. In general, the issue is not that children lack the aptitude for literacy; their educational systems are simply not equipped to address their specific literacy-learning needs—and this should change.

In this appendix, we present you four tools to assist you in adopting state literacy law on §5 GENERAL-EDUCATION MULTI-TIER SYSTEM OF SUPPORTS (MTSS) for Reading Development and Literacy Interventions.

Included are tools to assist your work: In this section, the Executive Summary provides an overview of MTSS and its properties; the Key Components outline the tiers and their areas of focus; the Roadmap and Specifics describe the intervention strategies in detail; and the Model Legislation is designed to help you and your community bring the focus and effectiveness of these system supports to your own state and district.

Executive Summary
Reading Interventions Grades K-12
Using Multi-Tier System Of Supports

Each school will provide continual data-driven assessment and Multi-Tier System of Supports (MTSS) intervention for students who are reading below grade-level proficiency. MTSS will be provided quickly and as needed.

Issue:

Approximately one-third of students read at advanced (3 percent) or proficient (30 percent) levels. Early identification and targeted interventions are the keys to improving these statistics. All teachers should be skilled reading literacy teachers to ensure that students comprehend content in in all subject areas. Research has shown that background knowledge is second only to vocabulary in enhancing reading comprehension outcomes for secondary readers.

Why this is important:

1. Up through third grade, children learn to read; after third grade, they read to learn. When they reach third grade, students enter a different phase of reading with the connected purposes of "reading for knowledge" (reading literacy) and of writing and speaking with structure and thought. To ensure students are reading literate, MTSS are imperative.
2. Each content area (e.g., math, science, social studies, and English language arts) has a unique vocabulary used to communicate concepts and explain processes. Students need to learn what these words mean and how to use them within the multiple contexts of reading, writing, and speaking.
3. Teachers and schools should not wait until a student is significantly behind grade-level reading before assessing skills and providing targeted supports. Each school should provide continual data-driven assessment and provide MTSS intervention quickly and as needed.

Goals of section:

1. For all schools and classrooms to ensure students' grade-level reading proficiency by offering Multi-Tier System of Supports in both instruction and intervention in general education.
2. To ensure that all students learn to apply critical analysis, inference, interpretation, and summation of printed materials, with the goal that students understand the text and respond through productive discussion and written answer.

How to achieve these goals:

1. Students should be identified early for reading failure through screenings and sustainable assessments that chronicle students' ongoing attainment of learning skills, including specific reading development markers, reading fluency, language, and writing.
2. Teachers in content areas will teach reading skills while delivering core content that meets state and district requirements.

Key Points:

MTSS involves considerable teacher and school-based knowledge in the use of evaluation, communication, and collaboration to guide instructional supports and to ensure continuous, organized planning for each student's progress. School culture should recognize that every content-area teacher is a literacy teacher because reading and writing are involved in every subject area. Reading and writing literacy strategies should be implemented as a school-wide program with a vision of high levels of student achievement in reading and subject-area literacy.

Key Components
For Reading and Literacy Interventions Grades K-12
Using Multi-Tier System Of Supports

The Goal: It Is Compulsory That General-Education Classrooms Provide System Supports For Students Who Struggle In Reading Development And Literacy Attainment.

Each school will provide continual student data-driven assessment and provide Multi-Tier System of Supports (MTSS also known as RTI—Response to Intervention) beginning in kindergarten for every student who struggles to meet monthly learning benchmarks. Intervention will be provided quickly and as needed for each student's reading literacy attainment.

MTSS are imperative for students' attainment of reading and subject-area literacy and achievement of state standards.

1. The major instructional strategies of MTSS use individualized data to determine the intensive and multicomponent methods appropriate for each student's reading, writing, and spelling proficiency.
2. MTSS are guided by student assessment in general-education classrooms and deliver tiers of instruction and intervention to individuals and analogous groups of students, allowing those who struggle with various aspects of learning to become proficient readers, writers, and users of the English language.
3. In grades K through 3, MTSS are designed for teachers of reading to scaffold instruction in small class settings at the first sign that a student or students are falling behind in lesson accomplishment. In grades 4 through 12, both teachers of reading and content-area teachers provide tiers of instruction and intervention to individuals and analogous groups to obtain subject-matter literacy.

Program Criteria for MTSS Standards for SEEDS in Grades Pre-K-3

Each state should systematically address the academic needs of all of SEEDS by implementing research-based MTSS.

Essential elements of a successful reading intervention include
Early screening, assessment, and identification of SEEDS in grades pre-K-3
Instruction and tiers of support delivered intensively in the areas of weakness in reading development skills
Intense instruction and intervention delivered by a highly qualified and certified teacher of reading
Sufficient duration of intervention until proficiency is reached in all reading development

The term "MTSS" refers to a comprehensive system of differentiated supports including evidence-based instruction, universal screening, progress monitoring, formative and summative assessments, research-based interventions matched to student needs, and educational decision-making using academic progress overtime.

Principles of Multi-Tier System of Supports (MTSS)		
1. Assumption and belief that all students can learn to read at grade level	2. Early intervention for students who demonstrate risk for literacy failure	3. Use of a multitier model of service delivery
4. Use of a problem-solving or standard-protocol method to make decisions within a multitier model in general education	5. Use of research-based, scientifically validated interventions/instruction to the extent available	
6. Monitoring of student progress to inform instruction	7. Use of data to make decisions	
Principles of Multi-Tier System of Supports (MTSS) for SEEDS who struggle in the area of reading:		
Tier I—Foundational Reading Instruction should involve		
1. The use of a scientifically based instructional program for all students	2. Ongoing assessment of progress and monitoring of reading achievement gains	
3. Teachers of reading using flexible grouping to target specific skills and differentiate instruction for all students		
Tier II—MTSS intervention components:		
1. Intended to meet the needs of SEEDS who do not respond quickly to foundational reading instruction skill development		
2. To be provided in a regular classroom setting		
3. Students will receive intensive small group reading instruction based on areas of skill weakness.		

4. To ensure adequate advancement and learning, student progress should be monitored at least every two weeks to be analyzed, interpreted, and documented.
5. A set of goals for each student will be identified and established.
Students who meet set criteria on targeted skills as a result of tier II interventions are reintegrated into the regular classroom setting (tier I).
If the student's progress shows no advancement and/or the student demonstrates characteristics associated with learning disorders at any time during or after the student's tier II intervention (maximum of ten weeks), the teacher of reading shall recommend a formal diagnostic assessment for the student.
Tier III—MTSS intensive instruction components:
1. Involves a small percentage of students who received tier II intervention and continue to show marked difficulty in acquiring the reading development necessary to reach grade-level proficiency
2. Intensive instruction that is more explicit and specifically designed to meet their individual needs
3. Progress monitoring at least every two weeks on targeted skills to ensure adequate progress and learning
4. Approximate time for tier III intensive instruction is eight to ten weeks.
After this intensity of instruction, the student can return to tier II intervention support before reintegration into the regular classroom setting (tier I).
If the student's progress shows no advancement and/or the student demonstrates characteristics associated with learning disorders at any time during or after the student's tier III intensive intervention, the teacher of reading shall recommend a formal diagnostic assessment for the student.

Grades 4-12: Reading Interventions and Strategies

In middle school, it is important to establish a school culture that recognizes that every content-area teacher is a reading teacher because reading is involved in every subject area.

Reading strategies will be implemented as a school-wide program in connection with a school culture and vision that work toward high levels of student achievement in reading literacy.

Specific interventions and strategies will be provided to support SEEDS.

Each school will provide SEEDS with demonstrated reading difficulties twenty-six to thirty-two weeks of supplemental reading interventions that directly address their vocabulary, comprehension, and word-reading challenges. To help support identification and MTSS:				
1. Students who are more than one grade level behind in reading should receive specific interventions daily. Through diagnostic assessment, teachers can determine which of the following are contributing to the reading difficulties and target their instruction:				
A. Word-reading problems	B. Word-meaning problems		C. Inadequate knowledge to understand text	
D. Unusually slow text reading		E. Inadequate use of reading comprehension strategies to promote reading comprehension		
2. Target instruction for each student by providing systems of support in three tiers with an outline of assessments of skill accomplishments and a timeline for stages of support				
3. During tier I intervention for grade 4-12 students who need intervention in word study, a certified teacher of reading provides students with approximately twenty-five lessons taught over seven to eight weeks depending on student mastery. Students' mastery determines their progress through the lessons. Lessons will include				
A. Daily instruction and practice with individual letter sounds, letter combinations, and affixes	B. Instruction and practice in applying a strategy to decode polysyllabic words by breaking them into known parts	C. Practice breaking words into parts to spell.	D. Daily word-reading strategies to apply reading in context in the form of sentences and passage-reading	E. Fluency instruction that promotes use of oral reading fluency data and pairing higher and lower readers for partner reading

F. Daily student engagement in repeated reading with their partner with the goal of increased accuracy and rate fluency	G. Modeling and providing feedback to students	H. Daily vocabulary	I. Comprehension during and after reading	J. Teachers assisting students in locating information in text and rereading to identify answers

4. During tier II intervention for grade 4-12 students who need intervention with vocabulary and comprehension, a certified teacher of reading provides students with lessons over seventeen to eighteen weeks depending on student mastery. Students' mastery determines their progress through the lessons. Lessons will include

A. Daily review of the word study strategies learned in tier I by applying the sounds and strategies to reading new words	B. Focus on word meaning	C. Word relatives and parts of speech	D. Application of word study for spelling words
E. Vocabulary words chosen from the text read in the fluency and comprehension component	F. Fluency and comprehension with an emphasis on reading and understanding text through discourse or writing	G. Content and vocabulary to understand the text prior to reading	H. Instruction in generating questions of varying levels of complexity and abstraction while reading

Tier III intervention continues the instructional emphasis on vocabulary and comprehension with more time spent on independent student application of skills and strategies. Tier III occurs over approximately eight to ten weeks.

Each content-area teacher will identify key content subject words for each student to learn and will teach at least two new words every day and review one from the previous day. There are several ways that these words can be taught, including

1. Using vocabulary maps that use the key word, pictures of the word, words that relate to the key word, a student-friendly definition, and how the word can be used in a historical context	2. Illustrating, showing a picture that represents the word, or reading one or two sentences that include the word, describing it in ways that allow students to make informed decisions about word meaning	3. Teaching key words within the context of a debate or structured discussion in which students use those key words in their written and oral arguments

Teachers should ask students to ask questions while they read and after they listen to the teacher read as they follow the text so that they will monitor comprehension and learning.	
Teachers should teach word-meaning strategies within content-area classes. Research supports two practices for helping students learn academic vocabulary:	
1. Teachers provide explicit instruction of academic or concept words that students need to learn to master the key ideas they are teaching. Teachers need to work with students to discuss what the word means and doesn't mean.	2. Teachers provide instruction in word-learning strategies. One means of equipping students to understand the content-area terms they encounter is to teach the component morphemes (prefixes, roots, and suffixes) and how they contribute to the meaning of words. Another word-learning strategy involves teaching word meanings directly through the use of a mnemonic word association and a picture that ties together the word clue and the definition.

Teachers should instruct students how to build and activate appropriate background knowledge for understanding text content. Research supports the following strategies for building background knowledge:	
1. Teach students to use text to support answers and consider whether they can locate text-based support for positions	2. Teach students to elaborate on why statements that they select can or cannot be supported based on the text

Teachers should teach students to use reading comprehension strategies while reading complex text. Research supports the following strategies for building reading comprehension:
1. Teach students to generate questions while reading to build comprehension skills.
2. Teach them how to generate main idea statements for single or multiple paragraphs. Students who are successfully taught this concept will be able to use the following three steps to generate a main idea statement:

A. Identify who or what is the focus of the paragraph or section	B. Determine the most important information about what the key person place/ thing has, is, or does	C. Succinctly state the who or what and most important information about him/her/ it in a sentence

CINTHIA COLETTI

Teachers should guide and engage students in text-related activities through classroom discussion and written assignments. Research supports the following strategies for encouraging reading for understanding:

A. Discussion in small groups that allows students the opportunity to return to texts a number of times to explore, discuss, and revise their developing understanding of the ideas and concepts. Each student in the small group will have a specific role.	B. Explicitly instruct students in how to summarize text.

Teachers should maximize all opportunities for students to read a range of printed material. Research supports the following strategies to enhance opportunities for students to read and respond to text:

A. Prepare students to read text by providing key ideas and key words.	B. Provide daily opportunities for students to read for a specific amount of time, then provide a prompt for student response.	C. Have students participate in partner reading and have them take turns reading the same passage.

Teachers should organize students into collaborative groups for reading tasks. Research supports the following strategies for collaborative groups:

A. Having students use collaborative strategic reading (CSR). The two importance phases for CSR are (1) learning the four reading comprehension strategies and (2) teaching students to use cooperative groups effectively as a means of applying the strategies.	B. Teachers should assign approximately four students to each CSR group to create a well-functioning team. Teachers assign students to roles, which rotate on a regular basis, in the group and teach them to perform their role.	C. The teacher's role in CSR, while students are working in their groups, is to ensure the students have been taught their role and know how to implement their responsibility.

Road Map and Specifics for State Handbook
Reading and Literacy Interventions Grades K-12
Using Multi-Tier System Of Supports

The Goal: It is compulsory upon general-education classrooms to provide system supports for students who struggle in reading development and literacy attainment.

Research shows that when students are (1) identified early (kindergarten and first-graders) for potential reading failure through universal screenings for dyslexia and specific learning disabilities, (2) monitored with systematic assessments at least twice a month in his and her general-education classroom, and (3) provided foundational reading development instruction by a certified teacher of reading who is capable of using data and benchmarks to determine progress and is skilled in (4) Multi-Tier System of Supports (MTSS) when progress slips, then and only then do the majority of diverse students in today's classrooms become skilled, proficient, grade-level readers. Then and only then is a student ready to meet the demands of becoming literate in a multitude of subjects beginning in grade 4 and continuing through high-school graduation.

Foundational reading development instruction driven by assessments chronicles a student's ongoing attainment of specific reading development markers, reading fluency, language, writing, and other learning skills needed for academic success. This type of assessment system involves considerable teacher and school-based knowledge in the use of evaluation, communication, and collaboration to guide instructional supports and ensure continuous, organized planning for each student's progress.

The major instructional strategies of MTSS use individualized data to determine intensive and multicomponent methods as appropriate for reading, writing, and spelling proficiency of each student. MTSS is designed for teachers of reading to scaffold instruction in small class settings at the first signs of a student or students falling behind lesson accomplishment. The reading achievement gap typically will be seen by a skilled teacher in kindergarten and can be ameliorated with MTSS.

Extensive research and numerous syntheses have been conducted in the area of reading instruction and intervention for reading difficulties

CINTHIA COLETTI

to be eradicated early. Success requires that teachers and schools no longer wait until a student is significantly behind grade-level reading before assessing skills and providing supports. This is standard practice today; a typical SEEDS student is not identified until third or fourth grade when the reading gap is so large that it becomes increasingly difficult and expensive to close without serious intervention and significant time and effort. This is why the literacy law provides for provide continual data driven student assessments and provides MTSS intervention quickly and as needed for each student's reading literacy attainment. With MTSS in force, students currently in grades K-3 will achieve grade-level reading proficiency before the fourth grade when they begin "reading to learn" subject-area materials.

However, for the current community of SEEDS students that have missed the opportunity to become reading literate by grade 4, specific interventions and strategies will be provided to support the SEEDS community of students in grades 4-12. They are already struggling and may be heading toward high-school dropout status due to no fault of his or her own but rather poor instruction in early elementary school. Thus, this law will ensure all schools (late elementary, middle and high) provide intense reading development interventions that serve as an alternative to English language arts class and literacy instruction in content subject areas of instruction.

Along with certified teachers of reading in all classrooms kindergarten through third grade, literacy success requires a school culture that recognizes that every "content-area teacher" is a literacy teacher as well, because reading and writing is involved in every subject area. Therefore, reading and writing literacy strategies are implemented as a school-wide program in connection with a school leadership, data systems, and vision that works toward high levels of student achievement in reading literacy. All classrooms provide every opportunity for students to read, practice their strategies, in every subject, every day, to enhance their development of the reading skills they need to become full literate.

Specifics of MTSS in Grades K-3

The term MTSS refers to a comprehensive system of differentiated supports that includes evidence-based instruction, universal screening, progress monitoring, formative and summative assessment, research-based interventions matched to student needs, and educational decision-making using academic progress overtime. All SEEDS have the opportunity to benefit from this process of instruction, intervention, and, if necessary, referral to special education.

Principles of Multi-Tier System of Supports: (1) Assumption and belief that all students can learn; (2) early intervention for students who demonstrate risk for literacy failure; (3) use of a multitier model of service delivery (to achieve high rates of student success, both the nature and intensity of instruction may be differentiated); (4) use of a problem-solving or standard-protocol method to make decisions within a multitier model; (5) use of research-based, scientifically validated instruction/intervention to the extent available; (6) monitoring of student progress to inform instruction; and (7) use of data to make decisions that direct instruction.

There are three tiers of instruction and intervention in MTSS for students who struggle to acquire reading development through to fluency skills through to achieving full reading literacy:

1. Tier I—Foundational Reading Development Instruction involves (1) the use of a scientifically based instructional program for all students, (2) screening, ongoing monitoring and assessment of student progress in reading achievement at each skill level, and (3) the use of flexible grouping by teachers of reading to target specific skills and differentiate instruction for all students.

2. Tier II—MTSS intervention is designed to meet the needs of SEEDS who do not respond quickly to foundational reading development instruction. MTSS are provided in the regular classroom setting, where students receive intensive small group reading instruction in general education. The teacher of reading emphasizes all essential components of early literacy during the reading intervention. Progress monitoring on the targeted skills of reading development occurs at least every two weeks to ensure students' adequate advancement and learning. A set of goals for each student is identified and established, and progress monitoring data will be analyzed, interpreted, and documented. Students who meet set criteria on targeted skills as a result of tier II interventions are reintegrated into the regular classroom setting (tier I).

CINTHIA COLETTI

3. If at any time during or after the student's tier II intervention (maximum of ten weeks), the student's progress in the essential components of reading shows no advancement and/or the student demonstrates characteristics associated with learning disorders such as dyslexia or specific learning disability, the teacher of reading shall recommend a formal diagnostic assessment for the student.

4. Tier III—MTSS intensive instruction addresses the small percentage of students who have received tier II intervention for not more than ten weeks in general education and continue to show marked difficulty in reaching grade-level reading development benchmarks. It is more explicit and is specifically designed to meet the individual needs of these students, who will be monitored on targeted skills at least every two weeks to ensure adequate progress and learning. The approximate time for tier III intensive instruction is eight to ten weeks. After this intensity of instruction, the students can return to tier II intervention support before reintegration into the regular classroom setting (tier I).

5. If at any time during or after tier III intensive instruction the student shows no progress in the essential components of reading development and/or does not reach grade-level reading attainment and/or demonstrates characteristics associated with a learning disorder such as dyslexia or specific learning disability, the teacher of reading will immediately recommend a formal diagnostic assessment.

6. A student that is struggling to close the reading gap will not spend more than twenty (20) weeks in a combination of tier II and tier III intervention without receiving a formal diagnostic assessment.

Specifics of MTSS Reading Interventions and Strategies for Older Students Grades 4-12

In elementary school grades K-3, reading is considered a separate subject; but in middle school, it is important to establish a school culture that recognizes every content-area teacher as a reading teacher, because reading is involved in every subject area. Therefore, reading strategies will be implemented as a school-wide program in connection with a school culture and vision that promote high levels of student achievement in reading literacy. Specific interventions and strategies will be provided to support SEEDS who have struggled to learn to read and are performing below grade level in reading. Schools will provide every opportunity for students to read and practice their strategies in every subject, every day, in order to develop the reading skills they need to become better readers and, ultimately, reading literate.

MTSS will be provided in each school and with three tiers of supports for intensive reading interventions to SEEDS students with reading problems in grades 4-12. While the expectation is that students will learn to read with understanding before entering middle and high school, the reality is that many students reach these schools unable to read grade-level text effectively and with understanding.

In MTSS tiers, SEEDS students with demonstrated reading difficulties one or more grade level behind are provided with, as an alternative to English language arts class in middle and high school, twenty-six to thirty-two weeks of supplemental reading interventions that directly address their vocabulary, comprehension, and word-reading challenges so they are able to perform significantly better in reading subject material text and can achieve grade-level reading literacy. Research supports identification and MTSS to help identify students who are more than one grade level behind in reading in order to provide daily reading intervention in English language arts.

Each day, during a dedicated period with a certified teacher of reading/teaching specialists, students with reading difficulties that are one grade level or more below expectations are provided with reading instruction, approximately forty to fifty minutes per day, focused specifically on their instructional needs. Providing students with specific MTSS interventions focused on their learning needs requires identifying whether a student's reading comprehension difficulties are a result of (a) word-reading problems (e.g., decoding unknown words), (b) word-meaning problems (e.g., vocabulary), (c) inadequate knowledge to understand text (e.g., background knowledge), (d) unusually slow text reading (e.g., fluency), and/or (e) inadequate use of strategies to promote reading comprehension. Through diagnostic assessment, teachers can determine which of the above are contributing to the reading difficulties and target their intervention instruction.

It is imperative that students receive MTSS that provides continual assessments of skill accomplishments and a timeline for stages of support.

CINTHIA COLETTI

Tier I intervention during English language arts is as follows:

1. During tier I, intervention for students in grades 4-12 typically is between twenty-five lessons taught over seven to eight weeks depending on student mastery. Tier I involves intervention in word study by a certified teacher of reading or teaching specialists.

2. The daily lessons are composed of *word study* to teach advanced decoding of polysyllabic words. Students' mastery of sounds and word reading determines their progress through the lessons. Students receive daily instruction and practice with individual letter sounds, letter combinations, and affixes. In addition, students receive instruction and practice in decoding and spelling polysyllabic words by breaking them into known parts. Word-reading strategies are applied daily to reading in context in the form of sentences and passage reading until automaticity is attained.

3. The daily lessons consist of high levels of teacher of reading or teaching specialists support and scaffolding provided to students in applying the *word-reading strategy to reading words and connected text and to spelling words.* The use of oral reading fluency data, along with the pairing of higher and lower readers for daily partner reading, facilitates fluency instruction and promotes increased fluency (accuracy and rate). Students take turns reading orally while their partner reads along and marks errors; after reading, partners are given time to go over errors and ask questions about unknown words. The higher reader always reads first. Partners read the passage three times each and graph the number of words read correctly. The teacher of reading is actively involved in modeling and providing feedback to students, teaching the meaning of a word through basic definitions and by providing examples and nonexamples of how to use it.

4. The daily lessons assist student in a *review of new vocabulary words daily* by matching words to appropriate definitions or examples of word usage. During and after reading, students *address relevant comprehension questions* of varying levels of difficulty (literal and inferential) while teachers assist them in locating information in text and rereading to identify answers.

Tier II intervention immediately follows tier I intervention based on successful data analysis. Tier II intervention is as follows:

1. During tier II intervention for students in grades 4-12, lessons occur over a period of seventeen to eighteen weeks depending on students' progress.

2. The daily lessons place emphasis on *vocabulary and comprehension*, with additional instruction and practice provided for applying the word study and fluency skills and strategies learned in tier I intervention. Word study and vocabulary are taught by applying the sounds and word study strategies learned in tier I to reading new words. Focus on word meaning is also part of word-reading practice, and students learn word relatives and parts of speech (e.g., politics, politician, politically). Finally, students review the application of word study to spelling words. Vocabulary words for instruction are chosen from the text read in the fluency and comprehension component.

3. Three lessons a week, teachers of reading/teaching specialists use subject matter lessons and materials to guide students through *reading and comprehending expository text;* while two lessons a week, teachers *use novels with lessons developed by the research team to guide students through narrative text.* Fluency and comprehension are taught with an emphasis on reading and understanding text through discourse or writing. After reviewing the content and vocabulary needed to understand the text, students read the text at least twice with an emphasis on reading for understanding. During and after the second reading, students discuss comprehension questions of varying levels of complexity and abstraction. Students also receive explicit instruction in generating questions of varying levels of complexity and abstraction while reading (e.g., literal questions, questions requiring students to synthesize information from text, and questions requiring students to apply background knowledge to information in text), in summarizing and identifying the main idea of the text, and in employing strategies for multiple-choice, short answer, and essay questions.

4. Tier II intervention immediately follows data provided success in tier I intervention.

Tier III intervention occurs over approximately eight to ten weeks with the goal of closing the student's reading gap and reintegration into English language arts curriculum. It continues the instructional emphasis on vocabulary, comprehension, and writing with the teacher of reading/teaching specialists at least once per week and emphasis toward more time spent on students' independent application of skills and strategies.

Specifics of MTSS in Content Areas

The role of content-area teachers assisting SEEDS students with literacy is as follows: to build grade-level subject literacy with vocabulary, dialogue, concepts, background knowledge, comprehension strategies, collaborations, and engagement. This is the primary reason all content-areas teachers should learn the basics of reading instruction and pass the basic reading instruction competence assessment (BRICA).

Each content-area teacher will identify key content subject words for each SEEDS student to learn and will teach at least two new words every day and review one from the previous day. This practice can be readily implemented across all content-area instruction to provide SEEDS students with opportunities to expand their academic vocabulary, increase their background knowledge, and better understand the key ideas that they are reading and studying.

One way a content-area teacher can do this is to select words in a unit that are high-priority and high-utility words. Assuming that a unit is three weeks long, they can then determine the key words students need to know, explicitly teaching them each week and also reviewing them in subsequent weeks. There are several ways that these words can be taught.

Vocabulary

Teachers can use vocabulary maps that present the key word, pictures of the word, related words, a student-friendly definition, and how the word can be used in a historical context. Teachers can illustrate the word, show a representative picture, or read one or two sentences that describe the word in ways that allow students to make informed decisions about its meaning. Then the students and the teacher can use this information to co-construct the meaning of the word. Key words can be taught within the context of a debate or structured discussion in which students use those key words in their written and oral arguments.

Dialogue

While students read, and after they follow the text while listening to the teacher read, teachers should monitor comprehension and learning by encouraging students to ask questions. Students who are actively engaged while listening and reading are more likely to understand and remember what they read or hear. Teachers can also promote this practice by instructing students to ask the class one of their questions. Students benefit from having question stems to help them develop these questions.

Concept Words

Teachers should teach word-meaning strategies within content-area classes. Concept words are the key to learning the big ideas of content as well as the necessary academic vocabulary for success. Each content area (e.g., math, science, social studies, and English language arts) has a unique vocabulary used to communicate concepts and explain processes. Students need to learn what these words mean and how to use them within the multiple contexts of reading, writing, and speaking.

Adolescents encounter approximately ten thousand new words per year, the majority of which are the complex terms of the content areas. Research supports two practices for helping students learn academic vocabulary:

(1) Teachers should provide explicit instruction of the academic or concept words integral to students' mastery of key ideas. These words need to be shown alongside a picture, video, or other demonstration to make the words vivid in students' minds. Teachers then need to work with students to discuss what the word does and doesn't mean. A critical step is to return to these words regularly throughout the lesson and throughout the instructional unit to ensure that students can

use them with understanding in their speaking and writing tasks. When teaching students the multiple meanings of words, teachers need to emphasize their meaning within the context of learning.

(2) Teachers should provide instruction in word-learning strategies. Although explicit instruction is important, the sheer number of words students need to learn requires that they develop strategies for independently determining the meanings of unfamiliar vocabulary words. One means of equipping students to understand the content-area terms they encounter is to teach the component morphemes (prefixes, roots, and suffixes) and how they affect meaning. Students taught to analyze words by morphemes were able to infer the meanings of untaught terms in subject-matter text.

Other research indicates the practice is particularly effective with SEEDS when done systematically and coupled with multiple opportunities to practice, such as the application of learned morphemes to words used in different content areas. Another word-learning strategy teaches word meanings directly through the use of a picture that ties together a mnemonic word association and the definition of the word.

Background Knowledge

Teachers should instruct students in how to build and activate appropriate background knowledge for understanding text content. Researchers report that background knowledge is second only to vocabulary in enhancing reading comprehension outcomes for secondary readers. A lack of prior knowledge makes understanding informational text particularly challenging. Research supports this strategy for building background knowledge: (1) teach students to use text to support answers and consider whether they can locate text-based support for positions and (2) teach students to elaborate on why statements can or cannot be supported by the text.

According to researchers, this technique requires students to link their background knowledge to the statements and to provide adequate justification for their responses. When used in connection with text-reading, it encourages students to return to important information to further elaborate on their responses. Students are asked to determine whether they can or cannot adequately support the statement using prior learning and text to support their views.

Comprehension Strategies

Teachers should teach students to use reading comprehension strategies while reading complex text. Too often, adolescents proceed through text with little understanding of what they are reading or awareness of when their comprehension has broken down. They need to be taught how to recognize when they do not adequately understand text and how to build comprehension. Research supports these strategies for reading comprehension:

(1) Teach students to generate questions while reading to build comprehension skills. Doing so prompts students to stop at regular intervals to think about what is being communicated and how the information relates across paragraphs. Studies have shown that this practice can increase comprehension of content-area text for students of different ability levels. The first level of questions is the most literal in that is based on facts that can be identified in one place in the text. The second level of questions combines information that is located in two different parts of the text, and the third level of questions relates information in the text to something the reader has experienced or learned previously.

(2) Teach students to be active readers and to monitor their own comprehension by generating main idea statements for single or multiple paragraphs. Adolescents and teens who learn to identify the explicitly or implicitly stated main ideas of a text have shown increased understanding and recall of important information. Referred to as either "paragraph shrinking" or "get the gist," these three steps have successfully taught students at a range of ability levels and language backgrounds to generate a main idea statement: identify who or what is the focus of the paragraph or section; determine the most important information about what the key person/place/thing has, is, or does; and succinctly state the who or what and most important information about him/her/it in a sentence.

Engagement

Teachers should guide and engage students in activities that are text related. Through both classroom discussion and written assignments, students will learn to apply critical analysis, inference, interpretation, and summation of printed material. The goal is to guide the student in understanding text and responding through productive discussion and written answers. Research supports the following strategies for encouraging reading for understanding:

(1) Foster discussion in small groups. Give students the opportunity to return to texts a number of times to explore, discuss, and revise their developing understanding of the ideas and concepts. This practice can be fostered through the use of reciprocal teaching, a multicomponent strategy intended to support student comprehension. In reciprocal teaching, the teacher leads the dialogue about the text until students learn to assume different roles independently: summarizer, questioner, clarifier, or predictor.

After reading a short section of text (generally a few paragraphs at first, but increasing to several pages with practice), the summarizer highlights the key points for the group. Then the questioner helps the group consider and discuss what was read by posing questions about anything that was unclear, puzzling, or related to other content information. In this portion of reciprocal teaching, students apply question generation skills that go beyond surface-level information.

The clarifier in the group of students is responsible for seeking out portions of text that will help answer the questions posed. However, all members of the group participate in discussing the information and connecting ideas. In doing so, students should return to the current selection and, possibly, other readings to look for textual evidence in support of their responses.

Finally, the predictor offers suggestions about what the group can expect to read in the next section of text. These predictions are focused on activating relevant background knowledge, setting a purpose for reading, and relating new information to that just discussed by the group.

(2) Teachers should instruct students in how to summarize text. Students who are explicitly taught to summarize text are better able to discern the relationships among main ideas and significant details. When students work collaboratively on summaries of expository text, such as in reciprocal teaching, they reach higher levels of comprehension and retain more content information. Teachers should thoroughly explain and model each step multiple times with different types of text before students will be able to complete them in collaborative groups or, eventually, on their own.

Maximize Students' Opportunities to Read

Teachers should maximize all opportunities for students to read printed material. Both middle- and high-school content-area teachers will have a range of readers in their classrooms, providing challenges for assignments that require text-reading. For this reason and others, many classroom teachers require students to read very little both inside and outside of their class time. Teachers, perceiving text-reading as inaccessible, also report that they increasingly rely on reading text aloud or using other media (e.g., videos) as a means for providing students with content knowledge. Reading and understanding text requires practice, and students need opportunities to read a range of text types (e.g., textbooks, letters, descriptions, original documents, poetry). Research supports the following strategies to enhance opportunities for students to read and respond to text:

(1) Prepare students to read text by providing key ideas and key words. Providing the big idea and connecting principles (or soliciting them from the class) before having students read the text will facilitate comprehension. Present the key words, including all proper nouns, prior to text reading; this can be done orally, on the board, or on a handout.
(2) Provide daily opportunities for students to read for a specific amount of time and provide a prompt for student response (e.g., two to three minutes for reading and one to two minutes for responding). Students can be asked to respond to predetermined prompts such as, "What is this section mostly about?" "How does the author describe _____?" "What did

you learn about _____?" Students can respond in writing using learning logs or they can respond orally by talking with a partner for one minute.

(3) Have students participate in partner reading (typically a better reader and a less able reader), asking them to take turns reading the same passage with the better reader going first. Students can partner-read for a specified amount of time (e.g., three minutes) and can use one to two minutes to write responses by determining the main idea, writing and answering a question, or summarizing the text.

Groupings

Teachers should organize students into collaborative strategic reading (CSR) groups for reading tasks. Student involvement and learning are greatly enhanced through well-structured collaborative groups designed to promote both individual and group accountability. These groups can be used within content-area classes and are associated with improved reading comprehension for students when implemented two or more times per week. Research supports the following strategies for collaborative groups.

Teachers should have students use CSR, which occurs in two important phases. The first phase involves learning the four reading comprehension strategies: (1) previewing text (preview), (2) monitoring comprehension while reading by identifying challenging key words and concepts (click and clunk), (3) thinking about the main idea while reading and putting it into one's own words (get the gist), and (4) summarizing text understanding after reading it (wrap-up). The second phase involves teaching students to use cooperative groups effectively as a means of applying the strategies. Once students have developed proficiency using the four strategies with teacher guidance, they are ready to use these same strategies in peer-led cooperative learning groups. Some teachers ask students to first work in pairs and then move into a group, while other teachers find it better to start with cooperative groups.

Forming CSRs will be a success if the teacher is aware that not all students will function equally well in a group and that groups are more effective when the teacher focuses on designing a well-functioning team. Teachers assign approximately four students to each group, considering that each group will need a leader, a student with high reading proficiency and one or two SEEDS students in order to represent varying abilities. Teachers assign students to roles in the group and teach them to perform their role. Roles rotate on a regular basis (e.g., every couple of weeks) so that students can experience a variety of roles. Student roles are an important aspect of effective implementation of cooperative learning and allow all group members to participate in a meaningful task and contribute toward the group's success.

The teacher's role in CSR, while students are working in their groups, is to ensure that the students have been taught their role and know how to implement their responsibility. Forming successful and productive groups is an important accomplishment because it allows the teacher to circulate among the groups, listen to students' participation, read students' learning logs, and most importantly, provide clear and specific feedback to improve the use and application of the strategies. Teachers can help by actively listening to students' conversations and clarifying difficult words, modeling strategy usage and application, and encouraging students to participate. It is expected that students will need assistance in learning to work in cooperative groups, implementing the strategies, and mastering academic content.

Summary

For SEEDS students to succeed in receiving a twenty-first-century education that leads to employment, MTSS in grades 4 through 12 is mandated until the student reaches grade-level reading and writing proficiency.

MODEL STATE LEGISLATION LANGUAGE
Reading Development And Literacy Interventions Using Multi-Tier System Of Supports In General-Education Classrooms Grades K-12

§5 General-Education Multi-Tier System Of Supports (MTSS) for reading development and literacy interventions

BE IT ENACTED BY THE LEGISLATURE OF THE STATE OF [insert state name] that all schools and classrooms offer each student in the SEEDS community, grades K-12, Multi-Tier System of Supports (MTSS) of intervention to ensure grade-level reading attainment. The schools in the state shall no longer wait until a student is significantly behind grade-level reading, but rather provide continual data-driven assessments, chronicle progress, and deliver remediation as needed for each student's grade-level literacy attainment. Students who are not reading fluently in grades 4-12 will be provided intense reading interventions that serve as an alternative to English language arts class. Additionally, content-areas teachers will teach reading skills while delivering core content that meets the state and district requirements.

§5.1 Program Criteria for MTSS Standards for SEEDS in Grades Pre-K-3

The state of [insert state name] is committed to systemically addressing the academic needs of all of SEEDS by implementing MTSS, for students most at risk for literacy failure. Based on present research, the state of [insert state name] provides in this section an overview MTSS for improving reading achievement for all students as a specific practice of research-based interventions to support students who are reading below grade level. Essentials elements of a successful reading intervention are outlined below and mandated by this law.

A. Early screening, assessment, and identification of SEEDS in grades pre-K-3.
B. Intense instruction and tiers of support will be delivered with intensity as mandated by [insert state name] Statute, Section

5.0 of this law. Optimally, a student who is struggling to read will be assessed and provided instruction in a group of three and no more than four students, and the student will receive this specialized reading instruction at least four, and preferably five, days a week.

C. Intense instruction and intervention will be delivered by a highly qualified and certified teacher of reading as required in [insert state name] Statute, Section 2.0 of this law. Recent studies highlight the difference that a highly trained accomplished teacher of reading can make in the overall success or failure of a reading program.

D. Sufficient duration: One of the most common errors in teaching SEEDS to read is to withdraw prematurely the instruction that seems to be working. A student who is reading accurately at or above grade level but not fluently at their independent reading level still requires intensive reading instruction.

§5.2 MTSS in Grades K-3

The term "MTSS" means a comprehensive system of differentiated supports that includes evidence-based instruction, universal screening, progress monitoring, formative assessments, summative assessments, research-based interventions matched to student needs, and educational decision-making using academic progress overtime. All SEEDS will have the opportunity to benefit from a process that helps them through instruction, intervention, and if necessary, referral to special education as mandated by this law.

A. [Insert state name] principles of Multi-Tier System of Supports (MTSS)
   1. Assumption and belief that all students can learn;
   2. Early intervention for students who demonstrate risk for literacy failure;
   3. Use of a multitier model of service delivery (to achieve high rates of student success, instruction may be differentiated in both nature and intensity);
   4. Use of a problem-solving or standard-protocol method to make decisions within a multitier model;

5. Use of research-based, scientifically validated interventions/ instruction to the extent available;
6. Monitoring of student progress to inform instruction; and
7. Use of data to make decisions.

B. The process described in this section of the law is for MTSS for SEEDS who struggle in the area of reading:

1. Tier I—Foundational Reading Instruction should involve (1) the use of a scientifically based instructional program for all students, (2) ongoing assessment of progress and monitoring of reading achievement gains, and (3) teachers of reading using flexible grouping to target specific skills and differentiate instruction for all students.

2. Tier II—MTSS intervention is designed to meet the needs of SEEDS who do not respond quickly to foundational reading instruction. MTSS will be provided in the regular classroom setting. These students will receive intensive small group reading instruction in general education. The teacher of reading will provide all the knowledge of [insert state name] Statute, Section 2.2 for Teachers of reading preparation in the reading intervention, emphasizing all essential components of early literacy. Progress monitoring on the student reading development will occur at least every two weeks on targeted skills to ensure adequate advancement and learning. A set of goals for each student will be identified and established. Progress monitoring data will be analyzed, interpreted, and documented. Students who meet set criteria on targeted skills as a result of tier II interventions are reintegrated into the regular classroom setting (tier I).

3. If at any time during the student's tier II intervention or after receiving tier II intervention (maximum of ten weeks), the student's progress in the essential components of reading shows no advancement and/or the student demonstrates characteristics associated with learning disorders such as dyslexia or specific learning disability, the teacher of reading shall recommend a formal diagnostic assessment for the student.

4. Tier III—MTSS intensive instruction involves a small percentage of students who have received tier

II intervention in general education and continue to show marked difficulty in acquiring necessary reading development to reach grade-level attainment. These students necessitate intensive instruction that is more explicit and specifically designed to meet their individual needs. These students will receive progress monitoring at least every two weeks on targeted skills to ensure adequate progress and learning. The approximate time for tier III intensive instruction is eight to ten weeks. After this intensity of instruction, the student can return to tier II intervention support before reintegration into the regular classroom setting (tier I).

5. If at any time during the student's tier III intensive instruction, or after receiving tier III intervention, the student's progress in the essential components of reading development shows no advancement and/or the student demonstrates characteristics associated with a learning disorder such as dyslexia or specific learning disability, the teacher of reading will immediately recommended a formal diagnostic assessment for the student.

§5.3 Reading Interventions and Strategies for Older Students Grades 4-12

In the state of [insert state name] grades K-3, reading is considered a separate subject; but in middle school, it is important for [insert name of state government department of education] to establish a school culture that recognizes that every content-area teacher is a reading teacher, because reading is involved in every subject area, [insert state name] Statute, Section 2.2 of this law. Therefore, reading strategies will be implemented as a school-wide program in connection with a school culture and vision that works toward high levels of student achievement in reading literacy. Specific interventions and strategies will be provided to support SEEDS who have struggled to learn to read and are performing below grade level in reading. [insert state name]'s schools will provide every opportunity for students to read, practice their strategies, in every subject, every day, to enhance their development of the reading skills they need to become better readers and, ultimately, reading literate.

A. Each school will provide intensive reading interventions to SEEDS in grades 4-12 with reading problems. While the expectation is that students will learn to read with understanding before attaining middle- and high-school status, the reality is that many students reach these schools unable to read grade-level text effectively and with understanding. SEEDS with demonstrated reading difficulties will be provided twenty-six to thirty-two weeks of supplemental reading interventions as an alternative to English language arts class in middle and high school that directly addresses their vocabulary, comprehension, and word-reading challenges so they are able to perform significantly better in reading subject material text and can achieve grade-level reading literacy. Research supports identification and MTSS to help with the following:

1. Identify students who are more than one grade level behind in reading and provide daily reading intervention. Using a dedicated period each day with a certified teacher-of-reading professional, students who have reading difficulties that are one or more grade levels below expectations are provided with daily reading instruction, approximately forty to fifty minutes per day, focused specifically on their instructional needs. Providing students specific interventions that are focused on their learning needs requires identifying whether a student's reading comprehension difficulties are a function of (a) word-reading problems (e.g., decoding unknown words), (b) word-meaning problems (e.g., vocabulary), (c) adequate knowledge to understand text (e.g., background knowledge), (d) unusually slow text reading (e.g., fluency), and/or (e) inadequate use of reading comprehension strategies to promote reading comprehension. Through diagnostic assessment, teachers can determine which of the above are contributing to the reading difficulties and target their instruction.

2. Target instruction for each student by providing systems of support in three tiers with an outline of assessments of skill accomplishments and a timeline for stages of support.

3. During tier I intervention for grade 4-12 students who need intervention in word study, a certified teacher of reading provides students with approximately twenty-five

lessons taught over seven to eight weeks depending on student mastery. The daily lessons are composed of word study to teach advanced decoding of multisyllabic words. Students' mastery of sounds and word reading determines their progress through the lessons. Students receive daily instruction and practice with individual letter sounds, letter combinations, and affixes. In addition, students receive instruction and practice in applying a strategy to decode multisyllabic words by breaking them into known parts. Students also practice breaking words into parts to spell. Word-reading strategies are applied to reading in context in the form of sentences and passage reading daily.

During tier I intervention, high levels of teacher of reading support and scaffolding are provided to students in applying the multisyllabic word-reading strategy to reading words and connected text, and spelling words. Fluency instruction is promoted by using oral reading fluency data and pairing higher and lower readers for partner reading. Students engage in repeated reading daily with their partner with the goal of increased fluency (accuracy and rate). Partners take turns reading orally while their partner reads along and marks errors. The higher reader always reads first. After reading, partners are given time to go over errors and ask questions about unknown words. Partners read the passage three times each and graph the number of words read correctly. The teacher of reading is actively involved in modeling and providing feedback to students. Vocabulary is taught daily by teaching the meaning of the words through basic definitions and providing examples and nonexamples of how to use the word. New vocabulary words are reviewed daily with students matching words to appropriate definitions or examples of word usage. Comprehension is taught during and after reading by asking students to address relevant comprehension questions of varying levels of difficulty (literal and inferential). Teachers assist students in locating information in text and rereading to identify answers.

4. During tier II intervention the instruction emphasis is on vocabulary and comprehension with additional instruction and practice provided for applying the word study and

fluency skills and strategies learned in tier I intervention. Lessons occur over a period of seventeen to eighteen weeks depending on students' progress. Word study and vocabulary are taught through daily review of the word study strategies learned in tier I by applying the sounds and strategy to reading new words. Focus on word meaning is also part of word-reading practice. Students are also taught word relatives and parts of speech (e.g., politics, politician, politically). Finally, students review application of word study to spelling words. Vocabulary words for instruction are chosen from the text read in the fluency and comprehension component. Three days a week, teachers use subject matter lessons and materials. Two days a week, teachers use novels with lessons developed by the research team. Fluency and comprehension are taught with an emphasis on reading and understanding text through discourse or writing. Students spend three days a week reading and comprehending expository subject matter text, one or two days a week reading and comprehending narrative text in novels. Content and vocabulary are needed to understand the text and are taught prior to reading. Students then read the text at least twice with an emphasis on reading for understanding. During and after the second reading, comprehension questions of varying levels of complexity and abstraction are discussed with students. Students also receive explicit instruction in generating questions of varying levels of complexity and abstraction while reading (e.g., literal questions, questions requiring students to synthesize information from text, and questions requiring students to apply background knowledge to information in text), identifying the main idea, summarizing, and employing strategies for multiple-choice, short answer, and essay questions.

5. Tier III intervention continues the instructional emphasis on vocabulary and comprehension with more time spent on independent student application of skills and strategies. Tier III occurs over approximately eight to ten weeks.

B. Each content-area teacher will identify key content subject words for each student to learn and teach at least two new words every day and review one from the previous day. This practice can be readily implemented across all content-area instruction and provides students with opportunities to expand their academic vocabulary, increase their background knowledge, and better understand the key ideas that they are reading and learning about. One way a content-area teacher can do this is to select words in a unit that are high-priority and high-utility words. Assuming that a unit is three weeks long, they can then determine the key words students need to know, explicitly teaching them each week and also reviewing them in subsequent weeks. There are several ways that these words can be taught:

1. Teachers can use vocabulary maps that use the key word, pictures of the word, words that relate to the key word, a student friendly definition, and how the word can be used in a historical context.

2. Teachers can illustrate, show a picture that represents the word, or read one or two sentences that include the word describing it in ways that allow students to make informed decisions about word meaning. Then the students and the teacher can use this information to co-construct the meaning of the word.

3. Key words can be taught within the context of a debate or structured discussion in which students use those key words in their written and oral arguments.

C. Teachers should ask students to ask questions while they read and after they listen to the teacher read while they are following the text so that they will monitor comprehension and learning. Students who are actively engaged while listening and reading are more likely to understand and remember what they read or hear. Teachers can promote that practice by instructing students to ask questions while they are reading. After students complete their reading, they can also be asked to develop one question to ask the class. Students benefit from having question stems to help them develop these questions.

D. Teachers should teach word-meaning strategies within content-area classes. Concept words are the center of learning the big ideas of content as well as the necessary academic vocabulary for success. Content areas (e.g., math, science, social studies, and English language arts) each have unique vocabulary used to communicate concepts and explain processes. Students need to learn what these words mean and how to use them within the multiple contexts of reading, writing, and speaking. Adolescents will encounter approximately ten thousand new words per year, the majority of which are the complex terms of the content areas. Research supports two practices for helping students learn academic vocabulary:

1. Teachers can provide explicit instruction of academic or concept words that students need to learn to master the key ideas they are teaching. These words need to be introduced to the student by showing them the words, showing them a picture, video, or other demonstration to make the words vivid. Teachers then need to work with students to discuss what the word means and doesn't mean. A critical step is to return to these words regularly throughout the lesson and throughout the instructional unit to assure that students can use them with understanding in their speaking and writing tasks. Teach students the meaning of words within the context of learning and also the multiple meanings of words.

2. Teachers need to provide instruction in word-learning strategies. Although explicit instruction is important, the sheer number of words students need to learn requires that they develop strategies for independently determining the meanings of unfamiliar vocabulary. One means of equipping students to understand the content-area terms they encounter is to teach the component morphemes (prefixes, roots, and suffixes) and how they contribute to the meaning of words. Students taught this process of analyzing words by morphemes were able to infer the meanings of untaught terms in subject-matter text. Other research indicates the practice is particularly effective with SEEDS when done systematically and coupled with multiple opportunities to practice. This can be facilitated by applying learned morphemes to words used in different content areas. Another word-learning strategy involves teaching word meanings directly through the use of a mnemonic word association and a picture that ties together the word clue and the definition.

E. Teachers should instruct students how to activate and build appropriate background knowledge for understanding text content. Researchers report that background knowledge is second only to vocabulary in enhancing reading comprehension outcomes with secondary readers. A lack of prior knowledge can make understanding informational text particularly challenging. Research supports this strategy for building background knowledge:

1. Teach students to use text to support answers and consider whether they can locate text-based support for positions, and

2. Teach students to elaborate on why statements that they select could or could not be supported based on the text.

   According to researchers, this technique requires students to identify related background knowledge in their memories to link to the statements and to provide adequate justification for their responses. When used in connection with text reading, it encourages students to return to important information to obtain further elaboration for their responses. Students would be asked to determine whether they could or could not adequately support the statement and use prior learning and text to support their views.

F. Teachers should teach students to use reading comprehension strategies while reading complex text. Students benefit from using reading comprehension strategies while reading complex text. Too often, adolescents proceed through text with little understanding of what they are reading or awareness of when their comprehension has broken down. They need to be taught to recognize when they do not adequately understand text and how to build comprehension. Research supports these strategies for reading comprehension:

1. Teach students to generate questions while reading to build comprehension skills. Learning to generate questions while reading is one way of getting students to stop at regular intervals to think about what is being communicated and how the information relates across paragraphs. Studies have shown that the practice can increase comprehension of content-area text for students of different ability levels.

The first level of questions is the most literal in that they are based on a fact that can be identified in one place in the text. The second level of questions combines information that is located in two different parts of the text. The third level of questions relates information in the text to something the reader has experienced or learned previously.

2. Another means of encouraging students to be active readers and to monitor their own comprehension is to teach them how to generate main idea statements for single or multiple paragraphs. Adolescents and teens that learn to identify the explicitly or implicitly stated main ideas of a text have shown increased understanding and recall of important information. Referred to as either "Paragraph Shrinking" or "Get the Gist," students at a range of ability levels and language backgrounds have been successfully taught to use three steps in generating a main idea statement:

   a. Identify who or what is the focus of the paragraph or section;

   b. Determine the most important information about what the key person place/thing has, is, or does;

   c. Succinctly state the who or what and most important information about him/her/it in a sentence.

G. Teachers should guide and engage students in activities that are text-related. Through both classroom discussion and written assignments, students will learn to apply critical analysis, inference, interpretation, and summation of printed material. The goal is to guide the student to understand text and respond through productive discussion and written answers. Research supports the following strategies for encouraging reading for understanding:

1. Foster discussion in small groups. Give students the opportunities to return to texts a number of times to explore, discuss, and revise their developing understanding of the ideas and concepts. This practice can be fostered through the use of reciprocal teaching, a multicomponent strategy intended to support student comprehension. In reciprocal teaching, the teacher leads the dialogue about the text until students learn to assume different roles independently: summarizer, questioner, clarifier, or

predictor. After reading a short section of text (generally a few paragraphs, at first, but increasing to several pages with practice), the summarizer highlights the key points for the group. Then, the questioner helps the group consider and talk about what was read by posing questions about anything that was unclear, puzzling, or related to other information that was learned. In this portion of reciprocal teaching, students can apply question generation skills that will support asking about more than surface-level information. The clarifier in the group of students is responsible for seeking out portions of text that will help answer the questions just posed. However, all members of the group participate in discussing the information and connecting ideas. In doing so, students need to return to the current selection and, possibly, other readings to look for text evidence in support of their responses. Finally, the predictor offers suggestions about what the group can expect to read in the next section of text. These predictions are focused on activating relevant background knowledge, setting a purpose for reading, and relating new information to that just discussed by the group.

2. Teachers should instruct students in how to summarize text. Students that are explicitly taught how to summarize text are better able to discern the relationships among main ideas and significant details. When students work collaboratively on summaries of expository text, such as in reciprocal teaching, they reach higher levels of comprehension and retain more content information. Teachers should thoroughly explain and model each step multiple times with different types of text before students will be able to complete them in collaborative groups or, eventually, on their own.

H. Teachers should maximize all opportunities for students to read printed material. Both middle and high school content-area teachers will have a range of readers in their classrooms, providing challenges for assignments that require text reading. For this reason, and others, many classroom teachers require students to read very little both inside and outside of their class time. Teachers also report that they increasingly rely on reading text aloud or using other media (e.g., videos) as a means for providing students with content knowledge perceiving text reading as inaccessible. Reading and understanding text requires practice, and students need opportunities to read a range of text types (e.g., textbooks, letters, descriptions, original documents, poetry). Research supports the following strategies to enhance opportunities for students to read and respond to text:

1. Prepare students to read text by providing key ideas and key words. Providing the big idea and connecting principles prior to having students read the text will facilitate comprehension. This goal can also be accomplished by soliciting the big idea and principle from the students. Present the key words orally, on the board, or on a handout, including all proper nouns, prior to text reading.

2. Provide daily opportunities for students to read for a specific amount of time, then, provide a prompt for student response (e.g., two to three minutes for reading and one to two minutes for responding). Students can be asked to respond to predetermined prompts such as, "What is this section mostly about?" "How does the author describe _____?" "What did you learn about _____?" Students can respond in writing using learning logs or they can respond orally by turning and talking with a partner for one minute.

3. Have students participate in partner reading (typically a better reader and a less able reader) and then ask them to take turns reading the same passage with the better reader reading the passage first and then the less able reader rereading the passage. Students can partner-read for a specified amount of time (e.g., three minutes) and can use one to two minutes to write responses by determining the main idea, writing and answering a question, or summarizing.

I. Teachers should organize students into collaborative groups for reading tasks. Student involvement and learning can be well enhanced through well-structured collaborative groups, designed to promote both individual and group accountability.

These groups can be used within content-area classes and are associated with improved reading comprehension for students when implemented two or more times per week. Research supports the following strategies for collaborative groups:

1. Having students use Collaborative Strategic Reading (CSR). CSR has two important phases: the first phase is learning the four reading comprehension strategies that include (1) previewing text (preview), (2) monitoring comprehension while reading by identifying key words and concepts that are challenging (click and clunk), (3) thinking about the main idea while reading and putting it into your own words (get the gist), and (4) summarizing text understanding after you read (wrap-up). The second phase is teaching students to use cooperative groups effectively as a means of applying the strategies. The focus of the practice described in this section is on implementing cooperative groups. Once students have developed proficiency using the four strategies with teacher guidance, they are ready to use these same strategies in peer-led cooperative learning groups. Some teachers ask students to first work in pairs and then move into a group, while other teachers find it better to start with cooperative groups.

2. Forming CSRs will be a success if the teacher is aware that all students will not function equally well in a group and that groups are more effective when the teacher selects students with the intent of designing a well-functioning team. Teachers assign approximately four students to each group, considering that each group will need a student with reading proficiency and a leader, thus providing a group that represents varying abilities. Teachers assign students to roles in the group and teach them to perform their role. Roles rotate on a regular basis (e.g., every couple of weeks) so that students can experience a variety of roles. Student roles are an important aspect of effective implementation of cooperative learning so that all group members are assigned a meaningful task and participate in the group's success.

3. The teacher's role in CSR, while students are working in their groups, is to ensure the students have been taught their role and know how to implement their responsibility.

Forming successful and productive groups is an important accomplishment because it allows the teacher to circulate among the groups, listen to students' participation, read students' learning logs, and most importantly, provide clear and specific feedback to improve the use and application of the strategies. Teachers can help by actively listening to students' conversations and clarifying difficult words, modeling strategy usage, encouraging students to participate, and modeling strategy application. It is expected that students will need assistance learning to work in cooperative groups, implementing the strategies, and mastering academic content.

§EFFECTIVE DATE. This section is effective [insert date].

EARLY CHILDHOOD EDUCATION

KEY ROLES IN FOUNDATIONAL
PRELITERACY INSTRUCTION

WHILE PREKINDERGARTEN EDUCATION shares little of the rigor or eclecticism of secondary and tertiary education, it is just a crucial period in a child's development of language and literacy skills. Studies show that children learn more between birth and age five than during any other five-year period of their life; and in a society that thrives on its youngest citizens' ability to reach their full potential early on, neglecting to cultivate such an essential skill as reading literacy comes at significant cost to the entire population. If we consider that the children for whom prekindergarten education is the most beneficial are those from low-income families, we realize that early care and education providers perform a critical role: the quality of their foundational literacy instruction may determine which children move into primary school ready to harness the power of written language and which children find themselves in the community of SEEDS.

The former option is clearly the more desirable, and it is an entirely realistic goal. The number of states providing free preschool for all four-year-olds is growing steadily, as is the demand for universal preschool throughout the United States. Preparation programs that offer both scientifically backed instructional methods and strategies and certification for early care and education providers are a necessity.

This appendix gives you four tools to assist you in adopting state literacy law on § New Qualifications, Licenses, and Certifications for

All Early Care Educators and Providers in Preliteracy Birth to Age Five: the Executive Summary presents the context for and benefits of preliteracy instruction; the Key Components outline the fundamentals of early literacy; the Roadmap and Specifics offer a more in-depth look at the responsibilities of early care providers; and the model state legislation is designed to help you and your community take a stand for the young children who deserve the chance to become capable and productive members of society.

Executive Summary
For Early Childhood Education Providers

Board-approved preparation programs will certify early care and education providers, who are responsible for instilling the foundations of language and literacy development in children from birth to age five.

Issue:

We in the modern era communicate through written text more than at any other time in human history, making the ability to read and write imperative for success in school and in the workforce. However, reading literacy acquisition is not an easy task for an alarming number of children in the United States, and currently only one-third of our students read proficiently. Scientific research has informed the systems and strategies needed to address reading failure beginning in primary education; but the path to proficient reading and skillful language use begins long before students enter kindergarten, and successful introduction of key early literacy skills will go a long way toward decreasing the percentage of struggling. Early care and education providers therefore play a vital role in securing bright futures for all our children.

Why this is important:

1. Teacher quality is the number-one predictor of a student's success, and teachers' impact is additive and cumulative.

2. A child's education is unquestionably an investment in the future of his or her country, and all techniques and practices intended for language development and literacy attainment should be rooted in scientific, data-validated findings.

Goals of instruction:

1. To inform all early care and education providers of predictors of early literacy success, keys to the development of a preliteracy foundation, and techniques and strategies for incorporating these into early instruction.
2. To certify all early care and education providers, identifying them as professionals in the cultivation of early and precursor literacy skills in young children.
3. To base all preliteracy instruction on validated scientific principles that are proven to foster literacy readiness and satisfactory preparedness for reading instruction in diverse student populations.

How effective preparation programs achieve these goals:

1. The program or collection of practices for early care and education providers should include instruction in and application of the areas of foundational preliteracy.
2. Board-approved provider, educator, and teacher preparation programs should use evidence-based best practices that lay the foundation for literacy readiness.
3. Preparation programs should afford early care and education providers an understanding of the application of scientific findings to effective activities and teaching strategies.

Key Points:

Preliteracy education relies just as much upon scientific principles and evidence as do primary and secondary instruction. The predictors of early literacy success are defined and measurable, and their ease of adaptation to activities and areas of instruction for diverse populations of young children has been repeatedly proven.

CINTHIA COLETTI

With the right tools and techniques in the hands of well-informed and well-prepared early care and education providers, children from birth to age five will acquire a strong base for the literacy skills that will advance them so far later in their lives.

Key Components
For Early Care And Education Providers

Preparation programs for early care and education providers should rely on replicated scientific research and evidence, and center the major components of foundational language development and literacy readiness.

The Scientific Principle:

Reading literacy is a process that begins in the first few years of a child's life. The purpose of early literacy instruction in prekindergarten education is to build a firm foundation of alphabetic and phonological principles that will aid the child in language and literacy development throughout his or her academic career, and for the rest of his or her life.

The Progression:

To these ends, early care and education providers should be well versed in the major components of early literacy; they should be able to adapt these principles to the real-world context of engaging children in language-development activities; and they should be certified for their profession.

1. Board-approved preparation programs, rooted in scientific research and data and proven to help children achieve literacy readiness, certify early care and education providers.
2. Early care and education providers receive instruction in the five main areas of foundational preliteracy.
3. Early care and education providers receive instruction in the application of early literacy principles to effective teaching strategies and tools.

The Key Components:

Basic Requirements for Foundational Preliteracy Instruction

The program or collection of practices for early care and education providers in preliteracy birth-age five should include, at a minimum, instruction in and application of the following five areas of foundational preliteracy:
1. Early literacy research
2. Language development
3. Shared book reading with an emphasis on vocabulary
4. Phonological awareness
5. The speech-to-print connection with an emphasis on alphabet knowledge

Predictors of Early Literacy Success

The program or collection of practices for early care and education providers should take into account the variables representing early or precursor literacy skills.	
1. Strong predictors of early literacy success include	
A. Alphabet Knowledge: knowledge of the names and sounds associated with printed letters	B. Phonological Awareness: the ability to detect, manipulate, or analyze the auditory aspects of spoken language (including the ability to distinguish or segment words, syllables, or phonemes), independent of meaning
C. Rapid Automatic Naming (RAN) of letters or digits: the ability to rapidly name a sequence of random letters or digits	D. Rapid Automatic Naming (RAN) of objects or colors: the ability to rapidly name a sequence of repeating random sets of pictures of objects (e.g., "car," "tree," "house," "man") or colors
E. Writing or writing name: the ability to write letters in isolation on request or to write one's own name	F. Phonological Memory: the ability to remember spoken information for a short period of time

2. Strategies for promoting early literacy		
A. Shared Book Reading: reading books with children, encouraging various forms of reader-child interactions around the material being read and the vocabulary used	B. Phonological Awareness Activities: rhyme, syllable, and sound activities that promote awareness of the smallest units of spoken language that can be manipulated independent of meaning	C. Connecting Speech-to-Print: helping children understand what they know—speech—and relate it to what they do not yet know—print—through alphabet knowledge and early writing activities

Preliteracy Language Development

Given the research-proven link between the major elements of spoken and written language development (listening, speaking, reading, and writing), early care and education providers should know how these language skills interrelate and contribute toward full literacy.

1. Important elements of language to be incorporated into preliteracy education include:

A. Phonology: the sound system	B. Vocabulary: words, relationships, and concepts	C. Morphology: meaningful word parts	D. Syntax: the rules for making sentences	E. Pragmatics: language use based on context and situation

2. Scaffolding helps children advance from what they know to what they need to learn

Shared Reading Benefits and Strategies

Shared book reading (reading with children, rather than to children) with an emphasis on vocabulary is a critical step in preparing children for the development of language skills and reading literacy. This activity		
1. Builds oral language and print awareness		
2. Builds vocabulary by introducing high-frequency words for mature language users		
3. Can be adapted for other shared book reading strategies, including		
A. Text Talk (vocabulary enrichment): a strategy developed to build mature vocabulary during shared book reading	B. The PEER Sequence: a strategy for building comprehension	C. CROWD: a strategy for building vocabulary and comprehension

Phonological Awareness

The program or collection of practices for early care and education providers should include an understanding of phonological awareness					
1. Phonological awareness is understanding that spoken language is made up of smaller parts: sentence into words, words into syllables, syllables into sounds.					
2. Phonological awareness includes a progression of rhyming skills from rote rhyming to recognizing rhyme to completing rhymes to generating rhymes.					
3. At the syllable level, the progression of rhyming skills is as follows:					
A. Blending		B. Segmenting		C. Deleting	
4. At the phonemic (sound) level, the progression of rhyming skills is as follows:					
A. Matching	B. Isolating	C. Blending	D. Segmenting and counting	E. Deleting	F. Manipulating

Connection between Spoken and Written Language

The program or collection of practices for early care and education providers should include speech-to-print connection with an emphasis on alphabet knowledge.			
1. Children need to use what they know—speech—to master what they do not yet know—print.			
2. Children need to learn to experience print in the following contexts:			
A. Recognizing print in their surroundings	B. Understanding that print carries meaning	C. Knowing that print is used for many purposes	D. Generating print through exploratory writing
3. With the help of early care and education providers, children should acquire the alphabetic principle through concepts of words and concepts of letters. They should			
A. Understand that sounds heard in spoken words are represented by letters		B. Know the sound that each letter or group of letters can make	
4. In order to impart this foundational literacy knowledge, early care and education providers should use such tools and techniques as			
A. Sound walls	B. Letter boxes and buckets	C. Variations on the alphabet song	
Once all of these components are incorporated into preliteracy education, states should develop a common early literacy language between pre-K early care and education providers and kindergarten teachers through a pre-K-K collaborative design.			

Road Map for Educators and Specifics for State Handbook For Early Childhood And Education Providers

Board—approved provider, educator, and teacher preparation programs will be implemented to certify early care educators and providers in preliteracy birth through age five. These programs will require instruction in the application of the research-based foundations of literacy and will be founded on research-proven instructional best practices. Replicated evidence should show that when these programs and practices are used, diverse student populations can achieve literacy readiness and can be satisfactory prepared for reading instruction in kindergarten.

The program or collection of practices for early care and education providers in preliteracy birth-age five should include, at a minimum, instruction in and application of the five areas of foundational preliteracy: (1) early literacy research, (2) language development, (3) shared book reading with an emphasis on vocabulary, (4) phonological awareness, and (5) the speech-to-print connection with an emphasis on alphabet knowledge.

Early literacy success: Strong predictors of an early success in literacy include (1) alphabet knowledge, knowledge of the names and sounds associated with printed letters; (2) phonological awareness, the ability to detect, manipulate, and analyze the auditory aspects of spoken language (including the ability to distinguish or segment words, syllables, or phonemes), independent of meaning; (3) rapid automatic naming (RAN) of letters or digits, the ability to rapidly name a sequence of random letters or digits; (4) rapid automatic naming (RAN) of objects or colors, the ability to rapidly name a sequence of repeating random sets of pictures of objects (e.g., "car," "tree," "house," "man") or colors; (5) writing or writing name, the ability to write letters in isolation on request or to write one's own name; and (6) phonological memory, the ability to remember spoken information for a short period of time.

Several strategies for promoting early literacy are shared book reading, which emphasizes reading with children rather than to them and encourages various forms of reader-child interactions around the material being read and the vocabulary used; phonological awareness activities, which use rhyme, syllable, and sound to promote awareness of the smallest units of spoken language that can be manipulated independent of meaning; and connecting speech-to-print, which helps children relate what they know—speech—to what they do not yet know—print—through alphabet knowledge and early writing activities.

Language Development: The four main areas of language development are listening, speaking, reading, and writing. Given the research-proven link between these major elements of spoken and written language, early care and education providers should know how they interrelate and how to incorporate them into preliteracy activities.

Important elements of language are phonology (the sound system), vocabulary (words, relationships, and concepts), morphology (meaningful word parts), syntax (the rules for making sentences), and pragmatics (language use based on context and situation). Scaffolding the introduction of and instruction surrounding each component helps children advance from what they know to what they need to learn, setting the proper pace for literacy preparedness.

Shared book reading: Shared book reading is more than just the act of reading to a child: when adults read with children, not just to them, and place emphasis on a particular element of language, children are in turn able to build their oral language and print awareness.

Early care and education providers can help to build children's vocabulary by using high-frequency words for mature language users and by using shared book reading strategies such as Text Talk, the PEER Sequence, and CROWD to both enrich vocabulary and enhance comprehension.

Phonological Awareness: Phonological awareness is not the same as phonics—it is about sounds, not letters. It is the understanding that spoken language is made up of smaller parts: sentence into words, words into syllables, syllables into sounds. Phonological awareness also involves a progression of rhyming skills from rote rhyming to recognizing rhyme to completing rhymes to generating rhymes.

At the syllabic level, these rhyming skills progress from blending to segmenting to deleting; at the phonemic (sound) level, the progression is from matching, to isolating, to blending, to segmenting and counting, to deleting, to manipulating.

Speech-to-Print Connection: Through exposure to the connection between spoken and written language, with an emphasis on alphabet knowledge, children are able to use their knowledge of speech to master print.

Children need to learn to identify and experience printed content by (1) recognizing print in their surroundings, (2) understanding that print carries meaning, (3) knowing that print is used for many purposes, and (4) experiencing print through exploratory writing.

Early care and education providers need to help children acquire the alphabetic principle—the understanding that sounds heard in spoken words can be represented by letters, and knowledge of the sound that each letter or group of letters can make—through concepts of words and letters. Tools and techniques for imparting this knowledge include sound walls, letter boxes and buckets, and variations on the alphabet song.

Once all of these components are incorporated into preliteracy education, states should develop a common early literacy language between pre-K early care and education providers and kindergarten teachers through a pre-K-K collaborative design.

MODEL STATE LEGISLATION LANGUAGE
EARLY CHILDHOOD AND EDUCATION PROVIDERS

Data Driven Preliteracy Instruction from birth to age five

Section §6

Guidelines for Early Childhood and Education Providers
Data-Driven Preliteracy Instruction from Birth to Age Five

BE IT ENACTED BY THE LEGISLATURE OF THE STATE OF New Qualifications, Licenses, and Certifications for All Early Care Educators and Providers in Preliteracy Birth to Age Five.

§6.1 Basic Requirements for Foundational Preliteracy Instruction

A. The state wil require certification of early care education teachers and providers. Board-approved provider, educator, and teacher preparation programs shall certify early care educators and providers in preliteracy birth to age five. The program will require instruction in the application of the research-based foundations of literacy. It will be founded on research-proven instructional best practices based on replicated evidence that shows that when these programs or practices are used, diverse student populations can be expected to achieve, at a minimum, literacy readiness and satisfactory preparedness for reading instruction in kindergarten.

B. The program or collection of practices for early care and education providers in preliteracy birth-age five should include, at a minimum, instruction in and application of the following five areas of foundational preliteracy:

1. Early Literacy Research;
2. Language Development;
3. Shared Book Reading with an emphasis on Vocabulary;
4. Phonological Awareness; and
5. The Speech-to-Print Connection with an emphasis on Alphabet Knowledge.

§6.2 Predictors of Early Literacy Success

The program or collection of practices for early care and education providers should take into account the variables representing early or precursor literacy skills.

A. Strong predictors of early literacy success include
   1. Alphabet Knowledge: knowledge of the names and sounds associated with printed letters;
   2. Phonological Awareness: the ability to detect, manipulate, or analyze the auditory aspects of spoken language (including the ability to distinguish or segment words, syllables, or phonemes), independent of meaning;
   3. Rapid Automatic Naming (RAN) of letters or digits: the ability to rapidly name a sequence of random letters or digits;
   4. Rapid Automatic Naming (RAN) of objects or colors: the ability to rapidly name a sequence of repeating random sets of pictures of objects (e.g., "car," "tree," "house," "man") or colors;
   5. Writing or writing name: the ability to write letters in isolation on request or to write one's own name; and
   6. Phonological Memory: the ability to remember spoken information for a short period of time.
B. Strategies for promoting early literacy:
   1. Shared Book Reading: reading books with children, encouraging various forms of reader-child interactions around the material being read and the vocabulary used;
   2. Phonological Awareness Activities: rhyme, syllable, and sound activities that promote awareness of the smallest

units of spoken language that can be manipulated independent of meaning; and

3. Connecting Speech-to-Print: helping children understand what they know—speech—and relate it to what they do not yet know—print—through alphabet knowledge and early writing activities.

§6.3 Preliteracy Language Development

Given the research-proven link between the major elements of spoken and written language development (listening, speaking, reading, and writing), early care and education providers should know how these language skills interrelate and contribute toward full literacy.

Important elements of language to be incorporated into preliteracy education include

A. Phonology: the sound system;
B. Vocabulary: words, relationships, and concepts;
C. Morphology: meaningful word parts;
D. Syntax: the rules for making sentences; and
E. Pragmatics: language use based on context and situation.
F. Scaffolding helps children advance from what they know to what they need to learn

§6.4 Shared Reading Benefits and Strategies

Shared book reading (reading with children, rather than to children) with an emphasis on vocabulary is a critical step in preparing children for the development of language skills and reading literacy. This activity

A. Builds oral language and print awareness;
B. Builds vocabulary by introducing high-frequency words for mature language users; and
C. Can be adapted for other shared book reading strategies, including
D. Text Talk (vocabulary enrichment): a strategy developed to build mature vocabulary during shared book reading;
E. The PEER Sequence: a strategy for building comprehension; and
F. CROWD: a strategy for building vocabulary and comprehension.

§6.5 Phonological Awareness

The program or collection of practices for early care and education providers should include an understanding of phonological awareness.

A. Phonological awareness is understanding that spoken language is made up of smaller parts: sentence into words, words into syllables, syllables into sounds
B. Phonological awareness includes a progression of rhyming skills from rote rhyming to recognizing rhyme to completing rhymes to generating rhymes.
C. at the syllable level, the progression of rhyming skills is as follows:
1. blending;
2. segmenting; and
3. deleting.
D. at the phonemic (sound) level, the progression of rhyming skills is as follows:
1. matching;
2. isolating;
3. blending;
4. segmenting and counting;
5. deleting; and
6. manipulating.

§6.6 Connection between Spoken and Written Language

The program or collection of practices for early care and education providers should include speech-to-print connection with an emphasis on alphabet knowledge.

A. Children need to use what they know—speech—to master what they do not yet know—print.
B. Children need to learn to experience print in the following contexts:
1. recognizing print in their surroundings;
2. understanding that print carries meaning;
3. knowing that print is used for many purposes; and
4. generating print through exploratory writing.

E. With the help of early care and education providers, children should acquire the alphabetic principle through concepts of words and concepts of letters. They should
  1. understand that sounds heard in spoken words are represented by letters; and
  2. know the sound that each letter or group of letters can make.
C. In order to impart this foundational literacy knowledge, early care and education providers should use such tools and techniques as
  1. sound walls;
  2. letter boxes and buckets; and
  3. variations on the alphabet song.

Once all of these components are incorporated into preliteracy education, states should develop a common early literacy language between pre-K early care and education providers and kindergarten teachers through a pre-K-K collaborative design.

§EFFECTIVE DATE. This section is effective [insert date].

RESPONSIBILITIES OF SCHOOL DISTRICTS AND SCHOOL BOARDS

THE SCHOOL DISTRICT and school board assume great responsibility for student academic success as well as for the effectiveness of each teacher, classroom, program, and system they direct.

Each district and school board should take a leadership role and comply with and implement with fidelity all components of the Literacy Policy and the procedures outlined. Every school system has specific leadership responsibilities for the implementation of the Policy, and the state will monitor and grade each requirement to ensure that district schools (1) adopt system policies and procedures for implementation of the Policy; (2) guarantee public notification regarding the school obligations for certified teachers of reading, teaching specialists, and content-area teachers' licensure; (3) provide training and professional development in the use and interpretation of student and classroom data; (4) provide reading development instruction for all teachers in grades kindergarten through third to pass the advanced reading instruction competence assessment for certification as a teacher of reading; (5) provide reading literacy instruction for content-area teachers to pass the basic reading instruction competence assessment; (6) provide informal training and professional development in reading literacy for system representatives, paraprofessionals, appropriate staff, and administrators on an annual basis; (7) assure that each school within the system selects personnel to oversee the assessment process for determination on curricula for foundational reading development, literacy, and professional development programs; (8) assure that MTSS programs for students with SEEDS meet the state criteria and follow the appropriate guidelines to include formal diagnostic assessment of students who do not make stipulated improvement in the time frames defined; and (9) assure that each school within the system follows the regulations for implementation of the Policy (Section 8) by providing for the functional and academic needs of all students identified as below proficient in grade-level reading.

It is the responsibility of the district and school board to provide data systems that are constructed to deliver continuous assessment, monitoring, evaluation, and communication about students' reading progress, teachers' knowledge and data acumen, and classroom effectiveness. In many districts, student/classroom data analysis has not been viewed as a high priority. To achieve the Literacy Policy, both district and school boards are mandated to use student data to analyze teachers, programs, and systems effectiveness. Data will be gathered to guide students' educational success by requiring that all district schools and education staff become familiar with data analysis, interpretation, and use to create plans to assist individual students achieve grade-level reading proficiency in grades K-12.

Responsibilities of the district school board further establish a data use plan that guides and supports teachers' knowledge and advancement in the use of data for directing instructional improvement. Data implementation should replace hunches and hypotheses with facts by using data rather than symptoms to identify areas of weakness in a student's academic development.

MODEL STATE LEGISLATION LANGUAGE RESPONSIBILITIES OF SCHOOL DISTRICTS AND SCHOOL BOARDS

§ 7 School District and School Boards Responsibilities to Literacy Policy

BE IT ENACTED BY THE LEGISLATURE OF THE STATE OF [insert state name] that every school district, school board, and school within jurisdiction must collect pertinent data on all students, teachers, and classrooms. Any student suspected of experiencing literacy failure must be provided assessments, analysis, and strategies to become grade-level proficient in reading literacy. A committee of persons knowledgeable about the student must review the relevant data and recommended strategies to determine a course for each student.

§7.1 [Insert name of state school board] Requirements

A. The local [insert name of the school board of education] for each school district, school, and charter school is responsible for ensuring compliance within their district of state Policy, rule, and procedures outlined in this Policy. Each school system has specific responsibilities for the implementation of the Policy, including

1. To create and adopt school system policies and procedures for implementation of the Policy;

2. To guarantee ongoing, clear public notification regarding the district's obligations toward assurance of certified teachers of reading in every grade K-3 classrooms to include teaching specialists, special education, ELL, and Title I instructors; assurance of data-validated/ evidenced-based Foundational Reading Development Instruction; and assurance of MTSS for SEEDS students;

3. To provide informational training and professional development about reading literacy for content-area teachers, system representatives, teachers, paraprofessionals, appropriate staff, and administrators on an annual basis as requested per [insert state name] Statute, Section 2 of this Policy;

4. To assure that each school within the system select personnel to oversee the assessment process for determination of program eligibility per [insert state name] Statute, Section 2.0 of this Policy;

5. To assure that programs for SEEDS students meet the state criteria and follow the appropriate guidelines to include formal diagnostic assessment of students; and

6. To assure that each school within the system follows the regulations for implementation of the Policy by providing for the functional and academic needs of students identified as not achieving grade-level reading proficiency.

B. Each Board of Education must
1. Ensure that procedures for using data systems and assessments to identifying a SEEDS student are implemented in the district and MTSS to bring all students to reading proficiency;
2. Ensure that procedures for providing appropriate instructional services and accommodations or modifications for the student are fully implemented in the district;
3. Ensure that the district or school complies with all applicable requirements of state educational programs.

§7.2 District Requirements

Each school district must

A. Administer K-3 universal screening at least three times during the kindergarten year. Every student in grades 1, 2, and 3 shall be assessed for appropriate reading progress every few weeks as identified in, [insert state name] Statute, Section 3 of this Policy;
B. Provide early identification, intervention, and support, [insert state name] Statute, Section 3 of this Policy;
C. Apply results of early assessment instruments to instruction and report to the district;
D. Implement procedures according to the State Board of Education;
E. Provide annual training of certified teachers of reading, staff, and paraprofessionals about SEEDS students;
F. Ensure the procedures for identification, instruction, and communication are in place;
G. Ensure the individuals responsible for administering and interpreting the necessary testing receive ongoing professional development in the assessments used;
H. Test for SEEDS students at appropriate times, as needed and in all grades;
I. Provide appropriate instruction, tier of supports, and accommodations for SEEDS and IEP students;

J. Purchase or develop programs that include descriptors listed in the state handbook;

K. Notify parents in writing before an assessment or identification procedure is used with an individual student;

L. Inform parents of all services and options available to eligible students;

M. Provide students with services of a teacher of reading and/or a teaching specialist certified and skilled in methods appropriate for SEEDS students' success;

N. Provide MTSS for students requiring specialized instruction, [insert state name] Statute, Section 5;

O. Provide a parent education program; and

P. Provide appropriate progress monitoring.

EFFECTIVE DATE. This section is effective [insert date].

IMPLEMENTATION OF THE LITERACY LAW

ENSURING STATE AND LOCAL CAPACITY TO TEACH READING LITERACY

A CLEAR, PRECISE, AND data-validated plan for rejuvenating American schools is a vital step toward long-term change and improvement, but it is only the first step. To advance from this point, we need to ensure that the new standards and procedures are being implemented as intended in districts, schools, and individual classrooms, and that the professionals overseeing this change are certified experts in teaching children to read.

While covering all these bases might seem a monumental task that could shift the focus from the central job of educating students, in practice, success requires only a firm commitment to the efficient and effective implementation of existing legislation. States can expedite successful reform by providing funds, information, and other key resources to school districts through an implementation infrastructure, while district and school leaders can do their part by ensuring that these offerings find their way into the classroom.

In this appendix, we present you with four tools to assist you in adopting state literacy law on §8 GUIDELINES AND STANDARDS FOR THE IMPLEMENTATION OF THE LAW. The Executive Summary outlines the necessary steps for transforming the United States education system; Key Components provide the details of certification and implementation; the Roadmap and Specifics relate the proposed changes to their intended outcomes; and the model state legislation is designed to help you and your community, with the help of your state and local leaders, take the initiative in the fight for our children's education and lifelong success.

Executive Summary
For The Implementation Of The Literacy Law

All state and local education agencies should support the purposeful implementation of the literacy law, giving teachers and school leaders the capacity to ensure foundational literacy skills for their students.

Issue:

Currently, only about one-third of the students in the United States read at a proficient or advanced level. Scientific research has informed the systems and strategies needed to target reading failure and guide struggling readers back toward the path to full literacy and lifelong success; but before this can happen, schools and districts should ensure that their teachers and curricula are prepared for change. The certification of teachers and the fidelity of implementation of the literacy law are keys steps in improving literacy and education outcomes in the future.

Why this is important:

1. Up through third grade, children learn to read; after third grade, they read to learn. If a student has not received quality instruction preparing them for grade 4 and beyond, instructional supports should be provided immediately, for as long as it takes the student to attain grade-level literacy.
2. Teacher quality is the number-one predictor of a student's success, and teachers' impact is additive and cumulative.
3. Nominal changes are only the first step: improper or poorly enforced policies and systems will not produce the desired outcome of improving students' attainment of language skills.

However, faithful implementation of data-validated teaching methods and intervention systems will make a significant difference in the success of schools and their students.

Goals of instruction:

1. For all teachers to demonstrate mastery of the skills needed to teach foundational and/or content-area reading and writing literacy.
2. To ensure that the state boards of education give their districts and schools the capacity to meet the requirements of the Common Core State Standards and the literacy law, through the provision of information, training, and resources.

How schools, school districts, and state and local education agencies achieve these goals:

1. All pre-K-third-grade teachers, along with all professionals in higher grades who teach reading instruction, English language learning instruction, Title I student instruction, or special-education instruction, will be required to pass the advanced reading instruction competence assessment in order to become a certified teacher of reading. All content-area teachers in grades 4 and up will be required to pass the basic reading instruction competence assessment.
2. Each state should provide funding for an "implementation infrastructure" in order to ensure that districts and schools have the resources and the knowledge capacity to improve student learning outcomes in accordance with the Common Core State Standards and the literacy law.
3. Each state should create a state literacy implementation team of two or more people to ensure that core features of the literacy law are put into practice.

Key Points:

The literacy law requires a school culture that values shared responsibility and teacher inclusion in data-based decision making so that all teachers have the capacity and support to be successful in ensuring that their students become proficient readers with the knowledge and skills to achieve the Standards.

Such outcomes are guaranteed by a combination of meaningful teacher certification or credentialing and faithful implementation of system policies and procedures.

Key Components
For The Implementation Of The Literacy Law

If teachers and school leaders are to have the capacity to ensure foundational literacy skills for all students, they should first have the support of local government in implementing the literacy law. This will be essential in achieving the Common Core State Standards.

The Scientific Principle:

Students should be consistently exposed to a sequenced progression of proven instructional methods. Reading literacy is a process, and the implementation of the law should therefore take place throughout a state or district and at each grade level, especially in the early grades when students are first learning to read. Likewise, system supports for struggling learners should be faithfully implemented and used to full effect.

The Progression:

To ensure implementation fidelity at all levels, teachers should follow credentialing or certification requirements; school districts should conduct screening and assessment to identify SEEDS students and provide adequate supports; and states should create an implementation infrastructure.

Teaching candidates pass either the advanced reading instruction competence assessment (to become a certified teacher of reading) or the basic reading instruction competence assessment (to become a content-area teacher).

School districts provide their administrators, staff, and parents with the necessary information regarding identification and instruction of students at risk for literacy failure

States rely on an implementation team to monitor the preparation of teaching candidates, the training of preparation program personnel, and the removal of systemic barriers to faithful implementation of the law.

The Key Components:

Reading Instruction Competence Assessments

The following professionals should pass the advanced reading instruction competence assessment to become a certified teacher of reading: those who
1. Teach classroom foundational reading instruction to all students in grades pre-K-3
2. Teach in elementary, middle, and high schools in any position that specializes in reading instruction
3. Specialize in English language learners instruction, Title I student instruction, or special-education instruction
All professionals who teach "content areas" should pass the basic reading instruction competence assessment for skill in teaching reading and writing literacy in their subject.

State Responsibilities

While significant implementation responsibility of effective instruction resides at district and school levels, the state should take responsibility for ensuring that district and school personnel have:		
1. Clear knowledge of system policies and procedures needed for implementation of the law		
2. Training and coaching for ensuring implementation fidelity of core features of effective literacy instruction		
A. Universal screening and progress monitoring	B. Multi-Tier System of Supports	C. Instruction designed to ensure that all students (especially SEEDS) attain grade-level reading proficiency

3. Systems in place for supporting data-based decisions to ensure each student's reading literacy attainment
4. Knowledge and understanding of systems change needed to ensure implementation fidelity of core features, especially those related to MTSS
5. Training and coaching for facilitating administrative support of effective instruction and purposeful implementation of core features

Guidelines and Standards for Implementation

To ensure that each school and charter school within a district follows all aspects of literacy law, the state will provide funding to build an implementation infrastructure, which will make available the appropriate and sufficient resources for state and local implementation capacity. The state will also create a literacy implementation team of two or more people, which will

1. Identify and define the state's core features of the literacy law

2. Provide training for state, regional, and local implementation teams to build implementation capacity for program and school administrators, to include the following core components of implementation science:

A. selection	B. training	C. coaching
D. evaluation of program fidelity	E. systems intervention	
F. facilitative administration	G. data systems to support decision-making	

3. Provide preservice and professional development training to all content-area teachers and teachers of reading, giving them the skills and knowledge to pass the basic or advanced reading instruction competence teaching assessment, identify student needs, and monitor student progress

4. Develop a system of oversight of teacher preparation programs in order to align such programs with state certification exams

5. Provide training for teacher preparation personnel in order to ensure the success of teaching candidates in passing state certification exams

6. Develop a communication protocol to help align policies and systems and to remove barriers to effective implementation of the core features of the law

The law provides that each school district, school, and charter school will
1. Provide parents, teachers, school administrators, staff, and all interested parties with public notice regarding the system's obligations toward all students (specifically SEEDS) who exhibit potential for literacy failure
2. Give notice of the school system's specific implementation plan
3. Ensure that teachers and administrators are aware of the state regulations regarding the following:

A. Literacy failure	B. Characteristics of SEEDS	C. State licensure requirements of teachers	D. Credentialing of teachers of reading in kindergarten, elementary, secondary, and special education	E. School system's policies for implementation of the law

4. Create district- and school-level implementation teams to ensure that		
A. Teachers and principals have the capacity to implement core features of the law	B. Systems are aligned to support implementation of the law	C. Barriers to effective implementation are removed so that all SEEDS attain grade-level reading proficiency by the end of third grade

4. Implement a program of universal screening for K-1 students
5. Implement a program of assessment for all pre-K-3 students and those displaying characteristics of SEEDS
6. Provide tier I instruction through a data-validated and evidence-based foundational reading development instruction program
7. Provide tier II of MTSS within thirty days of screening assessment if a SEEDS is identified
8. Provide tier III of MTSS within ten days of tier II instruction if the SEEDS student does not make adequate progress
9. Initiate referral for special education to SEEDS who have not responded to MTSS in regular education, under the timelines specified under state law

CINTHIA COLETTI

10. Initiate procedures for evaluation of eligibility under §504/ADAAA if the student is not eligible for special education	
11. Initiate procedures to implement the Standards for	
A. Reading and writing literacy	B. Speaking, listening, and language skills

Road Map for Educators and Specifics for State Handbook For The Implementation Of The Literacy Law

> Since sound and effective implementation requires change at the practice, organization, and systems level, processes should be purposeful to create change in the knowledge, behavior, and attitudes of all the human service professionals and partners involved.
>
> —Blasé, Van Dyke, and Fixsen, 2010

In order for teachers and school leaders to have the capacity to ensure that all students have the foundational literacy skills to achieve the Standards, the literacy law requires that state (SEA) and local education agencies (LEA) support purposeful implementation of the law.

The literacy law requires the state to ensure that all professionals who (1) teach classroom foundational reading instruction to all students in grades pre-K-3 and (2) teach in elementary, middle school, and high school in any position that specializes in reading instruction, English language learners instruction, Title I student instruction, and special-education instruction pass the advanced reading instruction competence assessment and become a certified teacher of reading. In addition, those professionals who (3) teach "content areas" are required to pass the basic reading instruction competence assessment for skill in teaching reading and writing literacy in their subject.

While significant implementation responsibility of effective instruction resides at district and school levels, the state should take responsibility for ensuring that district and school personnel have the following resources available to them: (1) clear knowledge of system policies and procedures needed for implementation of the law. (2) Training and coaching for ensuring implementation fidelity of core features of effective literacy instruction, including universal screening and progress monitoring, Multi-Tier System of Supports, and instruction designed to allow all students, especially SEEDS students, to attain grade-level reading proficiency. (3) Systems in place for supporting data-based decisions to ensure each student's reading literacy attainment. (4) Knowledge and understanding of systems change needed to ensure implementation fidelity of core features, especially those related to Multi-Tier System of Supports. (5) Training and coaching for facilitating administrative support of effective instruction and purposeful implementation of core features.

The literacy law requires a school culture that values shared responsibility and teacher inclusion in data-based decision-making, with the goal that all teachers have the capacity and support to be successful in ensuring that their students become proficient readers with the knowledge and skills to achieve the Standards. The literacy law requires that SEAs and LEAs develop a communication protocol to help align systems for and remove barriers to effective implementation of the core features of the law.

MODEL STATE LEGISLATION LANGUAGE FOR THE IMPLEMENTATION OF THE LITERACY LAW

Guidelines and Standards For the Implementation of the Law

§8 State Implementation Infrastructure; District and School Access to Policy Information, Training and Coaching, and System Supports; Teacher Certification and Credentialing

BE IT ENACTED BY THE LEGISLATURE OF THE STATE OF [insert state name] that the [insert the name of state board of education] is ultimately responsible for ensuring that each school district, schools within each district, and each charter school follows each and all aspects of this law. To that end, the state of [insert state name] shall provide funding to build an implementation infrastructure to ensure that appropriate and sufficient resources are made available to build state and local capacity to meet the requirements of this law. To that end, the state of [insert state name] shall create a state literacy implementation team consisting of at least two people to ensure that core features of the literacy law are put into practice. This team will:

A. Identify and define core features of the law including [insert state's] core features (e.g., teacher licensing requirements, use of Multi-Tier System of Supports, use of data-validated instruction).
B. Provide training for state, regional, and local implementation teams to build implementation capacity for program and school administrators that will include core components of implementation science including: selection, training, coaching, program fidelity and evaluation, systems intervention, facilitative administration, and data systems to support decision-making;
C. Provide preservice and professional development training so that all content-areas teachers and teachers of reading have the skills and knowledge to pass the [insert name of state] basic and/or advanced reading instruction competence teaching assessment, are knowledgeable about and can effectively implement appropriate instruction to meet the needs of all students, and have the knowledge and skills to monitor student progress toward attainment of literacy skills;
D. Develop a system of oversight of teacher preparation programs in order to align such programs with state certification exams;
E. Provide training for teacher preparation personnel in order to build capacity for ensuring that teacher candidates have the knowledge and skills needed to pass state certification exams; and
F. Develop a communication protocol to help align policies and systems and to remove barriers to effective implementation of the core features of the law.

The law, along with a state plan for building implementation capacity, will be readily available to the public through the [insert the name of state board of education] website [insert the web address (URL) of the state board of education], in print, and through an interpreter. Additionally, this law provides that each school district, school, and charter school shall

A. Provide to parents, teachers, school administrators, staff, and all interested parties public notice regarding the school system's specific implementation plan, in addition to the system's obligations toward all students, specifically SEEDS, exhibiting potential for literacy failure;

B. Ensure that teachers and administrators are aware of the state regulations regarding literacy failure; the characteristics of SEEDS; the state licensure requirements of teachers and credentialing of teachers of reading in kindergarten, elementary, secondary, and special education; and the school system's policies for implementation of the law;

C. Create district- and school-level implementation teams to ensure that teachers and principals have the capacity to implement core features of the law, systems are aligned to support implementation of the law, and barriers to effective implementation are removed so that all SEEDS attain grade-level proficiency in reading by the end of third grade;

D. Implement a program for universal screening for K-1 students, [insert state name] Statute, Section 3 of this law, and assessment for all grade pre-K-3 students and those students displaying characteristics of SEEDS;

E. Provide tier I instruction through a data-validated and evidence-based foundational reading instruction program;

F. Provide tier II of the MTSS, [insert state name] Statute, Section 5.0 of this law, within thirty days of screening or assessment if a SEEDS is found;

G. Provide tier III of the MTSS within ten days of tier II instruction should the SEEDS student not make adequate progress, [insert state name] Statute, Section 5.0 of this law;

H. Provide tier III of the MTSS within ten days of tier II instruction should the SEEDS student not make adequate progress, [insert state name] Statute, Section 5.0 of this law;

I. Initiate referral for special education under timelines specified under state law to SEEDS who have not responded to MTSS in regular education, [insert state name] Statute, Section 3.9 of this law;

J. Initiate procedures for evaluation of eligibility under §504/ADAAA if the student is not found to be eligible for special education; and

K. Initiate procedures to implement the Standards for reading and writing literacy and for speaking, listening, and language skills.

EFFECTIVE DATE. This section is effective [insert date].

COMPLIANCE WITH THE LITERACY POLICY

WITHOUT STRINGENT COMPLIANCE and consequence, Policy is neither an authoritative resource nor does it have the authority to hold individuals' and/or bureaucracies accountable for fulfilling its statutes. Therefore, to ratify either Literacy Policy without both monitoring compliance and assigning consequences would be a futile effort. The state's desire to accomplish the goals of significantly raising the floor of the current educational rankings and of providing its young people with a world-class education will not occur without strict adherence to the Literacy Policy and compliance with implementation fidelity.

The state must require that every college and university teacher preparation program, every school district, school, all personnel, and every teacher conform with Policy. It is up to the state's stewards, voted into office by its citizens, to take a leadership role in accordance with the guidelines and specification of each statute within this Policy. The reward will be that the chances are greatly increased for every student to achieve academic success and graduate from high school prepared for college and employment, equipped with the skills necessary for happiness, success, career, and lifetime learning.

Enacting this Literacy Policy requires an ethical code within the vocation of legislators, educators and citizens for both the good of the states' students and its future workforce. It is important to keep in mind that with strong legal compliance and governance in place, efficacy of the Policy's implementations can and will be accurately assessed by virtue of each student's achievement and the monitoring of legal compliance will be carried out successfully.

MODEL STATE LEGISLATION LANGUAGE FOR THE COMPLIANCE OF THE LITERACY POLICY

Section §9

Compliance

GUIDELINES FOR COMPLIANCE WITH THE POLICY

BE IT ENACTED BY THE LEGISLATURE OF THE STATE OF [insert state name] that the [insert the name of the state board of education] and school district, school, or governing body of an open-enrollment charter school, have equal responsibility for ensuring that each school complies with all applicable requirements of state Literacy Policy.

§9.1 Documentation

The intent of this recommended documentation is to ensure that a district, school, or charter school meets the needs of students and protects the rights of students and parents or guardians. The districts, schools, and charter schools will document the following in writing:

A. Documentation that the notice of evaluation has been given to parents or guardians;

B. Documentation that parents or guardians were given an explanation of their rights and provided a copy of the state Policy and IDEA 2004;

C. Documentation of the parent or guardian's consent for the evaluation;

D. Documentation of the evaluation data;

E. Documentation of the decisions made by the committee of knowledgeable persons concerning the disability, [insert state name] Statute, Sections 3.8-9, of this Policy, and if a disability exists, whether the disability substantially limits a major life activity; and

F. Documentation of the placement options and placement decisions, [insert state name] Statute, Sections 4 and 5 of this Policy.

§9.2 Procedures

Checklist of procedures to ensure compliance:

A. Notification to parents or guardians requesting permission to assess student for assessment or formal diagnostic;
B. Copy of state Literacy Policy and IDEA 2004 to be provided to the parents or guardians; and
C. Formal notification from the school district to inform and notify the teachers and parents or guardians of results from each measure or assessment administered to the student:
   1. List each measurement or assessment and describe the meaning and function of the measurement;
   2. Include identification, if one is determined, by the committee according to [insert state name] Statute, Section 3.8 of this Policy;
   3. Describe the next steps of the remediation and instruction process for the student, [insert state name] Statute, Section 5.0 of this Policy;
   4. Provide a timeline for remediation, future assessment dates, and procedure for progress reporting;
   5. Provide access to the ongoing data collected on the student; and
   6. Provide date for the next meeting with the parents or guardians and the school and teacher.

§9.3 Funding Implementation

It is the intention of the legislature that the costs relative to the implementation of the provisions of this Policy shall be covered by funds appropriated by the state. Such funds shall include those appropriated pursuant to [insert name of state education approved budget]. It is also supported by research that if the state is able to provide free and quality instruction to its young people, they will become graduates capable of contributing to the state's revenues. This is a payback that has been projected at $_____ [information can be found on the National Center for Education Statistics (NCES) site].

§9.4 Compliance/Funding Consequences

Requires the district or school to prepare a corrective action plan or improvement plan if the secretary of education determines that the district or school fails to comply with legislation. In the event of failure to comply with legislation, the state [insert secretary of education office name] (Secretary) may take the following actions:

A. District or school needs intervention assistance if the [insert secretary of education office name] determines, for two consecutive years, that there has been no improvement in AYP and the district or school needs assistance in implementing the requirements of this Policy, the Secretary takes one or more of the following actions:
   1. Places the entire entity on probation and posts this action for public awareness. Advises the district or school of available sources of technical assistance that may help address the areas in which the entity needs assistance, which may include assistance from the Office of Special Education Programs, other offices of the Department of Education, other federal agencies, technical assistance providers approved by the Secretary, and other federally funded nonprofit agencies, and requires the district, school, or charter school to work with appropriate entities. Such technical assistance may include
      a. Making provisions for advice by experts to address the areas in which the district or school needs assistance, including explicit plans for addressing the area for concern within a specified period of time;
      b. Assisting in identifying and implementing professional development, instructional strategies, and methods of instruction that are based on scientifically based research;
      c. Designating and using distinguished superintendents, principals, special-education administrators, special-education teachers, and other teachers to provide advice, technical assistance, and support; and

      d.   Devising additional approaches to providing technical assistance, such as collaborating with institutions of higher education, educational service agencies, national centers of technical assistance, and private providers of scientifically based technical assistance.

      e.   The entity will provide a plan of action and a timeline on all improvement strategies and a commitment to adhere to the Policy.

  2. Directs the use of funds from district or school on the area or areas in which school needs assistance to professional organization to prepare plan, evaluate data and provide recommendations;

  3. Identifies the district or school as a high-risk grantee and imposes special conditions on the grant; and

  4. Uses authority to replace the leadership at the school and apply criminal charges for breaking the Policy.

B. District or school needs intervention; the Secretary takes one or more of the following actions if the Secretary determines, for three or more consecutive years, that a district, school, or charter school needs intervention in implementing the requirements of this Policy, the following shall apply:

  1. The Secretary may take any of the actions described in Section 8.4.A.1.

  2. The Secretary takes following actions by changing the district or school-based leadership and teaching staff to correct the problem within one year by showing marked improvement 25 percent or more with compliance by the second year.

C. For each year of the determination, withholds not less than 20 percent and not more than 50 percent of the district or school funds until the Secretary determines by use of data that the district or school has sufficiently addressed the areas in which intervention is needed.

D. Seeks to recover funds:

  1. Withholds, in whole or in part, any further payments to the district or school;

  2. Needs substantial intervention. At any time that the Secretary determines that a district or school needs substantial intervention in implementing the requirements

of the Policy or that there is a substantial failure to comply with any condition, the Secretary takes one or more of the following actions:

a. Recovers funds

b. Withholds, in whole or in part, any further payments.

3. Refers the case to the Office of the Inspector General at the state [insert name state board].

EFFECTIVE DATE. This section is effective [insert date].

GENERAL PROVISIONS
OF LITERACY LAW

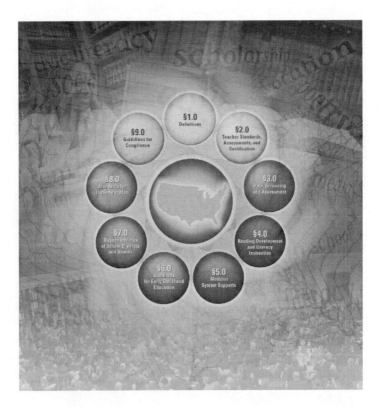

GENERAL PROVISIONS OF LITERACY POLICY

STATE LITERACY LAW

BE IT ENACTED BY THE LEGISLATOR OF THE STATE OF [insert state name] ON [insert date] THE LITERACY LAW. The Law warrants literacy proficiency for all students in the state of [insert name] and hereby requires that each college and university school of education, school district, school, local school board and local education agency provide in general education all component of literacy science to include teacher preparation, development and certification, classroom foundational reading development and reading literacy instruction, use of data to inform instruction that includes screening, assessments, strategies, and Multi-Tier System of Supports to achieve reading and writing literacy for all students.

[Insert state name] Literacy Law is hereby enacted in the following:

§1.0 Definitions;

1.1. Reading Development
1.2. Reading Literacy
1.3. Writing Literacy
1.4. Full Literacy
1.5. SEEDS Community of Students
1.6. Economically Disadvantaged Youngsters
1.7. English Language Learners (ELL) and/or Students with Limited English Proficiency (LEP)
1.8. Dyslexia
1.9. Specific Learning Disabilities
1.10. Teachers of Reading
1.11. Teaching Specialist
1.12. Content-area Teachers
1.13. Specific Language Impairment

§2.0 Standards, Certification, and Assessment for Teachers of Reading, Teaching Specialists, and Content-Area Teachers on Their Preparation, Professional Development, Knowledge and Skill;

2.1. All Education Professionals, Teachers of Reading, and Support Personnel Qualifications

§5.0 Multi-Tier System of Supports in General-Education Classrooms (MTSS);

§6.0 Guidelines for Early Childhood Education

§7.0 Responsibilities of School Districts and Boards;

§8.0 Guidelines and Standards for the Implementation of the Policy; and

§9.0 Guidelines for Compliance with the Policy

Section §1 Definitions

1.1 **Reading development** involves a progression of skills that begins with the ability to understand spoken words and culminates in the deep understanding of text. Reading development involves a range of complex language underpinnings including awareness of speech sounds (phonology), spelling patterns (orthography), word meaning (semantics), grammar (syntax) and patterns of word formation (morphology), all of which provide a necessary platform for reading fluency and comprehension. Attaining English literacy depends on the successful acquisition of these skills.

1.2 **Reading literacy** represents the lifelong, intellectual process of gaining meaning from print. It includes the ability to approach printed material with critical analysis, inference, and synthesis; to write with accuracy and coherence; and to use information and insights from text as the basis for informed decisions and creative thought. Reading literacy is a term that has evolved over time with changes in our society, economy, and culture. It goes beyond the development of reading's active and interactive skills and beyond comprehension of rich text. Reading literacy implies that there is a capacity for reflection on written material that initiates personal experiences as well as cognitive function. It moves from the schoolroom to the workplace, to citizenship, to lifelong learning. It affords the reader a set of linguistic tools that are increasingly important in modern society, from communication with peers and communities to interactions with large bureaucracies and complex legal systems. To attain reading literacy, individuals must be taught to utilize a wide range of reading and literacy skills that will develop into subject matter literacy—such as science or math literacy, and eventually into vocational literacy. Reading literacy is the foundation from which readers seek, use, and understand all textual matter; it unleashes the potential to enrich and extend one's personal life, and empowers one to participate fully in society.

1.3 **Writing literacy** is a term that has evolved and increased with the demands of a text-driven society. It has multiple components of discipline that reflect requirements to accurately write informative and explanatory texts. Writing literacy affords opportunity to convey ideas, concepts, and information clearly and accurately through the effective selection, organization, and analysis of content. Writing literacy implies that there is capacity for writing narratives to develop real or imagined experiences or events using effective technique, well-chosen details, and well-structured event sequences.

1.4 **Full literacy** is the ability to identify, understand, interpret, create, communicate, and compute using language and printed, written, and digital materials associated with varying contexts. Full literacy involves a continuum of learning in enabling individuals to achieve their goals, to develop their knowledge and potential, and to participate fully in their community and wider society.

1.5 **SEEDS** is an acronym (noun) that represents a community of students not performing at grade-level reading proficiency due to weak or improper instruction and lack of school supports. A term positive in its vision that is both inclusive and specific of a community of students who make up 67 percent of the student population according to National Assessment of Education Progress. The SEEDS community includes **S**truggling learners and readers encompassing *all* groups in society, **E**conomically disadvantaged youngsters, **E**nglish language learners, and students with **D**yslexia, **S**pecific learning disabilities and language impairment. Members of the **SEEDS** community are capable of achieving academic and lifelong success with multitier systems of reading literacy supports.

1.6 **Economically disadvantaged youngsters** are the students who often enter school significantly behind and less prepared than their more well-to-do peers. Their academic disadvantage is witnessed in everything from impoverished language input in early childhood (letter awareness and spoken vocabulary) to number awareness and self-control. If they are victims of poor quality or inappropriate reading instruction, these students can be even further behind their peers in language skills by the middle of second grade. Students in this category will require Multi-Tier System of Supports appropriate to their literacy needs beginning in pre-K through third grade. Many of these students are "Title I Eligible" and receive "Free and/or Reduced Lunch," meaning the federal Elementary and Secondary Act provide financial assistance to local educational agencies and schools with high numbers or high percentages of children from low-income families to help ensure that all children meet challenging state academic standards.

1.7   **English language learners (ELL) and/or students with limited English proficiency (LEP)** are students who have recently come to the United States from another country, have parents that speak a foreign language in their homes, or are older students of poor instruction often due to cultural-linguistic perception differences. ELL and LEP students are becoming the majority minority in many public schools. With more immigrants having arrived in the United States during the 1990s than any other single decade, the number of public school students in need of additional language instruction has increased dramatically in recent years (Bureau of US Citizenship and Immigration Services, 2001). A survey of state education agencies found that, in 2004, more than 5.5 million students with limited proficiency in English were enrolled in public schools across the nation, making up almost 10 percent of the total K-twelfth grade public school enrollment. The population of students who are ELL has grown 105 percent, while the general school population has grown only 12 percent since the 1990-91 school year. States report more than 460 languages spoken by students with limited proficiency in English (Kindler, 2002) with 80 percent of the students speaking Spanish. These burgeoning numbers pose unique challenges for educators striving to ensure that language-minority students achieve to high levels. Achievement data suggest that students with LEP lag far behind their peers. Nationwide, only 7 percent of these students scored "at or above proficient" in reading on the National Assessment of Educational Progress, compared to about 33 percent of students overall. Results in fourth-grade math, as well as eighth-grade reading and math, were similar. Findings support that limited oral language proficiency does not constrain a student's emergent reading and writing development. Limited English language students are capable of making sense of written input while they are working on becoming fluent speakers of English. This research orientation maintains that just as speaking, reading, and writing are interrelated in the emerging literacy of native speakers, they are equally related in the emerging literacy of second-language students.

1.8 **Dyslexia** is neurobiological in origin. It is characterized by difficulties with accurate or fluent word recognition and by poor spelling and decoding abilities. These difficulties typically result from a deficit in the phonological component of language that is often unexpected in relation to other cognitive abilities and the provision of effective classroom instruction. Secondary consequences may include problems in reading comprehension and reduced reading experience that can impede the growth of vocabulary and background knowledge (National Institutes of Child Health and Human Development [NICHD] and the International Dyslexia Association). Dyslexia is usually characterized by early difficulties with accurate or fluent word recognition and poor spelling, and by later difficulties with text-level fluency, leading to problems with written comprehension and sometimes writing. Students with dyslexia represent a continuum of underlying difficulties, typically beginning with weaknesses in the phonological component of language and in the speed of processing multiple, language-related components of reading. These difficulties can be found singly or, more typically, together. It is important to note that they are largely unexpected in relation to other, often-strong cognitive abilities in the student and the provision of otherwise effective instruction. Some students who have both decoding and fluency issues and who receive effective decoding instruction go on to have only fluency-based issues that affect comprehension and the quality of their reading and how much they read. Whatever the pathway, reduced reading can impede the growth of all language capacities, particularly vocabulary and grammar, which then can impede the development of background knowledge necessary for advances in learning. Further characteristics of students with dyslexia are often witnessed in rote math calculations, speech, word retrieval, and processing speed. Appropriate interventions can change the course of these students' academic careers. Dyslexia and specific learning disabilities represent approximately one-third of all literacy failure groups and may require intensive, appropriately matched intervention as early as possible. Kindergarten screening most often will identify these students early, so foundational reading instruction and systems of support can lead to good reading skills through life.

1.9 **Specific learning disability,** as defined by the Individuals with Disabilities Education Act of 2004, is a disorder in one or more of the basic psychological processes involved in understanding or using language, spoken or written, that may manifest itself in difficulty with listening, thinking, speaking, reading, writing, spelling, or doing mathematical calculations, and conditions such as perceptual disabilities, brain injury, minimal brain dysfunction, dyslexia, and developmental aphasia. Specific learning disability does not include learning problems or intellectual disabilities that create limitations in mental functioning that are mostly dealt with in special-education environments and are primarily the result of visual, hearing, or motor disabilities, mental retardation, or emotional disturbance. Specific learning disabilities can include metacognitive strategy development and self-regulation such as those with attention deficit and hyperactivity disorders and those with dysgraphia, both of whom display written expression problems. Research provides six clear classifications of learning disabilities: word reading (dyslexia), reading fluency, reading comprehension, written expression, mathematics calculation (dyscalculia), and mathematics problem solving. Each of these disabilities has a distinct cognitive correlate for which there is specific evidence-based intervention.

1.10 **Teachers of reading** are defined as educational professionals who have mastered the foundations of reading development and the use of formative data analysis to direct individual instruction that is required for teaching diverse student populations to read in grades K-3. Certified teachers of reading are essential to every student's academic foundation. They have received high-quality teacher preparation, professional development, advancement, and certification that warrants he or she has mastered the complexity of teaching reading, reading and writing literacy, speaking, listening, and language skills to all students. Teachers of reading will have passed the state's *advanced* reading instruction competence assessment, earning certification and demonstrating expertise in all aspects of reading literacy instruction; data analysis, interpretation, use, screening, monitoring, assessments, and strategies; and the Multi-Tier System of Supports necessary for all students to achieve grade-level reading literacy on or before third grade.

1.11 **Teaching specialists** (also known as literacy coaches, reading specialists, literacy specialists, and learning specialists) are teachers in elementary, middle school, and high school who specialize in reading/literacy instruction, English language learner instruction, Title I student instruction, and special-education instruction. Reading specialists, along with K-3 teachers of reading, are also certified, as teachers of reading, passing the advanced reading instruction competence assessment. Teachers with a certificate are considered to be advanced and highly important as a group of teachers within a school because they teach the foundational skills necessary for all educational attainment. Passing the advanced reading instruction competence assessment requires a solid knowledge base of a skilled expert in all aspects of reading instruction, data analysis and interpretation, screening, assessments, strategies, Multi-Tier System of Supports and interventions for all students to achieve grade-level reading literacy proficiency.

1.12 **Content-area teachers** are teachers of subject matter required in the state curricula and across curricula. Every teacher, regardless of content, is a reading and writing teacher because both are involved in every subject area. Reading and writing strategies and instruction should be implemented in all teacher preparation programs, professional development, and as a school-wide program in connection with school culture and vision that works toward high levels of student achievement in reading literacy. All requirements of the Literacy Policy and Standards highlight that all teachers and schools will provide every opportunity for students to read and practice their strategies in every subject, every day, to enhance their development of the literacy skills that are needed to become better readers and writers, and, ultimately, reading and writing literate.

1.13 **Specific language impairment** (SLI) is characterized by difficulty with language that is not caused by known neurological, sensory, intellectual, or emotional deficit. It can affect the development of vocabulary, grammar, and discourse skills, with evidence that certain morphemes may be especially difficult to acquire (including past tense, copula be, third person singular). Children with SLI may be intelligent and healthy in all regards except in the difficulty they have with language. They may in fact be extraordinarily bright and have high nonverbal IQs.

Section §2

Literacy Law for Teacher Preparation, Professional Development, and Advancement Programs

1. Teaching complex data-validated reading development and reading and writing literacy strategies to a diverse student population;
2. Screening, assessment, and data instruments to direct and advance student literacy skills;
3. Foundational reading instruction in the classroom that is data-validated;
4. SEEDS community reading instruction in general education;
5. Multi-Tier System of Supports and classroom implementation strategies; and
6. Student accommodations to assess knowledge attainment.

As a part of effective methods for achieving student reading literacy, these educational goals should be achieved by designing and implementing ongoing, quality instruction for teaching candidates, and quality professional development and advancement, or remedial support for all in-service teachers: K-3 grade teachers of reading, reading specialists, and content-area teachers.

§2.1. New Qualifications, Licenses, and Certifications for All Education Professionals

The state must issue licenses and certain certification(s) under its jurisdiction to persons qualified and competent for their respective positions in education.

A. The board requires a teaching candidate to successfully complete a basic reading instruction competence teaching assessment before being granted an initial teaching license to teach content areas in grades 4-12 to any and all pupils.

B. The board must require a teaching candidate to successfully complete an advanced reading instruction competence teaching assessment to receive a teacher of reading certification before being granted approval to provide instruction to any students in K-3 grades, for all Reading Specialists in elementary and secondary schools, and teachers in ELL, Title I, and special-education programs.

C. The board must require colleges and universities offering a board-approved teacher preparation program to provide remedial assistance, including a formal diagnostic component, to teaching candidates who wish to become K-3 classroom teachers and teaching specialist grades K-12, to persons enrolled in their institution who did not achieve a qualifying score on the advanced reading instruction competence teaching assessment to earn a teacher of reading certificate, and including those for whom English is a second language.

D. The colleges and universities must provide assistance in the specific academic areas of deficiency in which the person did not achieve a qualifying score.

E. Districts and schools must provide similar, appropriate, and timely remedial assistance that includes a formal diagnostic component and mentoring to those persons employed by the district/school who completed their teacher education program both in and outside the state, received a one-year license to teach in the state, and did not achieve a qualifying score on the advanced reading instruction competence teaching assessment to earn a certification, including those persons for whom English is a second language.

F. Districts and schools, shall report annually to the state on: the total number of teacher candidates during the most recent school year taking the basic reading instruction competence teaching assessment, and the teacher of reading/teaching specialists taking the advanced reading instruction competence teaching assessment; the number who achieve a qualifying score on the examination(s); the number who do not achieve a qualifying score on the examination(s); the distribution of all candidates' scores; the number of candidates who have taken the examination(s) at least once before; and the number of candidates who have taken the examination(s) at least once before and achieved a qualifying score.

G. A person who has completed an approved teacher preparation program and obtained a one-year license to teach, but has not successfully completed the skills basic reading instruction competence teaching assessment or the teacher of reading/ teaching specialists advanced reading instruction competence teaching assessment may renew the license for additional one-year periods, contingent upon the licensee

    1. Providing evidence of participating in an approved remedial assistance program provided by a school district or postsecondary institution that includes a formal diagnostic component in the specific areas in which the licensee did not obtain qualifying scores; and

    2. Attempting to successfully complete the skills reading instruction competence teaching assessment (s) during the period of the one-year extended license.

H. The state will grant continuing licenses only to those persons who have met board criteria for granting a continuing license, which includes successfully completing the basic reading instruction competence teaching assessment in reading, writing, and mathematics and, for teachers of reading, the teachers of reading certification as witnessed successfully passing the advanced reading instruction competence teaching assessment.

I. All colleges and universities approved by the state to prepare persons for teacher licensure must include in their teacher preparation programs a common core of teaching knowledge and skills to be acquired by all persons recommended for

CINTHIA COLETTI

teacher licensure. These common core standards shall meet the standards developed by the National Governors Association model standards for beginning teacher licensing and development.

J. Districts and schools shall report annually to the state on the performance of teacher candidates: For teachers of reading report on student reading achievement; for content teachers, report on common core assessments of knowledge and skills under this paragraph during the most recent school year.

§2.2 Requirements for All College and University Teacher Preparation Programs

Reading and writing literacy strategies at all colleges and universities to prepare persons for content-area classroom teacher licensure must be approved by the state and include research-based best practices in reading and writing, consistent with Statutes, Section 4.0 of this law, that enable the licensure candidate to know how to teach reading and writing literacy in the candidate's content areas and prepare the licensure candidate for the basic reading instruction teaching assessment.

Teachers of reading preparation for grade K-3 teachers and Title I, special education, ELL, and teaching specialist grades K-12 will implement instruction in research-based, best practices in reading and writing development, consistent with Statutes, Section 4.0 of this law, that enable the candidate to know how to teach reading, writing, speaking, listening, and language to each student using foundational knowledge, practices, and strategies so that all students will achieve continuous progress. To become a certified teacher of reading teachers and specialists will pass the advanced reading instruction teaching assessment through the implementation of

A. Board-approved teacher preparation programs for certifying teachers of reading in K-3 grade education. The program will require instruction in the application of comprehensive, foundational reading and instruction programs from Statutes, Section 4.0 of this law to include a program or collection of instructional practices that is based on valid, replicated evidence showing that when these programs or practices are used, diverse student populations can be expected to achieve, at a minimum, literacy and satisfactory reading progress.

The program or collection of practices for teachers of reading must include, at a minimum, instruction in ten areas of foundational reading instruction (Statutes, Section 4.0.A of this law), to include foundation concepts about oral and written language learning; knowledge of the structure of language; knowledge of SEEDS community and learning disorders; interpretation and administration of assessments for planning instruction; and structured language teaching of phonology, phonics, and word study, fluent automatic reading of text, vocabulary, text comprehension, and handwriting, spelling, and written expression. All certified teachers of reading must be effectively prepared and proficient in the following areas:

1. Foundational concepts about oral and written language learning that includes
   a. understanding and explaining the language processing requirements of proficient reading and writing, including phonological (speech sound) processing, orthographic (print) processing, semantic (meaning) processing, syntactic (sentence level) processing, and discourse (connected text level) processing,
   b. understanding and explaining other aspects of cognition and behavior that affect reading and writing, including attention, executive function, memory, processing speed, and graphomotor control,
   c. defining and identifying environmental, cultural, and social factors that contribute to literacy development, including language spoken at home, language and literacy experiences, and cultural values,
   d. knowing and identifying phases in the typical developmental progression of oral language (semantic, syntactic, and pragmatic), phonological skill, printed word recognition, spelling, reading fluency, reading comprehension, and written expression,
   e. understanding and explaining the known causal relationships among phonological skill, phonic decoding, spelling, accurate and automatic word recognition, text reading fluency, background

knowledge, verbal reasoning skill, vocabulary, reading comprehension, and writing,

f. knowing and explaining how the relationships among the major components of literacy development change with reading development (i.e., changes in oral language, including phonological awareness, phonics and word recognition, spelling, reading and writing fluency, vocabulary, reading comprehension skills and strategies, and written expression),

g. knowing reasonable goals and expectations for learners at various stages of reading and writing development, and

h. understanding first and second language acquisition stages, the impact of culture on student performance, knowledge regarding bilingual education and English as a second language programming and teaching methods, knowledge of how to interpret results of students' oral language proficiency in relation to the results of tests measuring academic achievement and cognitive processes, and understanding how to interpret results of similar or parallel tests given in more than one language.

2. Knowledge of the structure of language includes

a. phonology (the sound system), including how to identify, pronounce, classify, and compare the consonant and vowel phonemes of English,

b. orthography (the spelling system), including understanding the broad outline of historical influences on English spelling patterns, especially Anglo-Saxon, Latin (Romance), and Greek; defining "grapheme" as a functional correspondence unit or representation of a phoneme; recognizing and explaining common orthographic rules and patterns in English; knowing the difference between high frequency and irregular words; and identifying, explaining, and categorizing six basic syllable types in English spelling,

c. morphology, including identifying and categorizing common morphemes in English, for example,

Anglo-Saxon compounds, inflectional and derivational suffixes, Latin-based prefixes, roots, and derivational suffixes, and Greek-based combining forms,

d. semantics, including understanding and identifying examples of meaningful word relationships or semantic organization,

e. syntax, including defining and distinguishing among phrases, dependent clauses, and independent clauses in sentence structures; and identifying the parts of speech and the grammatical role of a word in a sentence, and

f. discourse organization, including explaining the major differences between narrative and expository discourse; identifying and constructing expository paragraphs of varying logical structures (e.g., classification, reason, sequence); and identifying cohesive devices in text and inferential gaps in the surface language of text.

3. Knowledge of SEEDS community and learning disorders includes

a. understanding the most common intrinsic differences between good and poor readers (i.e., cognitive, neurobiological, and linguistic),

b. recognizing the tenets of the NICHD definition of dyslexia and the US IDEA 2004 definition of specific learning disabilities,

c. recognizing that SEEDS and other reading difficulties exist on a continuum of severity,

d. identifying the distinguishing characteristics of SEEDS and related reading disorders (including developmental language comprehension disorder, attention deficit hyperactivity disorder, disorders of written expression or dysgraphia, mathematics learning disorder, nonverbal learning disorder, etc.)

e. identifying how symptoms of reading difficulty may change over time in response to development and instruction, and

f. understanding federal and state laws that pertain to learning disabilities, dyslexia, and ELL.

4. Interpretation and administration of assessments for planning instruction includes

a. understanding the differences among screening, diagnostic, outcome, and progress-monitoring assessments,

b. understanding basic principles of test construction, including reliability, validity, and norm-referencing, and knowing the most well-validated screening tests designed to identify students at risk for reading difficulties,

c. understanding the principles of progress-monitoring and the use of graphs to indicate progress,

d. knowing the range of skills typically assessed by diagnostic surveys of phonological skills, decoding skills, oral reading skills, spelling, and writing,

e. recognizing the content and purposes of the most common diagnostic tests used by psychologists and educational evaluators, and

f. interpreting measures of reading comprehension and written expression in relation to an individual child's component profile.

5. Structured language teaching of phonology includes

a. identifying the general and specific goals of phonological skill instruction,

b. knowing the progression of phonological skill development (i.e., rhyme, syllable, onset-rime, phoneme differentiation),

c. identifying the differences among various phonological manipulations, including identifying, matching, blending, segmenting, substituting, and deleting sounds,

d. understanding the principles of phonological skill instruction: brief, multicomponent, conceptual, and auditory-verbal,

e. understanding the reciprocal relationships among phonological processing, reading, spelling, and vocabulary, and

f. understanding the phonological features of a second language, such as Spanish, and how they interfere with English pronunciations and phonics.

6. Structured language teaching of phonics and word recognition includes

a. knowing or recognizing how to order phonics concepts from easier to more difficult,

b. understanding principles of explicit and direct teaching: model, lead, give guided practice, and review,

c. stating the rationale for multicomponent and multimodal techniques,

d. knowing the routines of a complete lesson format, from the introduction of a word recognition concept to fluent application in meaningful reading and writing, and

e. understanding research-based adaptations of instruction for students with weaknesses in working memory, attention, executive function, or processing speed.

7. Structured language teaching of fluent, automatic reading of text includes

a. understanding the role of fluency in word recognition, oral reading, silent reading, comprehension of written discourse, and motivation to read,

b. understanding reading fluency as a stage of normal reading development, as the primary symptom of some reading disorders, and as a consequence of practice and instruction,

c. defining and identifying examples of text at a student's frustration, instructional, and independent reading level,

d. knowing sources of activities for building fluency in component reading skills,

e. knowing which instructional activities and approaches are most likely to improve fluency outcomes,

f. understanding techniques to enhance student motivation to read, and

g. understanding appropriate uses of assistive technology for students with serious limitations in reading fluency.

8. Structured language teaching of vocabulary includes

a. understanding the role of vocabulary development and vocabulary knowledge in comprehension,

b. understanding the role and characteristics of direct and indirect (contextual) methods of vocabulary instruction,

c. knowing varied techniques for vocabulary instruction before, during, and after reading,

d. understanding that word knowledge is multifaceted, and

e. understanding the sources of wide differences in students' vocabularies.

9. Structured language teaching of text comprehension includes

a. being familiar with teaching strategies that are appropriate before, during, and after reading and that promote reflective reading,

b. contrasting the characteristics of major text genres, including narration, exposition, and argumentation,

c. understanding the similarities and differences between written composition and text comprehension, and the usefulness of writing in building comprehension,

d. identifying in any text the phrases, clauses, sentences, paragraphs, and academic language that could be a source of miscomprehension,

e. understanding levels of comprehension including the surface code, text base, and mental model (situation model), and

f. understanding factors that contribute to deep comprehension, including background knowledge, vocabulary, verbal reasoning ability, knowledge of literary structures and conventions, and use of skills and strategies for close reading of text.

10. Structured language teacher of handwriting, spelling, and written composition includes

a. knowing research-based principles for teaching letter naming and letter formation, both manuscript and cursive,

b. knowing techniques for teaching handwriting fluency,

c. recognizing and explaining the relationship between transcription skills and written expression,

d. identifying levels of students spelling development and orthographic knowledge,

e. recognizing and explaining the influences of phonological, orthographic, and morphemic knowledge on spelling,

f. understanding the major components and processes of written expression and how they interact (e.g., basic writing/transcription skills versus text generation),

g. knowing grade and developmental expectations for students' writing in the following areas: mechanics and conventions of writing, composition, revision, and editing processes, and

h. understanding appropriate uses of assistive technology in written expression.

B. The program or collection of teacher of reading practices must also include and integrate instructional strategies for continuously interpreting and administering student assessments and evaluations (Statutes, Section 3.0 of this law), and communicating the student's reading progress and needs to design and implement ongoing interventions (Statutes, Section 4.0 of this law) so that students of all ages and proficiency levels can read and comprehend text and apply higher level thinking skills.

C. Practicum for all teachers of reading certification shall include lesson planning and supervised practice both in teaching foundational reading instruction to whole classrooms and in delivering intervention to individuals or small groups of SEEDS. In addition, practicum for teaching specialists— special-education teachers, Title I instructors, and ELL instructors shall include documenting student progress with formal and informal assessments and completing an educational assessment of a student's progress.

D. Scientifically discredited notions of reading acquisition and instructional practices that are incompatible with science or inhibit student progress, such as using picture and context cues for decoding rather than self-monitoring and comprehension shall not be promoted in teacher preparation programs.

E. The guidelines shall be re-written to mandate rigor in the study of reading development to (include phonics) comply with this legislation. This shall be accomplished in consultation with an oversight panel consisting of persons with demonstrated mastery of the knowledge.

F. The [insert name state department of education], in consultation with an oversight panel consisting of persons with demonstrated mastery of knowledge in literacy approve a minor in reading, and ensure that the courses required in the reading minor of any teacher preparation program cover in depth the knowledge set forth in this legislation so as to ensure attaining a certificate to become a teacher of reading.

G. Syllabi changes are to be approved by the [insert name state department of education] in consultation with an oversight panel consisting of persons with demonstrated mastery of the knowledge of reading development and reading literacy, and experts in evaluation of the content and quality of teacher preparation programs who have conducted such reviews in other states.

H. The [insert name state department of education] shall designate funding for a higher education collaborative to provide professional development for reading administrators and instructors in institutions of higher education. The collaborative shall meet a minimum of three times per year and feature national reading experts as presenters on topics related to the knowledge of literacy and to preparing teacher candidates to become certified teachers of reading equipped with knowledge in all foundational reading skills.

§2.3 Reading Instruction Competence Teaching Assessment

The [insert state name] reading instruction competence teaching assessment examination must measure the knowledge, skill, and ability of kindergarten, elementary, secondary, ELL, Title I, and special-education teachers of reading in comprehensive, foundational reading and instructions, and Multi-Tier System of Supports as defined in Statutes, Section 4.0 of this law. The teaching-assessment examination must have been data-validated and previously administered in another state for over five years and be composed of multiple-choice and constructed-response questions designed to measure reading instruction knowledge and skills. Test content areas must assess foundations of reading development, development of reading comprehension, reading assessment and instruction, and integration of knowledge and understanding for reading literacy.

1. Basic Reading Instruction Competence Teaching Assessment
   Beginning (insert start date), all candidates for initial educator or professional educator licensure in Early Childhood Level Education (approximate ages birth through eight),

Early Childhood through Middle Childhood Level Education (approximate ages birth through eleven), Middle Childhood through Early Adolescent Level Education (approximate ages six through twelve or thirteen), and Special Education, and all persons entering or pursuing an approved certification as a teacher of reading as defined earlier shall pass a new exam covering basic knowledge of the foundations of reading development, development of reading comprehension, reading instruction and assessment, and integration of knowledge and understanding.

A. A basic reading instruction competence teaching assessment (BRICA) must have at least one hundred multiple-choice questions, worth 80 percent of the total possible points, and at least two open response questions, worth 20 percent of the total possible points, and must have been previously administered in another state for over five years.

B. If this BRICA is embedded in a comprehensive, multisubject licensure exam, there must be at least one hundred multiple-choice and two open-response reading questions, and there shall be a separate passing score for the reading portion of the exam.

C. The foundations of reading portion of a BRICA shall be worth 35 percent of the total possible points, and consist of multiple-choice questions covering the understanding of phonological and phonemic awareness, the understanding of concepts of print and the alphabetic principle, the role of phonics in promoting reading development, and the understanding of word analysis skills and strategies.

D. The development of reading comprehension portion of a BRICA shall be worth 27 percent of the total possible points, and consist of multiple-choice questions covering the understanding of vocabulary development, the understanding of how to apply reading comprehension skills and strategies to imaginative/literary texts, and the understanding of how to apply reading comprehension skills and strategies to informational/expository texts.

E. The reading assessment and instruction portion of a BRICA shall be worth 18 percent of the total possible points, and consist of multiple-choice questions covering the understanding of formal and informal methods for assessing reading development, and the understanding of multiple approaches to reading instruction.

F. The integration of knowledge and understanding portion of a BRICA shall be worth 20 percent of the total possible points, and consist of at least two open response questions requiring organized, developed analyses on topics related to foundations of reading development, development of reading comprehension, and/or reading assessment and instruction.

G. The Department of Public Instruction, in consultation with an oversight panel consisting of persons with demonstrated mastery of the knowledge set forth, shall select a BRICA and make a practice exam available by [insert date].

H. The passing score for a BRICA shall not be lower than 75 percent of the total possible points or 85 percent of the total possible points for prospective special-education teachers, reading teachers, and reading specialists. Persons entering or pursuing an approved program leading to certification as a reading teacher or reading specialist, who have previously passed a BRICA with a score of at least 85 percent, will not be required to retake the exam.

I. The Department of Public Instruction may grant a provisional license for up to a one-year term after failure and before retaking a BRICA if the individual candidate is actively involved in an approved remedial class or approved professional development as preparation for retaking the exam. No person shall be accepted into or continue in a program teaching grades pre-K-third-grade students, leading to certification as a teacher of reading or reading specialist without passing a BRICA.

J. Institutions of higher education are to provide free, approved remedial work for their candidates who fail a BRICA.

K. Districts are to provide free, approved professional development for new out-of-state hires who fail a BRICA. The Department of Public Instruction shall require districts to earmark a specific amount of funds annually for professional development in reading, based on the number of new out-of-state hires who have not yet passed a BRICA.

L. Providers of the remedial work and professional development in subsections J and K must be approved by the Department of Public Instruction after consultation with an oversight panel consisting of persons with demonstrated mastery of the knowledge set forth in this legislation.

M. Results of a BRICA are to be reported and made public annually, with first-time passage rates and overall passage rates tied to specific institutions of higher education for initial and professional license candidates and to individual districts for out-of-state hires.

N. Individuals who are certified in reading remediation or language therapy by a nationally recognized professional organization, have demonstrated success for at least two years in teaching SEEDS, and who pass a BRICA, plus an ARICA in Section 2.3.2 below with scores of at least 85 percent, may be hired by districts to provide professional development to teachers or administrators, or to work individually with SEEDS, or may be hired by parents to work with their own children in schools during school hours.

2. Advanced Reading Instruction Competence Teaching Assessment for Teachers of Reading Certification

In addition to the requirements of Section 2.3.1 of the basic reading instruction competence teaching assessment of this legislation, candidates for initial educator or professional educator certified as a teacher of reading, special-education teacher, Title I reading teacher, or ELL reading specialist shall pass a new advanced level exam covering reading processes and development, reading assessment, reading instruction, reading support systems, professional knowledge and roles of the teachers of reading, special-education teacher, Title I reading teacher, or ELL reading specialist (as appropriate to the candidate), and integration of knowledge and understanding. This examination is required for all in-service and preservice teachers in grades K-3, teachers of reading in all grades, special-education teachers, Title I reading teachers, and ELL reading specialists (as appropriate to the candidate).

A. An advanced reading instruction competence teaching assessment (ARICA) must have at least one hundred multiple-choice questions, worth 80 percent of the total possible points; at least two open response questions, worth 20 percent of the total possible points; and have been previously administered in another state for over five years.

B. The reading processes and development portion of an ARICA shall be worth 32 percent of the total possible points and consist of multiple-choice questions covering in depth the understanding of the connections among listening, speaking, reading, and writing; phonological and phonemic awareness; concepts of print and the alphabetic principle; the role of phonics knowledge in reading development; other word analysis skills and strategies; the development of vocabulary knowledge and skills; skills and strategies for comprehending literary/imaginative texts; and skills and strategies for comprehending expository and content-area texts.

C. The reading assessment portion of an ARICA shall be worth 16 percent of the total possible points and consist of multiple-choice questions covering the understanding of test construction and the interpretation of test results; characteristics and uses of formal and informal reading and writing assessments; the role of assessment in promoting reading and writing development; and the screening and diagnosis of reading difficulties and disabilities.

D. The reading instruction portion of an ARICA shall be worth 16 percent of the total possible points and consist of multiple-choice questions covering the understanding of research-based instructional strategies, programs, and methodologies for promoting early reading and writing development; research-based instructional strategies, programs, and methodologies for consolidating and expanding reading, writing, and spelling skills; the differentiation of reading instruction to meet the needs of individual students; and characteristics and uses of reading resources, materials, and technologies.

E. The professional knowledge and roles of the teachers of reading, special-education teacher, Title I reading teacher, or ELL reading specialist (as appropriate to the candidate) portion of an ARICA shall be worth 16 percent of the total possible points and consist of multiple-choice questions covering the understanding of the interpretation, evaluation, and application of reading research; the multiple roles of the candidate's prospective position in planning and implementing reading instruction in collaboration with other members of the school community; and the understanding of the role of professional development in promoting the effectiveness of the candidate's prospective position and other educators.

F. The integration of knowledge and understanding portion of an ARICA shall be worth 20 percent of the total possible points, and consist of at least two open response questions requiring organized, developed analyses on topics related to reading processes and development, reading assessment, reading instruction, and/or the professional knowledge and roles of the teachers of reading, special-education teacher, Title I reading teacher, and ELL reading specialist (as appropriate to the candidate).

G. The Department of Public Instruction, in consultation with an oversight panel consisting of persons with demonstrated mastery of the knowledge set forth, shall select an ARICA and make a practice exam available by [insert date].

H. The passing score for an ARICA shall not be lower than 85 percent of the total possible points.

I. The Department of Public Instruction may grant a provisional license for up to a one-year term after failure and before retaking an ARICA if the individual candidate is actively involved in an approved remedial class or approved professional development as preparation for retaking the exam.

J. Institutions of higher education are to provide free, approved remedial work for their candidates who fail an ARICA.

K. Districts are to provide free, approved professional development for in-service teachers and new out-of-state hires who fail an ARICA. The Department of Public

Instruction shall require districts to earmark a specific amount of funds annually for professional development in reading, based on the number of employees who have not yet passed an ARICA.

L. Providers of the remedial work and professional development in subsection N must be approved by the Department of Public Instruction after consultation with an oversight panel consisting of persons with demonstrated mastery of the knowledge set forth in this legislation.

M. Results of an ARICA are to be reported and made public annually, with first-time passage rates and overall passage rates tied to specific institutions of higher education for initial license candidates and to individual districts for out-of-state hires.

N. Individuals who are certified in reading remediation or language therapy by a nationally recognized professional organization, have demonstrated success for at least two years in teaching SEEDS, and who pass an ARICA, plus a BRICA in Section 2.3.1 with scores of at least 85 percent, may be hired by districts to provide professional development to teachers or administrators or to work individually with struggling readers, or may be hired by parents to work with their own children in schools during school hours.

§2.4 Reading Instruction Competence Teaching Assessment Reporting and Support

[Insert name of state board of education], no later than [insert date], shall adopt a reading instruction competence teacher assessment for all kindergarten, elementary, and secondary teachers; teachers of reading; special-education teachers; Title I reading teachers; and ELL reading specialists consistent with Statutes, Sections 2.0, 3.0, and 4.0 of this law.

A. [Insert name of state board of education] shall report to the Senate and House of Representatives committees having jurisdiction over prekindergarten through grade 12 education policy by [insert date], on the basic and advanced reading instruction competence teacher assessment that was adopted.

B. [Insert name of state board of education], in consultation with members of the professional reading community, shall establish an approved list of reading instruction program centers that offer staff development and remedial training necessary for all existing prekindergarten through grade 12 educators in reading and literacy to successfully pass either the basic or advanced reading instruction competence teacher assessment of this law (as appropriate to the candidate).

§2.5 Pretest and Grant for Candidates in an Approved Teacher Preparation Program

[Insert name of state board of education] shall provide teaching candidates and existing teachers reading instruction grants to improve their knowledge of teaching reading with the goal of passing the advanced reading instruction competence teacher assessment and becoming certified as a teacher of reading. A candidate taking the pretest is eligible for a grant to attend an approved reading instruction program if the candidate has successfully completed an examination of skills in reading, writing, mathematics, and reading literacy ([insert state name] Statutes, Section 2.1 of the law), commits to attend and complete an approved comprehension reading instruction program of his or her choosing, and commits to take both the basic and advanced reading instruction competence examination.

A. At the completion of the reading instruction program, no later than [insert date], a candidate enrolled in the final year of an approved teacher preparation program in kindergarten, elementary, secondary, or special education may apply to [insert name of state board of education] to take a [insert state name] reading instruction competence teaching assessment pretest.

B. No later than [insert date], schools providing instruction in kindergarten through grade 6 may apply to the [insert name of state board of education] in a manner prescribed by the [insert name of state board of education] for their teachers to take the [insert state name] reading instruction competence teaching assessment pretest.

C. A school is eligible for a grant for kindergarten, elementary, secondary, and special-education teachers to attend an approved reading instruction program if the teachers
   1. take the pretest;
   2. commit to attending and completing an approved reading instruction program of their choosing;
   3. take the basic and/or advanced reading instruction competence teaching assessment as determined by [insert state name] Statutes, Section 2.3 under this law.

§2.6 Passing Score on the [insert state name] Reading Instruction Competence Teaching Assessment

The [insert name of state board of education], in cooperation with the testing contractor providing the basic and advanced reading instruction competence teaching assessment, must use the reading instruction competence teaching assessment results on the pretest and posttest to determine a passing score on the [insert state name] reading instruction competence teaching assessment by [insert date].

Section § 3

Data Use and Systems in Schools to Progress Student Reading Literacy Achievement

1. collecting and interpreting both school and student data to include screening and systematic assessments of progress,
2. sharing data,
3. framing questions from analysis of multiple sets of data reports, and
4. creating plans to assist individual student achievement.

It is ratified that each district and school in the state of [insert name state] will:

1. establish a school-wide data use plan and ongoing review of implementation of that plan to monitor student progress toward goals;

2. guide and support teachers in use of data for instructional improvement to meet the needs of students and to support students in reaching their goals;
3. support and lead both students and their parents to be on track for postsecondary success by selecting goals and monitoring their progress toward those goals; and
4. ensure that school-level and student data needs are incorporated in district-wide data management systems planning and implementation.

It is adopted by [insert state name] that data be continuously utilized to provide new insights into student learning and how to improve it. This process is implemented so that facts, based on data, are utilized to identify the root causes of student learning problems, not just the symptoms.

With data, all districts, schools, and teachers will collect, analyze, and require:

1. clear assessment on students' needs;
2. the expertise to target resources to address students' needs;
3. the ability to set students' goals;
4. the aptitude to determine whether the goals are being reached; and
5. the ability to track the impact of staff development efforts.

This Policy implements and provides for the application of a data use plan under which students, pre-K-12 enrolled or enrolling in public schools in [insert state name], are screened and assessed for literacy failure or grade-level reading attainment as may be necessary, and are provided appropriate supports dependent on multiple factors and at multiple times until proficient grade-level reading skills are secured.

§3.1 General Procedures

Districts, schools, and charter schools must establish written procedures for screening, assessing, and recommending students at risk for literacy failure within General-Education settings. The state can no longer wait for these students to fail; all SEEDS will be provided with a systematic structure to learn. While districts, schools, and charter schools must follow federal and state guidelines, they must also develop internal procedures that address the needs of their student populations.

A. All entering kindergarten students will be screened for potential characteristics of SEEDS that could inhibit reading development. Kindergarten screening shall happen at least twice in the first semester of the year and once in the second semester.

B. Every student in grades 1, 2, and 3 shall be systematically assessed every two to three weeks during reading development stages of instruction to ensure they are reaching appropriate gains to achieve grade-level reading.

C. The Policy shall provide that, upon the request of a parent/ guardian, student, school nurse, classroom teacher, or other school personnel who have data to support that a student has a need for diagnostic testing in any grade, such testing will be conducted within thirty days.

§3.2 Screening Procedures

[Insert state name] is committed to data-driven instruction. State Policy requires universal screening. With the use of screening, teachers of reading can quickly assess if a child will experience reading difficulties and can provide early stage, targeted instruction by isolating the skills that need to be strengthened. Both research and practice support that these at-risk students, identified early through screening and provided a systemic process of a continuous cycle of assessment, data analysis, ongoing progress monitoring, and informed instruction, are most often aptly prepared to enter first grade on target for grade-level reading requirements and beyond.

A. All entering kindergarten students will be universally screened during the first, early weeks of reading instruction, again before the fall break, and also in the spring to evaluate reading progress. If a student is falling behind his or her peers, common characteristics will be identifiable early in these screening assessments. A teacher of reading will provide MTSS promptly to most quickly and assuredly ameliorate the areas of weakness.

B. If a student is found to be at serious risk for literacy failure, a systematic assessment will be provided, and the school district, school, or charter school must notify the students' parents/guardians. The school district, school, or charter school must also implement a MTSS and a reading program (accelerated and/or intensive) that appropriately addresses students' reading difficulties and enables them to "catch up" with their typically performing peers.

§3.3 Assessments for Reading Literacy

All students in prekindergarten, kindergarten and grades 1, 2, and 3 are to be systematically assessed for their reading development and comprehension grade-level skill attainment. The Policy acknowledges that early identification preferably happens in grades K-1, and that support systems will greatly improve every student's chances to realize reading literacy. It is understood that all students can be taught reading and literacy skills and perform at grade level. The purpose of this section is to ensure early intervention with SEEDS, with the goal of a successful school experience, and to bring to bear all resources that can be made available in a school setting to address any difficulty a student may have so that each student is ready and able to read for knowledge by grade 3. The following are requirements pursuant to this Policy:

A. Every student in public school shall be assessed for grade-level reading attainment. Every student in grades 1, 2, and 3 shall be systematically assessed, every two to three weeks during the year for grade-level reading skill attainment to ensure a successful skill progression.
B. In doing such assessments, students receiving below-grade-level scores shall be a top priority and the student will be provided support within a week (as defined in [insert state name] Statute, Section 4.0). When a student is identified and provided with systems of support, yet grade-level attainment is not accomplished within thirty days, then more intensive intervention is mandated (as defined in [insert state name] Statute, Section 4.0).
C. Assessments as required by [insert state name] Literacy, LD and Dyslexia Policy shall have one or more of the following results:

1. No indication of need for services;
2. Indication of need for MTSS (tier II) in general-education reading services to ameliorate SEEDS literacy failure, [insert state name] Statute, Section 4 of this Policy;
3. Indication of need for assistance to improve the effect of general-education reading instruction through intense intervention services (MTSS-tier III); or
4. Referral for further formal diagnostic assessment for the existence of SEEDS factors and eligibility for the receipt of special-education services.

D. If the student has not made adequate progress, the student shall receive a diagnostic assessment for all other issues of learning disorders such as seeking identification of dyslexia and specific learning disabilities as defined in [insert state name] Statute, Sections 1.8, 1.9, and 1.12 of this Policy, and/or social, cultural, and environmental factors that put a child at risk for literacy failure as that term has been defined in [insert state name] Statute, Section 1.2.

E. Students in need of services and/or assistance shall have it provided to them. Services shall be provided in accordance with [insert state name] state and federal Policy, [insert state name] Statute, Section 1.12 of the Policy.

F. New students enrolling in public schools shall be screened and assessed, if needed, for at-risk reading attainment at appropriate times in accordance with content-area subject teacher request, request of parents or guardians, or poor school progress.

G. [Name of state department of education and/or name of board of trustees of each school district board] shall provide for the treatment of any SEEDS determination or learning disorders, [insert state name] Statute, Section 3 of this Policy, and shall adopt any rules and standards necessary to administer this section.

H. The screenings/assessments required shall be done directly by specialists (certified teachers of reading, guidance counselors, pupil appraisal personnel, or any other professional employees of the school system) who have been appropriately trained, all of whom shall operate as advocates for the students identified as needing services or assistance. Persons who have not been trained to do such screenings/assessments shall do no screenings/assessments, consistent with the requirements established for such training by [insert state name]'s Literacy, LD and Dyslexia Policy. Screening/assessment specialists shall be professional employees of the school system who have been appropriately trained, all of whom shall have met the following requirements:

1. Screening/Assessment Specialists Training Requirements
   a. Identification and knowledge of the following:
      i. SEEDS pursuant to [insert state name] Statute, Section 1, of this Policy;
      ii. Characteristics of ADD and HD;
      iii. Characteristics of social, cultural, and emotional at risk literacy failure factors; and
      iv. Characteristics of gifted SEEDS (or twice exceptional in many states).
   b. Use of appropriate screening instruments.

I. Kindergarten screening instrument(s) state approved to determine developmental strengths and needs checklist:
   i. social/emotional factors at risk checklist;
   ii. informal reading/language inventories;
   iii. rapid automatic naming tests;
   iv. written language samples;
   v. informal mathematical assessment; and
   vi. norm-referenced tests.

J. Administration and interpretation of selected screening instruments
   1. Training of personnel to administer instruments; and
   2. Interpret screening results

K. Operation and procedures of school building level committee
   1. Membership;
   2. Referral process;
   3. Interventions in the classroom;
   4. Documentation; and
   5. Decision-making process;
   6. Selection of appropriate classroom strategies, accommodations, and modifications; and
   7. Child advocacy.

L. A private assessment can be obtained by the parents/guardian of the student. The school or district may take into account the assessment, administer additional assessments, or provide intervention based on the private assessment.

M. The federal ESEA requires annual testing of all students in reading and math in grades 3-8. Once in high school, all students must meet state-set proficiency standards, thus the state is compelled to ensure that ongoing assessment and progress monitoring of reading achievement gains are encouraged for all students.

N. Research indicates that there may be unexpected difficulties that students with dyslexia demonstrate in the area of reading, writing, and math despite the provision of effective foundational reading instruction and, thus, screening and assessment will identify and accelerate MTSS. Additionally, students with dyslexia and learning disabilities may be gifted and their difficulties more difficult to appreciate because of their intellect. The state of [insert state name] acknowledges formal assessment and diagnostics are necessary to understand these difficulties and the relationship to the student's cognitive abilities, reading fluency, writing, and math.

§3.4 Literacy Failure Diagnosis

A district-level committee may adopt a list of assessments/reading instruments for use in the district in addition to the assessments/reading instruments on the state's list based on data-validated research concerning reading skills development and reading comprehension (see www.literatenation.org for a list of state approved foundational reading instruction programs). A list of assessments/reading instruments adopted under this subsection must provide for diagnosing the reading development, fluency, and comprehension of students participating in a program.

Districts, schools, and charter schools must follow federal and state guidelines; they must also develop the following standards and procedures:

A. Schools administer assessments/reading instruments to diagnose student reading development, fluency, and comprehension;

B. Schools train specific educators in administering the assessments/reading instruments;

C. Schools apply the results of the assessments/reading instruments to the instructional program;

D. Districts shall adopt a list of assessments/reading instruments that schools may use to diagnose student reading development and comprehension;

E. Districts shall administer, at the kindergarten level and in grades 1, 2, and 3, an assessment/reading instrument on the list adopted by the district-level committee. The district shall administer the assessment/reading instrument in accordance with the state's recommendations;

F. District office shall:

   1. Report to the district-level committee the results of the assessment/reading instruments for each student;

   2. Report, in writing, to a student's parent or guardian the student's results on the assessment/reading instrument;

G. Districts shall notify the parent or guardian of each student in kindergarten and grades 1, 2, and 3 who is determined, on the basis of assessment/reading instrument results, to be a SEEDS. The district shall implement accelerated MTSS [insert state name] Statutes, Sections 4.2 and 4.3 of this Policy that provides reading instruction and strategies that address reading deficiencies in students;

H. Districts shall make a good faith effort to ensure that the notice required under this section is provided either in person or by regular mail, that the notice is clear and easy to understand, and is written in English and in the parent or guardian's native language.

§3.5 Data Gathering

At any time (from kindergarten through grade 12) that a student continues to struggle with one or more components of reading development and/or experiences reading literacy failure, districts, schools, and charter schools must collect additional information about the student. This information shall be analyzed and used to evaluate the student's underachievement and to determine what actions are needed to ensure the student's improved academic performance. Some of the information that the district or charter school collects is in the student's cumulative folder; other data is available from teachers and parents/guardians. Data collection is as follows:

A. To ensure that under achievement in SEEDS is not due to lack of appropriate instruction in reading, other criteria should be considered. This information should include data that demonstrates the student was provided appropriate instruction and data-based documentation of repeated assessments of achievement at reasonable intervals (progress monitoring), reflecting formal assessment of student progress during instruction. Additional information to be considered includes the results from some or all of the following:
   1. Vision screening;
   2. Hearing screening;
   3. Teacher reports of classroom concerns;
   4. Basal reading series assessment;
   5. Accommodations provided by classroom teachers;
   6. Academic progress reports (report cards);
   7. Samples of schoolwork;
   8. Parent conferences; and
   9. Speech and language screening through a referral process.
B. One of the actions that the district, school, or charter school has available is to recommend that SEEDS be administered a diagnostic assessment if the student demonstrates poor performance in one or more areas of reading and/or the related area of spelling that is unexpected for the student's age, grade, or intellectual development;
C. When the district, school, or charter school recommends a student be formally assessed, the following procedures for assessment must be adhered to as determined by [insert state name] Statute, Section 3.6 of this Policy.

§3.6 Formal Assessment

Students formal assessment diagnostic is dependent upon multiple factors including the student's reading performance, reading difficulties, poor response to supplemental scientifically based reading instruction (MTSS), teachers' input, and input from the parents or guardians. Additionally, the appropriate time for assessing is early in a student's school career, the earlier the better. While earlier is better, SEEDS should be recommended for assessment even if the reading difficulties appear later in a student's school career. (See www. literatenation.org for a list of formal assessment instruments.)

A. These procedures must be followed:
   1. Notify parents or guardians of proposal to perform a formal assessment diagnostic on a student;
   2. Inform parents or guardians of their rights;
   3. Obtain permission from the parent or guardian to assess the student; and
   4. Assess student, being sure that individuals/professionals who administer assessments have training in the evaluation of SEEDS, [insert state name] Statute, Section 3.3 of this Policy.

B. The notices and consent must be provided in the native language of the parent or guardian or other mode of communication used by the parent or guardian, unless it is clearly not feasible to do so.

C. Tests, assessments, diagnostics, and other evaluation materials must
   1. Be validated for the specific purpose for which the tests, assessments, and other evaluation materials are used;
   2. Include material tailored to assess specific areas of educational need and not merely materials that are designed to provide a single general intelligence quotient;
   3. Be selected and administered so as to ensure that when a test is given to a student with impaired sensory, manual, or speaking skills, the test results accurately reflect the student's aptitude or achievement level, or whatever other factor the test purports to measure, rather than reflecting the student's impaired sensory, manual, or speaking skills;
   4. Include multiple measures of a student's reading abilities, such as informal assessment information (e.g., anecdotal records, lists of books the student has read, audio recordings of the student's oral reading); and
   5. Be administered by trained personnel and in conformance with the instructions provided by the producer of the evaluation materials.

CINTHIA COLETTI

D. The district, school, or charter school administers measures that are related to the student's educational needs. Depending upon the student's age and stage of reading and intellectual development, the following reading areas should be assessed:
   1. Reading real and nonsense words in isolation (decoding);
   2. Phonological awareness;
   3. Letter knowledge (name and associated sound);
   4. Rapid naming;
   5. Reading fluency (rate and accuracy);
   6. Reading comprehension; and
   7. Written spelling.
E. Based on the student's individual academic difficulties and characteristics, additional areas that can be assessed include vocabulary, written expression, handwriting, and mathematics.

§3.7 English Language Learners (ELL)/Limited English Proficiency (LEP)

Much diversity exists among English language learners (ELLs). The identification and service delivery process for SEEDS must be in step with the student's linguistic environment and educational background. Involvement of a language proficiency assessment committee is recommended.

A. Additional data gathering may be required to include language proficiency documentation that includes the following:
   1. Home language survey;
   2. Assessment related to identification for limited English proficiency (oral language proficiency tests and norm-referenced tests);
   3. Linguistic environment and second-language acquisition development;
   4. Previous schooling in and outside of the United States; and
   5. Comprehensive oral language proficiency testing in English and the student's native language whenever possible.
B. These data gathering procedures are important to determine:
   1. Whether the student's current classroom setting is appropriate given his or her language abilities;
   2. The appropriate languages for assessing the student's academic achievement and cognitive processing;

3. The degree to which language proficiency in both the first and second language influences or explains the student's test performance on the academic achievement and cognitive processing measures; and

4. Whether the student's difficulties in reading are the result of a disability or a reflection of the normal process of second language acquisition.

C. Additionally, personnel involved in the evaluation process of ELLs for SEEDS must be trained in bilingual assessment and interpretation procedures. It is strongly recommended that personnel involved in the assessment and interpretation of assessment results have the following knowledge:

1. Understanding of first and second language acquisition stages;

2. Impact of culture on student performance;

3. Knowledge regarding bilingual education and English as a second language programming and MTSS teaching methods;

4. Knowledge in how to interpret results of student's oral language proficiency in relation to the results of the test measuring academic achievement and cognitive processes; and

5. Understanding of how to interpret results of similar or parallel tests given in more than one language.

D. To appropriately understand test results, the examiner(s)/committee of knowledgeable persons must interpret test results in light of the student's language development (in both English and the student's native language), educational history, linguistic background, socioeconomic issues, and any other pertinent factors that affect learning.

§3.8 SEEDS Determination

A. A district, school, or charter school team or committee of knowledgeable persons determines whether the student is a SEEDS, after reviewing all accumulated data, including the following areas:

1. Observations of the teacher, district, charter school staff, and/or parent/guardian;

2. Data gathered from the classroom (including student work and the results of classroom measures) and information found in the student's cumulative folder (including the developmental and academic history of the student);
3. Data-based documentation of student progress during instruction/intervention;
4. Results of administered assessments; and
5. All other accumulated data regarding the development of the student's learning and his or her educational needs.

B. Difficulties in the area of reading for SEEDS will reflect unexpectedly low performance for the student's age and educational level in the following areas:
1. Reading real words in isolation;
2. Decoding nonsense words;
3. Reading fluency (both rate and accuracy); and
4. Written spelling.

C. Unexpectedly low reading performance, including reading fluency, will be the result of a deficit in phonological processing, including the following:
1. Phonological awareness,
2. Rapid naming, and
3. Phonological memory.

D. Many SEEDS will have difficulty with the secondary characteristics of literacy, including reading comprehension, written composition, spelling, grammar, and rote math skills.

E. A committee of knowledgeable persons making a SEEDS determination must also incorporate the following considerations as authorized by this state Policy:
1. The student has received MTSS instruction, [insert state name] Statute, Section 4 of this Policy;
2. The student has an unexpected lack of appropriate academic progress (in the areas of reading and spelling) relative to their age/grade/intellectual development;
3. The student has adequate intelligence (an average ability to learn in the absence of print or in other academic areas);
4. The student exhibits characteristics associated with SEEDS; and
5. The student's lack of progress is not due to sociocultural factors such as language differences, irregular attendance, or lack of experiential background.

F. Based on the above information and guidelines, the committee of knowledgeable persons determines and identifies SEEDS and the committee of knowledgeable persons also determines whether the student has a disability under the federal Rehabilitation Act of 1973, §504 and the 2008 ADAAA. A student is considered to have a disability under §504 if the condition substantially limits the student's learning. Students with additional factors that complicate SEEDS may require additional support or referral to special education.

§3.9 Referral to Special Education

A. At any time during the assessment for reading failure identification process or instruction, students may be referred for evaluation for special education. At times, students will display additional factors or areas complicating their instruction and requiring more support than what is available through instruction (MTSS). At other times, students with severe at-risk characteristics or related disorders will be unable to make appropriate academic progress within any of the programs described in the procedures related to SEEDS. In such cases, a referral to special education for evaluation and possible identification as a child with a disability within the meaning of the IDEA 2004 (20 USC section 1400 et seq.), the federal Rehabilitation Act of 1973, §504, and the 2008 ADAAA should be made as needed. See [insert state name] Statute, Section 1.5 of this Policy.

B. If a SEEDS is found eligible for special education in the area of reading, the school district must include appropriate reading instruction on the student's Individualized Education Program (IEP). Appropriate reading instruction includes the descriptors listed at www.literatenation.org.

C. If a SEEDS is referred for special education, districts and charter schools must follow the Individuals with Disabilities Education Act (IDEA). In IDEA 2004, §1401 (30), SEEDS is considered one of a variety of etiological foundations for "specific learning disability." 34 CFR 300.8(c)(10) states that a "specific learning disability" means a disorder in one or more of the basic psychological processes involved in understanding or in using language, spoken or written, that may manifest in an imperfect ability to listen, think, speak, read, write, spell, or do mathematical calculations. The term includes such conditions as perceptual disability, brain injury, minimal brain dysfunction, dyslexia, and developmental aphasia. The term does not apply to students who have learning problems that are primarily the result of visual, hearing, or motor disabilities; of mental retardation; of emotional disturbance; or of environmental, cultural, or economic disadvantage.

Section §4

General Education: Foundational Reading Instruction; Speaking, Listening, And Language Instruction; Content-Area Reading Literacy Instruction; and Writing Literacy Instruction

§4.1 Foundational Reading Development Instruction in Grades K-3:

A. Foundational Reading Development Instruction programs shall consist of specific program content and a defined delivery system. The programs shall be taught by certified teachers of reading as defined in [insert state name] Statute, Section 2.0 of the Policy. The programs content shall consist of the following components:
1. Foundational Reading Development Instructional Content Components
    a. Language-based—A program that provides instruction that integrates all aspects of language: receptive (listening and reading); expressive (oral expression to include word finding and sequencing); written expression (spelling, mechanics, coherence); and handwriting.
    b. Phonological awareness—A language program that explicitly supports that words are made up of individual speech sounds and that those sounds can be manipulated: rhyming; recognition of initial, final, and medial sounds; recognition of vowel sounds; recognition and identification of the number of

syllables in a word; sound blending of phonemes (sounds) in words and detached syllables; phoneme segmentation of real words and detached syllables; and phoneme manipulation.

c. Phoneme-grapheme correspondence knowledge—A program that provides instruction on the system by which symbols represent sounds in a writing system: accurately pronouncing each phoneme represented by a given grapheme (symbol to sound); writing the graphemes that represent each given phoneme (sound to symbol); and blending rules.

d. Syllable instruction—A program that provides instruction in syllables and their application to reading both as a word or part of a word that contains one sounded vowel.

e. Linguistics—A program providing the science of language that includes phonology, morphology, syntax, and semantics; the study of the structure of a language and its relationship to other languages.

f. Meaning-based instruction—A program that provides instruction, through words and sentences, on how to best extract meaning in addition to teaching isolated letter-sound correspondence; instruction in morphology which includes identification of morphemes and their functional use in written and spoken words; instruction of syntax to include sentence construction, combining, and expansion in both narrative and expository text; instruction of semantics to include vocabulary acquisition, idioms, and figurative language; and instruction in comprehension of narrative and expository text.

g. Reading fluency instruction—A program that provides instruction on the imperative of reading fluency to include: accuracy; appropriate use of pitch, juncture, and stress; text phrasing; and the rate at which one reads. Instruction will provide for substantial practice and continual application of decoding and word recognition to work toward automaticity; and also opportunities for reading large amounts of text to achieve independent reading at grade-level with 95 percent accuracy and specific practices in skills being learned.

    h. Phonics—A program that provides instructional practices that emphasize how spellings are related to speech sounds in systematic ways.

B. Instructional Methodology and Delivery of Foundational Reading Instructional Content

    1. All teachers of reading shall be prepared to utilize the following techniques and strategies with a diverse student population in the classrooms. Foundational reading instruction with student-teacher interaction shall be delivered as follows:

        a. Systematic (structured), sequential, and cumulative instruction that is organized and presented in a way that follows a logical sequential plan, fits the nature of language (alphabetic principle) with no assumption of prior skills or language knowledge, and maximizes student engagement. This instruction proceeds at a rate commensurate with students' needs, ability levels, and demonstration of progress;

        b. Individualized instruction that meets the specific learning needs of each SEEDS in a small group setting to include a reading curriculum that matches each student's individual ability level;

        c. Intensive, highly concentrated instruction that maximizes student engagement, uses specialized methods and materials, and produces results;

        d. Meaning-based instruction that is directed toward purposeful reading and writing, with an emphasis on comprehension and composition, and independent thinking;

        e. Instruction that incorporates the simultaneous use of two or more sensory pathways (auditory, visual, kinesthetic, tactile) during teacher presentations and student practice.

    2. Instructional delivery that uses a simultaneous combination of internal learning pathways, visual, auditory, kinesthetic, and tactile to achieve proficiency in language processing.

3. Synthetic to analytic phonics delivery that teaches students the sounds of the letters first and then combines or blends these sounds to create words. Analytic phonics uses prior knowledge of letters and their corresponding sounds to decode and form new words.
4. Synthetic phonics methodology teaches students the sounds of the letters first and then combines or blends these sounds to create words. It is delivered to students as follows:
   a. Systematically. The material is organized and taught in a way that is logical and fits the nature of our language. This characteristic of the methodology refers to the way a system of rules governs how sounds combine to form words and words combine to form sentences to represent knowledge.
   b. Sequentially. The learner moves step-by-step, in order, from simple, well-learned material to that which is more complex, as he or she masters the necessary body of language skills.
   c. Cumulatively. Each step is incremental and based on those skills already learned.
   d. Individualized. Teaching is planned to meet the differing needs of learners who are similar to each other, but not ever exactly alike.
5. Automaticity of student reading performance requires a fluent processing of printed material. The goal is for the process to require little effort or attention, as in sight word recognition. Adequate student practice with decodable text is to be provided for mastery of automaticity skills and applications of concepts.

C. Implementation of the Foundational Reading Instruction Program is to be routinely provided to students within the regular school day for a minimum of [Insert state requirements (200-250)] minutes per week or a minimum of [Insert state requirements (40-50)] minutes each day. The instruction will be scheduled in two segments for students as follows: regular class instruction, out-of-class instruction, individual or small group instruction, a combination of these options, or any additional arrangements that may be developed by the committee.

§4.2 Grades K-5 Speaking, Listening, and Language Instruction
Speaking and Listening skills of increasing difficulty by grade level will be taught to students in grades K-5 for academic and lifelong expression, comprehension, cooperation, and collaboration.

A. Comprehension and collaboration in discussion with increased difficulty by grade level:
   1. Students will learn to engage effectively in a range of collaborative discussions (one-on-one, in groups, and teacher led) with diverse partners on grade-level topics and texts, building on others' ideas, and expressing their own ideas clearly.
   2. Students will learn to come to discussions prepared, having read or studied required material; explicitly draw on that preparation and other information known about the topic to explore ideas under discussion:
      a. Follow agreed-upon rules for discussions and carry out assigned roles.
      b. Pose and respond to specific questions by making comments that contribute to the discussion and elaborate on the remarks of others.
      c. Review the key ideas expressed and draw conclusions in light of information and knowledge gained from the discussions.
   3. Students will learn to summarize a written text read aloud or information presented in diverse media and formats, including visually, quantitatively, and orally.
   4. Students will learn to summarize the points a speaker makes and explain how each claim is supported by reasons and evidence.
B. Expression and presentation of knowledge and ideas in discussion with increased difficulty by grade level:
   1. Students will report on a topic or text or present an opinion; sequence ideas logically and use appropriate facts and relevant, descriptive details to support main ideas or themes; and speak clearly at an understandable pace.

2. Students will include multimedia components (e.g., graphics, sound) and visual displays in presentations when appropriate to enhance the development of main ideas or themes.
3. Students will learn to adapt speech to a variety of contexts and tasks, using formal English when appropriate to task and situation.

C. Conventions of Standard English in speaking and writing with increased difficulty by grade level:
1. Students will learn and demonstrate command of the conventions of standard English grammar and usage when writing or speaking.
2. Students will learn and explain the function of conjunctions, prepositions, and interjections in general and their function in particular sentences.
3. Students will learn to use the perfect verb tenses (e.g., I had walked; I have walked; I will have walked).
4. Students will learn to use verb tense to convey various times, sequences, states, and conditions.
5. Students will learn to recognize and correct inappropriate shifts in verb tense (e.g., either/or, neither/nor).

D. Command of the conventions of standard English—capitalization, punctuation, and spelling when writing with increased difficulty by grade level:
1. Students will learn to use punctuation to separate items in a series.
2. Students will learn to use a comma to separate an introductory element from the rest of the sentence.
3. Students will learn to use a comma to set off the words yes and no (e.g., Yes, thank you), to set off a tag question from the rest of the sentence (e.g., It's true, isn't it?), and to indicate direct address (e.g., Is that you, Steve?).
4. Students will learn to use underlining, quotation marks, or italics to indicate titles of works.
5. Students will learn to spell grade-appropriate words correctly, consulting references as needed.

E. Knowledge of language with increased difficulty by grade level:
1. Students will learn to use knowledge of language and its conventions when writing, speaking, reading, or listening.

2. Students will learn to expand, combine, and reduce sentences for meaning, reader and listener interest, and style.
3. Students will learn to compare and contrast the varieties of English (e.g., dialects, registers) used in stories, dramas, and poems.

F. Vocabulary acquisition and use with increased difficulty by grade level:
1. Students will learn to determine or clarify the meaning of unknown and multiple-meaning words and phrases based on grade 5 reading and content, choosing flexibly from a range of strategies.
2. Students will learn to use context (e.g., cause/effect relationships and comparisons in text) as a clue to the meaning of a word or phrase.
3. Students will learn to use common, grade-appropriate Greek and Latin affixes and roots as clues to the meaning of a word (e.g., photograph, photosynthesis).
4. Students will learn to consult reference materials (e.g., dictionaries, glossaries, thesauruses), both print and digital, to find the pronunciation and determine or clarify the precise meaning of key words and phrases.
5. Students will learn to demonstrate understanding of figurative language, word relationships, and nuances in word meaning.
6. Students will learn to interpret figurative language, including similes and metaphors, in context.
7. Students will learn to recognize and explain the meaning of common idioms, adages, and proverbs.
8. Students will learn to use the relationship between particular words (e.g., synonyms, antonyms, homographs) to better understand each of the words.
9. Students will learn to acquire and use accurately grade-appropriate general academic and domain-specific words and phrases, including those that signal contrast, addition, and other logical relationships (e.g., however, although, nevertheless, similarly, moreover, in addition).

§4.3 Grades 4-12 Reading Literacy Instruction in Content Areas

Reading literacy skills will be provided to all students by content area and English language arts as determined by the Standards to define college and career readiness expectations.

A. Key ideas and details in content-area reading literacy with increased difficulty by grade level:
  1. Read closely to determine what the text says explicitly and to make logical inferences from it; cite specific textual evidence when writing or speaking to support conclusions drawn from the text.
  2. Determine central ideas or themes of a text and analyze their development; summarize the key supporting details and ideas.
  3. Analyze how and why individuals, events, and ideas develop and interact over the course of a text.
B. Craft and structure content-area reading literacy with increased difficulty by grade level:
  1. Interpret words and phrases as they are used in a text, including determining technical, connotative, and figurative meanings, and analyze how specific word choices shape meaning or tone.
  2. Analyze the structure of texts, including how specific sentences, paragraphs, and larger portions of the text (e.g., a section, chapter, scene, or stanza) relate to each other and the whole.
  3. Assess how point of view or purpose shapes the content and style of a text.
C. Integration of knowledge and ideas in content-area reading literacy with increased difficulty by grade level:
  1. Integrate and evaluate content presented in diverse formats and media, including visually and quantitatively, as well as in words.
  2. Delineate and evaluate the argument and specific claims in a text, including the validity of the reasoning as well as the relevance and sufficiency of the evidence.
  3. Analyze how two or more texts address similar themes or topics to build knowledge or to compare author approaches.

D. Range of reading and level of text complexity for reading literacy with increased difficulty by grade level. Analyze and structure instruction with complex textual literature that requires increased comprehension proficiency and encourages independent analysis.

§4.4 Grades 4-8 Writing Literacy Instruction

Writing literacy skills will be provided to all students by teachers of content areas and English language arts as determined by the Standards, to define college and career readiness expectations.

A. In grades 4-8, with increased difficulty by grade level, students will be instructed on and master the skill of writing opinion pieces on topics or texts, supporting a point of view with reasons and information that increase in complexity:
   1. Introduce a topic or text clearly, state an opinion, and create an organizational structure in which related ideas are grouped to support the writer's purpose.
   2. Provide reasons that are supported by facts and details.
   3. Link opinion and reasons using words and phrases.
   4. Provide a concluding statement or section related to the opinion presented.
B. In grades 4-8, with increased difficulty by grade, students will be instructed on and master the skill of writing arguments to support claims in an analysis of substantive topics or texts, using valid reasoning and relevant and sufficient evidence:
   1. Introduce precise, knowledgeable claim(s), establish the significance of the claim(s), distinguish the claim(s) from alternate or opposing claims, and create an organization that logically sequences claim(s), counterclaims, reasons, and evidence.
   2. Develop claim(s) and counterclaims fairly and thoroughly, supplying the most relevant evidence for each while pointing out the strengths and limitations of both in a manner that anticipates the audience's knowledge level, concerns, values, and possible biases.
   3. Use words, phrases, and clauses as well as varied syntax to link the major sections of the text, create cohesion, and

clarify the relationships between claim(s) and reasons, between reasons and evidence, and between claim(s) and counterclaims.

4. Establish and maintain a formal style and objective tone while attending to the norms and conventions of the discipline in which they are writing.

5. Provide a concluding statement or section that follows from and supports the argument presented.

C. In grades 4-8, with increased difficulty by grade level, students will be instructed on and will master the skill of writing narratives to develop real or imagined experiences or events using effective technique, descriptive details, and clear event sequences:

1. Orient the reader by establishing a situation and introducing a narrator and/or characters; organize an event sequence that unfolds naturally.

2. Use dialogue and description to develop experiences and events or show the responses of characters to situations.

3. Use a variety of transitional words and phrases to manage the sequence of events.

4. Use concrete words and phrases and sensory details to convey experiences and events precisely.

5. Provide a conclusion that follows from the narrated experiences or events.

D. In grades 4-8, with increased difficulty by grade, students will be instructed on and will master the skill of the production and distribution of writing:

1. Produce clear and coherent writing in which the development and organization are appropriate to task, purpose, and audience.

2. With guidance and support from peers and teachers, develop and strengthen writing as needed by planning, revising, and editing.

3. With some guidance and support from teachers, use technology, including the Internet, to produce and publish writing as well as to interact and collaborate with others; demonstrate sufficient command of keyboarding skills.

CINTHIA COLETTI

E. In grades 4-8, with increased difficulty by grade level, students will be instructed on and master the writing skill of using research to build and present knowledge:
1. Conduct short research projects that build knowledge through investigation of different aspects of a topic.
2. Recall relevant information from experiences or gather relevant information from print and digital sources; take notes and categorize information; and provide a list of sources.
3. Draw evidence from literary or informational texts to support analysis, reflection, and research.

§4.5 Grades 9-12 Writing Literacy Instruction

Writing literacy skills will be provided to all students by content area and English language arts teachers as determined by the Standards to define college and career readiness expectations.

A. In grades 9-12, with increased difficulty by grade level, students will be instructed on and master the skill of writing informative/explanatory texts to examine and convey complex ideas, concepts, and information clearly and accurately through the effective selection, organization, and analysis of content.
1. Introduce a topic; organize complex ideas, concepts, and information so that each new element builds on that which precedes it to create a unified whole; include formatting (e.g., headings), graphics (e.g., figures, tables), and multimedia to aid comprehension:
2. Develop the topic thoroughly by selecting the most significant and relevant facts, extended definitions, concrete details, quotations, or other information and examples appropriate to the audience's knowledge of the topic.
3. Use appropriate and varied transitions and syntax to link the major sections of the text, create cohesion, and clarify the relationships among complex ideas and concepts.
4. Use precise language, domain-specific vocabulary, and techniques such as metaphor, simile, and analogy to manage the complexity of the topic.

5. Establish and maintain a formal style and objective tone while attending to the norms and conventions of the discipline in which they are writing.

6. Provide a concluding statement or section that follows from and supports the information or explanation presented (e.g., articulating implications or the significance of the topic).

B. In grades 9-12, with increased difficulty by grade level, students will be instructed on and master the skill of writing narratives to develop real or imagined experiences or events using effective technique, well-chosen details, and well-structured event sequences:

1. Engage and orient the reader by setting out a problem, situation, or observation and its significance, establishing one or multiple point(s) of view, and introducing a narrator and/or characters; create a smooth progression of experiences or events.

2. Use narrative techniques, such as dialogue, pacing, description, reflection, and multiple plot lines, to develop experiences, events, and characters.

3. Use a variety of techniques to sequence events so that they build on one another to create a coherent whole and build toward a particular tone and outcome (e.g., a sense of mystery, suspense, growth, or resolution).

4. Use precise words and phrases, telling details, and sensory language to convey a vivid picture of the experiences, events, setting, and characters.

5. Provide a conclusion that follows from and reflects on what is experienced, observed, or resolved over the course of the narrative.

C. In grades 9-12, with increased difficulty by grade level, students will be instructed on and master the skill of production and distribution of writing:

1. Produce clear and coherent writing in which the development, organization, and style are appropriate to task, purpose, and audience.

2. Develop and strengthen writing as needed by planning, revising, editing, rewriting, or trying a new approach,

focusing on addressing what is most significant for a specific purpose and audience.

3. Use technology, including the Internet, to produce, publish, and update individual or shared writing products in response to ongoing feedback, including new arguments or information.

D. In grades 9-12, with increased difficulty by grade level, students will be instructed on and master the writing skill of using research to build and present knowledge:

1. Conduct short as well as more sustained research projects to answer a question (including a self-generated question) or solve a problem; narrow or broaden the inquiry when appropriate; synthesize multiple sources on the subject, demonstrating an understanding of the subject under investigation.

2. Gather relevant information from multiple authoritative print and digital sources, using advanced searches effectively; assess the strengths and limitations of each source in terms of the task, purpose, and audience; integrate information into the text selectively to maintain the flow of ideas, while avoiding plagiarism and overreliance on any one source and following a standard format for citation.

3. Draw evidence from literary or informational texts to support analysis, reflection, and research.

Section §5

General-Education Multi-Tier System Of Supports (MTSS) for reading development and literacy interventions

§5.1 Program Criteria for MTSS Standards for SEEDS in Grades Pre-K-3

The state of [insert state name] is committed to systemically addressing the academic needs of all SEEDS by implementing MTSS, for students most at risk for literacy failure. Based on present research, the state of [insert state name] provides in this section an overview MTSS for improving reading achievement for all students as a specific practice of research-based interventions to support students who are reading below grade level. Essentials elements of a successful reading intervention are outlined below and mandated by this law.

A. Early screening, assessment, and identification of SEEDS in grades pre-K-3.
B. Intense instruction and tiers of support will be delivered with intensity as mandated by [insert state name] Statute, Section 5.0 of this law. Optimally, a student who is struggling to read will be assessed and provided instruction in a group of three and no more than four students, and the student will receive this specialized reading instruction at least four, and preferably five, days a week.
C. Intense instruction and intervention will be delivered by a highly qualified and certified teacher of reading as required in [insert state name] Statute, Section 2.0 of this law. Recent studies highlight the difference that a highly trained accomplished teacher of reading can make in the overall success or failure of a reading program.
D. Sufficient duration: One of the most common errors in teaching SEEDS to read is to withdraw prematurely the instruction that seems to be working. A student who is reading accurately at or above grade level but not fluently at their independent reading level still requires intensive reading instruction.

§5.2 MTSS in Grades K-3

The term "MTSS" means a comprehensive system of differentiated supports that includes evidence-based instruction, universal screening, progress monitoring, formative assessments, summative assessments, research-based interventions matched to student needs, and educational decision-making using academic progress overtime. All SEEDS will have the opportunity to benefit from a process that helps them through instruction, intervention, and if necessary, referral to special education as mandated by this law.

A. [Insert state name] principles of Multi-Tier System of Supports (MTSS)
    1. Assumption and belief that all students can learn;

2. Early intervention for students who demonstrate risk for literacy failure;

3. Use of a multitier model of service delivery (to achieve high rates of student success, instruction may be differentiated in both nature and intensity);

4. Use of a problem-solving or standard-protocol method to make decisions within a multitier model;

5. Use of research-based, scientifically validated interventions/ instruction to the extent interventions exist.

6. Monitoring of student progress to inform instruction; and

7. Use of data to make decisions.

B. The process described in this section of the law is for MTSS for SEEDS who struggle in the area of reading:

1. Tier I—Foundational Reading Instruction should involve (1) the use of a scientifically based instructional program for all students, (2) ongoing assessment of progress and monitoring of reading achievement gains, and (3) teachers of reading using flexible grouping to target specific skills and differentiate instruction for all students.

2. Tier II—MTSS intervention is designed to meet the needs of SEEDS who do not respond quickly to foundational reading instruction. MTSS will be provided in the regular classroom setting. These students will receive intensive small group reading instruction in general education. The teacher of reading will provide all the knowledge of [insert state name] Statute, Section 2.2 for Teachers of reading preparation in the reading intervention, emphasizing all essential components of early literacy. Progress monitoring on the student reading development will occur at least every two weeks on targeted skills to ensure adequate advancement and learning. A set of goals for each student will be identified and established. Progress monitoring data will be analyzed, interpreted, and documented. Students who meet set criteria on targeted skills as a result of tier II interventions are reintegrated into the regular classroom setting (tier I).

3. If at any time during the student's tier II intervention or after receiving tier II intervention (maximum of ten weeks), the student's progress in the essential components

of reading shows no advancement and/or the student demonstrates characteristics associated with learning disorders such as dyslexia or specific learning disability, the teacher of reading shall recommend a formal diagnostic assessment for the student.

4. Tier III—MTSS intensive instruction involves a small percentage of students who have received tier II intervention in general education and continue to show marked difficulty in acquiring necessary reading development to reach grade-level attainment. These students necessitate intensive instruction that is more explicit and specifically designed to meet their individual needs. These students will receive progress monitoring at least every two weeks on targeted skills to ensure adequate progress and learning. The approximate time for tier III intensive instruction is eight to ten weeks. After this intensity of instruction the student can return to tier II intervention support before reintegration into the regular classroom setting (tier I).

5. If at any time during the student's tier III intensive instruction, or after receiving tier III intervention, the student's progress in the essential components of reading development shows no advancement and/or the student demonstrates characteristics associated with a learning disorder such as dyslexia or specific learning disability, the teacher of reading will immediately recommended a formal diagnostic assessment for the student.

§5.3 Reading Interventions and Strategies for Older Students Grades 4-12

In the state of [insert state name] grades K-3 reading is considered a separate subject, but in middle school it is important for [insert name of state government department of education] to establish a school culture that recognizes that every content-area teacher is a reading teacher, because reading is involved in every subject area, [insert state name] Statute, Section 2.2 of this law. Therefore, reading strategies will be implemented as a school-wide program in connection with a school culture and vision that works toward high levels of student achievement in reading literacy. Specific interventions and strategies will be provided to support SEEDS who have struggled to learn to read and are performing below grade level in reading. [insert state name]'s schools will provide every opportunity for students to read, practice their strategies, in every subject, every day, to enhance their development of the reading skills they need to become better readers and, ultimately, reading literate.

A. Each school will provide intensive reading interventions to SEEDS in grades 4-12 with reading problems. While the expectation is that students will learn to read with understanding before attaining middle and high school status, the reality is that many students reach these schools unable to read grade-level text effectively and with understanding. SEEDS with demonstrated reading difficulties will be provided twenty-six to thirty-two weeks of supplemental reading interventions as an alternative to English language arts class in middle and high school, that directly addresses their vocabulary, comprehension, and word-reading challenges so they are able to perform significantly better in reading subject material text and can achieve grade-level reading literacy. Research supports identification and MTSS to help:

1. Identify students who are more than one grade level behind in reading and provide daily reading intervention. Using a dedicated period each day with a certified teacher-of-reading professional, students who have reading difficulties that are one or more grade levels below expectations are provided with daily reading instruction, approximately forty to fifty minutes per day, focused specifically on their instructional needs. Providing students specific interventions that are focused on their learning needs requires identifying whether a student's reading comprehension difficulties are a function of (a) word-reading problems (e.g., decoding unknown words), (b) word-meaning problems (e.g., vocabulary), (c) adequate knowledge to understand text (e.g., background knowledge), (d) unusually slow text reading (e.g., fluency), and/or (e) inadequate use of reading comprehension strategies to promote reading comprehension. Through diagnostic assessment, teachers can determine which of the

above are contributing to the reading difficulties and target their instruction.

2. Target instruction for each student by providing systems of support in three tiers with an outline of assessments of skill accomplishments and a timeline for stages of support.

3. During tier I intervention for grade 4-12 students who need intervention in word study, a certified teacher of reading provides students with approximately twenty-five lessons taught over seven to eight weeks depending on student mastery. The daily lessons are composed of Word Study to teach advanced decoding of multisyllabic words. Students' mastery of sounds and word reading determines their progress through the lessons. Students receive daily instruction and practice with individual letter sounds, letter combinations, and affixes. In addition, students receive instruction and practice in applying a strategy to decode multisyllabic words by breaking them into known parts. Students also practice breaking words into parts to spell. Word-reading strategies are applied to reading in context in the form of sentences and passage reading daily.

During tier I intervention, high levels of teacher of reading support and scaffolding are provided to students in applying the multisyllabic word-reading strategy to reading words and connected text, and spelling words. Fluency instruction is promoted by using oral reading fluency data and pairing higher and lower readers for partner reading. Students engage in repeated reading daily with their partner with the goal of increased fluency (accuracy and rate). Partners take turns reading orally while their partner reads along and marks errors. The higher reader always reads first. After reading, partners are given time to go over errors and ask questions about unknown words. Partners read the passage three times each and graph the number of words read correctly. The teacher of reading is actively involved in modeling and providing feedback to students. Vocabulary is taught daily by teaching the meaning of the words through basic definitions and providing examples and nonexamples of how to use the word. New vocabulary words are reviewed daily with students matching words to appropriate definitions or examples of word usage. Comprehension is taught during and after reading by asking students to address relevant comprehension questions of varying levels of difficulty (literal and inferential). Teachers assist students in locating information in text and rereading to identify answers.

4. During tier II intervention the instruction emphasis is on vocabulary and comprehension with additional instruction and practice provided for applying the word study and fluency skills and strategies learned in tier I intervention. Lessons occur over a period of seventeen to eighteen weeks depending on students' progress. Word study and vocabulary are taught through daily review of the word study strategies learned in tier I by applying the sounds and strategy to reading new words. Focus on word meaning is also part of word-reading practice. Students are also taught word relatives and parts of speech (e.g., politics, politician, politically). Finally, students review application of word study to spelling words. Vocabulary words for instruction are chosen from the text read in the fluency and comprehension component. Three days a week teachers use subject matter lessons and materials. Two days a week teachers use novels with lessons developed by the research team. Fluency and comprehension are taught with an emphasis on reading and understanding text through discourse or writing. Students spend three days a week reading and comprehending expository subject matter text. One and two days a week reading and comprehending narrative text in novels. Content and vocabulary are needed to understand the text and are taught prior to reading. Students then read the text at least twice with an emphasis on reading for understanding. During and after the second reading, comprehension questions of varying levels of complexity and abstraction are discussed with students. Students also receive explicit instruction in generating questions of varying levels of complexity and abstraction while reading (e.g., literal questions, questions requiring students to synthesize information from text, and questions requiring students to apply background knowledge

to information in text), identifying the main idea, summarizing, and employing strategies for multiple-choice, short answer, and essay questions.

5. Tier III intervention continues the instructional emphasis on vocabulary and comprehension with more time spent on independent student application of skills and strategies. Tier III occurs over approximately eight to ten weeks.

B. Each content-area teacher will identify key content subject words for each student to learn and teach at least two new words every day and review one from the previous day. This practice can be readily implemented across all content-area instruction and provides students with opportunities to expand their academic vocabulary, increase their background knowledge, and better understand the key ideas that they are reading and learning about. One way a content-area teacher can do this is to select words in a unit that are high-priority and high-utility words. Assuming that a unit is three weeks long, they can then determine the key words students need to know, explicitly teaching them each week and also reviewing them in subsequent weeks. There are several ways that these words can be taught:

1. Teachers can use vocabulary maps that use the key word, pictures of the word, words that relate to the key word, a student friendly definition, and how the word can be used in a historical context.

2. Teachers can illustrate, show a picture that represents the word, or read one or two sentences that include the word describing it in ways that allow students to make informed decisions about word meaning. Then the students and the teacher can use this information to co-construct the meaning of the word.

3. Key words can be taught within the context of a debate or structured discussion in which students use those key words in their written and oral arguments.

C. Teachers should ask students to ask questions while they read and after they listen to the teacher read while they are following the text so that they will monitor comprehension and learning. Students who are actively engaged while listening and reading are more likely to understand and remember what they read or hear. Teachers can promote that practice by instructing students to ask questions while they are reading. After students complete their reading they can also be asked to develop one question to ask the class. Students benefit from having question stems to help them develop these questions.

D. Teachers should teach word-meaning strategies within content-area classes. Concept words are the center of learning the big ideas of content as well as the necessary academic vocabulary for success. Content areas (e.g., math, science, social studies, and English language arts) each have unique vocabulary used to communicate concepts and explain processes. Students need to learn what these words mean and how to use them within the multiple contexts of reading, writing, and speaking. Adolescents will encounter approximately ten thousand new words per year, the majority of which are the complex terms of the content areas. Research supports two practices for helping students learn academic vocabulary:

1. Teachers can provide explicit instruction of academic or concept words that students need to learn to master the key ideas they are teaching. These words need to be introduced to the student by showing them the words, showing them a picture, video, or other demonstration to make the words vivid. Teachers then need to work with students to discuss what the word means and doesn't mean. A critical step is to return to these words regularly throughout the lesson and throughout the instructional unit to assure that students can use them with understanding in their speaking and writing tasks. Teach students the meaning of words within the context of learning and also the multiple meanings of words.

2. Teachers need to provide instruction in word-learning strategies. Although explicit instruction is important, the sheer number of words students need to learn requires that they develop strategies for independently determining the meanings of unfamiliar vocabulary. One means of equipping students to understand the content-area terms they encounter is to teach the component morphemes (prefixes, roots, and suffixes) and how they contribute

to the meaning of words. Research has demonstrated that students taught this process of analyzing words by morphemes were able to infer the meanings of untaught terms in subject-matter text. Other research indicates the practice is particularly effective with SEEDS when done systematically and coupled with multiple opportunities to practice. This can be facilitated by applying learned morphemes to words used in different content areas. Another word-learning strategy involves teaching word meanings directly through the use of a mnemonic word association and a picture that ties together the word clue and the definition.

E. Teachers should instruct students how to activate and build appropriate background knowledge for understanding text content. Researchers report that background knowledge is second only to vocabulary in enhancing reading comprehension outcomes with secondary readers. A lack of prior knowledge can make understanding informational text particularly challenging. Research supports this strategy for building background knowledge:

1. Teach students to use text to support answers and consider whether they can locate text-based support for positions, and

2. Teach students to elaborate on why statements that they select could or could not be supported based on the text.

According to researchers, this technique requires students to identify related background knowledge in their memories to link to the statements and to provide adequate justification for their responses. When used in connection with text reading, it encourages students to return to important information to obtain further elaboration for their responses. Students would be asked to determine whether they could or could not adequately support the statement and use prior learning and text to support their views.

F. Teachers should teach students to use reading comprehension strategies while reading complex text. Students benefit from using reading comprehension strategies while reading complex text. Too often, adolescents proceed through text with little understanding of what they are reading or awareness of when their comprehension has broken down. They need to be taught to recognize when they do not adequately understand text and how to build comprehension. Research supports these strategies for reading comprehension:

1. Teach students to generate questions while reading to build comprehension skills. Learning to generate questions while reading is one way of getting students to stop at regular intervals to think about what is being communicated and how the information relates across paragraphs. Studies have shown that the practice can increase comprehension of content-area text for students of different ability levels. The first level of questions is the most literal in that they are based on a fact that can be identified in one place in the text. The second level of questions combines information that is located in two different parts of the text. The third level of questions relates information in the text to something the reader has experienced or learned previously.

2. Another means of encouraging students to be active readers and to monitor their own comprehension is to teach them how to generate main idea statements for single or multiple paragraphs. Adolescents and teens that learn to identify the explicitly or implicitly stated main ideas of a text have shown increased understanding and recall of important information. Referred to as either "paragraph shrinking" or "get the gist," students at a range of ability levels and language backgrounds have been successfully taught to use three steps in generating a main idea statement:

    a. Identify who or what is the focus of the paragraph or section;

    b. Determine the most important information about what the key person place/thing has, is, or does;

    c. Succinctly state the 'who' or 'what' and most important information about him/her/it in a sentence.

G. Teachers should guide and engage students in activities that are text related. Through both classroom discussion and written assignments, students will learn to apply critical analysis, inference, interpretation, and summation of printed material. The goal is to guide the student to understand text and respond through productive discussion and written answers.

Research supports the following strategies for encouraging reading for understanding:

1. Foster discussion in small groups. Give students the opportunities to return to texts a number of times to explore, discuss, and revise their developing understanding of the ideas and concepts. This practice can be fostered through the use of reciprocal teaching, a multicomponent strategy intended to support student comprehension. In reciprocal teaching, the teacher leads the dialogue about the text until students learn to assume different roles independently: summarizer, questioner, clarifier, or predictor. After reading a short section of text (generally a few paragraphs, at first, but increasing to several pages with practice), the summarizer highlights the key points for the group. Then the questioner helps the group consider and talk about what was read by posing questions about anything that was unclear, puzzling, or related to other information that was learned. In this portion of reciprocal teaching, students can apply question generation skills that will support asking about more than surface-level information. The clarifier in the group of students is responsible for seeking out portions of text that will help answer the questions just posed. However, all members of the group participate in discussing the information and connecting ideas. In doing so, students need to return to the current selection and, possibly, other readings to look for text evidence in support of their responses. Finally, the predictor offers suggestions about what the group can expect to read in the next section of text. These predictions are focused on activating relevant background knowledge, setting a purpose for reading, and relating new information to that just discussed by the group.

2. Teachers should instruct students in how to summarize text. Students that are explicitly taught how to summarize text are better able to discern the relationships among main ideas and significant details. When students work collaboratively on summaries of expository text, such as in reciprocal teaching, they reach higher levels of comprehension and retain more content information.

Teachers should thoroughly explain and model each step multiple times with different types of text before students will be able to complete them in collaborative groups or, eventually, on their own.

H. Teachers should maximize all opportunities for students to read printed material. Both middle- and high-school content-area teachers will have a range of readers in their classrooms, providing challenges for assignments that require text reading. For this reason, and others, many classroom teachers require students to read very little both inside and outside of their class time. Teachers also report that they increasingly rely on reading text aloud or using other media (e.g., videos) as a means for providing students with content knowledge perceiving text reading as inaccessible. Reading and understanding text requires practice, and students need opportunities to read a range of text types (e.g., textbooks, letters, descriptions, original documents, poetry). Research supports the following strategies to enhance opportunities for students to read and respond to text:

1. Prepare students to read text by providing key ideas and key words. Providing the big idea and connecting principles prior to having students read the text will facilitate comprehension. This goal can also be accomplished by soliciting the big idea and principle from the students. Present the key words orally, on the board, or on a handout, including all proper nouns, prior to text reading.

2. Provide daily opportunities for students to read for a specific amount of time then provide a prompt for student response (e.g., two to three minutes for reading and one to two minutes for responding). Students can be asked to respond to predetermined prompts such as, "What is this section mostly about?" "How does the author describe _____?" "What did you learn about _____?" Students can respond in writing using learning logs or they can respond orally by turning and talking with a partner for one minute.

3. Have students participate in partner reading (typically a better reader and a less able reader) and then ask them to

take turns reading the same passage with the better reader reading the passage first and then the less able reader rereading the passage. Students can partner-read for a specified amount of time (e.g., three minutes) and can use one to two minutes to write responses by determining the main idea, writing and answering a question, or summarizing.

I. Teachers should organize students into collaborative groups for reading tasks. Student involvement and learning can be enhanced through well-structured collaborative groups, designed to promote both individual and group accountability. These groups can be used within content-area classes and are associated with improved reading comprehension for students when implemented two or more times per week. Research supports the following strategies for collaborative groups:

1. Having students use collaborative strategic reading (CSR). CSR has two important phases: the first phase is learning the four reading comprehension strategies that include (1) previewing text (preview), (2) monitoring comprehension while reading by identifying key words and concepts that are challenging (click and clunk), (3) thinking about the main idea while reading and putting it into your own words (get the gist), and (4) summarizing text understanding after you read (wrap-up). The second phase is teaching students to use cooperative groups effectively as a means of applying the strategies. The focus of the practice described in this section is on implementing cooperative groups. Once students have developed proficiency using the four strategies with teacher guidance, they are ready to use these same strategies in peer-led cooperative learning groups. Some teachers ask students to first work in pairs and then move into a group, while other teachers find it better to start with cooperative groups.

2. Forming CSRs will be a success if the teacher is aware that all students will not function equally well in a group and that groups are more effective when the teacher selects students with the intent of designing a well-functioning team. Teachers assign approximately four students to each group, considering that each group will need a student with

reading proficiency and a leader, thus providing a group that represents varying abilities. Teachers assign students to roles in the group and teach them to perform their role. Roles rotate on a regular basis (e.g., every couple of weeks) so that students can experience a variety of roles. Student roles are an important aspect of effective implementation of cooperative learning so that all group members are assigned a meaningful task and participate in the group's success.

3. The teacher's role in CSR, while students are working in their groups, is to ensure the students have been taught their role and know how to implement their responsibility. Forming successful and productive groups is an important accomplishment because it allows the teacher to circulate among the groups, listen to students' participation, read students' learning logs, and most importantly, provide clear and specific feedback to improve the use and application of the strategies. Teachers can help by actively listening to students' conversations and clarifying difficult words, modeling strategy usage, encouraging students to participate, and modeling strategy application. It is expected that students will need assistance learning to work in cooperative groups, implementing the strategies, and mastering academic content.

Section §6

Guidelines for Early Childhood and Education Providers Data Driven Preliteracy Instruction from Birth to Age Five

New Qualifications, Licenses, and Certifications for All Early Care Educators and Providers in Preliteracy Birth to Age Five.

Teachers of Reading

A. Board-approved provider, educator, and teacher preparation programs shall certify early care educators and providers in preliteracy birth to age five. The program will require instruction in the application of the research-based foundations of literacy. It will be founded on research-proven instructional best practices based on replicated evidence that shows that when these programs or practices are used, diverse student populations can be expected to achieve, at a minimum, literacy readiness and satisfactory preparedness for reading instruction in kindergarten.

§6.1 Basic Requirements for Foundational Preliteracy Instruction

B. The program or collection of practices for early care and education providers in preliteracy birth-age five should include, at a minimum, instruction in and application of the following five areas of foundational preliteracy:
1. Early Literacy Research;
2. Language Development;
3. Shared Book Reading with an emphasis on Vocabulary;
4. Phonological Awareness; and
5. The Speech-to-Print Connection with an emphasis on Alphabet Knowledge.

§6.2 Predictors of Early Literacy Success

The program or collection of practices for early care and education providers should take into account the variables representing early or precursor literacy skills.

A. Strong predictors of early literacy success include
1. Alphabet Knowledge: knowledge of the names and sounds associated with printed letters;
2. Phonological Awareness: the ability to detect, manipulate, or analyze the auditory aspects of spoken language (including the ability to distinguish or segment words, syllables, or phonemes), independent of meaning;
3. Rapid Automatic Naming (RAN) of letters or digits: the ability to rapidly name a sequence of random letters or digits;

    4. Rapid Automatic Naming (RAN) of objects or colors: the ability to rapidly name a sequence of repeating random sets of pictures of objects (e.g., "car," "tree," "house," "man") or colors;

    5. Writing or writing name: the ability to write letters in isolation on request or to write one's own name; and

    6. Phonological Memory: the ability to remember spoken information for a short period of time.

B. Strategies for promoting early literacy:

    1. Shared Book Reading: reading books with children, encouraging various forms of reader-child interactions around the material being read and the vocabulary used;

    2. Phonological Awareness Activities: rhyme, syllable, and sound activities that promote awareness of the smallest units of spoken language that can be manipulated independent of meaning; and

    3. Connecting Speech-to-Print: helping children understand what they know—speech—and relate it to what they do not yet know—print—through Alphabet Knowledge and early writing activities.

§6.3 Preliteracy Language Development

Given the research-proven link between the major elements of spoken and written language development (listening, speaking, reading, and writing), early care and education providers should know how these language skills interrelate and contribute toward full literacy.

Important elements of language to be incorporated into preliteracy education include:

1. Phonology: the sound system;
2. Vocabulary: words, relationships, and concepts;
3. Morphology: meaningful word parts;
4. Syntax: the rules for making sentences; and
5. Pragmatics: language use based on context and situation.
6. Scaffolding helps children advance from what they know to what they need to learn

§6.4 Shared Reading Benefits and Strategies

Shared book reading (reading with children, rather than to children) with an emphasis on Vocabulary is a critical step in preparing children for the development of language skills and reading literacy. This activity

1. Builds oral language and print awareness;
2. Builds vocabulary by introducing high frequency words for mature language users; and
3. Can be adapted for other shared book reading strategies, including
4. Text Talk (vocabulary enrichment): a strategy developed to build mature vocabulary during shared book reading;
5. The PEER Sequence: a strategy for building comprehension; and
6. CROWD: a strategy for building vocabulary and comprehension.

§6.5 Phonological Awareness

The program or collection of practices for early care and education providers should include an understanding of phonological awareness.

1. Phonological awareness is understanding that spoken language is made up of smaller parts: sentence into words, words into syllables, syllables into sounds
2. Phonological awareness includes a progression of rhyming skills from rote rhyming to recognizing rhyme to completing rhymes to generating rhymes.
3. At the syllable level, the progression of rhyming skills is as follows:
   a. blending;
   b. segmenting; and
   c. deleting.
4. At the phonemic (sound) level, the progression of rhyming skills is as follows:
   a. matching;
   b. isolating;

c. blending;
d. segmenting and counting;
e. deleting; and
f. manipulating.

§6.6 Connection between Spoken and Written Language

The program or collection of practices for early care and education providers should include speech-to-print connection with an emphasis on alphabet knowledge.

1. Children need to use what they know—speech—to master what they do not yet know—print
2. Children need to learn to experience print in the following contexts:
   a. recognizing print in their surroundings;
   b. understanding that print carries meaning;
   c. knowing that print is used for many purposes; and
   d. generating print through exploratory writing.
3. With the help of early care and education providers, children should acquire the alphabetic principle through concepts of words and concepts of letters. They should
   a. understand that sounds heard in spoken words are represented by letters; and
   b. know the sound that each letter or group of letters can make.
4. In order to impart this foundational literacy knowledge, early care and education providers should use such tools and techniques as
   a. sound walls;
   b. letter boxes and buckets; and
   c. variations on the alphabet song.

Once all of these components are incorporated into preliteracy education, the states will develop a common early literacy language between pre-K early care and education providers and kindergarten teachers through a pre-K-K collaborative design.

Section § 7

School District and School Boards Responsibilities to Literacy Policy

§7.1 [Insert name of state school board] Requirements

A. The local [insert name of the school board of education] for each school district, school, and charter school is responsible for ensuring compliance within their district with state Policy, rule, and procedures outlined in this Policy. Each school system has specific responsibilities for the implementation of the Policy, including:

1. To create and adopt school system policies and procedures for implementation of the Policy;

2. To guarantee ongoing, clear public notification regarding the district's obligations toward assurance of certified teachers of reading in all grade K-3 classrooms to include teaching specialists, special education, ELL, and Title I instructors; assurance of data-validated/evidenced-based Foundational Reading Development Instruction; and assurance of MTSS for SEEDS students;

3. To provide informational training and professional development about reading literacy for content-area teachers, system representatives, teachers, paraprofessionals, appropriate staff, and administrators on an annual basis per [insert state name] Statute, Section 2 of this Policy;

4. To assure that each school within the system select personnel to oversee the assessment process for determination of program eligibility per [insert state name] Statute, Section 2.0 of this Policy;

5. To assure that programs for SEEDS students meet the state criteria and follow the appropriate guidelines to include formal diagnostic assessment of students; and

6. To assure that each school within the system follows the regulations for implementation of the Policy by providing for the functional and academic needs of students identified as not achieving grade-level reading proficiency.

B. Each Board of Education must:
  1. Ensure that procedures for using data systems and assessments to identifying SEEDS students are implemented in the district and MTSS to bring all students to reading proficiency;
  2. Ensure that procedures for providing appropriate instructional services and accommodations or modifications for the student are fully implemented in the district;
  3. Ensure that the district or school complies with all applicable requirements of state educational programs.

§7.2 District Requirements

Each school district must:

A. Administer K-3 universal screening at least three times during the kindergarten year. Every student in grades 1, 2, and 3 shall be assessed for appropriate reading progress every two to three weeks as identified in, [insert state name] Statute, Section 3 of this Policy;
B. Provide early identification, intervention, and support, [insert state name] Statute, Section 3 of this Policy;
C. Apply results of early assessment instruments to instruction and report to the district;
D. Implement procedures according to the State Board of Education;
E. Provide annual training of certified teachers of reading, staff, and paraprofessionals about SEEDS students;
F. Ensure the procedures for identification, instruction, and communication are in place;
G. Ensure the individuals responsible for administering and interpreting the necessary testing receive ongoing professional development in the assessments used;
H. Test for SEEDS students at appropriate times, as needed and in all grades;
I. Provide appropriate instruction, tier of supports, and accommodations for SEEDS and IEP students;
J. Purchase or develop programs that include descriptors listed in the state handbook;

K. Notify parents in writing before an assessment or identification procedure is used with an individual student;
L. Inform parents of all services and options available to eligible students;
M. Provide students with services of a teacher of reading and/or a teaching specialist certified and skilled in methods appropriate for SEEDS students' success;
N. Provide MTSS for students requiring specialized instruction, [insert state name] Statute, Section 5;
O. Provide a parent education program; and
P. Provide appropriate progress monitoring.

Section §8

State Implementation Infrastructure; District and School Access to Policy Information, Training and Coaching, and System Supports; Teacher Certification and Credentialing

A. Identify and define core features of the law including [insert state's] core features (e.g., teacher licensing requirements, use of Multi-Tier System of Supports, use of data-validated instruction).
B. Provide training for state, regional, and local implementation teams to build implementation capacity for program and school administrators that will include core components of implementation science including: selection, training, coaching, program fidelity and evaluation, systems intervention, facilitative administration, and data systems to support decision-making;
C. Provide preservice and professional development training so that all content-areas teachers and teachers of reading have the skills and knowledge to pass the [insert name of state] basic and/or advanced reading instruction competence teaching assessment, are knowledgeable about and can effectively implement appropriate instruction to meet the needs of all students, and have the knowledge and skills to monitor student progress toward attainment of literacy skills;

CINTHIA COLETTI

D. Develop a system of oversight of teacher preparation programs in order to align such programs with state certification exams;

E. Provide training for teacher preparation personnel in order to build capacity for ensuring that teacher candidates have the knowledge and skills needed to pass state certification exams; and

F. Develop a communication protocol to help align policies and systems and to remove barriers to effective implementation of the core features of the law.

The law, along with a state plan for building implementation capacity, will be readily available to the public through the [insert the name of state board of education] website [insert the web address (URL) of the state board of education], in print, and through an interpreter. Additionally, this law provides that each school district, school, and charter school shall:

A. Provide to parents, teachers, school administrators, staff, and all interested parties public notice regarding the school system's specific implementation plan, in addition to the system's obligations toward all students, specifically SEEDS, exhibiting potential for literacy failure;

B. Ensure that teachers and administrators are aware of the state regulations regarding literacy failure; the characteristics of SEEDS; the state licensure requirements of teachers and credentialing of teachers of reading in kindergarten, elementary, secondary, and special education; and the school system's policies for implementation of the law;

C. Create district- and school-level implementation teams to ensure that teachers and principals have the capacity to implement core features of the law, systems are aligned to support implementation of the law, and barriers to effective implementation are removed so that all SEEDS attain grade-level proficiency in reading by the end of third grade;

D. Implement a program for universal screening for K-1 students, [insert state name] Statute, Section 3 of this law, and assessment for all grade pre-K-3 students and those students displaying characteristics of SEEDS;

E. Provide tier I instruction through a data-validated and evidence-based foundational reading instruction program;

F. Provide tier II of the MTSS, [insert state name] Statute, Section 5.0 of this law, within thirty days of screening or assessment if a SEEDS is found;

G. Provide tier III of the MTSS within ten days of tier II instruction should the SEEDS student not make adequate progress, [insert state name] Statute, Section 5.0 of this law;

H. Provide tier III of the MTSS within ten days of tier II instruction should the SEEDS student not make adequate progress, [insert state name] Statute, Section 5.0 of this law;

I. Initiate referral for special education under timelines specified under state law to SEEDS who have not responded to MTSS in regular education, [insert state name] Statute, Section 3.9 of this law;

J. Initiate procedures for evaluation of eligibility under §504/ADAAA if the student is not found to be eligible for special education; and

K. Initiate procedures to implement the Standards for reading and writing literacy and for speaking, listening, and language skills.

Section §9

Compliance
Guidelines For Compliance With The Policy

§9.1 Documentation

The intent of this recommended documentation is to ensure that a district, school, or charter school meets the needs of students and protects the rights of students and parents or guardians. The districts, schools, and charter schools will document the following in writing:

A. Documentation that the notice of evaluation has been given to parents or guardians;

B. Documentation that parents or guardians were given an explanation of their rights and provided a copy of the state Policy and IDEA 2004;

C. Documentation of the parent or guardian's consent for the evaluation;
D. Documentation of the evaluation data;
E. Documentation of the decisions made by the committee of knowledgeable persons concerning the disability, [insert state name] Statute, Sections 3.8-9, of this Policy, and if a disability exists, whether the disability substantially limits a major life activity; and
F. Documentation of the placement options and placement decisions, [insert state name] Statute, Sections 4 and 5 of this Policy.

§9.2 Procedures

Checklist of procedures to ensure compliance:

A. Notification to parents or guardians requesting permission to assess student for assessment or formal diagnostic;
B. Copy of state Literacy Policy and IDEA 2004 to be provided to the parents or guardians; and
C. Formal notification from the school district to inform and notify the teachers and parents or guardians of results from each measure or assessment administered to the student:
    1. List each measurement or assessment and describe the meaning and function of the measurement;
    2. Include identification, if one is determined, by the committee according to [insert state name] Statute, Section 3.8. of this Policy;
    3. Describe the next steps of the remediation and instruction process for the student, [insert state name] Statute, Section 5.0 of this Policy;
    4. Provide a timeline for remediation, future assessment dates, and procedure for progress reporting;
    5. Provide access to the ongoing data collected on the student; and
    6. Provide date for the next meeting with the parents or guardians and the school and teacher.

§9.3 Funding Implementation

It is the intention of the Legislature that the costs relative to the implementation of the provisions of this Policy shall be covered by funds appropriated by the state. Such funds shall include those appropriated pursuant to [insert name of state education approved budget]. It is also supported by research that if the state is able to provide free and quality instruction to its young people, they will become graduates capable of contributing to the state's revenues. This is a payback that has been projected at $_____ [information can be found on the National Center for Education Statistics (NCES) site].

§9.4 Compliance/Funding Consequences

Requires the district or school to prepare a corrective action plan or improvement plan if the secretary of education determines that the district or school fails to comply with legislation. In the event of failure to comply with legislation, the state [insert secretary of education office name] (Secretary) may take the following actions:

A. District or school needs intervention assistance if the [insert secretary of education office name] determines, for two consecutive years, that there has been no improvement in AYP and the district or school needs assistance in implementing the requirements of this Policy; the Secretary takes one or more of the following actions:
   1. Places the entire entity on probation and posts this action for public awareness. Advises the district or school of available sources of technical assistance that may help address the areas in which the entity needs assistance, which may include assistance from the Office of Special Education Programs, other offices of the Department of Education, other federal agencies, technical assistance providers approved by the Secretary, and other federally funded nonprofit agencies, and requires the district, school, or charter school to work with appropriate entities. Such technical assistance may include:
      a. Making provisions for advice by experts to address the areas in which the district or school needs assistance,

including explicit plans for addressing the area for concern within a specified period of time;

b. Assisting in identifying and implementing professional development, instructional strategies, and methods of instruction that are based on scientifically based research;

c. Designating and using distinguished superintendents, principals, special-education administrators, special-education teachers, and other teachers to provide advice, technical assistance, and support; and

d. Devising additional approaches to providing technical assistance, such as collaborating with institutions of higher education, educational service agencies, national centers of technical assistance, and private providers of scientifically based technical assistance.

e. The entity will provide a plan of action and a timeline on all improvement strategies and a commitment to adhere to the Policy.

2. Directs the use of funds from district or school on the area or areas in which school needs assistance to professional organization to prepare plan, evaluate data and provide recommendations;

3. Identifies the district or school as a high-risk grantee and imposes special conditions on the grant; and

4. Uses authority to replace the leadership at the school and apply criminal charges for breaking the Policy.

B. District or school needs intervention; the Secretary takes one or more of the following actions if the Secretary determines, for three or more consecutive years, that a district, school, or charter school needs intervention in implementing the requirements of this Policy, the following shall apply:

1. The Secretary may take any of the actions described in Section 8.4.A.1.

2. The Secretary takes following actions by changing the district or school-based leadership and teaching staff to correct the problem within one year by showing marked improvement 25 percent or more with compliance by the second year.

C. For each year of the determination, withholds not less than 20 percent and not more than 50 percent of the district or school funds until the Secretary determines by use of data that the district or school has sufficiently addressed the areas in which intervention is needed.

D. Seeks to recover funds:

1. Withholds, in whole or in part, any further payments to the district or school;

2. Needs substantial intervention. At any time that the Secretary determines that a district or school needs substantial intervention in implementing the requirements of the Policy or that there is a substantial failure to comply with any condition, the Secretary takes one or more of the following actions:

   a. Recovers funds

   b. Withholds, in whole or in part, any further payments.

3. Refers the case to the Office of the Inspector General at the state [insert name state board].

EFFECTIVE DATE. This Literacy Law is effective [insert date].

SUMMARY AND FACTS
BY CHAPTER

PART ONE: The Stories and the Facts of Literacy in the United States

Chapter One: Going Public

Across America, children are struggling to read. The reasons for their struggles vary widely, from economic disadvantage to specific learning disabilities, but the outcome is all too often the same: an unsuccessful academic record followed by bleak job prospects and a lifetime of self-doubt and self-blame. No one deserves this path, but as a society, we have done little to reach out to those who stray down it. While it may be tempting to place the blame for our students' plunging literacy attainment entirely on an ineffective education system, in truth, this is an issue that all of society has contributed toward and that we must address together. The struggling young readers of America are the future workforce, the future electorate, and the future global community. They are our future, and we cannot let them slip through the cracks.

Chapter Two: America's Plight

In the information age, literacy is key to success in school, work, and life in general. Our students need the ability to interact and communicate competently and dynamically—skills that are valuable not only in the top industries but also in every aspect of social, personal, and professional life. There is no denying that for society to function, all its members must make a meaningful contribution; and yet this cannot happen when two-thirds of the up-and-coming generation is less than fully literate. America is rapidly losing its hard-earned place among the leading industrial nations, but it is not yet past the point of recovery. If we are to rise to economic and cultural greatness once again, we must actively seek solutions: Rather than throwing more money at the problem and watching as it is swallowed by the gaps in our outmoded education system, we must fix the system itself.

Facts and Quotes

1. To reach a marketing audience of 50 million, the radio took 38 years, while Facebook took two.

   Social Media Marketing, Web Traffic Partners

2. The US Bureau of Labor Statistics reports that there are 3.1 million US jobs unfilled due to a shortage of qualified workers, while 12.8 million citizens are the documented unemployed.

   Bureau of Labor Statistics, Washington, DC (2012), accessed March 2012

3. 1,100 US manufacturers report job openings for skilled workers, while 83 percent of companies report moderate to serious shortages of labor.

   Association for Manufacturing Excellence, Rowling Meadows, Il, accessed February 2012

4. In terms of college graduation rates, the United States, in which 41 percent of citizens aged 25 to 34 hold college degrees, has made no progress in citizen education over the past forty years. Meanwhile, South Korea's college graduation rate

among the same age group has increased from 13 to 63 percent in just twenty years.

International Comparisons of Educational Attainment, Council of Graduate Schools, Nov. 1, 2011

5. According to the College Board, for every 100 US ninth-graders:

70 will graduate from high school.
44 will enter college.
30 will return to college for their sophomore year.
ONLY 21 will earn a bachelor's degree.

Reforming Schools through College Readiness, Excelerator, College Board, Feb. 12, 2012

6. Last year, of the 1.65 million students who took the SAT, only 43 percent met the "college and career benchmark" defined by the College Board. According to the Board, which was founded in 1900 and has data on student scores since 1972, the 2011 scores are the lowest in 40 years.

"43 Percent of 2011 College-Bound Seniors Met SAT College and Career Readiness Benchmark," College Board, accessed September 17, 2011

7. Between 1997 and 2007, China's enormous investment in its students' education doubled the number of colleges and quintupled the number of college graduates in the country.

Zakaria, Fareed. "The Real Challenge from China: Its People, Not Its Currency."[2] *Time Magazine*, Oct. 7, 2010

8. China's 400 million students typically start their formal education at age two and are expected to recognize 400 Chinese characters and write 100 midway through first grade.

Kristof, Nicholas D. "China's Winning Schools?" The *New York Times*, Jan. 15, 2011

9. The United States ranks twenty-fourth out of thirty-four developed countries in reading literacy.

Programme for International Student Assessment (PISA), Organisation for Economic Co-operation and Development (OECD), Paris, France (2009).

10. Despite the $1.15 trillion the US spends on public education every year—more money per student than any other country in the world—nearly seven out of ten US students read at a basic or below-basic level.

Kristof, Nicholas D. "China's Winning Schools?" The *New York Times*, Jan. 15, 2011

11. Students in Portugal, Hong Kong, Germany, Poland, Liechtenstein, Slovenia, Colombia, and Lithuania are improving academically at twice the rate of American students, while those in Latvia, Chile, and Brazil are improving at three times our rate.

Harvard Program on Education Policy and Governance (PEPG), Harvard Kennedy School, Cambridge, Massachusetts (2012)

12. While American students spend an average of 32 hours a week in school, children in Scandinavian countries have forty- to fifty-hour school weeks and Chinese students spend between eight-and-a-half and twelve hours a day in school.

"China's Children Too Busy for Playtime," *China Daily* (Xinhau), accessed September 15, 2011

13. The 2010-2011 classroom demographic of 3.4 million kindergartners consisted of 53 percent whites, 24 percent Hispanics, 13 percent African Americans, 4 percent Asians, and 1 percent American Indians or Alaska Natives.

Department of Education

14. Currently, 50 percent of new teachers quit the field altogether within the first five years.

Alliance for Excellent Education (2005). "Teacher attrition: A Costly Loss to the Nation and States," Issue Brief. Washington, DC: Alliance for Excellent Education.

Chapter Three: Road to Recovery

The weaknesses of the American education system present us, at the local and national levels alike, with a powerful opportunity to unite and drive change. It is time to stop making excuses for poor academic achievement and to start making improvements. The Common Core State Standards were created to do just that, and these significant educational reforms will find success—but only if we change our societal outlook as well. America must clearly define its vision of education and commit to realizing it through research-proven tactics, starting in the colleges of education and extending into each individual classroom. Many districts, and even entire states, have already set learning and literacy goals and are attaining them using such data-validated practices. Now, all that remains is for the nation as a whole to learn from its citizens and pass that knowledge on to its students.

Facts and Quotes

1. High school dropout rates in the United States have tripled in the past thirty years.

National Center for Education Statistics (NCES, 2011), Washington DC, accessed September, 2011

2. Countless studies demonstrate that all but 1 percent of all students can be taught to read using known methods.

Cardenas-Hagan, E. (2011). "Language and Literacy Development among English Language Learners. In *Multisensory Teaching of Basic Language Skills*, J. R. Birsh (ed.). Baltimore: Paul H. Brookes Publishing.

Chard, D. J., S. Vaughn, and B. Tyler. 2002. "A Synthesis of Research on Effective Interventions for Building Reading Fluency with Elementary Students with Learning Disabilities." *Journal of Learning Disabilities*.

Denton, C. A., and P. G. Mathes. 2003. "Intervention for Struggling Readers: Possibilities and Challenges." In *Preventing and Remediating Reading Difficulties: Bringing Science to Scale*, B. R. Foorman (ed.). Timonium, MD: York Press.

3. Studies conducted with functional magnetic resonance imaging show that under the tutelage of a skilled teacher, changes in students' brain activity allow them to develop and retain significantly better language skills.

Just, M., J. D. Gabrieli, A. Myler, T. Keller. 2009. "Focused Instruction Can Help Underperforming Brain Areas to Increase Their Proficiency." Center for Cognitive Brain Imaging, Carnegie Mellon University, Pittsburg, PA, The Department of Brain and Cognitive Sciences at Massachusetts Institute of Technology, Cambridge, MA.

Chapter Four: Collaborate and Prevail

The literacy movement is well on its way to finding success. Federal programs can be difficult to enact and sustain through changes in the administration, but state and local policies, organized by grassroots teams and supported by communities, have already made a significant difference in learning outcomes in nearly half of all states. For this trend to continue, we cannot fall back into complacency or otherwise lose momentum, and we cannot let America's economic situation stand in the way of achievement. While an undereducated populace carries a staggering price tag for the state and national government, an effective education system, starting with teacher preparation and certification and continuing through classroom practices and supports, is a tremendous boon to the economy. Most of all, an education system shaped by the Standards and informed by scientific research and findings will change the lives of millions of children who, whatever the cause of their academic troubles, absolutely deserve to achieve full literacy and reach their potential in life.

Facts and Quotes

1. In 2011, 21 percent of Hispanics/Latinos, 44 percent of whites, 57 percent of Asians, and 30 percent of blacks in America held an associate's degree or higher.

   Educational Attainment in the United States: 2011—Detailed Tables, United States Census Bureau, Feb 2011

2. In 2011, the Pacific Research Institute found that the state of California's failure to prepare a single cohort of freshmen for college-level work will cost students, schools, and the state up to $14 billion in remediation classes annually.

   Pacific Research Institute, California Index of Leading Education Indicators, Second Edition, San Francisco, CA, 2010.

3. On average, one in four California high school students scores proficient or higher on the English language arts section of the California Standards Test, and one in five California high school juniors are deemed college-ready in language arts on the Early Assessment Program test.

   Profile for California (State); Category: Education, Data Center: Kids Count, Annie E. Casey Foundation

   Early Assessment Program, California Department of Education

4. Over the past forty years, the amount of money the United States spends per student in public education every year has nearly tripled, from about $4,000 in 1971 to $11,000 in 2011.

   Total and current expenditures per pupil in public elementary and secondary schools: Selected years, 1919-20 through 2008-09, National Center for Education Statistics (NCES), Institute of Education Sciences (IES), 2011

5. Nationally, 1,230,000 students fail to graduate from secondary school every year.

   Alliance for Excellent Education—"The High Cost of High School Dropouts: What the Nation Pays for Inadequate High Schools" (Washington, DC: Author, 2008)

6. These 1.23 million nongraduates cost America over $319 billion in lost wages, taxes, and productivity in their lifetimes.

   "Demography as Destiny: How America Can Build a Better Future" (Washington, DC: Author, 2006).

7. According to the OECD, America spends over half a trillion dollars in public and private money every year on education, more than any of the other twenty-four industrialized nations.

   United States, Education at a Glance: OECD Indicators 2012, OECD

Part Two: Toolbox for Building a Cultural Movement to Drive A Seismic Shift in US Literacy Outcomes

Chapter Five: On the Edge of Action

Change is elusive—in the minds of many Americans, it originates at the higher levels of government, trickles through the political bureaucracy, and has, at best, a delayed and indirect effect on their own lives. Fortunately, this does not have to be the case, and we must free ourselves of these misconceptions if we intend to make a difference in national literacy statistics and economic growth. Change can happen at the grassroots level, and community efforts to improve education have indeed already succeeded in many states. Years of scientific research have informed us of the ingredients for education reform: teacher preparation and certification, data-validated instruction and evaluation, student support, and faithful implementation. Now you, too, can join the cause, by familiarizing yourself with the facts, gathering a coalition of friends and allies, and pledging to take the first step toward a more literate America.

Facts and Quotes

1. In state-by-state rankings, California—the world's eighth leading economy—students rank 46th in reading and math achievement, 41st in high school graduation, and 49th in young adult high school diploma holdings. California also ranks 23rd in the number of citizens holding a bachelor's degree or higher; in 1960 the state was 8th.

   Fensterwald, John. "Sobering NAEP Scores: Achievement Gap Grows Sharply in San Diego." *Thoughts on Public Education*, Silicon Valley Education Foundation, Dec. 9, 2011.

2. Since 2003, Massachusetts has required teachers to pass a competency assessment in reading instruction and literacy; the state now boasts the highest 4th- and 8th-grade NAEP scores in the US.

   NAEP Results: State-level for Massachusetts, Massachusetts Department of Elementary and Secondary Education

Chapter Six: Knowledge Calibration

Teacher knowledge is the primary factor in what students learn, how they learn, and how far their education will take them. For this reason, any successful education reform must guarantee that teaching candidates are knowledgeable in their area of instruction before they can be certified or credentialed. This is a special concern with teachers of reading, who at this point in time are unlikely to have received special training in the science of reading development and the assessment of reading troubles. Once these requirements are implemented, however, the benefits for students, teachers, schools, and the nation as a whole will be dramatic. Just as students deserve the best reading instruction for their future success, teachers deserve the best preparation for the enormous responsibility and privilege of shaping the next generation of thinkers.

Facts and Quotes

1. America's NAEP scores for 4th graders show that our nation is 17th in the world in reading.

   "The Nation's Report Card on 4th Grade Reading 2011," *Voices for America's Children*, 2011

2. Studies conducted on teachers' literacy-related knowledge and reading education curricula show that university professors are not very well-informed about word structure (phonemes and graphemes).

   McCombes-Tolis, J., and R. Feinn. 2008. "Comparing Teachers' Literacy-Related Knowledge to Their State's Standards for Reading." *Reading Psychology* 29: 236-265.

   Joshi, R. M., E. Binks, L. Graham, E. Ocker-Dean, D. Smith, and R. Boulware-Gooden. 2009. "Do Textbooks Used in University Reading Education Courses Conform to the Instructional Recommendations of the National Reading Panel?" *Journal of Learning Disabilities* 42: 458-463.

3. Teachers' knowledge of the subject they teach is the major teacher characteristic related to student achievement.

   Miller and Chait, 2008

4. Harvard researchers have identified five levels of increasing progressive differentiation in a teacher's mastery of his or her field: declarative, situated, stable, expert, and reflective knowledge.

   Snow, C. E., P. Griffin, and M. S. Burns. 2005. *Knowledge to Support the Teaching of Reading: Preparing Teachers for a Changing World.* San Francisco, CA: Jossey-Bass.

5. After analyzing 222 reading course syllabi from 72 institutions, the National Council on Teacher Quality found that 85 percent of the programs ignored scientific research on reading.

    What Education Schools Aren't Teaching about Reading and What Elementary Teachers Aren't Learning

Chapter Seven: Actions of the Potentate

For centuries now, America has led the world in freedom and progress. The nation's recent slip in educational achievement is a cause for concern and a call to action, but it does not at all indicate that the basic principles upon which America was founded have ceased to propel us forward. On the contrary, in order to succeed in the movement for education and literacy, we must return to our roots and embrace the spirit of equity, self-reliance, and social justice that first brought this country to the forefront. An effective message to potential champions and allies will reflect all of these ideals in its phrasing and imagery. To fully bring your message to life, arm yourself with both facts and success stories and always be ready to reach out.

Facts and Quotes

1. More than 46 million Americans are living in poverty—the highest rate in over fifty years.

    Sabrina Tavernise. "Soaring Poverty Casts Spotlight on "Lost Decade." The *New York Times* (Washington). September 13, 2011.

Chapter Eight: Leverage Social Media to Drive Change! Twitter Power for Literacy Educators and Activists

The world is changing rapidly, and for those of us who did not grow up with computers in our pockets and a massive global audience at our fingertips, the question of where to start (and whether to start at all) can be difficult. However, social media is an enormously valuable tool when it comes to sending a message and starting a movement. Even for the busiest of activists, Twitter is extremely helpful for communicating with allies, sharing findings, and soliciting new ideas. It is relatively simple to learn, and the benefits and rewards continue for as long as you remain loyal to your online community of partners and followers.

Facts and Quotes

1. Twitter was used to organize protests in Egypt from 2010 to 2011, Tunisia from 2009 to 2010, Iran in 2009, and Moldova in 2009.

   "Exploring the Role of Twitter and Social Media in Revolutions." Frontline Club News, Frontline Club London, Feb. 14, 2011

2. During the summer of 2011, a grassroots effort called Save Our Schools used Twitter to recruit members, disseminate information, attract the attention of traditional press, and organize a march in Washington, DC.

   Save Our Schools

Chapter Nine: First Helping My Child— Then Creating Community Change

For parents of children who struggle to read, simply navigating the school system and seeking individualized solutions can be emotionally draining. However, if we continue to address this problem on a case-by-case, child-by-child basis, we do nothing to change the system as a whole. Instead, if your child is having trouble at school, view his or her struggles as an opportunity to help all students. By first learning the facts about dyslexia and other learning disabilities and by comparing them to your family's situation, you complete the transition from concerned parent to determined agent of change. As you meet with your child's teacher and school personnel to discuss your options, be sure to ask questions that will determine the best course of action for your child and reveal any shortcomings in the school's procedures for intervention and support. Doing so will pave the way for positive reform at all levels of education in your district and beyond.

Facts and Quotes

1. While states and schools use different terms for struggling readers, the words "dyslexia" and "learning disability" are used in federal law.

   Learning Disabilities: Issues on Definition, National Joint Committee on Learning Disabilities, American Speech-Language-Hearing Association (ASHA), 1991

2. Two programs used in most states to provide services to children at risk for reading failure are Response to Intervention (RtI) and Multi-Tier System of Supports (MTSS).

   Multi-Tier System of Supports/Response to Intervention, National Center for Learning Disabilities, 2013

3. A common and effective assessment tool used to evaluate students who struggle with reading is DIBELS Next.

   Dynamic Measurement Group

4. Under the Individuals with Disabilities Education Act (IDEA), parents can request an assessment for special education for their child at any time.

   Special Education Law: the Individuals with Disabilities Education Act (IDEA), Understanding Special Education, 2009

Chapter Ten: Challenges Breed Opportunity—You Can Do This

The state of American education and the state of the American economy are tightly linked—which is why it is so critical for literacy activists and education reformers to act now. As the economy slowly recovers from recession, industries are pushing for more domestic job openings, and we must continue to meet their demands by adequately preparing our children for successful careers and rewarding personal lives. Already, in cities across the country, parents and other ordinary citizens have accomplished the seemingly impossible by demanding and enacting change in their education systems. The spirit of the literacy movement is born anew in everyone who chooses to stand up for the children of America; and with focus, determination, and the guidance of facts and anecdotes, you too can make a tremendous difference in millions of young lives.

Facts and Quotes

1. Currently, over half a million children in the United States are homeless, and nearly one in every five children lives below the poverty line.

    Homeless Children and Youth, Child Trends Databank, Sept 2012

    Children in Poverty, Child Trends Databank, Oct 2012

2. China's "2020 vision for universal high schools and world-class universities" succeeded a decade ahead of time, and the major Chinese population centers are at the top of global educational statistics. Other countries such as Singapore and Finland have made similar gains in short periods of time.

    Qualitative Advances of China's Basic Education since Reform and Opening up: A Brief Overview, Education Resources Information Center (ERIC)

    Finland, Organisation for Economic Co-operation and Development (OECD)

    Singapore, Organisation for Economic Co-operation and Development (OECD)

3. Beginning in 1996, concerned parents and staff in the Brownsville, Texas, school district established the Brownsville Reads Task Force to reverse the trends of reading failure and dropout in the district. According to the Neuhaus Education Center in Houston, Texas, Brownsville students who had received Language Enrichment in second grade performed significantly higher on state-mandated reading tests in the

third and fifth grades than students who had not received LE instruction.

International Dyslexia Association

4. Los Angeles Unified School District, the second-largest school district in the US, spends over $30,000 a year per student in grades K-12, but the district's high school graduation rate is only 40.6 percent.

Seiler, John. "LAUSD Spends $30K Per Student." *Cal Watchdog*, Aug. 20, 2010

Chapter Eleven: Nuts and Bolts of Enacting Legislation

Once you have succeeded in forming a community devoted to improving education and literacy outcomes for all American students, you are ready to find a champion and brave the legislative waters. Seeing your ideas formalized in state legislation represents a huge triumph for the movement, but it is hardly a passive process, and you must not hesitate to reach out to your representatives and lawmakers along the way. This can be done in person, in writing, or by telephone; the most important thing is to be confident in your goal. As you compete for the attention and support of your state legislators, always be sympathetic to opposing perspectives, as these will help you to understand educational issues more fully and tailor your call to action to various interests. Always keep in mind those who have chosen this path before you and found success at the end.

Chapter Twelve: Tricks of the Trade

At first, the work of transforming the education system of a community, let alone an entire state, may seem daunting and even impossible. However, as long as you engage your allies and legislative champion, teaching yourself and others the facts and prognoses of literacy in America, you can only move forward. Understanding state and national agendas, state infrastructure, and community organization goes a long way toward enhancing your power and efficacy; in addition, sharing the right statistics and asking the right questions will take you far in your journey. Ultimately, success requires personal connection, which will bring your cause to the forefront and your message to life.

Facts and Quotes

1. The Common Core State Standards set requirements for literacy in English language arts, history, social studies, science, technology, and new media subjects.

   National Governors Association Center for Best Practices and the Council of Chief State School Officers, Introduction, Common Core State Standards, citing website http://www. corestandards.org/assets/CCSSI_ELA%20Standards.pdf (accessed September 12, 2011).

FACTS AND CITATIONS
BY CATEGORY

DEMOGRAPHICS

1. More than 46 million Americans are living in poverty—the highest rate in over fifty years.

   Sabrina Tavernise. "Soaring Poverty Casts Spotlight on Lost Decade." The *New York Times* (Washington) September 13, 2011.

2. The 2010-2011 classroom demographic of 3.4 million kindergartners consisted of 53 percent whites, 24 percent Hispanics, 13 percent African Americans, 4 percent Asians, and 1 percent American Indians or Alaska Natives.

   Department of Education

3. Currently, over half a million children in the United States are homeless, and nearly one in every five children lives below the poverty line.

   Homeless Children and Youth, Child Trends Databank, Sept 2012

   Children in Poverty, Child Trends Databank, Oct 2012

PRIMARY EDUCATION

1. America's NAEP scores for 4th graders show that our nation is 17th in the world in reading.

   The Nation's Report Card on 4th Grade Reading 2011, Voices for America's Children, 2011

2. Beginning in 1996, concerned parents and staff in the Brownsville, Texas, school district established the Brownsville Reads Task Force to reverse the trends of reading failure and dropout in the district. According to the Neuhaus Education Center in Houston, Texas, Brownsville students who had received Language Enrichment in second grade performed significantly higher on state-mandated reading tests in the third and fifth grades than students who had not received LE instruction.

   International Dyslexia Association

3. Countless studies demonstrate that all but 1 percent of all students can be taught to read using known methods.

   Cardenas-Hagan, E. 2011. "Language and Literacy Development among English Language Learners. In *Multisensory Teaching of Basic Language Skills*, J. R. Birsh (ed.). Baltimore: Paul H. Brookes Publishing.

   Chard, D. J., S. Vaughn, and B. Tyler. 2002. "A Synthesis of Research on Effective Interventions for Building Reading Fluency with Elementary Students with Learning Disabilities." *Journal of Learning Disabilities*.

   Denton, C. A., and P. G. Mathes. 2003. "Intervention for Struggling Readers: Possibilities and Challenges." In *Preventing and Remediating Reading Difficulties: Bringing Science to Scale*, B. R. Foorman (ed.). Timonium, MD: York Press.

SECONDARY EDUCATION

1. High school dropout rates in the United States have tripled in the past thirty years.

   National Center for Education Statistics (NCES, 2011), Washington DC, accessed September 2011

2. Nationally, 1,230,000 students fail to graduate from secondary school every year.

   Alliance for Excellent Education—The High Cost of High School Dropouts: What the Nation Pays for Inadequate High Schools (Washington, DC: Author, 2008)

3. These 1.23 million nongraduates cost America over $319 billion in lost wages, taxes, and productivity in their lifetimes.

   Demography as Destiny: How America Can Build a Better Future (Washington, DC: Author, 2006).

4. Last year, of the 1.65 million students who took the SAT, only 43 percent met the "college and career benchmark" defined by the College Board. According to the Board, which was founded in 1900 and has data on student scores since 1972, the 2011 scores are the lowest in 40 years.

   "43 Percent of 2011 College-Bound Seniors Met SAT College and Career Readiness Benchmark," College Board, accessed September 17, 2011

5. In state-by-state rankings, California—the world's eighth leading economy—students rank 46th in reading and math achievement, 41st in high school graduation, and 49th in young adult high school diploma holdings.

   Fensterwald, John. "Sobering NAEP Scores: Achievement Gap Grows Sharply in San Diego." *Thoughts on Public Education*, Silicon Valley Education Foundation, Dec. 9, 2011.

DEGREE ATTAINMENT

1. According to the College Board, for every 100 US ninth-graders:

   70 will graduate from high school.
   44 will enter college.
   30 will return to college for their sophomore year.
   ONLY 21 will earn a bachelor's degree.
   Reforming Schools through College Readiness, Excelerator, College Board, Feb. 12, 2012

2. In 2011, 21 percent of Hispanics/Latinos, 44 percent of whites, 57 percent of Asians, and 30 percent of blacks in America held an associate's degree or higher.

   Educational Attainment in the United States: 2011—Detailed Tables, United States Census Bureau, Feb 2011

3. In terms of college graduation rates, the United States, in which 41 percent of citizens aged 25 to 34 hold college degrees, has made no progress in citizen education over the past forty years. Meanwhile, South Korea's college graduation rate among the same age group has increased from 13 to 63 percent in just twenty years.

   International Comparisons of Educational Attainment, Council of Graduate Schools, Nov. 1, 2011

4. America has slipped from first to twelfth place in college graduation rates among the top twenty-two developed countries.

   United Nations Educational, Scientific and Cultural Organization (UNESCO), UNESCO/OECD World Education Indicators (WEI) Programme, Paris (2005)

5. The state of California ranks 23rd in the nation in the number of citizens holding a bachelor's degree or higher; in 1960 the state was 8th.

Fensterwald, John. "Sobering NAEP Scores: Achievement Gap Grows Sharply in San Diego." *Thoughts on Public Education*, Silicon Valley Education Foundation, Dec. 9, 2011.

EDUCATORS

1. Since 2003, Massachusetts has required teachers to pass a competency assessment in reading instruction and literacy; the state now boasts the highest 4th- and 8th-grade NAEP scores in the US.

   NAEP Results: State-level for Massachusetts, Massachusetts Department of Elementary and Secondary Education

2. Studies conducted on teachers' literacy-related knowledge and reading education curricula show that university professors are not very well-informed about word structure (phonemes and graphemes).

   McCombes-Tolis, J., and R. Feinn. 2008. "Comparing Teachers' Literacy-Related Knowledge to their State's Standards for Reading." *Reading Psychology* 29: 236-265.

   Joshi, R. M., E. Binks, L. Graham, E. Ocker-Dean, D. Smith, and R. Boulware-Gooden. 2009. "Do Textbooks Used in University Reading Education Courses Conform to the Instructional Recommendations of the National Reading Panel?" *Journal of Learning Disabilities* 42: 458-463.

3. Harvard researchers have identified five levels of increasing progressive differentiation in a teacher's mastery of his or her field: declarative, situated, stable, expert, and reflective knowledge.

   Snow, C. E., P. Griffin, and M. S. Burns. 2005. *Knowledge to Support the Teaching of Reading: Preparing Teachers for a Changing World*. San Francisco, CA: Jossey-Bass.

4. After analyzing 222 reading course syllabi from 72 institutions, the National Council on Teacher Quality found that 85 percent of the programs ignored scientific research on reading.

What Education Schools Aren't Teaching About Reading and What Elementary Teachers Aren't Learning

5. Teachers' knowledge of the subject they teach is the major teacher characteristic related to student achievement.

Miller and Chait, 2008

EDUCATION IN CHINA

1. Between 1997 and 2007, China's enormous investment in its students' education doubled the number of colleges and quintupled the number of college graduates in the country.

Zakaria, Fareed. "The Real Challenge from China: Its People, Not Its Currency."[2] *Time Magazine*, Oct. 7, 2010

2. China's 400 million students typically start their formal education at age two and are expected to recognize 400 Chinese characters and write 100 midway through first grade.

Kristof, Nicholas D. "China's Winning Schools?" The *New York Times*, Jan. 15, 2011

3. Chinese students spend between eight-and-a-half and twelve hours a day in school.

"China's Children Too Busy for Playtime," *China Daily* (Xinhau), accessed September 15, 2011.

4. China's "2020 vision for universal high schools and world-class universities" succeeded a decade ahead of time, and the major Chinese population centers are at the top of global educational

statistics. Other countries such as Singapore and Finland have made similar gains in short periods of time.

Qualitative Advances of China's Basic Education since Reform and Opening up: A Brief Overview, Education Resources Information Center (ERIC)

Finland, Organisation for Economic Co-operation and Development (OECD)

Singapore, Organisation for Economic Co-operation and Development (OECD)

EDUCATION IN OTHER COUNTRIES

1. Students in Portugal, Hong Kong, Germany, Poland, Liechtenstein, Slovenia, Colombia, and Lithuania are improving academically at twice the rate of American students, while those in Latvia, Chile, and Brazil are improving at three times our rate.

   Harvard Program on Education Policy and Governance (PEPG), Harvard Kennedy School, Cambridge, Massachusetts (2012)

2. While Korea is sending 85 percent of its students to college, forty-seven percent of America's urban students drop out of high school.

   America's Promise Alliance, Johns Hopkins University, Everyone Graduates Center, Civic Enterprises, Alliance for Excellent Education, "Building a Grad Nation: Progress and Challenge in Ending the High School Dropout Epidemic" (Washington, DC, 2010).

3. While American students spend an average of 32 hours a week in school, children in Scandinavian countries have forty- to fifty-hour school weeks.

   "China's Children Too Busy for Playtime," *China Daily* (Xinhau), accessed September 15, 2011

EXPENDITURES

1. Despite the $1.15 trillion the US spends on public education every year—more money per student than any other country in the world—nearly seven out of ten US students read at a basic or below-basic level

    Kristof, Nicholas D. "China's Winning Schools?" The *New York Times*, Jan. 15, 2011

2. Over the past forty years, the amount of money the United States spends per student in public education every year has nearly tripled, from about $4,000 in 1971 to $11,000 in 2011.

    Total and current expenditures per pupil in public elementary and secondary schools: Selected years, 1919-20 through 2008-09, National Center for Education Statistics (NCES), Institute of Education Sciences (IES), 2011

    School Finance: Federal, State, and Local K-12 School Finance Overview, Federal Education Budget Project, Dec. 13, 2012

3. According to the OECD, America spends over half a trillion dollars in public and private money every year on education, more than any of the other twenty-four industrialized nations.

    United States, Education at a Glance: OECD Indicators 2012, OECD

4. Los Angeles Unified School District, the second-largest school district in the US, spends over $30,000 a year per student in grades K-12, but the district's high school graduation rate is only 40.6 percent.

    Seiler, John. "LAUSD spends $30K per student." *Cal Watchdog*, Aug. 20, 2010

5. In 2011, the Pacific Research Institute found that the state of California's failure to prepare a single cohort of freshmen for college-level work will cost students, schools, and the state up to $14 billion in remediation classes annually.

   Pacific Research Institute, California Index of Leading Education Indicators, Second Edition, San Francisco, CA, 2010.

UNEMPLOYMENT

1. The US Bureau of Labor Statistics reports that there are 3.1 million US jobs unfilled due to a shortage of qualified workers, while 12.8 million citizens are the documented unemployed.

   Bureau of Labor Statistics, Washington, DC (2012), accessed March 2012

2. 1,100 US manufacturers report job openings for skilled workers, while 83 percent of companies report moderate to serious shortages of labor.

   Association for Manufacturing Excellence, Rowling Meadows, Il, accessed February 2012

Organization for Economic Co-operation and Development (OECD)

1. The United States ranks twenty-fourth out of thirty-four developed countries in reading literacy.

   Programme for International Student Assessment (PISA), Organisation for Economic Co-operation and Development (OECD), Paris, France (2009).

LEARNING DIFFICULTY AND DISABILITY

1. While states and schools use different terms for struggling readers, the words "dyslexia" and "learning disability" are used in federal law.

   Learning Disabilities: Issues on Definition, National Joint Committee on Learning Disabilities, American Speech-Language-Hearing Association (ASHA), 1991

2. Two programs used in most states to provide services to children at risk for reading failure are Response to Intervention (RtI) and Multi-Tier System of Supports (MTSS).

   Multi-Tier System of Supports/Response to Intervention, National Center for Learning Disabilities, 2013

3. A common and effective assessment tool used to evaluate students who struggle with reading is DIBELS Next.

   Dynamic Measurement Group

4. Under the Individuals with Disabilities Education Act (IDEA), parents can request an assessment for special education for their child at any time.

   Special Education Law: the Individuals with Disabilities Education Act (IDEA), Understanding Special Education, 2009

COMMON CORE

1. The Common Core State Standards set requirements for literacy in English language arts, history, social studies, science, technology, and new media subjects.

   National Governors Association Center for Best Practices and the Council of Chief State School Officers, Introduction, Common Core State Standards, citing website http://www. corestandards.org/assets/CCSSI_ELA%20Standards.pdf (accessed September 12, 2011).

SOCIAL MEDIA

1. To reach a marketing audience of fifty million, the radio took thirty-eight years, while Facebook took two.

   Social Media Marketing, Web Traffic Partners

2. Twitter was used to organize protests in Egypt from 2010 to 2011, Tunisia from 2009 to 2010, Iran in 2009, and Moldova in 2009.

   "Exploring the role of Twitter and Social Media in Revolutions." Frontline Club News, Frontline Club London, Feb. 14, 2011

3. During the summer of 2011, a grassroots effort called Save Our Schools used Twitter to recruit members, disseminate information, attract the attention of traditional press, and organize a march in Washington, DC.

   Save Our Schools

ACKNOWLEDGEMENT AND APPLAUSE
FOR BRILLIANT TEAMWORK

M Y MOST IMPORTANT acknowledgement is for my two children. I am grateful for their emotional intelligence, leadership, values, and the powerful, inspirational messages that are witnessed through their accomplishments and their positive impact on others. Without them, I would have never entered the world of education.

The effort to write this book, to curate the science, and to bring the very best expertise to bear is quite simply a blessing, as well as being both enlightening and daunting. My growing and deep respect for educators has enabled me to understand the very different cultures of the K-12 system and higher-education worlds. The goal is to successfully bridge these worlds in this work—recognizing that it is essential for making major progress in national education outcomes for all students.

The true origins of this book began a decade ago with a clinical trial on reading interventions in more than two dozen Pennsylvania public schools. I knew so little about the education system at that time. Yet guidance was generous as I learned the education ropes through numerous lenses of perspective. Quickly, educational foundations of learning became apparent: the significance of screening children early and using data to direct their instruction, of advancing teacher knowledge and skill with intensity and support, and the meaning of quality school-based leadership. This experience and others that followed created the building blocks for me to understand the complexity of components needed to ensure a literate, prosperous American culture. Huge appreciation goes out to David Myers, Joe Torgesen, John Gabrieli, and Donna Durno.

One of the first requests I received to write a book came from my colleague, Guinevere Eden, when I was asked to chair the Government

Affairs Committee of the International Dyslexia Association. Hah! Not being a writer, lawyer, lobbyist, or scientist, I refused often, obviously to no avail. Time has passed and several years of hunting and gathering produced two bodies of work (the book, *The Power to Act*, followed by the handbook, *Literacy Policy*) that elevated the "discussion," and were catalysts to write *Blueprint*. In time all this work helped to energize a national movement with a mission to create a fundamental shift in the culture of the classroom where students do more thinking, sense-making, explaining, exploring, and adding to their worlds, and literacy is achieved before the third grade so this can happen. Each and every one of our team members knows how much they contributed to evolving my thinking. From the very beginning, we formed a family and continue to grow. This work would not have been possible without the unwavering support of these friends and colleagues—who know who they are and how important they are to me. Thank you!

The main reason we are able to self-publish this book (all rights will be the property of Literate Nation to share in any media) is because of guidance, friendship, and grants from the Emily Hall Tremaine Foundation. Thank you, Tremaines and Suzanne Lang.

All research and writing has been in collaboration with, is supported by, and continues to be reinforced across a number of individuals, organizations, universities, experts in associated fields, and alliance partners. In fact, more than two hundred talented minds have contributed to the fabric of *Blueprint for a Literate Nation*. I thank each and every one of you.

Great assistance has been provided by the staff and researchers at the Haan Foundation for Children, the Coletti Institute for Education and Career Achievement, Literate Nation's grassroots organization, and the Strategic Education Research Partnership. They have done the heavy lifting, to include thousands of hours of research and all for less than a dime of remuneration. We are a team of purposeful "literacy change-making pioneers" with award-winning experts leading with passion, respect, and proof that living core values often means paying forward. I hail you, my mentors and friends, in so many ways.

May you, too, pay forward and reach out and thank everyone for this labor of love—for our children and our country.

My dear editors and advisors: Rosemary Bowler, Carolyn Cowen, Dorothy Morrison, Sinclair Sherrill, Maryanne Wolf, Richard Bradford, Susan Smartt, Cecillia Retelle, Eric and Elise Berendt, Glenn

McCoy, Claire Mullins, Patricia Ross, and Jill St. Anne. You have each added so much of yourselves to this work and to my psyche. I stand in awe of your support and friendship.

And most importantly, a hug of deep appreciation to my impressive family, who often long for me to stop this work that seems to be on a 24/7 continuum. Yes, they are my inspiration, and in equal measure, they drag me away from travel, phones, conferences, and the computers when I need it most. They give me perspective and balance in a world that yields little. Darren, Tiffany, Gianmarco, Dad, Jeffrey, Michael, Carol, Lisa, Brittany, Brian, Kimberlee, Nicky, Donald, Viteks, Tommy, Shell, Cassady, Samantha, and Kodiak, your love lifts me.

*　　*　　*

Cinthia Coletti in collaboration with Literate Nation, the Haan Foundation for Children, Coletti Institute for Education and Career Achievement, numerous institutes of higher education, numerous teacher associations, Strategic Education Research Partnership Institute, California Business for Education Excellence, International Dyslexia Association, International Reading Association, Literacy How, Tufts University Center for Reading and Language Research, Dyslexia Advantage, and oh so many more alliance partners.

BIOGRAPHIES

Cinthia Coletti/Haan

Ms. Cinthia Coletti is a top-notch business leader by trade and an education advocate by choice. She is fueled with passion for the success of all children and our nation. She currently oversees the executive management of several nonprofit organizations and facilitates a number of projects in the fields of literacy, STEM, education, data, legislation, and neuroscience. She directs the Power4Kids Reading Initiative of clinical trials in education, the Haan Foundation for Children, the newly endowed Coletti Institute for Education and Career Achievement, and the national organization, Literate Nation. Ms. Coletti serves as chair of Syndacon Corporation and Coletti Investments, LLC.

Prior to dedicating her skills to science and education, Cinthia enjoyed over twenty years of success in the business community as an entrepreneur, CEO, and in senior management positions. She was a founding team member in Southern Pacific Railroad's landmark launch of SPRINT through to its acquisition by GTE, seven years after inception. She was the managing director of Ford Aerospace's cutting-edge Starnet Division. Subsequent ventures were a series of successful mergers and acquisitions in the telecommunication and software industries.

Coletti also serves on the board of directors of several lauded science and educational organizations, including the Strategic Educational Research Partnership (SERP/National Academies of Science); the California Business for Education Excellence (CBEE/EDResults); the Harvard Medical School, Program in Education, Afterschool and Resiliency (PEAR); the Department of Education Policy and Leadership at Southern Methodists University; the UCSF Neuroscience Initiative, Leadership Council; and more. She has authored two books on education prior to this book, *The*

Power to Act: Transforming Literacy and Education and *Literacy Policy: Ground-breaking Blueprint for State Legislation*. Ms. Coletti is a frequent speaker, has received many prestigious honors and awards in the fields of telecommunications, education, science, advocacy, and dyslexia, and was one of the top-fifty Bay Area's philanthropists for 2012 in *Gentry Magazine*, a leading publication in Silicon Valley and San Francisco.

An advocate for education and literacy reform in Washington, DC, and in the states, Ms. Coletti focuses her work on quality research, teacher advancement, project-based learning, universal student educational success, and school-based leadership. She is adamant that American students receive a world-class education, become capable of lifelong learning, and compete in the global workforce and economy. She actively supports the role played by data in public-education transformation efforts, understanding that student, teacher, and school achievement data must be analyzed, understood, and compared to make informed decisions that affect students' progress and build United States human capital.

Margie Gillis, EdD

Dr. Gillis is a research affiliate at Haskins Laboratories and president of Literacy How. She has been teaching children of all ages to read for nearly forty years. At the University of Connecticut, she studied with Isabelle Liberman, a Haskins scientist who discovered the role of phonemic awareness in learning to read. Upon graduating, she worked as a special educator in both public and private schools for twenty years, becoming a certified academic language therapist. In 1998, Margie earned her doctorate of education in special education from the University of Louisville, where she began her work training teachers of reading. Two years later, she became an early reading success fellow at Haskins Laboratories. She founded Literacy How in 2009 to continue the professional development work she began at Haskins; in this capacity, she directs twelve mentors who work in public and private schools in Connecticut. While most of the work of Literacy How focuses on teachers in regular classrooms, the mentors also work with special education and reading teachers to build their knowledge and skills to increase their effectiveness with struggling readers. Since 2000, Haskins and Literacy How mentors have worked with more than eight hundred teachers in over one hundred Connecticut schools.

Dr. Gillis has also served on many state committees, including the RTI task force and the LD Guidelines task force—both charged with setting state policy that incorporates scientifically based reading research in assessing and delivering optimum classroom instruction. This state policy work led to her recent involvement with groundbreaking legislation passed in Connecticut to ensure that preservice and certified teachers have the requisite knowledge to teach children to read. As a result of this legislation, she is currently at work on two research projects to investigate best literacy practices and implementation in twenty schools in nine Connecticut districts.

She is a director and past president of the Connecticut Branch of the International Dyslexia Association, as well as a member of IDA's Professional Development Committee. Dr. Gillis is also the past president and cofounder of Smart Kids with Learning Disabilities, an advocacy organization for parents. The tag line for Literacy How is "Empower teaching excellence" because the more teachers know about language and literacy acquisition and development, the more successful their students will be in developing reading proficiency.

Carolyn D. Cowen

Carolyn is an educator and social entrepreneur known for developing, launching, and managing programs and initiatives that improve the teaching-learning landscape for people with learning differences, particularly those with dyslexia. Currently, she serves as an advising social media editor/strategist for the International Dyslexia Association Examiner and for Degrees2 Dreams. She also serves as a founding member on the Literate Nation board of directors.

Most recently, she was executive director of Carroll School's Center for Innovative Education, where she oversaw various outreach and professional-development programs, convened the Dyslexia Leadership Summit, and spearheaded the Dyslexia Geno-Phenotyping Initiative. Prior to that, she was executive director of the Learning Disabilities Network—a nonprofit she cofounded and operated for twenty years that provided services to individuals with LD, their families, and professionals working on their behalf.

In her thirty-five-year career in education and nonprofits, Carolyn has worn many hats, including teacher, reading therapist, speaker, author, editor, consultant, professional-development planner, executive director, think-tank convener, fund-raiser, funder, and research coordinator. Carolyn earned her master's degree in reading education and learning disabilities from Harvard University (during the Jeanne Chall era). She received the Alice H. Garside Award from the New England Branch of the International Dyslexia Association (IDA) and chaired IDA's nominating committee.

These days, Carolyn is especially interested in new-media/print literacy intersections, social media as a tool for driving change, and creative ways nonprofits can "power the mission with the message."

Elenn Steinberg

Elenn Steinberg began her journey into the world of education and literacy sixteen years ago, when her son's school informed her that he was at risk for reading failure. At that point, she could never have predicted the journey that would result in her becoming a passionate voice for students, a highly skilled reading interventionist, an advocate for families, a consultant, and a nationally known speaker in the areas of dyslexia, literacy, student self-advocacy, and literacy legislation.

In her work as both a member and cochair of the Colorado Special Education Advisory Committee, Ms. Steinberg was able to work with the Colorado Department of Education in various capacities, including the development of the Colorado Reading Summit and the decision-making process of the Response to Intervention implementation in Colorado. As a board member and president of six years, Elenn built parent, family, and educator programs for the Rocky Mountain branch of the International Dyslexia Association that have received local and national acclaim.

Furthermore, she was the local chair of the 2005 national IDA conference and continues to lead Reading in the Rockies, Colorado's leading literacy conference addressing the needs of students with dyslexia and literacy challenges. She is a founding board member and vice president of Advocacy for Literate Nation, a national organization dedicated to literacy for all students. Elenn also serves as cochair of the Government Affairs Committee for the International Dyslexia Association.

Richard Long, PhD

Dr. Long is the director of government relations for the International Reading Association and the executive director of government relations for the National Title I Association. He has been working for over thirty-five years to improve education for all high-need children—those who are economically disadvantaged, disabled, or part of a language minority. He works with members of Congress, the administration, and other advocate groups to advance the goal of improving education for all children. Recently, Long has written on improving literacy education for urban students, the relationship of reading and writing instruction, and the role of the federal government in supporting professional development. His latest book, *Hidden Cauldron: The Paradox of American Education Reform*, is due to be published later this year.

Long earned his master's and doctorate in educational counseling, as well as his undergraduate degree in psychology, at George Washington University. In addition, he has worked on the staff of Congressman James W. Symington (D-MO) and held consultancies with several state education agencies, including the US Department of Education, the World Health Organization, and USA TODAY, among others.

Long lives in Virginia with his wife of thirty-two years and two adult sons.

REFERENCES, SCIENCE, AND RESOURCES

The fact is that fourth-grade students not proficient in reading are all too likely to become the nation's least-skilled, lowest-income, least-productive, and most-costly citizens of tomorrow. Worse: this is not a difficult fix, we can do it.

Cinthia Coletti (Haan)
Leveraging Literacy Legislation
IDA Conference
Chicago, 2011

MATERIALS USED FOR Synthesizing and Curating the *Blueprint for a Literate Nation* and *State Literacy Law*

Table of Contents

Compliance and Implementation Science

Barber, M., Fullan, M., Mackey, T. (2009). Building excellent education systems: From concept to implementation at scale. IARTV Publications.

Evers, W. (1998). What's Gone Wrong in America's Classrooms. Stanford, CA: Hoover Institution Press.

Fixsen, D., Naoom, S., Blase, K., and Wallace, F. (2007). Implementation: The missing link between research and practice. The APSAC Advisor.

Fullen, M. (2011). Choosing the wrong drivers for whole system reform. Shaping our Common Future. Center for Strategic Seminar Series.

Goldstone, R. L, and Son, J. Y. (2005). The transfer of scientific principles using concrete and idealized simulations. The Journal of the Learning Sciences.

Hallinger, P. (2011). What have we learned from 30 years of empirical research. Leadership for Learning.

Olshfski, D. F., Cunningham, R. B. (2008). Agendas and Decisions: How State Government Executives and Middle Managers Make and Administer Policy. State University of New York Press.

Southworth, G. (2009). School leadership: What we know and what it means for schools, their leaders and policy. Centre for Strategic Education Seminar Series.

Tudball, L., Rizvi, K., Mullane, K., and Fleming, D. (May 2011). Current activities and future challenges of education. International Education Advisory Group.

Zbar, V., Kimber, R., and Graham, M. (2010). Getting the preconditions for school improvement in place: How to make it happen. CSE Publication.

Data Science

Austin, G., and Bernard, B. (2007). The state data system to assess learning barriers, supports, and engagement: Implications for school reform efforts, prepared for the EdSource California Education Policy Convening, Sacramento. December, 2010, from http://www.wested.org/chks/pdf/edsourcepolicy.pdf

Bernhardt, V. L. (2006). Using data to improve student learning in school districts. New York: Eye on Education.

Bernhardt, V. (1998). Data analysis for comprehensive school-wide improvement. Larchmont, NY: Eye on Education, Inc.

Bernhardt, V. L. (2000). Intersections: New routes open when one type of data crosses another. Journal of Staff Development. June, 2011, from http://eff.csuchico.edu/downloads/Intersct.pdf

Berninger, V. W., and Amtmann, D. (2003). Preventing written expression disabilities through early and continuing assessment and intervention for handwriting and/or spelling problems: Research into practice. In H. L. Swanson, K. R. Harris, and S. Graham (Eds.), Handbook of Learning Disabilities. New York: Guilford Press.

Blink, R. (2007). Data-driven instructional leadership. Larchmark, NY: Eye on Education.

Brunner, C., Fasca, C., Heinze, J., Honey, M., Light, D., Mandinach, E., et al. (2005). Linking data and learning: The Grow Network study. Journal of Education for Students Placed At Risk.

Bryk, A. S., Sebring, P. B., Allensworth, E., Luppescu, S. and Easton, J. Q. (2010). Organizing schools for improvement: Lessons from Chicago. Chicago: The University of Chicago Press.

Choppin, J. (2002, April). Data use in practice: Examples from the school level. Paper presented at the annual meeting of the American Educational Research Association (AERA), New Orleans, LA.

Deno, S. L. (2003). Developments in curriculum-based measurement. Journal of Special Education, Volume 37.

Fiarman, S. E. (2007). Planning to assess progress: Mason Elementary School refines an instructional strategy. In K. P. Boudett and J. L. Steele (Eds.), Data wise in action: Stories of schools using data to improve teaching and learning. Cambridge, MA: Harvard Education Press.

Deno, S. L. (2003). Developments in curriculum-based measurement. Journal of Special Education, Volume 37.

Glazerman, S. Loeb, S., Goldhaber, D., Staiger, D., Raudenbush, S., and Whitehurst, G. (2010). Evaluating teachers: The important role of value-added. Brookings Institution.

Good, R. H., Simmons, D. C., and Kame'enui, E. J. (2001). The importance and decision-making utility of a continuum of fluency-based indicators of foundational reading skills for third-grade high-stakes outcomes. Scientific Studies of Reading, Volume 5.

Farr, R., and Tone, B. (1994). Portfolio and performance assessment: Helping students evaluate their progress as readers and writers. Fort Worth, TX: Harcourt, Brace.

Foorman, B. R., Fletcher, J. M., and Francis, D. J. (2004). Early reading assessment. In W. M. Evers and H. J. Walberg (Eds.), Testing student learning, evaluating teaching effectiveness. Stanford, CA: The Hoover Institution.

Fuchs, L. S., Fuchs, D., Hamlett, C. L., Walz, L., and Germann, G. (1993). Formative evaluation of academic progress: How much growth should we expect? School Psychology Review.

Good, R. H., Simmons, D. C., and Kame'enui, E. J. (2001). The importance and decision-making utility of a continuum of fluency-based indicators of foundational reading skills for third-grade high-stakes outcomes. Scientific Studies of Reading.

Halverson, R., Grigg, J., Prichett, R., and Thomas, C. (2007). The new instructional leadership: Creating data-driven instructional systems in schools. Journal of School Leadership.

Hamilton, L., Halverson, R., Jackson, S., Mandinach, E., Supovitz, J., and Wayman, J. (2009). Using student achievement data to support instructional decision making (NCEE 2009). Washington, DC: National Center for Education Evaluation and Regional Assistance, Institute of Education Sciences, US Department of Education. February, 2011, from http://ies.ed.gov/ncee/wwc/publications/practiceguides/.

Hasbrouck, J., and Haager, D. (Eds.). (2007). Monitoring children's progress in academic learning. Perspectives on Language and Literacy, Volume 33.

Hogan, T. P., Catts, H. W., and Little, T. D. (2005). The relationship between phonological awareness and reading: Implications for the assessment of phonological awareness. Language, Speech, and Hearing Services in Schools, Volume 36.

Hosp, M. K., Hosp, J. L., and Howell, K. W. (2007). The ABC's of CBM: A practical guide to curriculum-based measurement. New York: Guilford Press.

Hudson, R. F., Lane, H. B., and Pullen, P. C. (2005). Reading fluency assessment and instruction: What, why, and how? The Reading Teacher.

Ingram, D., Louis, K. S., and Schroeder, R. G. (2004). Accountability policies and teacher decision making: Barriers to the use of data to improve practice. Teacher College Record.

Jenkins, J. R., Johnson, E., and Hileman, J. (2004). When is reading also writing: Sources of individual differences on the new reading performance assessments. Scientific Studies of Reading, Volume 8.

Keenan, J. M., Betjemann, R. S., and Olson, R. K. (2008). Reading comprehension tests vary in the skills they assess: Differential dependence on decoding and oral comprehension. Scientific Studies of Reading, Volume 12.

Knapp, M. S., Swinnerton, J. A., Copland, M. A., and Monpas-Huber, J. (2006). Data-informed leadership in education. Seattle, WA: University of Washington, Center for the Study of Teaching and Policy.

Lachat, M. A., and Smith, S. (2005). Practices that support data use in urban high schools. Journal of Education for Students Placed At Risk.

May, H., and Robinson, M. A. (2007). A randomized evaluation of Ohio's Personalized Assessment Reporting System (PARS). Philadelphia, PA: Consortium for Policy Research in Education.

Moody, L., and Dede, C. (2008). Models of data-based decision-making: A case study of the Milwaukee Public Schools. In E. B. Mandinach and M. Honey (Eds.), Data-driven school improvement: Linking data and learning. New York: Teachers College Press.

Murnane, R. J., Sharkey, N. S. and Boudett, K. P. (2005). Using student-assessment results to improve instruction: lessons from a workshop. Journal of Education for Students Placed at Risk.

Supovitz, J. A., and Klein, V. (2003). Mapping a course for improved student learning: How innovative schools systematically use student performance data to guide improvement. Philadelphia, PA: University of Pennsylvania, Consortium for Policy Research in Education.

Thorn, C. A. (2001). Knowledge management for educational information systems: What is the state of the field? Education Policy Analysis Archives.

Torgesen, J. K. (2004). Avoiding the devastating downward spiral: The evidence that early intervention prevents reading failure. American Educator, Volume 28.

Troia, G. (Ed.). (2009). Instruction and assessment for struggling writers: Evidence-based practices. New York: Guilford Press.

Wayman, J. C. (2005). Involving teachers in data-driven decision making: Using computer data systems to support teacher inquiry and reflection. Journal of Education for Students Placed At Risk.

Wayman, J. C., Brewer, C., and Stringfield, S. (2009, April). Leadership for effective data use. Paper presented at the annual meeting of the American Educational Research Association (AERA), San Diego, CA.

Wayman, J. C., Cho, V., and Johnston, M. T. (2007). The data-informed district: A district-wide evaluation of data use in the Natrona County School District. Austin, TX: The University of Texas.

Wayman, J. C., and Conoly, K. (2006). Managing curriculum: Rapid implementation and sustainability of a district wide data initiative. ERS Spectrum.

Wayman, J. C., Midgley, S., and Stringfield, S. (2006). Leadership for data-based decision-making: Collaborative educator teams. In A. B. Danzig, K. M.

Wayman, J. C., and Stringfield, S. (2006). Technology-supported involvement of entire faculties in examination of student data for instructional improvement. American Journal of Education.

Wayman, J. C. (2005). Involving teachers in data-driven decision making: Using computer data systems to support teacher inquiry and reflection. Journal of Education for Students Placed At Risk.

Wayman, J. C., Stringfield, S., and Yakimowski, M. (2004). Software enabling school improvement through analysis of student data. Baltimore, MD: Center for Research on the Education of Students Placed at Risk.

Grassroots and Social Media

Chambers, E. T. (2010). Roots for Radicals. Organizing for power, action, and justice. New York, NY. Continuum International Publishing Group.

Cross, C. T., (2004).Political Education: National Policy Comes of Age. New York, NY. Teachers College Press.

Deckers, E. and Lacy, K. (2011). Branding yourself: How to use social media to invent or re-invent yourself. Indianapolis, IN: Pearson Education, Inc.

Eadie, D. (2001). Extraordinary Board Leadership. The seven keys to high-impact governance. Gaithersburg, MD. Aspen Publishers.

Fullan, M. (2001). Leading in a culture of change. San Francisco, CA: Jossey-Bass.

Gegan, M. (2002). Going Public. An organizer's guide to citizen action. Boston, MA. Anchor Books, Random House.

Gladwell, M. (2000). The Tipping Point: How little things can make a big difference. Boston: Little, Brown, and Company.

Hess, F. M. (2010). The same thing over and over: How school reformers get stuck in yesterday's ideas. Cambridge, MA: Harvard University Press.

Luntz, F. (2010). The Language of Choice in Education. Worddoctors.com.

Kaufmann (2009). Kauffman Thought Book. Discovery consists of seeing what everybody has seen and thinking what nobody has thought. Kansas City, MO. Ewing Marion Kauffman Foundation Press.

Kawasaki, G. (2011). Enchantment: The art of changing hearts, minds, and actions. London: Penguin Book Ltd.

Perry, T., Moses, R., Wynne, J., Cortes, E., and Delpit, L. (2008). Quality Education as a Constitutional Right: Creating a Grassroots Movement to Transform Public Schools. Random House.

Olshifski, D. F., Cunningham, R. (2008). Agendas and Decisions. How State governments executives and middle managers make and administer policy. Albany, NY. State University of New York Press.

Sen, R., Klein, K. (2003). Stir It Up: Lessons in Community Organizing and Advocacy. Jossey-Bass.

Smith, S. N. (2009). Stoking the Fires of Democracy, Our Generation's Introduction to Grassroots Organizing. Pierce.

Wolf, M. (2010). Cassandra's Thoughts about Reading and Time. In Sherman, G. F. and Cowen, C. D. (Eds.). Perspectives: Dyslexia with 2020 Vision—where will we be in 10 years, 36 (1): 39-40

High School Dropout Facts and Prevention

Alexander, K., Entwisle, D., and Horsey, C. (1997). From first grade forward: Early foundations of high school dropout. Sociology of Education.

Allen, J. P., Philliber, S., Herrling, S., and Kuperminc, G. P. (1997). Preventing teen pregnancy and academic failure: Experimental evaluation of a developmentally based approach. Child Development.

Bacon, Tina P. (2002). Evaluation of the Too Good for Drugs and Violence High School Prevention Program. Tampa, Fla.: Hillsborough County Antidrug Alliance Criminal Justice/Substance Abuse Coordination Section.

Barrington, B. L., and Hendricks, B. (1989). Differentiating Characteristics of High School Graduates, Dropouts, and Nongraduates. The Journal of Educational Research.

Battin-Pearson, S., Newcomb, M. D., Abbott, R. D., Hill, K. G., Catalano, R. F., and Hawkins, J. D. (2000). Predictors of early high school dropout: A test of five theories. Journal of Educational Psychology.

Chicago Public Schools (n.d.). Chicago Public Schools Toolkit. May, 2011, from http://www.cpstoolkit.com/default.aspx

Dynarski, M., and Gleason, P. (2002). How can we help? What we have learned from federal dropout prevention studies. Journal of Education for Students Placed at Risk.

Dynarski, M., Gleason, P., Rangarajan, A., and Wood, R. (1998). Impacts of dropout prevention programs: Final report. A research report from the School Dropout Demonstration Assistance Program evaluation. Princeton, NJ: Mathematica Policy Research.

Ensminger, M., and Slusarick, A. (1992). Paths to high school graduation or dropout: A longitudinal study of a first grade cohort. Sociology of Education.

Farrell, A. D., Meyer, A. L., Sullivan, T. N., and Kung, E. M. (2003). Evaluation of the Responding In Peaceful and Positive Ways (RIPP) seventh grade violence prevention curriculum. Journal of Child and Family Studies.

Garnier, H. E., Stein, J. A., and Jacobs, J. (1997). The process of dropping out of high school: A 19-year perspective. American Educational Research Journal.

Gleason, P., and Dynarski, M. (2002). Do we know whom to serve: Issues in using risk factors to identify dropouts. Journal of Education for Students Placed at Risk.

Harrell, A. V., Cavanaugh, S. E., and Sridharan, S. (1998). Impact of the Children at Risk Program: Comprehensive final report II. Washington, DC: The Urban Institute.

Hecht, M. L., Marsiglia, F. F., Elek—Fisk, E., Wagstaff, D. A., Kulis, S., and Dustman, P. A. (2003). Culturally grounded substance use prevention: An Evaluation of the keepin' it R.E.A.L. Prevention Science.

Hurwitz, E., Menacker, J. and Weldon, W. (1996). Critical issue: Developing and maintaining safe schools. North Central Regional Education Laboratory. July, 2011, from http://www.ncrel.org/sdrs/areas/issues/envrnmnt/drugfree/sa200.htm

Jimerson, S. R., Anderson, G. E., and Whipple, A. D. (2002). Winning the battle and losing the war: Examining the relation between grade retention and dropping out of high school. Psychology in the Schools.

Kemple, J., Herlihy, C., and Smith, T. (2005). Making progress toward graduation: Evidence from the talent development high school model. New York: MDRC.

Kemple, J., and Herlihy, C. (2004). The Talent Development High School model: Context, components, and initial impacts on ninth-grade students' engagement and performance. New York: MDRC.

Larson, K. A., and Rumberger, R. W. (1995). ALAS: Achievement for Latinos through Academic Success. In H. Thornton (Ed.), Staying in school. Minneapolis, MN: University of Minnesota, Institute on Community Integration.

Letgers, N. E., Balfanz, R., Jordan, W. J., and McPartland, J. M. (2002). Comprehensive reform for 9 urban high schools: A talent development approach. New York: Teachers College Press.

LoSciuto, L., Rajala, A. K., Townsend, T. N., and Taylor, A. S. (1996). An outcome evaluation of Across Ages: An intergenerational mentoring approach to drug prevention. Journal of Adolescent Research.

McPartland, J. A., and Nettles, S. M. (1991). Using community adults as advocates or mentors for at-risk middle school students: A two-year evaluation of Project RAISE. American Journal of Education.

Morris, J. D., Ehren, B. J., and Lenz, B. K. (1991). Building a model to predict which fourth through eighth graders will drop out of high school. Journal of Experimental Education.

Quint, J. (2006). Meeting five critical challenges of high school reform: Lessons from research on three reform models. New York: MDRC.

Roderick, M., and Engel, M. (2001). The grasshopper and the ant: Motivational responses of low-achieving students to high-stakes testing. Educational Evaluation and Policy Analysis.

Sinclair, M. F., Christenson, S. L., Evelo, D. L., and Hurley, C. M. (1998). Dropout prevention for youth with disabilities: Efficacy of a sustained school engagement procedure. Exceptional Children.

Smink, J. (1990). Mentoring programs for at-risk youth: A dropout prevention research report. Clemson, SC: National Dropout Prevention Center.

Snipes, J. C., Holton, G. I., Doolittle, F., and Sztejnberg, L. (2006). Striving for student success: The effect of Project GRAD on high school student outcomes in three urban school districts. New York, NY: MDRC.

Swanson, Christopher B., (2009). Cities in Crisis: A Special Analytic Report on High School Graduation. EPE Research Center, and supported by America's Promise Alliance and the Bill and Melinda Gates Foundation.

Wehlage, G. G. (1989). Dropping out: Can schools be expected to prevent it? In L. Weis, E. Farrar, and H. G. Petrie (Eds.), Dropouts from school: Issues, dilemmas, and solutions. Albany, NY: State University of New York Press.

Identification

Catts, H., Fey, M., Zhang, X., and Tomblin, J. B. (2001). Estimating the risk of future reading difficulties in kindergarten children: A research-based model and its clinical implementation. Language, Speech, Hearing Services in Schools.

Scarborough, H. S. (1998). Early identification of children at risk for reading disabilities: Phonological awareness and some other promising predictors. In B. K. Shapiro, P. J. Accardo, and A. J. Capute (Eds.), Specific reading disability: A view of the spectrum. Timonium, MD: York Press.

Multi-Tier System of Supports Reading Literacy and Writing

Blachman, B. A., Schatschneider, C., Fletcher, J. M., Francis, D. J., Clonan, S., Shaywitz, B., et al. (2004). Effects of intensive reading remediation for second and third graders. Journal of Educational Psychology.

Catone, W. V., and Brady, S. (2005). The inadequacy of individual educational program goals for high school students with word-level reading difficulties. Annals of Dyslexia, Number 55.

Chard, D. J., Vaughn, S., and Tyler, B (2002). A synthesis of research on effective interventions for building reading fluency with elementary students with learning disabilities. Journal of Learning Disabilities.

Cromley, J. G., and Azevedo, R. (2007). Testing and refining the direct and inferential mediation model of reading comprehension. Journal of Educational Psychology.

De La Paz, S. (1999). Self-regulated strategy instruction in regular education settings: Improving outcomes for students with and without learning disabilities. Learning Disabilities Research and Practice.

De La Paz, S., and Graham, S. (1997a). Effects of dictation and advanced planning instruction on the composing of students with writing and learning problems. Journal of Educational Psychology.

De La Paz, S. (2005). Teaching historical reasoning and argumentative writing in culturally and academically diverse middle school classrooms. Journal of Educational Psychology.

Denton, C. A., and Hocker, J. L. (2006). Responsive reading instruction: Flexible intervention for struggling readers in the early grades. Longmont, CO: Sopris West.

Denton, C. A., and Mathes, P. G. (2003). Intervention for struggling readers: Possibilities and challenges. In B. R. Foorman (Ed.), Preventing and remediating reading difficulties: Bringing science to scale. Timonium, MD: York Press.

Diamond, L., and Gutlohn, L. (2006). Vocabulary handbook. Berkeley, CA: Consortium on Reading Excellence.

Dole, J. A., Valencia, S. W., Greer, E. A., and Waldrop, J. L. (1991). Effects of two types of prereading instruction on the comprehension of narrative and expository text. Reading Research Quarterly.

Gersten, R., Fuchs, L., Williams, J., and Baker, S. (2001). Teaching reading comprehension strategies to students with learning disabilities: A review of research. Review of Educational Research.

Fletcher, J. M., Denton, C. A., Fuchs, L., and Vaughn, S. R. (2005). Multi-tiered reading instruction: Linking general education to special education. In S. O. Richardson and J. W. Gilger (Eds.), Research-based education and Intervention: What we need to know. Baltimore, MD: International Dyslexia Association.

Fletcher, J. M., Denton, C. A., Fuchs, L., and Vaughn, S. R. (2005). Multi-tiered reading instruction: Linking general education to special education. In S. O. Richardson and J. W. Gilger (Eds.), Research-based education and intervention: What we need to know.

Foorman, B. R. (2007). Primary prevention in classroom reading instruction. Teaching Exceptional Children.

Foorman, B. R., Nixon, S. (Fall, 2005). Curriculum integration in a multi-tiered instructional approach. Perspectives, IDA. Baltimore, MD.

Foorman, B. R., Carlson, C. D., and Santi, K. L. (2007). Classroom reading instruction and teacher knowledge in the primary grades. In D. Haager, J. Klingner, and S. Vaughn (Eds.), Evidence-based reading practices for response to intervention. Baltimore, MD: Brookes Publishing Co.

Foorman, B. R., and Ciancio, D. J. (2005). Screening for secondary intervention: Concept and context. Journal of Learning Disabilities.

Fuchs, D., Fuchs, L., and Burish, P. (2000). Peer-Assisted Learning Strategies (PALS): An evidence-based practice to promote reading achievement. Learning Disabilities Research and Practice.

Gajria, M., and Salvia, J. (1992). The effects of summarization instruction on text comprehension of students with learning disabilities. Exceptional Children.

Gersten, R., Fuchs, L. S., Williams, J. P., and Baker, S. (2001). Teaching reading comprehension strategies to students with learning disabilities. Review of Educational Research.

Graesser, A. C., and Person, N. K. (1994). Question asking during tutoring. American Educational Research Journal.

Graham, S. (1999). Handwriting and spelling instruction for students with learning disabilities. Learning Disabilities Quarterly.

Graham, S., Harris, and Larsen, L. (2001). Prevention and intervention of writing difficulties for students with Learning Disabilities. Learning Disability Research and Practice.

Graham. S., and Harris, K. R. (2003). Students with learning disabilities and the process of writing: A meta-analysis of SRSD studies. In L. Swanson, K. R. Harris, and S. Graham (Eds.). Handbook of research on learning disabilities. New York: Guilford.

Graner, P. S., Faggella-Luby, M. N., and Fritschmann, N. S. An overview of responsiveness to intervention: What practitioners ought to know. Topics in Language Disorders.

Grossen, B., Hagen-Burke, S., and Burke, M. D. (2002). An experimental study of the effects of considerate curricula in language arts on reading comprehension and writing. Lawrence, KS: University of Kansas, Institute for Academic Access.

Hall, S. (2008). Implementing response to intervention: A principal's guide. Thousand Oaks, CA: Corwin Press.

Hasbrouck, J., and Tindal, G. (2006). Oral reading fluency norms: A valuable assessment tool for reading teachers. Reading Teacher.

Honig, B., Diamond, L., and Gutlohn, L. (2008). Teaching Reading Sourcebook. Berkeley, CA: Consortium on Reading Excellence (CORE).

Jitendra, A K., Hoppes, M. K., and Xin, Y. P. (2000). Enhancing main idea comprehension for students with learning problems: The role of a summarization strategy and self-monitoring instruction. The Journal of Special Education.

Jitendra, A., Edwards, L., Sacks, G., and Jacobson, L. (2004). What research says about vocabulary instruction for students with learning disabilities. Exceptional Children.

Joseph, L. M., and Schisler, R. (2009). Should adolescents go back to the basics?: A review of teaching word reading skills to middle and high school students. Remedial and Special Education, Number 30.

Kamil, M. L., Borman, G. D., Dole, J., Kral, C. C., Salinger, T., and Torgesen, J. (2008). Improving adolescent literacy: Effective classroom and intervention practices: A Practice Guide. Retrieved, from National Center for Education Evaluation and Regional Assistance, Institute of Education Sciences, US Department of Education. July, 2011, from http://ies.ed.gov/ncee/wwc

Klingner, J. K., Vaughn, S., Arguelles, M. E., Hughes, M. T., and Leftwich, S. A. (2004). Collaborative Strategic Reading: Real world lessons from classroom teachers. Remedial and Special Education.

Lesaux, N. K., Kieffer, M. J., Faller, E., and Kelley, J. (2010). The effectiveness and ease of implementation of an academic vocabulary intervention for linguistically diverse students in urban middle schools. Reading Research Quarterly.

Levin, J. R. (2008). The unmistakable professional promise of a young educational psychology research and scholar. Educational Psychologist.

Lovett, M. W., Barron, R. W., and Benson, N. J. (2003). Effective remediation of word identification and decoding difficulties in school-age children with reading disabilities. In H. L. Swanson, K. R. Harris, and S. Graham (Eds.), Handbook of Learning Disabilities. New York: Guilford Press.

Lumbelli, L., Paoletti, G., and Frausin, T. (1999). Improving the ability to detect comprehension problems: From revising to writing. Learning and Instruction.

Mason, L., and Graham, S. (2008). Writing instruction for adolescents with learning disabilities: Programs of intervention research. Learning Disabilities Research and Practice.

Mastropieri, M. A., Scruggs, T. E., Spencer, V., and Fontana, J. (2003). Promoting success in high school world history: Peer tutoring versus guided notes. Learning Disabilities Research and Practice.

Mastropieri, M. A., Scruggs, T. E., Levin, J. R., Gaffney, J., and McLoone, B. (1985). Mnemonic vocabulary instruction for learning disabled students. Learning Disability Quarterly.

Mathes, P. G., Denton, C. A., Fletcher, J. M., Anthony, J. L., Francis, D. J., and Schatschneider, C. (2005). The effects of theoretically different instruction and student characteristics on the skills of struggling readers. Reading Research Quarterly, Number 40.

McCray, A. D., Vaughn, S., and Neal, L. I. (2001). Not all students learn to read by third grade: Middle school students speak out about their reading disabilities. Journal of Special Education.

McMaster, K. L., Fuchs, D., and Fuchs, L. S. (2006). Research on peer-assisted learning strategies: The promise and limitations of peer-mediated instruction. Reading and Writing Quarterly.

Moats, L. C., Foorman, B. R., and Taylor, W. P. (2006). How quality of writing instruction impacts high-risk fourth graders' writing. Reading and Writing: An Interdisciplinary Journal.

Moje, E. B. (2007). Science literacy Q & A. April, 2011, from Council of Chief State School Officers website: http://www.ccsso.org/content/pdfs/Science_Complete%20Set_Final.pdf

Murphy, P., and Graham, S. (2010). Word processing programs and weaker writers/readers: A meta-analysis of research findings. Reading and Writing: An Interdisciplinary Journal. National Commission on Writing (2003, April). The neglected R: The need for a writing revolution.

Nagy, W. E., Berninger, V. W., and Abbott, R. D. (2006). Contributions of morphology beyond phonology to literacy outcomes of upper elementary and middle-school students. Journal of Educational Psychology.

Neuhaus, G. F., Foorman, B. R., Francis, D. J., Carlson, C. D. (2001). Measures of information processing in rapid automatized naming (RAN) and their relation to reading. Journal of Experimental Child Psychology.

Pullen, P. C., Lane, H. B., Lloyd, J. W., Nowak, R., and Ryals, J. (2005). Effects of explicit instruction on decoding of struggling first grade students: A data-based case study. Education and Treatment of Children.

Pittelman, S. D., Levin, K. M., and Johnson, D. D. (1985). An investigation of two instructional settings in the use of semantic mapping with poor readers. Madison, WI: Wisconsin Center for Educational Research, University of Wisconsin.

Riccomini, P. J., Sanders, S., and Jones, J. (2008). The key to enhancing students' mathematical vocabulary knowledge. Journal on School Educational Technology.

Rieth, H. J., Bryant, D. P., and Kinzer, C. K. (2002). An analysis of the impact of anchored instruction on teaching and learning activities in two ninth-grade language arts classes. Remedial and Special Education.

Rogers, L., and Graham, S. (2008). A meta-analysis of single subject design writing intervention research. Journal of Educational Psychology

Saenz, L. M., Fuchs, L. S., and Fuchs, D. (2005). Peer-assisted learning strategies for English language learners with learning disabilities. Exceptional Children.

Scammacca, N., Roberts, G., Vaughn, S., Edmonds, M., Wexler, J., Reutebuch, C. K., and Torgesen, J. K. (2007). Interventions for adolescent struggling readers: A meta-analysis with implications for practice. Portsmouth, NH: RMC Research Corporation, Center on Instruction.

Spencer, V. G., Scruggs, T. E., and Mastropieri, M. A. (2003). Content area learning in middle school social studies classrooms and student with emotional or behavioral disorders: A comparison of strategies. Behavioral Disorders.

Surber, J. R., and Schroeder, M. (2007). Effect of prior domain knowledge and headings of processing of informative text. Contemporary Educational Psychology.

Therrien, W. J., Wickstrom, K., and Jones, K. (2006). Effect of a combined repeated reading and question generation intervention on reading achievement. Learning Disabilities Research and Practice.

Trabasso, T., and Bouchard, E. (2002). Teaching readers how to comprehend text strategically. In C. C. Pressley and M. Pressley, Comprehension instruction: Research-based best practices. New York, NY: Guilford.

Van Garderen, D. (2004). Reciprocal teaching as a comprehension strategy for understanding mathematical word problems. Reading and Writing Quarterly.

Vaughn, S., Klinger, J. K., and Bryant, D. P. (2001). Collaborative strategic reading as a means to enhance peer-mediated instruction for reading comprehension and content area learning. Remedial and Special Education.

Vaughn, S., Martinez, L. R., Linan-Thompson, S., Reutebuch, C. K., Carolson, C. D., and Francis, D. J. (2009). Enhancing social studies vocabulary and comprehension for seventh-grade English language learners: Findings from two experimental studies. Journal of Research on Educational Effectiveness.

Vaughn, S., Wanzek, J., Woodruff, A. L., and Linan-Thompson, S. (2007). A three-tier model for preventing reading difficulties and early identification of students with reading disabilities. In D. Haager, J. Klingner, and S. Vaughn (Eds.), Evidence-based reading practices for response to intervention. Baltimore: Brookes.

Veit, D. T., Scruggs, T. E., and Mastropieri, M. A. (1986). Extended mnemonic instruction with learning disabled students. Journal of Educational Psychology.

Welch, M. (1992). The PLEASE strategy: A metacognitive learning strategy for improving the paragraph writing of students with mild disabilities. Learning Disability Quarterly.

Reading Literacy Early Childhood and Elementary School

General

Adams, M. J. (1998). The three-cueing system. In F. Lehr and J. Osborn (Eds.), Literacy for all: Issues in teaching and learning. New York: Guilford Press.

Adams, M. (1990). Beginning to read: Learning and thinking about print. Cambridge, MA: MIT Press.

Best, R. M., Floyd, R. G., and McNamara, D. S. (2008). Differential competencies contributing to children's comprehension of narrative and expository texts. Reading Psychology.

Bickart, T. (1998). Summary report of preventing reading difficulties in young children (National Academy of Sciences). Washington, DC: US Department of Education.

CINTHIA COLETTI

Brady, S., Gillis, M., Smith, T., Lavalette, M., Liss-Bronstein, L., Lowe, E., et al. (2009). First grade teachers' knowledge of phonological awareness and code concepts: Examining gains from an intensive form of professional development. Reading and Writing: An Interdisciplinary Journal.

Brown, A. L., and Palinscar, A. S. (1984). Reciprocal teaching of comprehension: Fostering and monitoring activities. Cognition and Instruction.

Cardenas-Hagan, E. (2011). Language and literacy development among English language learners in J. R. Birsh, (Ed.). Multisensory teaching of basic language skills. Baltimore: Paul H. Brookes Publishing.

Cardenas-Hagan, E. (1998). Esperanza: A multisensory Spanish language program. Brownsville, TX: Valley Speech, Language and Learning Center.

Cepeda, N.J., Pashler, H., Vul, E., Wixted, J. T., and Rohrer, D. (2006). Distributed practice in verbal recall tasks: A review and quantitative synthesis. Psychological Bulletin.

Chan, K. S. (1991). Promoting strategy generalization through self-instructional training in students with reading disabilities. Journal of Learning Disabilities. Cognition and Technology Group at Vanderbilt. (2002).

Cunningham, A. E., and Stanovich, K. E. (1997). Early reading acquisition and its relation to reading experience and ability ten years later. Developmental Psychology, Volume 39.

Denton, C. A., Fletcher, J. M., Anthony, J. L., and Francis, D. J. (2006). An evaluation of intensive intervention for students with persistent reading difficulties. Journal of Learning Disabilities, Volume 39.

Denton, C., Foorman, B., and Mathes, P. (2003). Schools that "Beat the Odds": Implications for reading instruction. Remedial and Special Education, Volume 24.

Denton, C., Vaughn, S., and Fletcher, J. (2003). Bringing research-based practice in reading intervention to scale. Learning Disabilities Research and Practice, Volume 18.

Fletcher, J. M., Lyon, G. R., Fuchs, L. S., and Barnes, M. A. (2007). Learning disabilities: From identification to intervention. New York: Guilford Press.

Fletcher, J. M., Foorman, B. R., Denton, C., and Vaughn, S. (2006). Scaling research on beginning reading: Consensus and conflict. In M. Constas and R. Sternberg (Eds.), Translating educational theory and research into practice. Mahwah, NJ: Lawrence Erlbaum Associates.

Foorman, B. R., and Moats, L.C. (2004). Conditions for sustaining research-based practices in early reading instruction. Remedial and Special Education.

Foorman, B. R., Francis, D. J., Davidson, K., Harm, M., and Griffin, J. (2004). Variability in text features in six grade 1 basal reading programs. Scientific Studies in Reading.

Foorman, B. R., Goldenberg, C., Carlson, C., Saunders, W., Pollard-Durodola, S.D. (2004). How teachers allocate time during literacy instruction in primary-grade English language learner classrooms. In M. McCardle and V. Chhabra (Eds.), The voice of evidence: Bringing research to the classroom. Baltimore, MD: Brookes Publishing Co.

Foorman, B. R., Kalinowski, S. J., and Sexton, W. L. (in press). Standards-based educational reform is one important step toward reducing the achievement gap. In A. Gamoran (Ed.), Standards-based reform and the poverty gap: Lessons from "No Child Left Behind Washington, DC: Brookings Institution.

Foorman, B. R., Perfetti, C. A., Pesetsky, D., Rayner, K., and Seidenberg, M. S. (2001). How psychological science informs the teaching of reading. Psychological Science in the Public Interest.

Foorman, B.R., and Santi, K. L. (in press). The teaching of reading. In L. J. Saha and A.G. Dworkin (Eds.), The New International Handbook of Teachers and Teaching. Norwell, MA: Springer.

Francis, D.F., Santi, K. L., Barr, C., Fletcher, J. M., Varisco, A., and Foorman, B.R. (in press). Form effects on the estimation of students' oral reading fluency using DIBELS. Journal of School Psychology.

Francis, D. J., Carlson, C.D., Fletcher, J. M., Foorman, B.R., Goldenberg, C.R., Vaughn, S., Miller, J., Iglesias, A., and Papanicolaou, A. (2005). Oral literacy development of Spanish-speaking children: A multi-level program of research on language minority children and the instruction, school and community contexts, and interventions that influence their academic outcomes. Perspectives, IDA. Baltimore, MD.

Fuchs, L., Fuchs, D., Bentz, J., Phillips, N., and Hamlett, C. (1994). The nature of students' interactions during peer tutoring with and without prior training and experience. American Educational Research Journal.

Fuchs, L. S., Fuchs, D., Hosp, M. K., and Jenkins, J. R. (2001). Oral reading fluency as an indicator of reading competence: A theoretical, empirical, and historical analysis. Scientific Studies of Reading.

Genesee, F., Paradis, J., and Crago, M. (2004). Dual language development and disorders: A handbook on bilingualism and second language learning. Baltimore: Brookes.

Ghatala, E. S., Levin, J. R., Foorman, B. R., and Pressley, M. (1989). Improving children's regulations of their reading PREP time. Contemporary Educational Psychology.

Hart, B., and Risley, T. R. (1995). Meaningful differences in the everyday experience of young American children. Baltimore: Brookes Publishing.

Henry, M. (2003). Unlocking literacy. Baltimore: Brookes Publishing.

Hirsch, E. D. (2001). Overcoming the language gap. American Educator, Volume 25.

Kamil, M. K., Mosenthal, P. B., Pearson, P. D., and Barr, R. (2000). Handbook for reading research (Vol. III). Mahwah, NJ: Erlbaum.

McCardle, P., Chhabra, V. (2004). The Voice of Evidence in Reading Research. Brookes Publishing.

McCutchen, D., Abbott, R. D., and Green, L. B. (2002).Beginning literacy: Links among teacher knowledge, teacher practice, and student learning. Journal of Learning Disabilities.

Mehta, P., Foorman, B.R., Branum-Martin, L., and Taylor, W. P. (2005). Literacy as a unidimensional multilevel construct: Validation, sources of influence, and implications in a longitudinal study in grades 1-4. Scientific Studies of Reading.

Moats, L. C. (2000). Speech to print: Language essentials for teachers. Baltimore: Brookes.

Moats, L. C., and Foorman, B.R. (1998). Scholastic Spelling. NY: Scholastic, Inc.

Moats, L.C., and Foorman, B.R. Literacy achievement in the primary grades in high poverty schools: Lessons learned from a five-year research program. In S. B. Neuman (ed.), Literacy achievement for young children from poverty. Baltimore: Brookes Publishing Co.

National Reading Panel. (2000). Teaching children to read: An evidence-based assessment of the scientific research literature on reading and its implications for reading instruction. Washington, DC: National Institutes of Health.

Paynter, D. E., Bodrova, E., and Doty, J. K. (2005). For the love of words: Vocabulary instruction that works, Grades K-6. San Francisco: Jossey-Bass.

Rayner, K., and Pollatsek, A. (1989). The Psychology of Reading Hillsdale, NJ: Erlbaum.

RAND Reading Study Group. (2002). Reading for understanding: Toward a research and development program in reading comprehension. Santa Monica, CA: RAND Corporation. (http://www. rand.org.multi/achievementforall/reading/readreport.html.)

Rayner, K., Foorman, B., Perfetti, C.A., Pesetsky, D., and Seidenberg, M.S. (2002). How should reading be taught? Scientific America.

Rowe, K. J. (1995). Factors affecting students' progress in reading: key findings from a longitudinal study. Literacy, Teaching and Learning.

Saunders, W. M., Foorman, B.R., Carlson, C.D. (November, 2006). Do we need a separate block of time for oral English language development, Elementary School Journal.

Schatschneider, C., Fletcher, J., Francis, D., Carlson, C., and Foorman, B. (2004). Kindergarten prediction of reading skills: A longitudinal comparative study. Journal of Educational Psychology.

Seals, L., Pollard-Durodola, S., Foorman, B.R., and Bradley, A. (2007). Vocabulary power: Lessons for Students Who Use African American Vernacular English (Teacher's Manual Level 2 and Student Workbook Level 2). Baltimore, MD: Brookes Publishing Co.

Shaywitz, S. (2003). Overcoming dyslexia: A new and complete science-based program for reading problems at any level. New York: Knopf.

Snow, C. E., Burns, M. S., and Griffin, P. (1998). Preventing reading difficulties in young children. Washington, DC: National Academy Press.

Stahl, S. A., and Fairbanks, M. M. (1986). The effects of vocabulary instruction: A model-based meta-analysis. Review of Educational Research.

Snow, C., Griffin, P., and Burns, S. (2006). Knowledge to support the teaching of reading. San Francisco: Jossey-Bass.

Spear-Swerling, L., and Sternberg, R. J. (2001). What science offers teachers of reading. Learning Disabilities Research and Practice.

Spear-Swerling, L. (2004). A road map for understanding reading disability and other reading problems: Origins, intervention, and prevention. In R. Ruddell and N. Unrau (Eds.), Theoretical models and processes of reading: Vol. 5. Newark, DE: International Reading Association.

Stanovitch, P. J., and Stanovich, K. E. (2003). Using Research and Reason in Education: How Teachers Can Use Scientifically Based Research to Make Curricular and Instruction Decisions.

Stanovich, K. E. (2000). Progress in understanding reading: Scientific foundations and new frontiers. New York: Guilford Press.

Stone, A. C., Silliman, E. R., Ehren, B. J., and Apel, K. (Eds.). (2004). Handbook of language and literacy: Development and disorders. New York: Guilford Press.

Taylor, B. M., Frye, B. J., Maruyama, G. M. (1990). Time spent reading and reading growth. American Educational Research Journal.

Torgesen, J. K. (2002). The Prevention of Reading Difficulties. Journal School Psychology.

Vadasy, P. F., Sanders, E. A., Peyton, J. A., and Jenkins, J. R. (2002). Timing and intensity of tutoring: A closer look at the conditions for effective early literacy tutoring. Learning Disabilities Research and Practice.

Vellutino, F. R., Tunmer, W. E., Jaccard, J. J., and Chen, R. (2007). Components of reading ability: Multivariate evidence for a convergent skills model of reading development. Scientific Studies of Reading, Volume 11.

Wolf, M. (2007). Proust and the Squid, the Story and the Science of the Reading Brain. Harper Collins.

CINTHIA COLETTI

Wolf, M., and Bowers, P. G. (1999). The double-deficit hypothesis for the developmental dyslexias. Journal of Educational Psychology.

Wolfe, M. B., and Mienko, J. A. (2007). Learning and memory of factual content from narrative and expository text. British Journal of Educational Psychology.

Early Childhood and Emergent Literacy

Adams, M. J. (1990). Beginning to read: Thinking and learning about print. Cambridge, MA: MIT Press.

Adams, M. J., Foorman, B.R., Lundberg, I., and Beeler, T. (1998). Phonemic awareness in young children: A classroom curriculum. Baltimore, MD: Brookes Publishing Co.

Ball, E. W., and Blachman, B. A. (1988). Phoneme segmentation training: Effect on reading readiness. Annals of Dyslexia.

Chard, D. J., Simmons, D. C., and Kameenui, E. J. (1998). Word recognition: Research bases. In D. C. Simmons and E. J. Kameenui (Eds.), What reading research tells us about children with diverse learning needs: Bases and basics (pp. 239-278). Mahwah, NJ: Erlbaum.

Dickinson, D., and Tabors, P. O. (Eds.). (2001). Beginning literacy. Baltimore: Brookes.

Hiebert, E. H. (1993). Young children's literacy experiences in home and school. In S. R. Yussen and M. C. Smith (Eds.), Reading across the lifespan. New York: Springer-Verlag.

Leseman, P. M., and Jong, P. F. (1998). Home literacy: Opportunity, instruction, cooperation and social-emotional quality predicting early reading achievement. Reading Research Quarterly.

McCabe, A. (1992). Language games to play with your child. New York: Plenum Press.

McGee, L. M., and Richgels, D. J. (2000). Literacy beginnings: Supporting young readers and writers (3rd ed.). Needham, MA: Allyn and Bacon.

Newman, S. B., and Dickinson, D. K. (2001). Handbook of early literacy research. New York: Guilford Press.

Snow, C. E., Burns, M. S., and Griffin, P. (1998). Preventing Reading Difficulties in Young Children. National Academy Press.

Teale, W. H., and Sulzby, E. (1986). Emergent literacy as a perspective for examining how young children become readers and writers. In W. H. Teale and E. Sulzby (Eds.), Emergent literacy: Writing and reading. Stanford, CT: Ablex.

Troia, G. A., Roth, F. P., and Graham, S. (1998). An educator's guide to phonological awareness: Assessment measures and intervention activities for children. Focus on Exceptional Children.

Van Kleeck, A. (1990). Emergent literacy: Learning about print before learning to read. Topics in Language Disorders.

Whitehurst, G. L., and Lonigan, C. J. (1998). Child development and early literacy. Child Development.

Yopp, H. K. (1992). Developing phonemic awareness in young children. The Reading Teacher.

Shared Relationships

Barnhart, J. E. (1990). Differences in story retelling behaviors and their relation to reading comprehension in second graders. In J. Zutell and S. McCormick (Eds.), Literacy theory and research: Analyses from multiple paradigms Chicago: National Reading Conference.

Catts, H. W. (1993). The relationship between speech-language impairments and reading disabilities. Journal of Speech and Hearing Research.

Dickson, S. V., Simmons, D. C., and Kameenui, E. J. (1998). Text organization: Research bases. In D. C. Simmons and E. J. Kameenui (Eds.), What reading research tells us about children with diverse learning needs: Bases and basics. Mahwah, NJ: Erlbaum.

Ehri, L. C. (2000). Learning to read and learning to spell: Two sides of a coin. Topics in Language Disorders.

Silliman, E. R., Jimerson, T. L., and Wilkinson, L. C. (2000). A dynamic systems approach to writing assessment in students with language learning problems. Topics in Language Disorders.

Sulzby, E. (1996). Roles of oral and written language as children approach conventional literacy. In C. Pontecorvo, M. Orsolini, B. Burge, and L. B. Resnick (Eds.), Children's early text construction. Mahway, NJ: Erlbaum.

Torgesen, J. K. (1999). Assessment and instruction for phonemic awareness and word recognition skill. In H. W. Catts and A. G. Kamhi (Eds.), Language and reading disabilities Boston, MA: Allyn and Bacon.

Watson, L. R., Crais, E., and Layton, T. L. (2000). Handbook of early language development in children: Assessment and treatment. San Diego, CA: Delmar.

Reading Literacy High School and Middle School

Alfassi, M. (2004). Reading to learn: Effects of combined strategy instruction on high school students. The Journal of Educational Research.

Alfassi, M. (1998). Reading for meaning: The efficacy of reciprocal teaching in fostering reading comprehension in high school students in remedial reading classes. American Educational Research Journal.

Apel, K., and Swank, L. K. (1999). Second chances: Improving decoding skills in the older student. Language, Speech, and Hearing Services in Schools.

Archer, A. A., Gleason, M. M., and Vachon, V. (2005). REWARDS PLUS reading strategies applied to social studies passages. Longmont, CO: Sopris West.

Baumann, J., Edwards, E. C., Boland, E., and Olejnik. S. (2003). Vocabulary tricks: Effects of instruction in morphology and context on fifth-grade students' ability to derive and infer word meanings. American Educational Research Journal.

Baumann, J. F., Edwards, E. C., Font, G., Tereshinski, C. A., Kame'enui, E. J., and Olejnik, S. (2002). Teaching morphemic and contextual analysis to fifth-grade students. Reading Research Quarterly.

Borkowski, J. G. (1992). Metacognitive theory: A framework for teaching literacy, writing, and math skills. Journal of Learning Disabilities.

Brown, R. (2002). Straddling two worlds: Self-directed comprehension instruction for middle schoolers. In C.C. Block, and M. Pressley (Eds.), Comprehension instruction: Research-based best practices. New York, NY: Guilford.

Bower, G. H., Black, J.B., and Turner, T.J. (1979). Scripts in memory for text. Cognitive Psychology.

Cornoldi, C., and Oakhill, J. (Eds.). (1996). Reading comprehension difficulties: Processes and intervention. Mahwah, NJ: Erlbaum.

Cutting, L. E., and Scarborough, H. S. (2006). Prediction of reading comprehension: Relative contributions of word recognition, language proficiency, and other cognitive skills can depend on how comprehension is measured. Scientific Studies of Reading, Number 10.

Deshler, D. D., and Lenz, B. K. (1989). The strategic instructional approach. International Journal of Disability, Development, and Education.

Gholson, B., and Craig, S.D. (2006). Promoting constructive activities that support learning during computer-based instruction. Educational Psychology Review.

Lovett, M. W., Lacerenze, L., and Borden, S. L. (2000). Putting struggling readers on the PHAST track: A program to integrate phonological and strategy-based remedial reading instruction and maximize outcomes. Journal of Learning Disabilities.

Ruddell, R. B., Ruddell, M. R., and Singer, H. (Eds.). (1994). Theoretical models and processes of reading (4th ed.). Newark, DE: International Reading Association.

Santi, K. L., York, M., Foorman, B.R., and Francis, D. J. (2009). Mentoring: A framework for success. Insight.

Smith, B. L., Holliday, W. G., and Austin, H. W. (2010). Students' comprehension of science textbooks using a question-based reading strategy. Journal of Research in Science Teaching.

Snow, C. E., Lawrence, J., and White, C. (2009). Generating knowledge of academic language among urban middle school students. Journal of Research on Educational Effectiveness.

Taboada, A., and Guthrie, J. (2006). Contributions of student questioning and prior knowledge to construction of knowledge from reading information text. Journal of Literacy Research.

School Administration

Adams, M. J. (1998). The three-cueing system. In F. Lehr and J. Osborn (Eds.), Literacy for all: Issues in teaching and learning. New York: Guilford Press.

Black, P., Harrison, C., Lee, C., Marshall, B., and Wiliam, D. (2003). Assessment for learning: Putting it into practice. Maidenhead, UK: Open University Press.

Blankstein, A. (2004). Failure is not an option: six principles that guide student achievement in high performing schools. Thousand Oaks, CA: Corwin Press.

Crawford, E. C., and Torgesen, J. K. (2006, July). Teaching all children to read: Practices from Reading First schools with strong intervention outcomes. Presented at the Florida Principal's Leadership Conference, Orlando, from *http://www.fcrr.org/science/sciencePresentationscrawford.htm*

Coben, S. S., Thomas, C. C., Sattler, R. O., and Morsink, C. V. (1997). Meeting the challenge of consultation and collaboration: Developing interactive teams. Journal of Learning Disabilities.

Cunningham, A. E., and Stanovich, K. E. (1998). What reading does for the mind. American Educator.

Denton, C., Foorman, B., and Mathes, P. (2003). Schools that "Beat the Odds": Implications for reading instruction. Remedial and Special Education.

Denton, C., Vaughn, S., and Fletcher, J. (2003). Bringing research-based practice in reading intervention to scale. Learning Disabilities Research and Practice.

Fishbaugh, M. S. (1997). Models of collaboration. Boston: Allyn and Bacon.

Good, R. H., Simmons, D. C., and Kame'enui, E. J. (2001). The importance and decision-making utility of a continuum of fluency-based indicators of foundational reading skills for third-grade high-stakes outcomes. *Scientific Studies of Reading.*

Hamilton, C., and Shinn, M. R. (2003). Characteristics of word callers: An investigation of the accuracy of teachers' judgments of reading comprehension and oral reading skills. School Psychology Review.

Hosp, M. K., Hosp, J. L., and Howell, K. W. (2007). The ABC's of CBM: A practical guide to curriculum-based measurement. New York: Guilford Press

Idol, L., Nevin, A., and Paolucci-Whitcomb, P. (1994). Collaborative consultation (2nd ed.). Austin, TX: Pro-Ed.

CINTHIA COLETTI

Landi, N., Perfetti, C.A., Bolger, D. J., and Foorman, B.R. (2006). The role of discourse context in developing word form representations: A paradoxical relation between reading and learning. Journal of Experimental Child Psychology,

Halverson, R., and Thomas, C. N. (2007). The roles and practices of student services staff as data-driven instructional leaders. In M. Mangin and S. Stoelinga (Eds.), Instructional teachers leadership roles: Using research to inform and reform. New York: Teachers College Press.

Herman, R., Dawson, P., Dee, T., Greene, J., Maynard, R., Redding, S., and Darwin, M. (2008). Turning around chronically low-performing schools: A practice guide. Washington, DC. Assistance, Institute of Education Sciences, US Department of Education. May, 2011, from http://ies.ed.gov/ncee/wwc/publications/practiceguides.

Hill, D., Lewis, J., and Pearson, J. (2008). Metro Nashville Public Schools student assessment staff development model. Nashville, TN: Vanderbilt University, Peabody College.

Hughes, S. (2010). Five critical success factors for project managers. PM Hut, July, 2011, from *http://www.pmhut.com/five-critical-success-factors-for-project-managers.*

McCardle, P., and Chhabra, V. (2004). The voice of evidence in reading research. Baltimore: Brookes.

Murphy, J., Weil, M., Hallinger, P., and Mittman, A. (1982). Academic press: translating high expectations into school policies and classroom practices. Educational Leadership.

Pedriana, A. (2009). Leaving Johnny Behind. Learning Dynamics Press.

Prelock, P. A., Miller, B. L., and Reed, N. L. (1995). Collaborative partnerships in a language in the classroom program. Language, Speech, and Hearing Services in Schools.

Risko, V. J., and Bromley, K. (2001). Collaboration for diverse learners. Newark, DE: International Reading Association.

Snow, C., Griffin, P., and Burns, S. (2006). Knowledge to support the teaching of reading. San Francisco: Jossey-Bass.

Spear-Swerling, L., and Sternberg, R. J. (2001). What science offers teachers of reading. Learning Disabilities Research and Practice

Stanovich, K. E. (2000). Progress in understanding reading: Scientific foundations and new frontiers. New York: Guilford Press

Whitehurst, G. J. (2002). Improving teacher quality. Spectrum: The Journal of State Government, Summer, 2002. Washington, DC.

Villa, R. A., Thousand, J. S., Nevin, A. I., and Malgeri, C. (1996). Instilling collaboration for inclusive schooling as a way of doing business in public schools. Remedial and Special Education.

State Educators and Institutes of Higher Education

Abbott, D. V. (2008). A functionality framework for educational organizations: Achieving accountability at scale. In E. Mandinach and M. Honey (Eds.), Data driven school improvement: Linking data and learning. New York: Teachers College Press.

Abledinger, J. and Kowal, J. (2010). Shooting for stars: Cross sector lessons for retaining high performing educators. Chapel Hill, NC: Public Impact.

Balfanz, R. (2007, August). Locating and transforming the low performing high schools which produce the nation's dropouts. Presented August 16, 2007, at Turning Around Low-Performing High Schools: Lessons for Federal Policy from Research and Practice.

Bryk, A. S., Sebring, P. B., Allensworth, E., Luppescu, S., and Easton, J. Q. (2010). Organizing schools for improvement: Lessons from Chicago. Chicago: The University of Chicago Press.

Borman, B. A. Jones, and W. F. Wright (Eds.), Learner-centered leadership: Research, policy, and practice. Mahwah, NJ: Lawrence Erlbaum Associates.

Cirino, P., Pollard-Durodola, S.D., Foorman, B.R., and Carlson, C.D., and Francis, D. J. (March, 2007). Teacher characteristics, classroom instruction, and student literacy and language outcomes in bilingual kindergarteners. Elementary School Journal, Number 107.

Copland, M.A. (2003). Leadership of inquiry: Building and sustaining capacity for school improvement. Educational Evaluation and Policy Analysis.

Goodwin, B. (2010). Changing the odds for student success: What matters most. Denver, CO.: Mid-continent Research for Education and Learning (McREL).

Gunn, J. H., and King, B. (2003). Trouble in paradise: Power, conflict, and community in an interdisciplinary teaching team. Urban Education.

Feger, S., and Arruda, E. (2008). Professional learning communities: Key themes from the literature. Providence, RI: Brown University, Education Alliance.

Foorman, B.R., and Nixon, S. (2006). The influence of public policy on research and practice in reading. Topics in Language Disorders.

Foorman, B. R., Schatschneider, C., Eakin, M. N., Fletcher, J. M., Moats, L. C., and Francis, D. J. (2006). The impact of instructional practices in grades 1 and 2 on reading and spelling achievement in high poverty schools. Contemporary Educational Psychology.

Halverson, R., Prichett, R. B., and Watson, J. G. (2007). Formative feedback systems and the new instructional leadership. Madison, WI: University of Wisconsin.

Herman, R., Dawson, P., Dee, T., Greene, J., Maynard, R., Redding, S., and Darwin, M. (2008). Turning around chronically low-performing schools: A practice guide, Washington, DC: National Center for Education Evaluation and Regional Assistance, Institute of Education Sciences, US Department of Education. May, 2011, from http://ies.ed.gov/ncee/wwc/publications/practiceguides.

Louis, K. S., Leithwood, K., Wahlstrom, K. L., and Anderson, S. (2010). Investigating the links to improved student learning: Final report of research findings to the Wallace Foundation. Minneapolis: University of Minnesota.

Mieles, T., and Foley, E. (2005). Data warehousing: Preliminary findings from a study of implementing districts. Providence, RI: Annenberg Institute for School Reform.

Murphy, J. (2006). Preparing school leaders: An agenda for research and action. Lanham, MD: Rowman and Littlefield.

National Reading Panel. (2000). Teaching children to read: An evidence-based assessment of the scientific research literature on reading and its implications for reading instruction. Washington, DC: National Institutes of Health.

RAND Reading Study Group. (2002). Reading for understanding: Toward a research and development program in reading comprehension. Santa Monica, CA: RAND Corporation, may, 2011 from *http://www.rand.org.multi/achievementforall/reading/readreport.html.*

Shirm, A., Stuart, E., and McKie, A. (2006). The Quantum Opportunity Program demonstration: Final impacts. Washington, DC: Mathematica Policy Research, Inc.

Stoll, L., Bolam, R., McMahon, A., Wallace, M., and Thomas, S. (2006). Professional learning communities: A review of the literature. Journal of Educational Change.

Supovitz, J. A. (2006). The case for district-based reform: Leading, building, and sustaining school improvement. Cambridge, MA: Harvard Education Press.

Walsh, K., Glaser, D., and Wilcox, D. D. (2006). What education schools aren't teaching about reading and what elementary teachers aren't learning. Washington, DC: National Council on Teacher Quality.

Waters, J. T., Marzano, R. J., and McNulty, B. A. (2003). Balanced leadership: What 30 years of research tells us about the effect of leadership on student achievement. Aurora, CO: Mid-continent Research for Education and Learning. June, 2011, from http://www. mcrel.org/PDF/LeadershipOrganizationDevelopment/5031RR_ BalancedLeadership.pdf

Teacher Knowledge and Professional Development

Beck, I. L., McKeown, M. G., Hamilton, R. L., and Kucan, L. (1997). Questioning the Author: An approach for enhancing student engagement with text. Delaware: International Reading Association.

Bos, C., Mather, N., Dickson, S., Podhajski, B., and Chard, D. (2001). Perceptions and knowledge of preservice and in-service educators about early reading instruction. Annals of Dyslexia, Volume 51.

Brady, S., Gillis, M., Smith, T., Lavalette, M., Liss-Bronstein, L., Lowe, E., et al. (2009). First grade teachers' knowledge of phonological awareness and code concepts: Examining gains from an intensive form of professional development. Reading and Writing: An Interdisciplinary Journal, Volume 22.

Crawford, E. C., and Torgesen, J. K. (2006, July). Teaching all children to read: Practices from Reading First schools with strong intervention outcomes. Presented at the Florida Principal's Leadership Conference, Orlando. Retrievable from http://www.fcrr.org/science/ sciencePresentationscrawford.ht

Cunningham, A. E., Perry, K. E., Stanovich, K. E., and Stanovich, P. J. (2004). Disciplinary knowledge of K-3 teachers and their knowledge calibration in the domain of early literacy. Annals of Dyslexia, Volume 54.

CONNECT (1997). Professional Development Criteria: A study guide for effective professional development. Colorado Statewide Systemic Initiative for Mathematics and Science (CONNECT). Denver: CO. May, 2011, from http://www.mcrel.org/PDF/ProfessionalDevelopment/6804TG_ProfDevelopCriteria.pdf

Cochran-Smith, M., and Lytle, S. L. (1993). Inside-outside: Teacher research and knowledge. New York: Teachers College Press.

Cook, C. J. (1997). Critical issue: Evaluating professional growth and development. North Central Regional Educational Laboratory. June, 2011, from http://www.ncrel.org/sdrs/areas/issues/educatrs/profdevl/pd500.htm

Elmore, R. F. (2000). Building a new structure for school leadership. Washington, DC: The Albert Shanker Institute.

Feger, S., and Arruda, E. (2008). Professional learning communities: Key themes from the literature. Providence, RI: Brown University, Education Alliance.

Garet, M., Porter, A. C., Desimone, L., Birman, B., and Yoon, K. S. (2001). What makes professional development effective? Results from a national sample of teachers. American Education Research Journal (AERA).

Harris, D. N., and Sass, T. R. (2007). Teacher training, teacher quality, and student achievement. University of Wisconsin-Madison.

Institute for Educational Leadership—IEL (2001). Leadership for student learning: Redefining the teacher as a leader. School leadership for the 21st century initiative: A report of the task force on teacher leadership. Washington, DC: Institute for Educational Leadership. April, 2011, from http://www.iel.org/programs/21st/reports/teachlearn.pdf

Kennedy, M. (1998). Form and substance of in-service teacher education (Research Monograph). Madison: University of Wisconsin-Madison, National Institute for Science Education.

Kameenui, E. J. (Ed.). (1997). Effective teaching strategies that accommodate diverse learners. Upper Saddle River, NJ: Prentice Hall.

Kowal, J., and Hassel, E. A. (2010). Measuring teacher and leader performance: Cross-sector lessons for excellent evaluations. Chapel Hill, NC: Public Impact. March, 2011, from *http://www.publicimpact.com/images/stories/performance_measurement_2010.pdf*

Mahoney, J. W. (2010). Discerning, developing and rewarding effective teachers. American Association of School Administrators. June, 2011, from *http://resources.aasa.org/ConferenceDaily/handouts2011/2170-1.pdf*

Mastropieri, M. A., and Scruggs, T. E. (1997). Best practices in promoting reading comprehension in students with learning disabilities: 1976 to 1996. Remedial and Special Education.

Moats, L., Carreker, S., Davis, R. (2010). Knowledge and Practice Standards for Teachers of Reading. International Dyslexia Association, Baltimore, MD.

Murphy, J. (2004). Leadership for literacy: Research-based practice, preK-3. Thousand Oaks, CA: Corwin Press.

Pressley, M. (1998). Reading instruction that works: The case for balanced teaching. New York: Guilford Press.

Snow-Renner, R., and Lauer, P. A. (2005). Professional development analysis. Mid-continent Research for Education and Research (McREL). Denver: CO. Aug, 2011, from http://www.mcrel.org/PDF/ProfessionalDevelopment/5051IR_Prof_dvlpmt_analysis.pdf

Weisberb, D., Sexton, S., Mulhern, J., and Keeling, D. (2009). The widget effect: Our national failure to acknowledge and act on differences in teacher effectiveness. The New Teacher Project. July, 2011, from http://www.gatesfoundation.org/learning/Documents/the-widget-effect.pdf

Writing Instruction

Bangert-Drowns, R. (1993). The word processor as an instructional tool: A meta-analysis of word processing in writing instruction. Review of Educational Research.

Bangert-Drowns, R. L., Hurley, M. M., and Wilkinson, B. (2004). The effects of school-based writing-to-learn interventions on academic achievement: A meta-analysis. Review of Educational Research.

Benson, N. L., (1979). The effects of peer feedback during the writing process on writing performance, revision behavior, and attitude toward writing (Master's thesis). University of Colorado, Boulder, CO.

Bereiter, C., and Scardamalia, M. (1987). The psychology of written composition. Hillsdale, NJ: Erlbaum.

Berninger, V. W., Abbott, R. D., Jones, J., Gould, L., Anderson-Youngstrom, M., Shimada, S., et al. (2006). Early development of language by hand: Composing, reading, listening, and speaking connections; three letter-writing modes; and fast mapping in spelling. Developmental Neuropsychology, Volume 29.

Berkowitz, S. J. (1986). Effects of instruction in text organization on sixth-grade students' memory for expository reading. Reading Research Quarterly.

Clarke, L. K. (1988). Invented versus traditional spelling in first graders' writings: Effects on learning to read and spell. Research in the Teaching of English.

De La Paz, S., and Graham, S. (2002). Explicitly teaching strategies, skills, and knowledge: Writing instruction in middle school classrooms. Journal of Educational Psychology.

Denner, P. R. (1987). Comparison of the effects of episodic organizers and traditional note taking on story recall. ERIC.

Edwards, L. (2003). Writing instruction in kindergarten: Examining an emerging area of research for children with writing and reading difficulties. Journal of Learning Disabilities, Volume 36.

Englert, C. S., Raphael, T. E., Anderson, L. M., Anthony, H. M., Stevens, D., and Fear, K. (1991). Making writing strategies and self-talk visible: Cognitive strategy instruction in writing in regular and special education classrooms. American Educational Research Journal.

Englert, C. S., Wu, X., and Zhao, Y. (2005). Cognitive tools for writing: Scaffolding the performance of students through technology. Learning Disabilities Research and Practice, Volume 20.

Goldring, A., Russell, M., and Cook, A. (2003). The effects of computers on student writing: A meta-analysis of studies from 1992-2002. Journal of Technology, Learning, and Assessment.

Graham, S., and Perin, D. (2007). Writing next: Effective strategies to improve writing of adolescents in middle and high schools—A report to Carnegie Corporation of New York. Washington, DC: Alliance for Excellent Education.

Graham, S., McArthur, C.A., and Fitzgerald, J. (Eds.). (2007). Best practices in writing instruction. New York: Guilford Press.

Graham, S., and Perin, D. (2007). Writing next: Effective strategies to improve writing of adolescents in middle and high schools. New York: Carnegie Corporation of New York.

Graham, S., and Perin, D. (2007). A meta-analysis of writing instruction for adolescent students. Journal of Educational Psychology.

Graham, S., and Hebert, M. (2010). Writing to reading: Evidence for how writing can improve reading. Alliance for Excellence in Education. Washington, DC.

Graves, D. H. (1983). Writing: Teachers and children at work. Portsmouth, NH: Heinemann.

Guastello, E. F. (2001). Parents as partners: Improving children's writing. Celebrating the voices of literacy: The twenty-third yearbook of the College Reading Association: College Reading Association.

Harris, K. R., and Graham, S. (1996). Making the writing process work: Strategies for composition and self-regulation. Cambridge, MA: Brookline Books.

Hayes, J., and Flower, L. (1980). Identifying the organization of the writing process. In L. W. Gregg and E. R. Steinberg (Eds.), Cognitive processes in writing. Hillsdale, NJ: Erlbaum.

Hillocks, G. (1986). Research on written composition: New directions for teaching. Urbana, IL: National Council of Teachers of English.

Levy and S. Ransdell (Eds.), (2008). The science of writing: Theories, methods, individual differences, and applications. Mahwah, New Jersey: Lawrence Erbaum Associates.

Neville, D., and Searls, E. (1991). A meta-analytic review of the effects of sentence-combining on reading comprehension. Reading Research and Instruction.

Pritchard, R.J. (1987). Effects on student writing of teacher training in the National Writing Project Model. Written Communication.

Pritchard, R.J., and Marshall, J.C. (1994). Evaluation of a tiered model for staff development in writing. Research in the Teaching of English.

Olson, V. B. (1990). The revising processes of sixth-grade writers with and without peer feedback. Journal of Educational Research.

Ross, J. A., Rolheiser, C., and Hogboam-Gray, A. (1999). Effects of self-evaluation training on narrative writing. Assessing Writing.

Roth, F. P. (2000). Narrative writing: Development and teaching with children with writing difficulties. Topics in Language Disorders.

Saddler, B., and Graham, S. (2005). The effects of peer-assisted sentence combining instruction on the writing performance of more and less skilled young writers. Journal of Educational Psychology.

Scardamalia, M., and Bereiter, C. (1986). Research on written composition. In M. C. Wittrock (Ed.), Handbook of research on teaching. NY: Macmillan.

Schunk, D. H., and Swartz, C. W. (1993). Writing strategy instruction with gifted students: Effects of goals and feedback on self-efficacy and skills. Roeper Review.

Senechal, M., LeFeure, J., Thomas, E. M., and Daley, K. E. (1998). Differential effects of home literacy experiences on the development of oral and written language. Reading Research Quarterly.

Silliman, E. R., Jimerson, T. L., and Wilkinson, L. C. (2000). A dynamic systems approach to writing assessment in students with language learning problems. Topics in Language Disorders.

Taylor, B. M., and Beach, R. W. (1984). The effects of text structure instruction on middle-grade students' comprehension and production of expository text. Reading Research Quarterly.

Wong, B. Y. L., Kuperis, S., Jamieson, D., Keller, L., and Cull-Hewitt, R. (2002). Effects of guided journal writing on students' story understanding. The Journal of Educational Research.

Wong, B. Y. L. (2000). Writing strategies instruction for expository essays for adolescents with and without learning disabilities. Topics in Learning Disorders.

Zellermayer, M., Salomon, G., Globerson, T., and Givon, H. (1991). Enhancing writing-related metacognitions through a computerized writing partner. American Educational Research Journal.

INDEX

A

ability levels, 385, 396, 428, 442-43, 531, 551

abstraction, 415, 424, 439, 547

academic progress, appropriate, 353-54, 369, 527-28

academic vocabulary, 416, 425-26, 440-41, 548-49

accommodations, 259, 344-45, 347, 350, 361, 364, 466, 520, 523, 561

activists, 138, 141-42, 152, 154, 157-58, 240, 579

ADAAA, 261, 354, 369, 479, 528, 564

administration of assessments, 249, 286, 291, 294, 500, 502

administrators, 33, 169, 185, 190-91, 217, 230, 260, 301, 304, 463, 465, 471, 474, 478, 510, 513, 560, 563

advanced decoding of multisyllabic words, 438, 546

advocacy program, 184-85

agencies, local education, 63, 262, 267, 347, 362, 469-70, 475, 487, 492

Alliance for the Accreditation and Certification of Structured Language Education, 107

alphabetic principle, 233, 247-48, 300, 302, 385, 396, 455, 457, 462, 508, 511, 531, 559

alphabet knowledge, 257-58, 322, 452-53, 455-57, 459-61, 556-57, 559

American education, 64, 69, 130, 194, 581

system, 36, 573

ARICA (advanced reading instruction competence assessment), 76, 113-14, 229, 248-49, 260, 270, 273, 275, 279-81, 287-90, 301-4, 306, 385, 463, 470-73, 475, 477, 495, 497-98, 510-13, 515, 562

ASHA (American Speech-Language-Hearing Association), 581, 594

Asians, 79, 572, 575, 585, 588

assessment information, informal, 351, 365, 524

assessment process, 463, 465, 560

assessment/reading instrument, 363, 522

results, 363, 522

assessment results, reading instruction competence teaching, 306, 515

assessments

basic reading instruction competence, 76, 113, 247, 276, 279, 390, 425, 463, 470-72, 475

H

I

K

CINTHIA COLETTI

M

CINTHIA COLETTI

T

teaching specialists, 95, 114, 229, 246-47, 260, 263, 270, 272, 277, 280, 289, 297, 385, 407, 423, 463, 465, 467, 487, 495, 498, 506, 560, 562

technical assistance, 483, 566-67

text

automatic reading of, 250, 284, 291, 295, 500, 504

decodable, 386, 397, 532

deep understanding of, 93, 265, 490

identifying examples of, 284, 296, 504

imaginative/literary, 247, 300, 508

informational, 300, 381, 392-93, 404, 406, 427, 442, 508, 539, 541, 550

narrative, 424, 439, 547

previewing, 431, 446, 554

structure of, 330, 379, 389, 401, 536

subject-matter, 427, 441, 550

surface language of, 283, 293, 314, 502

text-based support, 416, 427, 442, 550

text complexity, level of, 254, 390, 402, 537

text content, understanding, 257, 416, 427, 442, 550

text generation, 285, 297, 332, 505

text phrasing, 384, 396, 530

textual evidence, 379, 389, 401, 429, 536

text understanding, summarizing, 431, 446, 554

tier II

instruction, 261, 474, 478, 564

interventions, 256, 413, 415, 420, 424, 435, 438, 543, 547

TIMSS (Trends in International Mathematics and Science Study), 42

tone, objective, 380, 391-92, 403, 405, 538, 540

V

verb tense, 377, 388, 399, 534

vocabulary, 104, 166, 175, 233-34, 250, 256-58, 268, 271, 281-85, 291-92, 295-97, 307, 312, 327-28, 330, 352, 366, 392, 405, 409, 414-15, 422, 424-25, 427, 437-39, 442, 452-54, 456-57, 459-60, 493, 496, 500-501, 503-5, 525, 539, 545-48, 550, 556-58

development, 247, 300, 328, 508

instruction, 284, 296, 322, 327, 504

knowledge, 248, 284, 296, 302, 327, 504, 511

words, 415, 423-24, 438-39, 546-47

W

word analysis skills, understanding of, 247, 300, 508

word meanings (semantics), 93, 224, 265, 327-28, 378, 389, 400, 415, 424, 427, 439-40, 490, 535, 547-48

word recognition, 249, 282-84, 292, 295, 312, 323, 325, 384, 386, 396, 501, 503-4, 530

fluent, 268, 493

Edwards Brothers Malloy
Thorofare, NJ USA
March 20, 2014